Mastering CMake

Fourth Edition

**Ken
Martin** & **Bill
Hoffman**

With contributions from:
Andy Cedilnik, Brad King, Alex Nuendorf

Published by Kitware Inc.

Join the CMake community at www.cmake.org

Leaders in Visualization Technology

© 2005 - 2007 Kitware, Inc.
http://www.kitware.com

The publisher Kitware, Inc. offers discounts on this book when ordered in bulk quantities. For more information contact Kitware, Inc. at kitware@kitware.com. You may also order directly from Kitware's electronic store at http://www.kitware.com/products.

Contributors to this work include those listed on the title page as well as:
Cover Design: Sébastien Barré
Technical Contributors: World-Wide CMake Developer Community at www.cmake.org.

Printed and produced in Colombia.
ISBN-10: 1-930934-20-3
ISBN-13: 978-1-930934-20-7

Contents

## Chapter 1

Why CMake?

If you have ever maintained the build and installation process for a software package, you will be interested in CMake. CMake is an open source build manager for software projects that allows developers to specify build parameters in a simple portable text file format. This file is then used by CMake to generate project files for native build tools including Integrated Development Environments such as Microsoft Visual Studio or Apple's Xcode, as well as UNIX, Linux, NMAKE, and Borland style makefiles. CMake handles the difficult aspects of building software such as cross platform builds, system introspection, and user customized builds, in a simple manner that allows users to easily tailor builds for complex hardware and software systems.

For any project, and especially cross platform projects, there is a need for a unified build system. Many projects today ship with both a UNIX makefile (or Makefile.in) and a Microsoft Visual Studio workspace. This requires that developers constantly try to keep both build systems up to date and consistent with each other. To target additional build systems such as Borland or Xcode requires even more custom copies of these files, creating an even bigger problem. This problem is compounded if you try to support optional components (such as including jpeg support if libjpeg is available on the system). CMake solves this by consolidating these different operations into one simple easy to understand file format.

If you have multiple developers working on a project, or multiple target platforms then the software will have to be built on more than one computer. Given the wide range of installed software and custom options that are involved with setting up a modern computer, chances are two computers running the same OS will be slightly different. CMake provides many benefits for single platform multi-machine development environments including:

- The ability to automatically search for programs, libraries, and header files that may be required by the software being built. This includes the ability to consider environment variables and Window's registry settings when searching.

- The ability to build in a directory tree outside of the source tree. This is a useful feature found on many UNIX platforms; CMake provides this feature on Windows as well. This allows a developer to remove an entire build directory without fear of removing source files.

- The ability to create complex custom commands for automatically generated files such as Qt's moc (www.trolltech.com), The Insight Toolkit's CABLE wrappers (public.kitware.com/Cable/HTML/Index.html) and SWIG (www.swig.org) wrapper generators. These commands are used to generate new source files during the build process that are in turn compiled into the software.

- The ability to select optional components at configuration time. For example, several of VTK's libraries are optional, and CMake provides an easy way for users to select which libraries are built.

- The ability to automatically generate workspaces and projects from a simple text file. This can be very handy for systems that have many programs or test cases, each of which requires a separate project file, typically a tedious manual process to create using an IDE.

- The ability to easily switch between static and shared builds. CMake knows how to create shared libraries and modules on all platforms supported. Complicated platform-specific linker flags are handled, and advanced features like built in run time search paths for shared libraries are supported on many UNIX systems.

- Automatic generation of file dependencies and support for parallel builds on most platforms.

When developing cross platform software, CMake provides a number of additional features:

- The ability to test for machine byte order and other hardware specific characteristics.

- A single set of build configuration files that work on all platforms. This avoids the problem of developers having to maintain the same information in several different formats inside a project.

- Support for building shared libraries on all platforms that support it.

- The ability to configure files with system dependent information such as the location of data files and other information. CMake can create header files that contain information such as paths to data files and other information in the form of #define macros. System specific flags can also be placed in configured header files. This has advantages over command line -D options to the compiler because it allows other build systems to use the CMake built library without having to specify the exact same command line options used during the build.

1.1   The History of CMake

CMake was developed starting in 1999 as part of the Insight Toolkit (ITK, www.itk.org) funded by the US National Library of Medicine. ITK is a large software project that works on many platforms and can interact with many other software packages. To support this, a powerful, yet easy to use, build tool was required. Having worked with build systems for large projects in the past, the developers designed CMake to address these needs. Since then CMake has continuously grown in popularity with many projects and developers adopting it for its ease of use and flexibility. Since 1999 CMake has been under active development and has matured to the point where it is a proven solution for a wide range of build issues. The most telling example of this is the successful adoption of CMake as the build system of the K Desktop Environment (KDE), arguably the largest open source software project in existence.

One of the recent additions to CMake is the inclusion of software testing support in the form of CTest. Part of the process of testing software involves building the software, possibly installing it, and determining what parts of the software are appropriate for the current system. This makes CTest a logical extension of CMake as it has much of this information already. In a similar vein a new CMake feature is CPack which is designed to support cross platform distribution of software. It provides a cross platform approach to creating native installations for your software making use of existing popular packages such as NSIS, RPM, Cygwin, and PackageMaker.

Other recent additions to CMake include support for Apple's Xcode IDE and support for Microsoft's Visual Studio 8. With CMake, once you write your input files you get support for new compilers and build systems for free because the support for them is built into new releases of CMake, not tied to your software distribution. Another recent addition to CMake is support for cross compiling to other operating systems or embedded devices. Many commands in CMake now properly handle the differences between the host system and the target platform when cross compiling.

1.2   Why Not Use Autoconf?

Before developing CMake its authors had experience with the existing set of available tools. Autoconf combined with automake provides some of the same functionality as CMake, but to use these tools on a Windows platform requires the installation of many additional tools not found natively on a Windows box. In addition to requiring a host of tools, autoconf can be difficult to use or extend and impossible for some tasks that are easy in CMake. Even if you do get autoconf and its required environment running on your system, it generates makefiles that will force users to the command line. CMake on the other hand, provides a choice allowing developers to generate project files that can be used directly from the IDE to which Windows and Xcode developers are accustomed.

While autoconf supports user specified options, it does not support dependent options where one option depends on some other property or selection. For example, in CMake you could have a user option to use multithreading be dependent on first determining if the user's system has multithreading support. CMake provides an interactive user interface making it easy for the user to see what options are available and how to set them.

For UNIX users, CMake also provides automated dependency generation that is not done directly by autoconf. CMake's simple input format is also easier to read and maintain than a combination of Makefile.in and configure.in files. The ability of CMake to remember and chain library dependency information has no equivalent in autoconf/automake.

1.3   Why Not Use JAM, qmake, SCons, or ANT?

Other tools such as ANT, qmake, SCons, and JAM have taken different approaches to solving these problems and they have helped us to shape CMake. Of the four, qmake is the most similar to CMake although it lacks much of the system interrogation that CMake provides. Qmake's input format is more closely related to a traditional makefile. ANT, JAM and SCons are also cross-platform although they do not support generating native project files. They do break away from the traditional makefile oriented input with ANT using XML, JAM using its own language, and SCons using python. A number of these tools directly run the compiler as opposed to letting the system's build process perform that task. Many of these tools require other tools such as Python or Java to be installed before they will work.

1.4   Why Not Script It Yourself?

Some projects use existing scripting languages such as Perl or Python to configure build processes. Although similar functionality can be achieved with systems like this, over-use of tools can make the build process more of an Easter egg hunt than a simple-to-use build system. Before installing your software package users are forced to find and install version 4.3.2 of this, and 3.2.4 of that, before they can even start the build process. To avoid that problem, it was decided that CMake would require no more tools than the software it was being used to build would require. At a minimum using CMake requires a C compiler, that compiler's native build tools, and a CMake executable. CMake was written in C++, requires only a C++ compiler to build and precompiled binaries are available for most systems. Scripting it yourself also typically means you will not be generating native Xcode or Visual Studio workspaces making Mac and Windows builds limited.

1.5   On What Platforms Does CMake Run?

CMake runs on a wide variety of platforms including Microsoft Windows, Mac OSX, and most UNIX or UNIX-like platforms. At the time of the writing of this book CMake was tested nightly on the following platforms: Windows 98/2000/XP/Vista, AIX, HPUX, IRIX, Linux, Mac OSX, Solaris, OSF, QNX, CYGWIN, MinGW, and FreeBSD.   You can check www.cmake.org for a current list of tested platforms.

Likewise, CMake supports most common compilers. It supports the GNU compiler on all CMake supported platforms. Other tested compilers include Visual Studio 6, 7, and 8, Intel C, SGI CC, Mips Pro, Borland, Sun CC and HP aCC. CMake should work for most UNIX-style compilers out of the box. If the compiler takes arguments in a strange way, then see the section *Porting CMake to New Platform* on page 197 for information on how to customize CMake for a new compiler.

Platforms	Compilers / Build Systems
Windows 98/ME	Visual Studio 6, .Net, 2003, 2005 NMAKE Borland Intel
Windows NT/2000/XP	Visual Studio 6, .Net, 2003, 2005 NMAKE Borland Intel
Windows Cygwin	gcc all versions
Windows Mingw	gcc all versions
Linux (versions after 1999)	KDevelop Intel gcc all versions
Solaris/SunOS	SunPro cc, CC gcc all versions
IRIX	Mips Pro, SGI cc, CC gcc all versions
HPUX	HP cc, aCC gcc all versions
AIX	Visual Age C++ xlC gcc all versions
Mac OSX 10.2 or later	Xcode gcc all versions
FreeBSD	gcc all versions

OSF	Compaq (DEC) C and C++
	gcc all versions

Figure 1-Listing of supported platforms, compilers, and build systems

## Chapter 2

Getting Started

2.1 Getting and Installing CMake on Your Computer

Before using CMake you will need to install or build the CMake binaries on your system. On many systems you may find that CMake is already installed or is available for install with the standard package manager tool for the system. Cygwin, Debian, FreeBSD and Mac OSX Fink all have CMake distributions. If your system does not have a CMake package, you can find CMake precompiled for most common architectures at www.cmake.org. If you do not find your system precompiled, then you can build CMake from source. To build CMake you will need a modern C++ compiler that supports the Standard Template Library (STL).

2.2 UNIX and Mac Binary Installations

If your system provides CMake as one of its standard packages, follow your system's package installation instructions. If your system does not have CMake, or has an out of date version of CMake, you can download precompiled binaries from www.cmake.org. The binaries from www.cmake.org come in the form of a compressed tar file. The tar file contains a README file and an enclosed tar file. The README file contains a manifest of the files contained in the enclosed tar file, and some instructions. To install, simply extract the enclosed tar file into a destination directory (typically /usr/local). However, it can be any directory, and does not require root privileges for installation.

2.3   Windows Binary Installation:

For Windows CMake has a NullSoft install file called cmake-(version)-win32.exe available
for download from www.cmake.org. To install this file, simply run the executable on the
windows machine on which you want to install CMake. You will be able to run CMake from
the Start Menu after it is installed.

2.4   Building CMake Yourself

If binaries are not available for your system, or if binaries are not available for the version of
CMake you wish to use, you can build CMake from the source code. You can obtain the
CMake source code by following the instructions at www.cmake.org. Once you have the
source code it can be built in two different ways. If you do have a version of CMake on your
system you can use it to build other versions of CMake. Generally the current development
version of CMake can always be built from the previous release of CMake. This is how new
versions of CMake are built on most Windows systems.

The second way to build CMake is by running its bootstrap build script. To do this you
change directory into your CMake source directory and type

```
./bootstrap
make
make install
```

The make install step is optional since CMake can run directly from the build directory if
desired. On UNIX, if you are not using the GNU C++ compiler, you need to tell the bootstrap
script which compiler you want to use. This is done by setting the environment variable CXX
before running bootstrap. If you need to use any special flags with your compiler, set the
CXXFLAGS environment variable. For example, on the SGI with the 7.3X compiler, you would
build CMake like this:

```
cd CMake
(setenv CXX CC; setenv CXXFLAGS "-LANG:std"; ./bootstrap)
make
make install
```

2.5   Basic CMake Usage and Syntax

Using CMake is simple. The build process is controlled by creating one or more CMakeLists
files (actually CMakeLists.txt but this guide will leave off the extension in most cases) in each

of the directories that make up a project. The CMakeLists files should contain the project description in CMake's simple language. The language is expressed as a series of commands. Each command is evaluated in the order that it appears in the CMakeLists file. The commands have the form

```
command (args...)
```

where `command` is the name of the command, and `args` is a white-space separated list of arguments. (Arguments with embedded white-space should be double quoted.) CMake is case insensitive to command names as of version 2.2. So where you see command you could use `COMMAND` or `Command` instead. Older versions of CMake only accepted uppercase commands.

CMake supports simple variables that can be either strings or lists of strings. Variables are referenced using a `${VAR}` syntax. Multiple arguments can be grouped together into a list using the `set` command. All other commands expand the lists as if they had been passed into the command with white-space separation. For example, `set(Foo a b c)` will result in setting the variable `Foo` to `a b c`, and if `Foo` is passed into another command `command(${Foo})` it would be equivalent to `command(a b c)`. If you want to pass a list of arguments to a command as if it were a single argument simply double quote it. For example `command("${Foo}")` would be invoked passing only one argument equivalent to `command( "a b c" )`.

System environment variables and Windows registry values can be accessed directly in CMake. To access system environment variables the syntax `$ENV{VAR}` is used. CMake can also reference registry entries in many commands using a syntax of the form `[HKEY_CURRENT_USER\\Software\\path1\\path2;key]` where the paths are built from the registry tree and key.

2.6   Hello World for CMake

For starters let us consider the simplest possible CMakeLists file. To compile an executable from one source file the CMakeLists file would contain two lines:

```
project (Hello)
add_executable (Hello Hello.c)
```

To build the Hello executable you follow the process described in Running CMake (See section 2.7) to generate the makefiles or Microsoft project files. The `project` command indicates what the name of the resulting workspace should be and the `add_executable` command adds an executable target to the build process. That's all there is to it for this simple example. If your project requires a few files it is also quite easy, just modify the add_executable line as shown below.

```
add_executable (Hello Hello.c File2.c File3.c File4.c)
```

add_executable is just one of many commands available in CMake. Consider the more complicated example below.

```
project (HELLO)

set (HELLO_SRCS Hello.c File2.c File3.c)

if (WIN32)
  set(HELLO_SRCS ${HELLO_SRCS} WinSupport.c)
else (WIN32)
  set(HELLO_SRCS ${HELLO_SRCS} UnixSupport.c)
endif (WIN32)

add_executable (Hello ${HELLO_SRCS})

# look for the Tcl library
find_library (TCL_LIBRARY
  NAMES tcl tcl84 tcl83 tcl82 tcl80
  PATHS /usr/lib /usr/local/lib
  )

if (TCL_LIBRARY)
  target_link_library (Hello ${TCL_LIBRARY})
endif (TCL_LIBRARY)
```

In this example the set command is used to group together source files into a list. The if command is used to add either WinSupport.c or UnixSupport.c to this list based on whether or not CMake is running on Windows. And finally the add_executable command is used to build the executable with the files listed in the variable HELLO_SRCS. The find_library command looks for the Tcl library under a few different names and in a few different paths. An if command checks if the TCL_LIBRARY was found and if so adds it to the link line for the Hello executable target. Note the use of the # character to denote a comment line. All characters from the # to the end of the line are considered to be part of the comment.

2.7 How to Run CMake?

Once CMake has been installed on your system, using it to build a project is easy. There are two main directories CMake uses when building a project: the source directory and the binary directory. The source directory is where the source code for your project is located. This is also where the CMakeLists files will be found. The binary directory is where you want CMake to put the resulting object files, libraries, and executables. Typically CMake will not write any files to the source directory, only the binary directory. If you want you can set the source and binary directories to be the same. This is known as an in-source build in contrast to out-of-source builds where they are different.

CMake supports both in-source and out-of-source builds on all operating systems. This means that you can configure your build to be completely outside of the source code tree which makes it very easy to remove all of the files generated by a build. Having the build tree differ from the source tree also makes it easy to support having multiple builds of a single source tree. This is useful when you want to have multiple builds with different options but just one copy of the source code. Now let us consider the specifics of running CMake on different platforms. We will cover the process for Windows and then UNIX.

Running CMake for Windows / Microsoft Visual C++

Run `CMakeSetup.exe`, which should be in your Start menu under Program Files. There may also be a shortcut on your desktop, or if you built from source, it will be in the build directory. A GUI will appear similar to what is shown in Figure 1. The top two entries are the source code and binary directories. They allow you to specify where the source code is for what you want to compile and where the resulting binaries should be placed. You should set these two values first. If the binary directory you specify does not exist, it will be created for you. If the binary directory has been configured by CMake before then it will automatically set the source tree.

The "Cache Values" area is where you can specify different options for the build process. The example shown in Figure 1 is for VTK which has a large number of options. More obscure variables may be hidden, but can be seen if you click on the "Show Advanced Values" check-button. Once you have specified the source code and binary directories you should click the Configure button. This will cause CMake to read in the CMakeLists files from the source code directory and then update the cache area to display any new options for the project that were exposed by other options you may have selected. Adjust your cache settings if desired and click the Configure button again. Values that changed during the configure process will be highlighted in red. To be sure you have seen all possible values you should click Configure until no values are red and you are happy with all the settings.

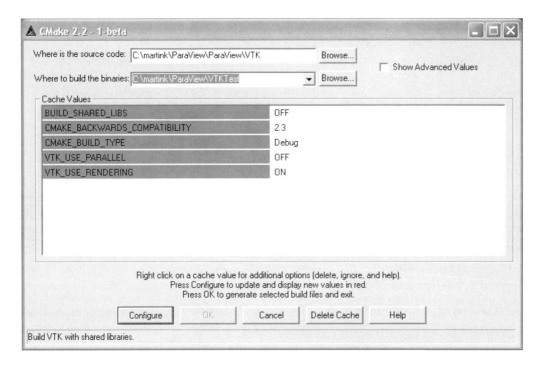

Figure 1 - The CMakeSetup Interface on Windows

The first time you configure a project, CMake will prompt you to select a Generator as shown
in Figure 2. Your choice of generator determines what build files CMake will produce. If you
select NMake Makefiles then CMake will produce makefiles suitable for NMake. Selecting a
version of Visual Studio will cause CMake to produce Microsoft Visual C++ workspaces
instead. Once you are done configuring, click the "OK" button.

Figure 2 – Selecting a Generator

It is important that you make sure that your environment is suitable for running CMakeSetup.
If you are using an IDE such as Visual Studio then your environment will be setup correctly
for you. If you are using nmake or MinGW then you need to make sure that the compiler can

run from your environment. You can either directly set the required environment variables for your compiler or use a shell in which they are already set. For example, Microsoft Visual Studio 7 has an option on the start menu for creating a Visual Studio Command Prompt. This opens up a command prompt window that has its environment already setup for Visual Studio. You should run CMakeSetup from this command prompt if you want to use nmake makefiles. The same approach applies to MinGW. You should run CMakeSetup from a MinGW shell that has a working compiler in its path.

When CMakeSetup finishes it will have generated the build files in the binary directory you specified. If Visual Studio was selected as the generator, a MSVC workspace (or solution) file is created. This file's name is based on the name of the project you specified in the PROJECT command at the beginning of your CMakeLists file. For most other generator types, makefiles are generated. The next step in this process is to open the workspace with MSVC. Once open, the project can be built in the normal manner of Microsoft Visual C++. The ALL_BUILD target can be used to build all of the libraries and executables in the package. If you are using a makefile build type, then continue reading the next section Running CMake on UNIX.

Running CMake on UNIX

On most UNIX platforms, if the curses library is supported, CMake provides an executable called ccmake. This interface is a terminal-based text application that is very similar to the Windows GUI. To run ccmake, change directory (cd) to the directory where you want the binaries to be placed. This can be the same directory as the source code for what we call in-source builds or it can be a new directory you create. Then run ccmake with the path to the source directory on the command line. For in-source builds use "." for the source directory. This will start the text interface as shown in Figure 3 (in this case the cache variables are from VTK and most are set automatically.)

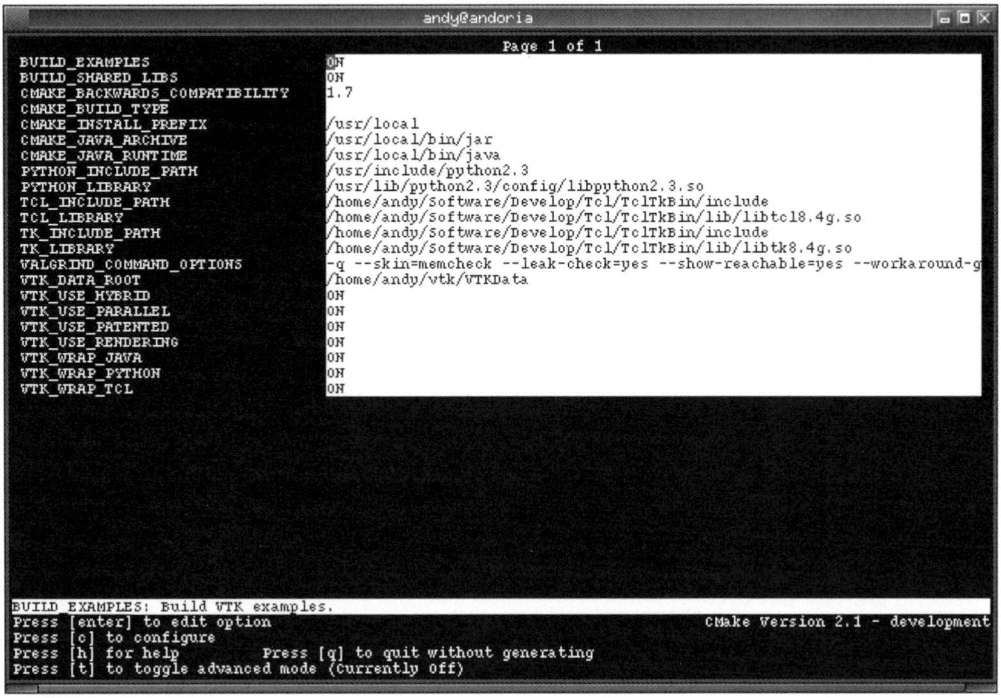

Figure 3 - ccmake running on UNIX

Brief instructions are displayed in the bottom of the window. If you hit the "c" key, it will configure the project. You should always configure after changing values in the cache. To change values, use the arrow keys to select cache entries, and then the enter key to edit them. Boolean values will toggle with the enter key. Once you have set all the values as you like, you can hit the "G" key to generate the makefiles and exit. You can also hit "h" for help, "q" to quit, and "t" to toggle the viewing of advanced cache entries. Two examples of CMake usage on the UNIX platform follow for a hello world project called Hello. In the first example, an in-source build is performed.

```
cd Hello
ccmake .
make
```

In the second example, an out-of-source build is performed.

```
mkdir Hello-Linux
cd Hello-Linux
ccmake ../Hello
make
```

You also have the option of running a Qt based GUI as shown in Figure 4. This GUI was developed by Clinton Stimpson and runs on Windows, UNIX/Linux, and Mac OSX. It is actively being developed as of the writing of this book and is included in the CMake source code but you will need an installation of Qt on your system prior to building this GUI. The top two entries are the source code and binary directories. They allow you to specify where the source code is for what you wanted to compile and where the resulting binaries should be placed. You should set these two values first. If the binary directory you specify does not exist, it will be created for you.

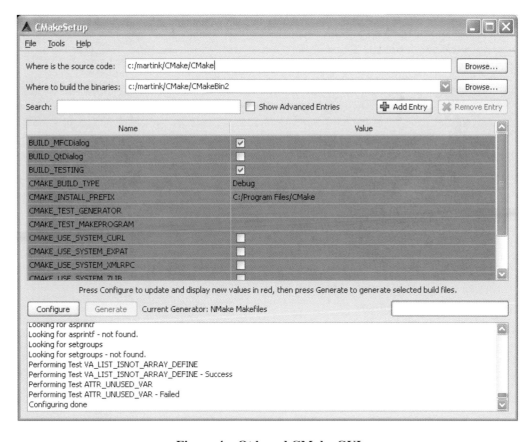

Figure 4 – Qt based CMake GUI

The middle area is where you can specify different options for the build process. More obscure variables may be hidden, but can be seen if you click on the "Show Advanced Entries" check-button. Once you have specified the source code and binary directories you should click the Configure button. This will cause CMake to read in the CMakeLists files from the source code directory and then update the cache area to display any new options for the project. Adjust your cache settings if desired and click the Configure button again. New values that were created by the configure process will be colored red. To be sure you have seen all possible values you should click Configure until no values are red and you are happy with all the settings. Once you are done configuring, click the Generate button, this will produce the appropriate files and then exit.

Running CMake on Mac OSX

Two options are available for running CMake on a Mac OSX system. You can use ccmake from a shell window following the same instructions as for UNIX, or you can run the Qt-based GUI as on UNIX.

Running CMake from the Command Line

From the command line, CMake can be run as an interactive question and answer session or as a non-interactive program. To run in interactive mode, just pass the "-i" option to CMake. This will cause CMake to ask you for a value for each entry in the cache file for the project. CMake will provide reasonable defaults just like it does in the GUI and curses based interfaces. The process stops when there are no longer any more questions to ask. An example of using the interactive mode of CMake is provided below.

```
$ cmake -i -G "NMake Makefiles" ../CMake
Would you like to see advanced options? [No]:
Please wait while cmake processes CMakeLists.txt files....

Variable Name: BUILD_TESTING
Description: Build the testing tree.
Current Value: ON
New Value (Enter to keep current value):

Variable Name: CMAKE_INSTALL_PREFIX
Description: Install path prefix, prepended onto install
directories.
Current Value: C:/Program Files/CMake
New Value (Enter to keep current value):

Please wait while cmake processes CMakeLists.txt files....

CMake complete, run make to build project.
```

Using CMake to build a project in non-interactive mode is a simple process if the project has few or no options. For larger projects like VTK, using `ccmake`, `cmake -i`, or `CMakeSetup` is recommended. To build a project with a non-interactive CMake, first change directory to where you want the binaries to be placed. For an in-source build you then run `cmake .` and pass in any options using the `-D` flag. For out-of-source builds the process is the same except you run `cmake` and also provide the path to the source code as its argument. Then type `make` and your project should compile. Some projects will have install targets as well so you can type `make install` to install them.

Specifying the Compiler to CMake

On some systems you may have more than once compiler to choose from or your compiler may be in a non-standard place. In these cases you will need to specify to CMake where your desired compiler is located. There are three ways to specify this; the generator can specify the compiler, an environment variable can be set, or a cache entry can be set. Some generators are tied to a specific compiler, for example the Visual Studio 6 generator always uses the Microsoft Visual Studio 6 compiler. For makefile based generators CMake will try a list of usual compilers until it finds a working compiler. The list can be found in the files:

```
Modules/CMakeDeterminCCompiler.cmake and
Modules/CMakeDetermineCXXCompiler.cmake
```

The lists can be preempted with environment variables that can be set before CMake is run. The `CC` environment variable specifies the C compiler while `CXX` specifies the C++ compiler. You can specify the compilers directly on the command line by using `-DCMAKE_CXX_COMPILER=cl` for example. If those are not set, CMake will try the following list of compilers:

```
c++ g++ CC aCC cl bcc xlC.
```

Once CMake has been run and picked a compiler, you can change the selection by changing the cache entries `CMAKE_CXX_COMPILER` and `CMAKE_C_COMPILER` although this is not recommended. The problem with doing this is that the project you are configuring may have already run some tests on the compiler to determine what it supports. Changing the compiler typically does not cause these tests to be rerun which can lead to incorrect results. If you must change the compiler, start over with an empty binary directory. The flags for the compiler and the linker can also be changed by setting environment variables. Setting `LDFLAGS` will initialize the cache values for link flags, while `CXXFLAGS` and `CFLAGS` will initialize `CMAKE_CXX_FLAGS` and `CMAKE_C_FLAGS` respectively.

Dependency Analysis

CMake has powerful built-in dependency analysis capabilities for C and C++ source code files. CMake also has limited support for Fortran and Java dependencies. Since Integrated Development Environments (IDEs) support and maintain dependency information, CMake skips this step for those build systems. However, makefiles with a make program do not know how to automatically compute and keep dependency information up-to-date. For these builds, CMake automatically computes dependency information for C and C++ files. Both the generation and maintenance of these dependencies are automatically done by CMake. Once a project is initially configured by CMake, users only need to run make, and CMake does the rest of the work. CMake's dependencies fully support parallel builds for multiprocessor systems.

Although users do not need to know how CMake does this work, it may be useful to look at the dependency information files for a project. This information for each target is stored in four files called `depend.make`, `flags.make`, `build.make`, and `DependInfo.cmake`. `depend.make` stores the depend information for all the object files in the directory. `flags.make` contains the compile flags used for the source files of this target. If they change then the files will be recompiled. `DependInfo.cmake` is used to keep the dependency information up-to-date and contains information about what files are part of the project and what languages they are in. Finally the rules for building the dependencies are stored in `build.make`. If a dependency is out of date then all the dependencies for that target will be recomputed keeping the dependency information current.

2.8   Editing CMakeLists Files

CMake provides a few tools to help you in editing your CMakeLists files. For developers who use Emacs or Vim as their editors, CMake includes indentation and syntax highlighting modes. These can be found in the Docs directory of the source distribution or downloaded from the cmake web site. The file `cmake-mode.el` is the Emacs mode and `cmake-indent.vim` and `cmake-syntax.vim` are used by vim. Within Visual Studio the CMakeLists files are listed as part of the project and you can edit them simply by double clicking on them. Within any of the supported generators (makefiles, Visual Studio, etc) if you edit a CMakeLists file and rebuild there are rules that will automatically invoke CMake to update the generated files (e.g. makefiles or project files) as required. This helps to assure that your generated files are always in sync with your CMakeLists files.

Since CMake computes and maintains dependency information, the CMake executables must always be available (though they don't have to be in your PATH) when make or an IDE is being run on CMake generated files. This means that if a CMake input file changes on disk, your build system will automatically re-run CMake and produce up-to-date build files. For this reason you generally should not generate makefiles or projects with CMake and move them to another machine that does not have CMake installed.

2.9   Setting Initial Values for CMake

While CMake works well in an interactive mode, sometimes you will need to setup cache entries without running a GUI. This is common when setting up nightly dashboards or if you will be creating many build trees with the same cache values. In these cases the CMake cache can be initialized in two different ways. The first way is to pass the cache values on the CMake command line using `-DCACHE_VAR:TYPE=VALUE` arguments. For example consider the following nightly dashboard script for a UNIX machine:

```
#!/bin/tcsh

cd ${HOME}

# wipe out the old binary tree and then create it again
rm -rf Foo-Linux
mkdir Foo-Linux
cd Foo-Linux

# run cmake to setup the cache
cmake -DBUILD_TESTING:BOOL=ON <etc...> ../Foo

# generate the dashboard
ctest -D Nightly
```

The same idea can be used with a batch file on windows. The second way is to create a file to be loaded using CMake's `-C` option. In this case instead of setting up the cache with `-D` options it is done though a file that is parsed by CMake. The syntax for this file is standard CMakeLists syntax and typically it is just a series of `set` commands such as:

```
#Build the vtkHybrid kit.
set (VTK_USE_HYBRID ON CACHE BOOL "doc string")
```

In some cases there might be an existing cache and you want to force the cache values to be set a certain way. For example say you want to turn Hybrid on even if the user has previously run CMake and turned it off. Then you can do:

```
#Build the vtkHybrid kit always.
set (VTK_USE_HYBRID ON CACHE BOOL "doc" FORCE)
```

Another option is that you want to set and then hide options so the user will not be tempted to adjust them later on. This can be done using the following commands:

```
#Build the vtkHybrid kit always and don't distract
#the user by showing the option.
set (VTK_USE_HYBRID ON CACHE INTERNAL "doc" FORCE)
mark_as_advanced (VTK_USE_HYBRID)
```

You might be tempted to directly edit the cache file or to "initialize" a project by giving it an initial cache file. This may not work and could cause additional problems in the future. First, the syntax of the CMake cache is subject to change. Secondly cache files have full paths in them that make them unsuitable for moving between binary trees. So if you want to initialize a cache file use one of the two standard methods described above.

That is all there is to installing and running CMake for simple projects. In the following chapters we will consider CMake in more detail and how to use it on more complex software projects.

## Chapter 3

Key Concepts

3.1   Main Structures

This chapter provides an introduction to CMake's key concepts. As you start working with CMake you will run into a variety of concepts such as targets, generators, and commands. In CMake these concepts are implemented as C++ classes and are referenced in many of CMake's commands. Understanding these concepts will provide you with the working knowledge you need to create effective CMakeLists files.

Before going into detail on CMake's classes it is worth understanding their basic relationships. At the lowest level there are source files. These correspond to typical C or C++ source code files. Source files are combined into targets. A target is typically an executable or library. A directory represents a directory in the source tree and typically has a CMakeLists file and one or more targets associated with it. Every directory has a local generator that is responsible for generating the makefiles or project files for that directory. All of the local generators share a common global generator that oversees the build process. And finally the global generator is created and driven by the cmake class itself.

Figure 5 shows the basic class structure of CMake. We will now consider CMake's concepts in a bit more detail. CMake's execution begins by creating an instance of the `cmake` class and passing the command line arguments to it. This class manages the overall configuration process and holds information that is global to the build process such as the Cache values. One of the first things the `cmake` class does is to create the correct global generator based on the user's selection of what generator to use (such as Visual Studio 7, Borland makefiles, or UNIX makefiles). At this point the `cmake` class passes control to the global generator it created by invoking the configure and generate methods.

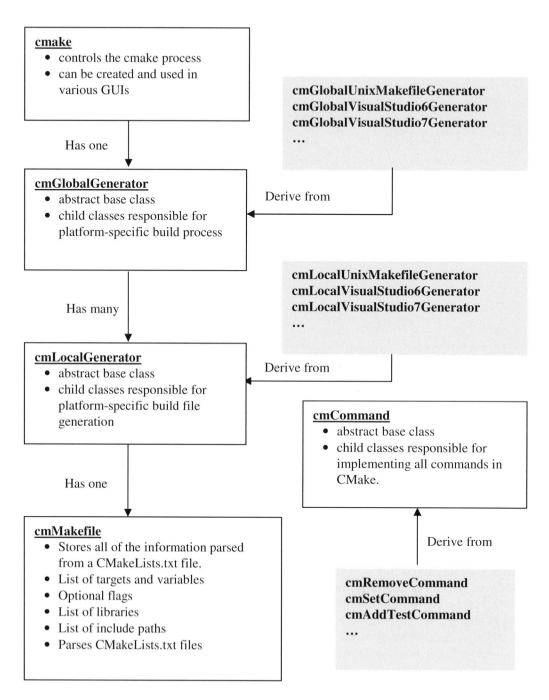

Figure 5 - CMake Internals

The global generator is responsible for managing the configuration and generation of all of the makefiles (or project files) for a project. In practice most of the work is actually done by local generators which are created by the global generator. One local generator is created for each directory of the project that is processed. So while a project will have only one global generator it may have many local generators. For example, under Visual Studio 7 the global generator creates a solution file for the entire project while the local generators create a project file for each target in their directory.

Under "UNIX Makefiles", the local generators create most of the makefiles and the global generator simply orchestrates the process and creates the main top-level makefile. Implementation details vary widely among generators. The Visual Studio 6 generators make use of .dsp and .dsw file templates and perform variable replacements on them. The Visual Studio 7 generators directly generate the XML output without using any file templates. The makefile generators including UNIX, NMAKE, Borland, etc use a set of rule templates and replacements to generate the makefiles.

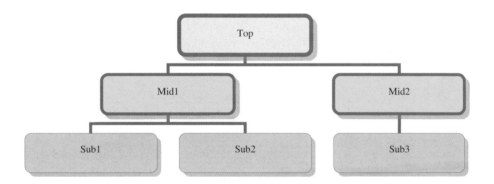

Figure 6 - Sample Directory Tree

Each local generator has an instance of the class cmMakefile. cmMakefile is where the results of parsing the CMakeLists files are stored. Specifically, for each directory in a project there will be a single cmMakefile instance which is why the cmMakefile class is often referred to as the directory. This is clearer for build systems that do not use Makefiles. That instance will hold all of the information from parsing that directory's CMakeLists file (see Figure 6.) One way to think of the cmMakefile class is as a structure that starts out initialized with a few variables from its parent directory, and then is filled in as the CMakeLists file is processed. Reading in the CMakeLists file is simply a matter of CMake executing the commands it finds in the order it encounters them.

Each command in CMake is implemented as a separate C++ class and has two main parts. The first part of a command is the InitialPass method. The InitialPass method receives the arguments and the `cmMakefile` instance for the directory currently being processed, and then performs its operations. In the case of the `set` command, it processes its arguments and if the arguments are correct it calls a method on the `cmMakefile` to set the variable. The results of the command are always stored in the `cmMakefile` instance. No information is ever stored in a command. The last part of a command is the FinalPass. The FinalPass of a command is executed after all commands (for the entire CMake project) have had their InitialPass invoked. Most commands do not have a FinalPass, but in some rare cases a command must do something with global information that may not be available during the initial pass.

Once all of the CMakeLists files have been processed the generators use the information collected into the `cmMakefile` instances to produce the appropriate files for the target build system (such as makefiles).

3.2   Targets

Now that we have discussed the overall process of CMake, let us consider some of the key items stored in the `cmMakefile` instance. Probably the most important item is targets. Targets represent executables, libraries, and utilities built by CMake. Every `add_library`, `add_executable`, and `add_custom_target` command creates a target. For example, the following command will create a target named foo that is a static library with `foo1.c` and `foo2.c` as source files.

```
add_library (foo STATIC foo1.c foo2.c)
```

The name foo is now available for use as a library name everywhere else in the project, and CMake will know how to expand the name into the library when needed. Libraries can be declared to be of a particular type such as `STATIC`, `SHARED`, `MODULE`, or left undeclared. `STATIC` indicates that the library must be built as a static library. Likewise `SHARED` indicates it must be built as a shared library. `MODULE` indicates that the library must be created so that it can be dynamically loaded into an executable. On many operating systems this is the same as `SHARED` but on other systems such as OSX it is different. If none of these options are specified that indicates that the library could be built as either shared or static. In that case CMake uses the setting of the variable `BUILD_SHARED_LIBS` to determine if the library should be `SHARED` or `STATIC`. If it is not set, then CMake defaults to building static libraries.

Likewise executables have some options. By default an executable will be a traditional console application that has a `main (int argc, const char*argv[])`. If `WIN32` is specified after the executable name then the executable will be compiled as a MS Windows executable and the operating system will call WinMain instead of main at startup. `WIN32` has no effect on non-Windows systems.

In addition to storing their type, targets also keep track of general properties. These properties can be set and retrieved using the `set_target_properties` and `get_target_property` commands or the more general `set_properties` and `get_property` commands. The most commonly used property is `LINK_FLAGS` which is used to specify link flags for a specific target. Targets store a list of libraries that they link against which are set using the `target_link_libraries` command. Names passed into `this` command can be full paths to libraries, or the name of a library from an `add_library` command. They also store the link directories to use when linking, the install location for the target, and custom commands to execute after linking.

For each library CMake creates, it keeps track of all the libraries on which that library depends. This is important for static linking. Since static libraries do not link to the libraries on which they depend, it is important for CMake to keep track of the libraries so they can be specified on the link line of the executable being created. For example,

```
add_library (foo foo.cxx)
target_link_libraries (foo bar)

add_executable (foobar foobar.cxx)
target_link_libraries (foobar foo)
```

This will link the libraries foo and bar into the executable foobar even though only foo was explicitly linked into foobar. With shared or dll builds this linking is not always needed, but the extra linkage is harmless. For static builds, this is required. Since the foo library uses symbols from the bar library foobar will most likely also need bar since it uses foo.

3.3   Source Files

The source file structure is in many ways similar to a target. It stores the filename, extension, and a number of general properties related to a source file. Like targets you can set and get properties using `set_source_files_properties` and `get_source_file_property or the more generic versions`.. The most common properties include:

COMPILE_FLAGS

> Compile flags specific to this source file. These can include source specific –D and –I flags.

GENERATED

> The `GENERATED` property indicates that the source file is generated as part of the build process. In this case CMake will treat it differently for computation of dependencies because the source file may not exist when CMake is first run.

OBJECT_DEPENDS

Adds additional files on which this source file should depend. CMake automatically performs dependency analysis to determine the usual C and C++ dependencies. This parameter is used rarely in cases where there is an unconventional dependency or the source files do not exist at dependency analysis time.

ABSTRACT
WRAP_EXCLUDE

CMake doesn't directly use these properties. Some loaded commands and extensions to CMake look at these properties to determine how and when to wrap a C++ class into languages such as Tcl, Python, etc.

3.4   Directories, Generators, Tests, and Properties

In addition to targets and source files you may find yourself occasionally working with other classes such as directories, generators, and tests. Normally such interactions take the shape of setting or getting properties from these objects. All of these classes have properties associated with them as do source files and targets. A property is just a key-value pair attached to a specific object such as a target. The most generic way to access properties is through the `set_properties` and `get_property` commands. Those commands allow you to set or get a property from any class in CMake that has properties. Some of the properties for targets and source files have already been covered. Some useful properties for a directory include:

ADDITIONAL_MAKE_CLEAN_FILES

This property specifies a list of additional files that will be cleaned as a part of the "make clean" stage. By default CMake will clean up any generated files that it knows about, but your build process may use other tools that leave files behind. This property can be set to a list of those files so that they also will be properly cleaned up.

EXCLUDE_FROM_ALL

This property indicates if all the targets in this directory and all sub directories should be excluded from the default build target. If it is not, then with a Makefile for example typing make will cause these targets to be built as well. The same concept applies to the default build of other generators.

LISTFILE_STACK

This property is mainly useful when trying to debug errors in your CMake scripts. It returns a list of what list files are currently being processed, in order. So if one CMakeLists file does an include command then that is effectively pushing the included CMakeLists file onto the stack.

A full list of properties supported in CMake can be obtained by running `cmake` with the `-help-property-list` option.

The generators and directories are automatically created for you as CMake processes your source tree, but they do have some useful properties. For example on a directory you can query for the `LISTFILE_STACK` which will return a list, in order, of what CMakeLists files are currently being processed.

3.5   Variables and Cache Entries

CMakeLists files use variables much like any programming language. Variables are used to store values for later use and can be a single value such as "ON" or "OFF" or they can represent a list such as (`/usr/include /home/foo/include /usr/local/include`). A number of useful variables are automatically defined by CMake and are discussed in Appendix A - Variables.

Variables in CMakeLists files by default have a scope limited to the current CMakeLists file, any subdirectory CMakeLists files, and any files that they include using the `INCLUDE` command. Variables in CMake are referenced using a `${VARIABLE}` notation and variables are defined in the order of execution of the `set` commands. Consider the following example:

```
# FOO is undefined

set (FOO 1)
# FOO is now set to 1
set (FOO 0)
# FOO is now set to 0
```

This may seem straight forward but consider the following example:

```
set (FOO 1)

if (${FOO} LESS 2)
   set (FOO 2)
else (${FOO} LESS 2)
   set (FOO 3)
endif (${FOO} LESS 2)
```

Clearly the `if` statement is true which means that the body of the `if` statement will be executed. That will set the variable FOO to 2. When the `else` statement is encountered FOO will have a value of 2. Normally in CMake the new value of FOO would be used but the `else` statement is a rare exception to the rule and always refers back to the value of the variable when the `if` statement was executed. So in this case the body of the `else` clause will not be executed. To further understand the scope of variables consider this example:

```
set (foo 1)

# process the dir1  subdirectory
add_subdirectory (dir1)

# include and process the commands in file1.cmake
include (file1.cmake)

set (bar 2)
# process the dir2 subdirectory
add_subdirectory (dir2)

# include and process the commands in file2.cmake
include (file2.cmake)
```

In this example because the variable `foo is defined in the beginning it` will be defined while processing both dir1 and dir2. In contrast `bar` will only be defined when processing dir2. Likewise `foo` will be defined when processing both file1.cmake and file2.cmake whereas `bar` will only be defined while processing file2.cmake.

Variables can also represent a list of values. In these cases when the variable is expanded it will be expanded into multiple values. Consider the following example:

```
# set a list of items
set (items_to_buy apple orange pear beer)

# loop over the items
foreach (item ${items_to_buy})
  message ( "Don't forget to buy one ${item}" )
endforeach (item ${items_to_buy})
```

In some cases you might want to allow the user building your project to set a variable from the CMake user interface. In that case the variable must be a cache entry. Whenever CMake is run it produces a cache file in the directory where the binary files are to be written. The values of this cache file are displayed by the CMake user interface. There are a few purposes to this cache. The first is to store the user's selections and choices so that if they should run CMake again they don't need to reenter that information. For example, the `option` command creates a Boolean variable and stores it in the cache.

```
option (USE_JPEG "Do you want to use the jpeg library")
```

The above line would create a variable called USE_JPEG and put it into the cache. That way the user can set that variable from the user interface and its value will remain in case the user should run CMake again in the future. To create a variable in the cache you can use commands like option or find_file or you can use the standard set command with the CACHE option.

```
set (USE_JPEG ON CACHE BOOL "include jpeg support?")
```

When you use the cache option you must also provide the type of the variable and a documentation string. The type of the variable is used by the GUI to control how that variable is set and displayed. Variable types include BOOL, PATH, FILEPATH, and STRING. The documentation string is used by the GUI for providing online help.

The other purpose of the cache is to store key variables that are expensive to determine. These variables may not be visible or adjustable by the user. Typically these values are system dependent variables such as CMAKE_WORDS_BIGENDIAN which require CMake to compile and run a program to determine their value. Once these values have been determined, they are stored in the cache to avoid having to recompute them every time CMake is run. Generally CMake tries to limit these variables to properties that should never change (such as the byte order of the machine you are on). If you significantly change your computer, either by changing the operating system, or switching to a different compiler, you will need to delete the cache file (and probably all of your binary tree's object files, libraries, and executables).

Variables that are in the cache also have a property indicating if they are advanced or not. By default when a CMake GUI is run (such as ccmake or CMakeSetup) the advanced cache entries are not displayed. This is so that the user can focus on the key cache entries that they should consider changing. The advanced cache entries are other options that the user can modify but typically will not. It is not unusual for a large software project to have fifty or more options and the advanced property lets a software project divide them into key options for most users and advanced options for advanced users. Depending on the project there may even be no non-advanced cache entries. To make a cache entry advanced the mark_as_advanced command is used with the name of the variable (a.k.a. cache entry) to make advanced.

A few final points should be made concerning variables and their interaction with the cache. If a variable is in the cache, it can still be overridden in a CMakeLists file using the set command without the CACHE option. Cache values are checked only if the variable is not found in the current cmMakefile instance before CMakeLists file processing begins. The set command will set the variable for processing the current CMakeLists file (and subdirectories as usual) without changing the value in the cache.

```
# assume that FOO is set to ON in the cache

set (FOO OFF)
# sets foo to OFF for processing this CMakeLists file
# and subdirectories; the value in the cache stays ON
```

Once a variable is in the cache, its "cache" value can not normally be modified from a CMakeLists file. The reasoning behind this is that once CMake has put the variable into the cache with its initial value, the user may then modify that value from the GUI. If the next invocation of CMake overwrote their change back to the set value, the user would never be able to make a change that CMake wouldn't overwrite. So a set (FOO ON CACHE BOOL "doc") command will typically only do something when the cache doesn't have the variable in it. Once the variable is in the cache, that command will have no effect.

In the rare event that you really want to change a cached variable's value you can use the FORCE option in combination with the CACHE option to the set command. The FORCE option will cause the set command to override and change the cache value of a variable.

3.6   Build Configurations

Build configurations allow a project to be built in different ways for debug, optimized, or any other special set of flags. CMake supports by default Debug, Release, MinSizeRel, and RelWithDebInfo configurations. Debug has the basic debug flags turned on. Release has the basic optimizations turned on. MinSizeRel has the flags that produce the smallest object code, but not necessarily the fastest code. RelWithDebInfo builds an optimized build with debug information as well.

CMake handles the configurations in slightly different ways depending on what generator is being used. The conventions of the native build system are followed when possible. This means that configurations impact the build in different ways when using makefiles versus using Visual Studio project files.

The Visual Studio IDE also supports the notion of Build Configurations. A default project in Visual Studio usually has Debug and Release configurations. From the IDE you can select build Debug, and the files will be built with Debug flags. The IDE puts all of the binary files into directories with the name of the active configuration.   This brings about an extra complexity for projects that build programs that need to be run as part of the build process from custom commands. See the CMAKE_CFG_INTDIR variable and the custom commands section for more information about how to handle this issue. The variable CMAKE_CONFIGURATION_TYPES is used to tell CMake which configurations to put in the workspace.

With makefile based generators, only one configuration can be active at the time CMake is run, and it is specified by the CMAKE_BUILD_TYPE variable. If the variable is empty then no flags are added to the build. If the variable is set to the name of a configuration, then the appropriate variables and rules (such as CMAKE_CXX_FLAGS_<ConfigName>) are added to the compile lines. Makefiles do not use special configuration subdirectories for object files. To build both debug and release trees, the user is expected to create multiple build directories with the out of source build feature of CMake, and set the CMAKE_BUILD_TYPE to the desired selection for each build. For example,

```
# With source code in the directory MyProject
# to build MyProject-debug create that directory, cd into it and
(ccmake ../MyProject -DCMAKE_BUILD_TYPE:STRING=Debug)
# the same idea is used for the release tree MyProject-release
(ccmake ../MyProject -DCMAKE_BUILD_TYPE:STRING=Release)
```

## Chapter 4

Writing CMakeLists files

This chapter will cover the basics of writing effective CMakeLists files for your software. It will cover all of the basic commands and issues you will need to handle most projects. It will also discuss how to convert existing UNIX or Windows projects into CMakeLists files. While CMake can handle extremely complex projects, for most projects you will find this chapter's contents will tell you all you need to know. CMake is driven by the CMakeLists.txt files written for a software project. The CMakeLists files determine everything from what options to put into the cache, to what source files to compile. In addition to discussing how to write a CMakeLists file this chapter will also cover how to make them robust and maintainable. The basic syntax of a CMakeLists.txt file and key concepts of CMake have already been discussed in chapters 2 and 3. This chapter will expand on those concepts and introduce a few new ones.

4.1   CMake Syntax

CMakeLists files follow a simple syntax consisting of comments, commands, and white space. A comment is indicated using the # character and runs from that character until the end of the line. A command consists of the command name, opening parenthesis, white space separated arguments and a closing parenthesis. All white space (spaces, line feeds, tabs) are ignored except to separate arguments. Anything within a set of double quotes is treated as one argument as is typical for most languages. The backslash can be used to escape characters preventing the normal interpretation of them. The subsequent examples in this chapter will help clear up some of these syntactic issues. You might wonder why CMake decided to have its own language instead of using an existing language such as Python, Java, or TCL. The main reason is that we did not want to make CMake require an additional tool to run. By requiring one of these other languages all users of CMake would be required to have that language installed and potentially a specific version of that language. This is on top of the CMake language extensions that would be required to do some of the CMake work for both performance and capability reasons.

4.2   Basic Commands

While the previous chapters have already introduced many of the basic commands for CMakeLists files, this chapter will review and expand on them. The first command the top-level CMakeLists file should have is the PROJECT command. This command both names the project and optionally specifies what languages will be used by it. Its syntax is as follows:

```
project (projectname [CXX] [C] [Java] [NONE])
```

If no languages are specified then CMake defaults to supporting C and C++. If the NONE language is passed then CMake includes no language specific support. Whenever C++ language support is specified then C language support will also be loaded.

For each project command that appears in a project, CMake will create a top level IDE project file. The project will contain all targets that are in the CMakeLists.txt file or any of its sub directories as specified by the add_subdirectory command. If the EXCLUDE_FROM_ALL option is used in the add_subdirectory command, then the generated project will not appear in the top level makefile or IDE project file. This is useful for generating sub projects that do not make sense as part of the main build process. Consider that a project with a number of examples could use this feature to generate the build files for each example with one run of cmake, but not have the examples built as part of the normal build process.

The set command is probably one of the most used commands since it is used for defining and modifying variables and lists. Complimenting the set command are the remove and separate_arguments commands. The remove command can be used to remove a value from a variable list while the separate_arguments command can be used to take a single variable value (as opposed to a list) and break it into a list based on spaces.

The add_executable and add_library commands are the main commands for defining what libraries and executables to build and what source files comprise them. For Visual Studio projects the source files will show up in the IDE as usual but any header files the project uses will not be there. To have the header files show up as well you simply add them to the list of source files for the executable or library. This can be done for all generators. Any generators that do not use the header files directly (such as Makefile based generators) will simply ignore them.

4.3   Flow Control

In many ways writing a CMakeLists file is like a writing a program in a simple language. Like most languages CMake provides flow control structures to help you along your way. CMake provides three flow control structures;

- conditional statements (e.g. `if`)

- looping constructs (e.g. `foreach` and `while`)

- procedure definitions (e.g. `macro`)

First we will consider the `if` command. In many ways the `if` command in CMake is just like the `if` command in any other language. It evaluates its expression and based on that either executes the code in its body or optionally the code in the `ELSE` clause. For example:

```
if (FOO)
   # do something here
else (FOO)
   # do something else
endif (FOO)
```

One difference you might notice is that the conditional of the `if` statement is repeated in the `else` and `endif` clauses. These conditionals are only used for matching `else` and `endif` clauses with their matching `if` clause. As such they must exactly match the original conditional of the `if` statement. The following code would not work:

```
set (FOO 1)

if (${FOO})
   # do something
endif (1)
# ERROR, it doesn't match the original if conditional
```

Fortunately CMake provides verbose error messages in the case where an `if` statement is not properly matched with an `endif`. This should help you to track down any problems with matching conditionals. Requiring the conditionals on the `else` and `endif` commands also has the added benefit of helping to document your CMakeLists file. With a long `if` statement it can be easy to lose track of what `if` statement the `endif` is closing. `if` statements can be nested to any depth and any command can be used inside of an `if` or `else` clause.

The `if` command has a limited set of operations that you can use. It does not support general purpose C style expressions such as `${FOO}` `&&` `${BAR}` `||` `${FUBAR}` instead it supports a limited subset of expressions that should work for most cases. Specifically `if` supports:

if (variable)

> True if the variable's value is not empty, 0, FALSE, OFF, or NOTFOUND.

if (NOT variable)

>   True if the variable's value is empty, `0`, `FALSE`, `OFF`, or `NOTFOUND`

if (variable1 AND variable2)

>   True if both variables would be considered true individually.

if (variable1 OR variable2)

>   True if either variable would be considered true individually.

if (COMMAND command-name)

>   True if the given name is a command that can be invoked.

if (DEFINED variable)

>   True if the given variable has been set, regardless of what value it was set to.

if (EXISTS file-name)
if (EXISTS directory-name)

>   True if the named file or directory exists.

if (IS_DIRECTORY name)
if (IS_ABSOLUTE name)

>   True if the given name is a directory, or absolute path respectively.

if (name1 IS_NEWER_THAN name2)

>   True if the file specified by name1 has a more recent modification time than the file specified by name2.

if (variable MATCHES regex)
if (string MATCHES regex)

>   True if the given string or variable's value matches the given regular expression.

if (variable EQUAL number)
if (string EQUAL number)
if (variable LESS number)
if (string LESS number)
if (variable GREATER number)
if (string GREATER number)

>   True if the given string or variable's value is a valid number and the inequality test is true.

if (variable STRLESS string)

if (string STRLESS string)

if (variable STRGREATER string)

if (string STRGREATER string)

if (variable STREQUAL string)

if (string STREQUAL string)

> True if the given string or variable's value is lexicographically less than (or greater than , or equal to) than the string on the right.

Similar to C and C++ these expressions can be combined to create more powerful conditionals. For example consider the following conditionals:

```
if (1 LESS 2 AND 3 LESS 4)
  message ("sequence of numbers")
endif (1 LESS 2 AND 3 LESS 4)

if (1 AND 3 AND 4)
  message ("series of true values")
endif (1 AND 3 AND 4)

if (NOT 0 AND 3 AND 4)
  message ("a false value")
endif (NOT 0 AND 3 AND 4)

if (0 OR 3 AND 4)
  message ("or statements")
endif (0 OR 3 AND 4)

if (EXISTS ${PROJECT_SOURCE_DIR}/Help.txt AND COMMAND IF)
  message ("Help exists")
endif (EXISTS ${PROJECT_SOURCE_DIR}/Help.txt AND COMMAND IF)

set (fooba 0)

if (NOT DEFINED foobar)
  message ("foobar is not defined")
endif (NOT DEFINED foobar)

if (NOT DEFINED fooba)
  message ("fooba not defined")
endif (NOT DEFINED fooba)
```

In compound `if` statements there is an order of precedence that specifies the order that the operations will be evaluated. For example, in the statement below, the NOT will be evaluated first then the AND, not the other way around. Thus the statement will be false and the message never printed. Had the AND been evaluated first the statement would be true.

```
if (NOT 0 AND 0)
  message ("This line is never executed")
endif (NOT 0 AND 0)
```

CMake defines the order of operations such that EXISTS, COMMAND, and DEFINED operators, are evaluated first, then any EQUAL, LESS, GREATER, STREQUAL, STRLESS, STRGREATER, and MATCHES operators. The NOT operators are evaluated next and finally the AND, and OR, expressions will be evaluated. With operations that have the same level of precedence, such as AND and OR, they will be evaluated from left to right. Current CMake does not support using parentheses to order evaluation of the expression.

The `foreach`, `while`, and `macro` commands are the best way to reduce the size of your CMakeLists files and keep them maintainable. The `foreach` command enables you to execute a group of CMake commands repeatedly on the members of a list. Consider the following example adapted from VTK:

```
foreach (tfile
         TestAnisotropicDiffusion2D
         TestButterworthLowPass
         TestButterworthHighPass
         TestCityBlockDistance
         TestConvolve
         )
  add_test(${tfile}-image ${VTK_EXECUTABLE}
    ${VTK_SOURCE_DIR}/Tests/rtImageTest.tcl
    ${VTK_SOURCE_DIR}/Tests/${tfile}.tcl
    -D ${VTK_DATA_ROOT}
    -V Baseline/Imaging/${tfile}.png
    -A ${VTK_SOURCE_DIR}/Wrapping/Tcl
    )
endforeach ( tfile )
```

The first argument of the `foreach` command is the name of the variable that will take on a different value with each iteration of the loop. The remaining arguments are the list of values over which to loop. In this example the body of the `foreach` loop is just one CMake command, `add_test`. In the body of the `foreach` loop any time the loop variable (`tfile` in this example) is referenced it will be replaced with the current value from the list. In the first iteration, occurrences of ${tfile} will be replaced with TestAnisotropicDiffusion2D. In the next iteration, ${tfile} will be replaced with TestButterworthLowPass. The FOREACH loop will continue to loop until all the arguments have been processed.

It is worth mentioning that FOREACH loops can be nested and that the loop variable is replaced prior to any other variable expansion. This means that in the body of a FOREACH loop you can construct variable names using the loop variable. In the code below the loop variable tfile is expanded, and then concatenated with _TEST_RESULT. That new variable name is then expanded and tested to see if it matches FAILED.

```
if ( ${${tfile}}_TEST_RESULT} MATCHES FAILED)
   message ("Test ${tfile} failed.")
endif ( ${${tfile}}_TEST_RESULT} MATCHES FAILED)
```

The while command provides for looping based on a test condition. The format for the test expression in the while command is the exact same as that for the if command described earlier. Consider the following example which is used by CTest. Note that CTest updates the value of CTEST_ELAPSED_TIME internally.

```
#######################################################
# run paraview and ctest test dashboards for 6 hours
#
while (${CTEST_ELAPSED_TIME} LESS 36000)
   set (START_TIME ${CTEST_ELAPSED_TIME})
   ctest_run_script ( "dash1_ParaView_vs71continuous.cmake" )
   ctest_run_script ( "dash1_cmake_vs71continuous.cmake" )
endwhile (${CTEST_ELAPSED_TIME} LESS 36000)
```

While the foreach and while commands allow you to handle repetitive tasks that occur in sequence, the macro command supports repetitive tasks that may be scattered throughout your CMakeLists files. Once a macro is defined it can be used by any CMakeLists files processed after its definition. The first argument is the name of the macro to create. All additional arguments are formal parameters to the macro.

```
# define a simple macro

macro (assert TEST COMMENT)
   if (NOT ${TEST})
     message ("Assertion failed: ${COMMENT}")
   endif (NOT ${TEST})
endmacro (assert)
```

```
# use the macro
find_library (FOO_LIB foo /usr/local/lib)
assert ( ${FOO_LIB} "Unable to find library foo" )
```

The simple example above creates a macro called `assert`. The macro is defined to take two arguments. The first argument is a value to test and the second argument is a comment to print out if the test fails. The body of the macro is a simple `if` command with a `MESSAGE` command inside of it. The macro body ends when the `endmacro` command is found. The macro can be invoked simply by using its name as if it were a command. In the above example if `FOO_LIB` was not found a message would be displayed indicating the error condition.

The `macro` command also supports defining macros that take variable argument lists. This can be useful if you want to define a macro that has optional arguments or multiple signatures. Variable arguments can be referenced using `ARGC` and `ARGV0`, `ARGV1`, etc. instead of the formal parameters. `ARGV0` represents the first argument to the macro while `ARGV1` represents the next and so forth. You can even use a mixture of formal arguments and variable arguments as shown in the example below.

```
# define a macro that takes at least two arguments
# (the formal arguments) plus an optional third argument

macro (assert TEST COMMENT)
  if (NOT ${TEST})
    message ("Assertion failed: ${COMMENT}")

    # if called with three arguments then also write the
    # message to a file specified as the third argument
    if (${ARGC} MATCHES 3)
      file (APPEND ${ARGV2} "Assertion failed: ${COMMENT}")
    endif (${ARGC} MATCHES 3)

  endif (NOT ${TEST})
endmacro (ASSERT)

# use the macro
find_library (FOO_LIB foo /usr/local/lib)
assert ( ${FOO_LIB} "Unable to find library foo" )
```

In this example the two required arguments are `TEST` and `COMMENT`. These required arguments can be referenced by name, as they are in this example, or they can be referenced using `ARGV0` and `ARGV1`. If you want to process the arguments as a list you can use the `ARGV` and `ARGN` variables. `ARGV` (as opposed to `ARGV0`, `ARGV1`, etc) is a list of all the arguments to the macro while ARGN is a list of all the arguments after the formal arguments. Inside your macro you can use the foreach command to iterate over ARGV or ARGN as desired.

4.4   Regular Expressions

A few CMake commands, such as if and string, make use of regular expressions or can take a regular expression as an argument. In its simplest form, a regular-expression is a sequence of characters used to search for exact character matches. However, many times the exact sequence to be found is not known, or only a match at the beginning or end of a string is desired. Since there are a few different conventions for specifying regular expressions, CMake's standard is described below. The description is based on the open source regular expression class from Texas Instruments that is used by CMake for parsing regular expressions.

Regular expressions can be specified by using combinations of standard alphanumeric characters and the following regular expression meta-characters:

^   Matches at beginning of a line or string

$ Matches at end of a line or string

.   Matches any single character other than a newline

[ ]   Matches any character(s) inside the brackets

[^]   Matches any character(s) not inside the brackets

[-]   Matches any character in range on either side of a dash

*   Matches preceding pattern zero or more times

+   Matches preceding pattern one or more times

?   Matches preceding pattern zero or once only

()   Saves a matched expression and uses it in a later replacement

(|)   Matches either the left or right side of the bar

Note that more than one of these meta-characters can be used in a single regular expression in order to create complex search patterns. For example, the pattern [^ab1-9] indicates to match any character sequence that does not begin with the characters "a" or "b" or numbers in the series one through nine. The following examples may help clarify regular expression usage:

- The regular expression "^hello" matches a "hello" only at the beginning of a search string. It would match "hello there" but not "hi,\nhello there".

- The regular expression "long$" matches a "long" only at the end of a search string. It would match "so long", but not "long ago".

- The regular expression "t..t..g" will match anything that has a "t" then any two characters, another "t", any two characters and then a "g". It will match "testing", or "test again" but would not match "toasting"

- The regular expression "[1-9ab]" matches any number one through nine, and the characters "a" and "b". It would match "hello 1" or "begin", but would not match "no-match".

- The regular expression "[^1-9ab]" matches any character that is not a number one through nine, or an "a" or "b". It would NOT match "1ab2" or "b2345a", but would match "no-match".

- The regular expression "br* " matches something that begins with a "b", is followed by zero or more "r"s, and ends in a space. It would match "brrrr ", and "b ", but would not match "brrh ".

- The regular expression "br+ " matches something that begins with a "b", is followed by one or more "r"s, and ends in a space. It would match "brrrr ", and "br ", but would not match "b " or "brrh ".

- The regular expression "br? " matches something that begins with a "b", is followed by zero or one "r"s, and ends in a space. It would match "br ", and "b ", but would not match "brrr " or "brrh ".

- The regular expression "(..p)b" matches something ending with pb and beginning with whatever the two characters before the first p encountered in the line were. It would find "repb" in "rep drepaqrepb". The regular expression "(..p)a" would find "repa qrepb" in "rep drepa qrepb"

- The regular expression "d(..p)" matches something ending with p, beginning with d, and having two characters in between that are the same as the two characters before the first p encountered in the line. It would match "drepa qrepb" in "rep drepa qrepb".

4.5   Checking Versions of CMake

CMake is an evolving program and as new versions are released, new features or commands may be introduced. As a result, there may be instances where you might want to use a command that is in a current version of CMake but not in previous versions. There are a couple of ways to handle this. One option is to use the `if` command to check whether a new command exists. For example:

```
# test if the command exists

if (COMMAND some_new_command)
  # use the command
  some_new_command ( ARGS...)
endif (COMMAND some_new_command)
```

The above approach should work for most cases, but if you need more information you can test against the actual version of CMake that is being run by evaluating the `CMAKE_MAJOR_VERSION` and `CMAKE_MINOR_VERSION` variables as in the following example:

```
# look for newer versions of CMake

if (${CMAKE_MAJOR_VERSION}.${CMAKE_MINOR_VERSION} GREATER 1.6)
  # do something special here
endif (${CMAKE_MAJOR_VERSION}.${CMAKE_MINOR_VERSION}
       GREATER 1.6)
```

When writing your CMakeLists files you might decide that you do not want to support old versions of CMake. To do this you can place the following command at the top of your CMakeLists file:

```
cmake_minimum_required (VERSION 2.2)
```

This indicates that the person running CMake on your project must have at least CMake version 2.2. If they are running an older version of CMake then an error message will be displayed telling them that the project requires at least the specified version of CMake.

Finally, in some cases a new release of CMake might come out that no longer supports some commands you were using (although we try to avoid this). In these cases you can either update your project to work with the new version of CMake or set the `CMAKE_BACKWARDS_COMPATIBILITY` variable to the older version of CMake. Generally, by setting this variable, old commands that are no longer supported by CMake will still work. Users who are building your software can set the CMAKE_BACKWARDS_COMPATIBILITY variable if they have a newer version of CMake.

4.6   Using Modules

Code reuse is a valuable technique in software development and CMake has been designed to support it. Allowing CMakeLists files to make use of reusable modules enables the entire CMake community to share reusable sections of code. For CMake these sections of code are called modules and can be found in the Modules subdirectory of your CMake installation. Modules are simply sections of CMake commands put into a file. They can then be included into other CMakeLists files using the include command. For example, the following commands will include the FindTCL module from CMake and then add the Tcl library to the target FOO.

```
include (FindTCL)

target_link_libraries (FOO ${TCL_LIBRARY})
```

A module's location can be specified using a full path to the module file, or by letting CMake find the module by itself. CMake will look for modules in the directories specified by CMAKE_MODULE_PATH and if it cannot find it there, it will look in the Modules subdirectory of CMake. This way projects can overwrite modules that CMake provides to customize them for their needs. Modules can be broken into a few main categories:

Find Modules

These modules determine the location of software elements such as header files or libraries.

System Introspection Modules

These modules test the system for properties such as the size of a float, support for ANSI C++ streams, etc.

Utility Modules

These modules provide added functionality such as support for situations where one CMake project depends on another and other convenience routines.

Now let us consider these three types of modules in more detail. CMake includes a large number of Find modules. The purpose of a Find module is to locate software elements such as header or library files. If they cannot be found then they provide a cache entry so that the user can set the required properties. Consider the following module that finds the PNG library.

```
#
# Find the native PNG includes and library
#

# This module defines
# PNG_INCLUDE_DIR, where to find png.h, etc.
# PNG_LIBRARIES, the libraries to link against to use PNG.
# PNG_DEFINITIONS - You should call
# ADD_DEFINITIONS (${PNG_DEFINITIONS}) before compiling code
# that includes png library files.
# PNG_FOUND, If false, do not try to use PNG.

# also defined, but not for general use are
# PNG_LIBRARY, where to find the PNG library.

# None of the above will be defined unless zlib can be found.

# PNG depends on Zlib
include ( FindZLIB.cmake )

if (ZLIB_FOUND)
  find_path (PNG_PNG_INCLUDE_DIR png.h
  /usr/local/include
  /usr/include
  )

  find_library (PNG_LIBRARY png
  /usr/lib
  /usr/local/lib
  )

  if (PNG_LIBRARY)
    if (PNG_PNG_INCLUDE_DIR)
      # png.h includes zlib.h. Sigh.
      set (PNG_INCLUDE_DIR
          ${PNG_PNG_INCLUDE_DIR} ${ZLIB_INCLUDE_DIR} )
      set (PNG_LIBRARIES ${PNG_LIBRARY} ${ZLIB_LIBRARY})
      set (PNG_FOUND "YES")

      if (CYGWIN)
        if (BUILD_SHARED_LIBS)
          # No need to define PNG_USE_DLL here, because
          # it's default for Cygwin.
        else (BUILD_SHARED_LIBS)
```

```
        set (PNG_DEFINITIONS -DPNG_STATIC)
      endif (BUILD_SHARED_LIBS)
    endif (CYGWIN)

  endif (PNG_PNG_INCLUDE_DIR)
 endif (PNG_LIBRARY)

endif (ZLIB_FOUND)
```

The top of the module clearly documents what the module will do and what variables it will set. Next it includes another module, the FindZLIB module that determines if the ZLib library is installed. Next, if ZLib is found, the `find_path` command is used to locate the PNG include files. The first argument is the name of the variable to store the result in, the second argument is the name of the header file to look for, the remaining arguments are paths to search for the header file. If it is not found in the system path then the variable is set to `PNG_PNG_INCLUDE_DIR-NOTFOUND` allowing the user to set it.

Note that the paths to search for the PNG library can include hard coded directories, registry entries, and directories made up of other CMake variables. The next command finds the actual PNG library using a `find_library` command. This command performs additional checks to find a proper library name, such as, for example, adding "lib" in front of the name and ".so" at the end of the name on Linux systems.

After the finds, some CMake variables are set that developers using FindPNG can use in their projects (such as the include paths, and library name). Finally `PNG_FOUND` is set correctly which lets developers know that the PNG library was properly found.

This structure is fairly common to all Find modules in CMake. Usually they are fairly short but in some cases, such as `FindOpenGL`, they can be a few pages long. Usually they are independent of other modules but there is no restriction that they cannot use other modules.

System introspection modules provide information about the target platform or compiler. Many of these modules have names prefixed with `Test` or `Check`, such as `TestBigEndian` and `CheckTypeSize`. Many of the system introspection modules actually try compiling code to determine the correct result. In these cases the source code is usually named the same as the module but with a `.c` or `.cxx` extension instead. System introspection modules are covered in more detail in chapter 7.

CMake includes a few Utility modules to help make using CMake a little easier. `CMakeExportBuildSettings` and `CMakeImportBuildSettings` provide tools to help verify that two C++ projects are compiled with the same compiler and key flags. The `CMakePrintSystemInformation` module prints out a number of key CMake settings to aid in debugging.

Using CMake with SWIG

One example of how modules can be used is to look at wrapping your C/C++ code into another language using SWIG. SWIG (Simplified Wrapper and Interface Generator) www.swig.org is a tool that reads annotated C/C++ header files and creates wrapper code (glue code) in order to make the corresponding C/C++ libraries available to other programming languages such as TCL, Python, or Java. CMake supports SWIG with the `find_package` command. Although SWIG can be used from CMake using custom commands, the SWIG package provides several macros that make building SWIG projects with CMake simple. To use the SWIG macros, first you must call the `find_package` command with the name SWIG. Then you need to include the file referenced by the variable `SWIG_USE_FILE`. This will define several macros and set up CMake to easily build SWIG based projects.

Two very useful macros are `SWIG_ADD_MODULE` and `SWIG_LINK_LIBRARIES`. `SWIG_ADD_MODULE` works much like the `add_library` command in CMake. The command is invoked like this:

```
SWIG_ADD_MODULE (module_name language source1 source2 … sourceN)
```

The first argument is the name of the module to create. The next argument is the target language SWIG is producing a wrapper for. The rest of the arguments consist of a list of source files used to create a shared module. The big difference is that SWIG `.i` interface files can be used directly as sources. The macro will create the correct custom commands to run SWIG and generate the C or C++ wrapper code from the SWIG interface files. The sources can also be regular C or C++ files that need to be compiled in with the wrappers.

The `SWIG_LINK_LIBRARIES` macro is used to link support libraries to the module. This macro is used because depending on the language being wrapped by SWIG, the name of the module may be different. The actual name of the module is stored in a variable called `SWIG_MODULE_${name}_REAL_NAME` where `${name}` is the name passed into the `SWIG_ADD_MODULE` macro. For example, `SWIG_ADD_MODULE(foo tcl foo.i)` would create a variable called `SWIG_MODULE_foo_REAL_NAME` which would contain the name of the actual module created.

Now consider the following example that uses the SWIG example found in SWIG under Examples/python/class.

```
# Find SWIG and include the use swig file
find_package (SWIG REQUIRED)

include (${SWIG_USE_FILE})

# Find python library and add include path for python headers
```

```
find_package (PythonLibs)
include_directories (${PYTHON_INCLUDE_PATH})

# set the global swig flags to empty
set (CMAKE_SWIG_FLAGS "")

# let swig know that example.i is c++ and add the -includeall
# flag to swig
set_source_files_properties (example.i PROPERTIES CPLUSPLUS ON)
set_source_files_properties (example.i
                             PROPERTIES SWIG_FLAGS "-includeall")

# Create the swig module called example
# using the example.i source and example.cxx
# swig will be used to create wrap_example.cxx from example.i
SWIG_ADD_MODULE (example python example.i example.cxx)
SWIG_LINK_LIBRARIES (example ${PYTHON_LIBRARIES})
```

This example first uses `find_package` to locate SWIG. Next it includes the `SWIG_USE_FILE` defining the SWIG cmake macros. Next, it finds the python libraries and sets up CMake to build with the python library. Notice that the SWIG input file example.i is used like any other source file in CMake, and properties are set on the file telling SWIG that the file is C++ and that the SWIG flag –includeall should be used when running SWIG on that source file. The module is created by telling SWIG the name of the module, the target language and the list of source files. Finally, the python libraries are linked to the module.

Using CMake with Qt

Projects using the popular widget toolkit Qt from Trolltech www.trolltech.com can be built with CMake. CMake supports multiple versions of Qt including versions 3 and 4. The first step is to tell CMake what versions of Qt to look for. Many Qt applications are designed to work with Qt3 or Qt4 but not both. If your application is designed for Qt4 then you can use the FindQt4 module, for Qt3 you would use the FindQt3 module. If your project can work with either version of Qt then you can use the generic FindQt module. All of the modules provide helpful tools for building Qt projects. The following is a simple example of building a project that uses Qt4.

```
find_package ( Qt4 )

if (QT4_FOUND)
  include (${QT_USE_FILE})

  # what are our ui files?
  set (QTUI_SRCS qtwrapping.ui)
```

```
QT4_WRAP_UI (QTUI_H_SRCS ${QTUI_SRCS})
QT4_WRAP_CPP (QT_MOC_SRCS TestMoc.h)

add_library (myqtlib ${QTUI_H_SRCS} ${QT_MOC_SRCS})
target_link_libraries (myqtlib ${QT_LIBRARIES} )

add_executable (qtwrapping qtwrappingmain.cxx)
target_link_libraries (qtwrapping myqtlib)

endif (QT4_FOUND)
```

Using CMake with FLTK

CMake also supports the The Fast Light Toolkit (FLTK) with special FLTK CMake commands. The `FLTK_WRAP_UI` command is used to run the fltk fluid program on a .fl file and produce a C++ source file as part of the build. The following example shows how to use FLTK with CMake.

```
find_package (FLTK)
if (FLTK_FOUND)
  set (FLTK_SRCS
       fltk1.fl
       )
  FLTK_WRAP_UI (wraplibFLTK ${FLTK_SRCS})
  add_library (wraplibFLTK ${wraplibFLTK_UI_SRCS} )
endif (FLTK_FOUND)
```

4.7   Specifying Optimized or Debug Libraries with a Target

On Windows platforms it is often required to link debug libraries with debug libraries and optimized libraries with optimized libraries. CMake helps satisfy this requirement with the `target_link_libraries` command which takes an optional flag that is debug or optimized. So, if a library is preceded with either debug or optimized, then that library will only be linked in with the like configuration type. For example:

```
add_executable (foo foo.c)
target_link_libraries (foo debug libdebug optimized libopt)
```

In this case foo will be linked against libdebug if a debug build was selected and against libopt if an optimized build was selected.

4.8   Shared Libraries and Loadable Modules

Shared libraries and loadable modules are very powerful tools for software developers. They can be used to create extension modules or plugins for off-the-shelf software, and can be used to decrease the compile/link/run cycles for C and C++ programs. However despite years of use, the cross platform creation of shared libraries and modules remains a black art understood by only a few developers. CMake has the ability to aid developers in the creation of shared libraries and modules. CMake knows the correct tools and flags to use in order to produce the shared libraries for most modern operating systems that support them. Unfortunately, CMake can not do all the work, and developers must sometimes alter source code and understand the basic concepts and common pitfalls associated with shared libraries before they can be used effectively. This section will describe many of the issues required to take advantage of shared libraries and loadable modules.

A shared library should be thought of more like an executable than a static library, and on most systems actually requires executable permissions to be set on the shared library file. This means that shared libraries can link to other shared libraries when they are created in the same way as an executable. Unlike a static library where the atomic unit is the object file, for shared libraries, the entire library is the atomic unit. This can cause some unexpected linker errors when converting from static to shared libraries. If an object file is part of a static library, but the executable linking to the library does not use any of the symbols in that object file, then the file is simply excluded from the final linked executable. With shared libraries, all the object files that make up the library and all of the dependencies that they require come as one unit. For example, suppose you had a library with an object file defining the function `DisplayOnXWindow()` which required the X11 library. If you linked an executable to that library, but did not call the `DisplayOnXWindow()` function, the static library version would not require X11, but the shared library version would require the X11 library. This is because a shared library has to be taken as one unit, and a static library is only an archive of object files from which linkers can choose which objects are needed. This means that static linked executables can be smaller, as they only contain the object code actually used.

Another difference between shared and static libraries is library order. With static libraries the order on the link line can make a difference. This is because most linkers only use the symbols that are needed in a single pass over all the given libraries. So, the library order should go from the library that uses the most other libraries to the library that uses no other libraries. CMake will preserve and remember the order of libraries and library dependencies of a project. This means that each library in a project should use the `target_link_libraries` command to specify all of the libraries that it directly depends on. The libraries will be linked with each other for shared builds, but not static builds. However, the link information is used in static builds when executables are linked. An executable that only links library libA will get libA plus libB and libC as long as libA's dependency on libB and libC was properly specified using `target_link_libraries (libA libB libC)`.

At this point, one might wonder why shared libraries would be preferred over static libraries. There are several reasons. First, shared libraries can decrease the compile/link/run cycle time. This is because the linker does not have to do as much work when linking to shared libraries because there are fewer decisions to be made about which object files to keep. Also, often times, the executable does not even need to be re-linked after the shared library is rebuilt. So, developers can work on a library compiling and linking only the small part of the program that is currently being developed, and then re-run the executable after each build of the shared library. Also, if a library is used by many different executables on a system, then there only needs to be one copy of the library on disk and often times in memory as well.

In addition to the concept of a software library, shared libraries can also be used on many systems as run time loadable modules. This means that a program can at run time, load and execute object code that was not part of the original software. This allows developers to create software that is both open and closed. (For more information see Object Oriented Software Construction by Bertrand Meyer.) Closed software is software that can not be modified. It has been through a testing cycle and can be certified to perform specific tasks with regression tests. However, a seemingly opposite goal is sought after by developers of object oriented software. This is the concept of Open software that can be extended by future developers. This can be done via inheritance and polymorphism with object systems. Shared libraries that can be loaded at run time, allow for these seemingly opposite goals to be achieved in the same software package. Many common applications support the idea of plugins. The most common of these applications is the web browser. Internet Explorer uses plugins to support video over the web and 3D visualization. In addition to plugins, loadable factories can be used to replace C++ objects at run time as is done with VTK.

Once it is decided that shared libraries or loadable modules are the right thing for a particular project, there are a few issues that developers need to be aware of. The first question that must be answered is which symbols are exported by the shared library? This may sound like a simple question, but the answer is different from platform to platform. On most, but not all UNIX systems, the default behavior is to export all the symbols much like a static library. However, on Windows systems, developers must explicitly tell the linker and compiler which symbols are to be exported and imported from shared libraries. Often times this is a large problem for UNIX developers moving to Windows. There are two ways to tell the compiler/linker which symbols to export/import on Windows. The first more common approach is to decorate the code with a Microsoft™ C/C++ language extension. The second approach is to create an extra file called a .def file. This file is a simple ASCII file containing the names of all the symbols to be exported from a library.

The Microsoft™ extension uses the `__declspec` directive. If a symbol has `__declspec( dllexport )` in front of it, it will be exported, and if it has `__declspec( dllimport )` it will be imported. Since the same file may be shared during the creation and use of a library, it must be both exported and imported in the same source file. This can only be done with the preprocessor. The developer can create a macro called `LIBRARY_EXPORT` that is defined to `dllexport` when building the library and `dllimport` when using the library. CMake helps this process by automatically defining ${LIBNAME}_EXPORTS when building a DLL (dynamic link library, a.k.a. a shared library) on windows.

The following code snippet is from the VTK library vtkCommon, and is included by all the files in the vtkCommon library:

```
#if defined(WIN32)

 #if defined(vtkCommon_EXPORTS)
  #define VTK_COMMON_EXPORT __declspec( dllexport )
 #else
  #define VTK_COMMON_EXPORT __declspec( dllimport )
 #endif
#else
  #define VTK_COMMON_EXPORT
#endif
```

The example checks for Windows and checks the vtkCommon_EXPORTS macro provided by CMake. So, on UNIX VTK_COMMON_EXPORT is defined to nothing, and on Windows during the building of vtkCommon.dll it is defined as __declspec(dllexport), and when the file is being used by another file, it is defined to __declspec(dllimport).

The second approach requires a .def file to specify the symbols to be exported. This file could be created by hand, but for a large and changing C++ library that could be time consuming and error prone. CMake's custom commands can be used to run a pre-link program that will create a .def file from the compiled object files automatically. In the following example, a Perl script called makedef.pl, the script runs the DUMPBIN program on the .obj files and extracts all the exportable symbols and writes a .def file with the correct exports for all the symbols in the library mylib.

```
----CMakeLists.txt-----

project (myexe)

set (SOURCES mylib.cxx mylib2.cxx)

# create a list of all the object files
string (REGEX REPLACE "\\.cxx" ".obj" OBJECTS "${SOURCES}")

# create a shared library with the .def file
add_library (mylib SHARED ${SOURCES}
  ${CMAKE_CURRENT_BINARY_DIR}/mylib.def
  )
```

```
# set the .def file as generated
set_source_files_properties (
  ${CMAKE_CURRENT_BINARY_DIR}/mylib.def
  PROPERTIES GENERATED 1
  )

# create an executable
add_executable (myexe myexe.cxx)

# link the executable to the dll
target_link_libraries(myexe mylib)

#convert to windows slashes
set (OUTDIR
  ${CMAKE_CURRENT_BINARY_DIR}/${CMAKE_CFG_INTDIR}
  )

string (REGEX REPLACE "/" "\\\\" OUTDIR ${OUTDIR})

# create a custom pre link command that runs
# a perl script to create a .def file using dumpbin
add_custom_command (
  TARGET mylib PRE_LINK
  COMMAND perl
  ARGS ${CMAKE_CURRENT_SOURCE_DIR}/makedef.pl
  ${CMAKE_CURRENT_BINARY_DIR}\\mylib.def mylib
  ${OUTDIR} ${OBJECTS}
  COMMENT "Create .def file"
  )
```

```
---myexe.cxx----
#include <iostream>
#include "mylib.h"
int main()
{
  std::cout << myTen() << "\n";
  std::cout << myEight() << "\n";
}
```

```
---mylib.cxx--
int myTen()
{
   return 10;
}
```

```
--mylib2.cxx---
int myEight()
{
   return 8;
}
```

There is a significant difference between Windows and most UNIX systems with respect to the requirement of symbols. DLL's on Windows are required to be fully resolved, and this means that they must link every symbol at creation. UNIX systems allow shared libraries to get symbols from the executable or other shared libraries at run time. On UNIX systems that support this feature, CMake will compile with the flags that allow executable symbols to be used by shared libraries. This small difference can cause large problems. A common, but hard to track down bug with DLL's happens with C++ template classes and static members. Two DLL's can end up with separate copies of what is supposed to be a single global static member of a class. There are also problems with the approach taken on most UNIX systems. The start up time for large applications with many symbols can be long since much of the linking is deferred to run time.

Another common pitfall occurs with C++ global objects. These objects require that constructors must be called before they can be used. The main that links or loads C++ shared libraries MUST be linked with the C++ compiler, or globals like cout may not be initialized before they are used causing strange crashes at start up time.

Since executables that link to shared libraries must be able to find the libraries at run time, special environment variables and linker flags must be used. There are tools that can be used to show which libraries an executable is actually using. On many UNIX systems there is a tool called ldd (otool –L on MacOSX) that shows which libraries are used by an executable. On Windows, a program called depends can be used for the same type of information. On many UNIX systems there are also environment variables like LD_LIBRARY_PATH that tell the program where to find the libraries at run time. Where supported CMake will add run time library path information into the linked executables, so that LD_LIBRARY_PATH is not required. That feature can be turned off by setting the cache entry CMAKE_SKIP_RPATH to false. This may be desirable for installed software that should not be looking in the build tree for shared libraries. On Windows there is only one PATH environment variable that is used for both DLL's and finding executables.

4.9   Shared Library Versioning

When an executable is linked to a shared library, it is important that the copy of the shared library loaded at runtime matches that expected by the executable. On some UNIX systems, a shared library has an associated "soname" intended to solve this problem.   When an executable links against the library, its soname is copied into the executable. At runtime, the dynamic loader uses this name from the executable to search for the library.

Consider a hypothetical shared library "foo" providing a few C functions that implement some functionality. The interface to foo is called an Application Programming Interface (API). If the implementation of these C functions changes in a new version of foo, but the API remains the same, then executables linked against foo will still run correctly. When the API changes, old executables will no longer run with a new copy of foo, so a new API version number must be associated with foo.

This can be implemented by creating the original version of foo with an soname and file name such as libfoo.so.1. A symbolic link such as libfoo.so -> libfoo.so.1 will allow standard linkers to work with the library and create executables. The new version of foo can be called libfoo.so.2 and the symbolic link updated so that new executables use the new library. When an old executable runs, the dynamic loader will look for libfoo.so.1, find the old copy of the library, and run correctly. When a new executable runs, the dynamic loader will look for libfoo.so.2 and correctly load the new version.

This scheme can be expanded to handle the case of changes to foo that do not modify the API. We introduce a second set of version numbers that is totally independent of the first. This new set corresponds to the software version providing foo. For example, some larger project may have introduced the existence of library foo starting in version 3.4. In this case, the file name for foo might be libfoo.so.3.4, but the soname would still be libfoo.so.1 because the API for foo is still on its first version. A symbolic link from libfoo.so.1 -> libfoo.so.3.4 will allow executables linked against the library to run. When a bug is fixed in the software without changing the API to foo, then the new library file name might be libfoo.so.3.5, and the symbolic link can be updated to allow existing executables to run.

CMake supports this soname-based version number encoding on platforms supporting soname natively. A target property for the shared library named "VERSION" specifies the version number used to create the file name for the library. This version should correspond to that of the software package providing foo. On Windows the VERSION property is used to set the binary image number, using major.minor format.   Another target property named "SOVERSION" specifies the version number used to create the soname for the library. This version should correspond to the API version number for foo. These target properties are ignored on platforms where CMake does not support this scheme.

The following CMake code configures the version numbers of shared library foo:

```
set_target_properties (foo PROPERTIES VERSION 1.2 SOVERSION 4)
```

This results in the following library and symbolic links:

```
libfoo.so.1.2
libfoo.so.4 -> libfoo.so.1.2
libfoo.so -> libfoo.so.4
```

If only one of the two properties is specified, the other defaults to its value automatically. For example, the code

```
set_target_properties (foo PROPERTIES VERSION 1.2)
```

results in the following shared library and symbolic link:

```
libfoo.so.1.2
libfoo.so -> libfoo.so.1.2
```

CMake makes no attempt to enforce sensible version numbers. It is up to the programmer to utilize this feature in a productive manner.

4.10 Installing Files

Software is typically installed into a directory separate from the source and build trees. This allows it to be distributed in a clean form and isolates users from the details of the build process. CMake provides the `install` command to specify how a project is to be installed. This command is invoked by a project in the CMakeLists file and tells CMake how to generate installation scripts. The scripts are executed at install time to perform the actual installation of files. On Makefile generators (UNIX, NMake, Borland, MinGW, etc.), the user simply runs `"make install"` (or "`nmake install`") and the make tool will invoke CMake's installing module. On GUI based systems (Visual Studio, Xcode, etc.) the user simply builds the target called `INSTALL`.

Each call to the `install` command defines some installation rules. Within one CMakeLists file (source directory) these rules will be evaluated in the order in which the corresponding commands are invoked. The order across multiple directories is not specified.

The `install` command has several signatures designed for common installation use cases. A particular invocation of the command specifies the signature as the first argument. The signatures are TARGETS, FILES, PROGRAMS, DIRECTORY, SCRIPT, and CODE.

install (TARGETS ...)

> Install the binary files corresponding to targets built inside the project.

install (FILES ...)

> General-purpose file installation. It is typically used for installation of header files, documentation, and data files required by your software.

install (PROGRAMS ...)

> Installs executable files not built by the project, such as shell scripts. It is identical to `install (FILES)` except that the default permissions of the installed file include the executable bit.

install (DIRECTORY ...)

> Install an entire directory tree. This may be used for installing directories with resources such as icons and images.

install (SCRIPT ...)

> Specify a user-provided CMake script file to be executed during installation. Typically this is used to define pre-install or post-install actions for other rules.

install (CODE ...)

> Specify user-provided CMake code to be executed during the installation. This is similar to `install (SCRIPT)` but the code is provided inline in the call as a string.

The TARGETS, FILES, PROGRAMS, DIRECTORY signatures are all meant to create install rules for files. The targets, files, or directories to be installed are listed immediately after the signature name argument. Additional details are specified using keyword arguments followed corresponding values. Keyword arguments provided by most of the signatures are as follows.

DESTINATION

> Specifies the location in which the installation rule will place files. This argument must be followed by a directory path indicating the location. If the directory is specified as a full path it will be evaluate at install time as an absolute path. If the directory is specified as a relative path it will be evaluated at install time relative to the installation prefix. The prefix may be set by the user through the cache variable CMAKE_INSTALL_PREFIX. A platform-specific default is provided by CMake: "/usr/local" on UNIX and "<SystemDrive>/Program Files/<ProjectName>" on Windows, where SystemDrive is something like "C:" and ProjectName is the name given to the top-most PROJECT command.

PERMISSIONS

Specifies file permissions to be set on the installed files. This option is needed only to override the default permissions selected by a particular INSTALL command signature. Valid permissions are OWNER_READ, OWNER_WRITE, OWNER_EXECUTE, GROUP_READ, GROUP_WRITE, GROUP_EXECUTE, WORLD_READ, WORLD_WRITE, WORLD_EXECUTE, SETUID, and SETGID. Some platforms do not support all of these permissions. On such platforms the corresponding permission names are ignored.

CONFIGURATIONS

Specifies a list of build configurations for which an installation rule applies (Debug, Release, etc.). For Makefile generators the build configuration is specified by the CMAKE_BUILD_TYPE cache variable. For Visual Studio and Xcode generators the configuration is selected when the INSTALL target is built. An installation rule will be evaluated only if the current install configuration matches an entry in the list provided to this argument. Configuration name comparison is case-insensitive.

COMPONENT

Specifies the installation component for which the installation rule applies. Some projects divide their installations into multiple components for separate packaging. For example, a project may define a "Runtime" component that contains the files needed to run a tool, a "Development" component containing the files needed to build extensions to the tool, and a "Documentation" component containing the manual pages and other help files. The project may then package each component separately for distribution by installing only one component at a time. By default all components are installed. Component-specific installation is an advanced feature intended for use by package maintainers. It requires manual invocation of the installation scripts with an argument defining the COMPONENT variable to name the component desired. Note that component names are not defined by CMake. Each project may define its own set of components.

OPTIONAL

Specifies that it is not an error if the input file to be installed does not exist. If the input file exists it will be installed as requested. If it does not exist it will be silently not installed.

Projects typically install some of the library and executable files created during their build process. The install command provides the TARGETS signature for this purpose:

```
install (TARGETS targets...
        [[ARCHIVE|LIBRARY|RUNTIME]
         [DESTINATION <dir>]
         [PERMISSIONS permissions...]
         [CONFIGURATIONS [Debug|Release|...]]
```

```
          [COMPONENT <component>]
          [OPTIONAL]
        ] [...])
```

The `TARGETS` keyword is immediately followed by a list of the targets created using `add_executable` or `add_library` to be installed. One or more files corresponding to each target will be installed.

Files installed with this signature may be divided into three categories: `ARCHIVE`, `LIBRARY`, and `RUNTIME`. These categories are designed to group target files by typical installation destination. The corresponding keyword arguments are optional, but if present specify that other arguments following them apply only to target files of that type. Target files are categorized as follows:

executables - `RUNTIME`

>   Created by `add_executable` (.exe on Windows, no extension on UNIX)

loadable modules - `LIBRARY`

>   Created by `add_library` with the `MODULE` option (.dll on Windows, .so on UNIX)

shared libraries - `LIBRARY`

>   Created by `add_library` with the `SHARED` option on UNIX-like platforms (.so on most UNIX, .dylib on Mac)

dynamic-link libraries - `RUNTIME`

>   Created by `add_library` with the `SHARED` option on Windows platforms (.dll)

import libraries - `ARCHIVE`

>   Linkable file created by a dynamic-link library that exports symbols (.lib on most Windows, .dll.a on Cygwin and MinGW).

static libraries - `ARCHIVE`

>   Created by `add_library` with the `STATIC` option (.lib on Windows, .a on UNIX, Cygwin, and MinGW)

Consider a project that defines an executable `myExecutable` that links to a shared library `mySharedLib`. It also provides a static library `myStaticLib` and a plugin module to the executable called `myPlugin` that also links to the shared library. The executable, static library, and plugin file may be installed individually using the commands

```
install (TARGETS myExecutable DESTINATION bin)
install (TARGETS myStaticLib DESTINATION lib/myproject)
install (TARGETS myPlugin DESTINATION lib)
```

The executable will not be able to run from the installed location until the shared library to which it links is also installed. Installation of the library requires a bit more care in order to support all platforms. It must be installed to a location searched by the dynamic linker on each platform. On UNIX-like platforms the library is typically installed to `lib` while on Windows it should be placed next to the executable in `bin`. An additional challenge is that the import library associated with the shared library on Windows should be treated like the static library and installed to `lib/myproject`. In other words we have three different kinds of files created with a single target name that must be installed to three different destinations! Fortunately this problem can be solved using the category keyword arguments. The shared library may be installed using the command

```
install (TARGETS mySharedLib
         RUNTIME DESTINATION bin
         LIBRARY DESTINATION lib
         ARCHIVE DESTINATION lib/myproject)
```

This tells CMake that the `RUNTIME` file (.dll) should be installed to `bin`, the `LIBRARY` file (.so) should be installed to `lib`, and the `ARCHIVE` (.lib) file should be installed to `lib/myproject`. On UNIX the `LIBRARY` file will be installed and on Windows the `RUNTIME` and `ARCHIVE` files will be installed.

If the above sample project is to be packaged into separate runtime and development components we must assign the appropriate component to each target file installed. The executable, shared library, and plugin are required in order to run the application, so they belong in a `Runtime` component. Meanwhile the import library (corresponding to the shared library on Windows) and the static library are required only to develop extensions to the application and therefore belong in a `Development` component.

Component assignments may be specified by adding `COMPONENT` arguments to each command above. However we may also combine all the installation rules into a single command invocation. This single command is equivalent to all the above commands with components added. Files generated by each target are installed using the rule for their corresponding category.

```
Install (TARGETS myExecutable mySharedLib myStaticLib myPlugin
         RUNTIME DESTINATION bin          COMPONENT Runtime
         LIBRARY DESTINATION lib          COMPONENT Runtime
         ARCHIVE DESTINATION lib/myproject COMPONENT Development)
```

Projects may install files other than those that are created with `add_executable` or `add_library`, such as header files or documentation. General-purpose installation of files is specified using the `FILES` signature:

```
install (FILES files... DESTINATION <dir>
         [PERMISSIONS permissions...]
         [CONFIGURATIONS [Debug|Release|...]]
         [COMPONENT <component>]
         [RENAME <name>] [OPTIONAL])
```

The `FILES` keyword is immediately followed by a list of files to be installed. Relative paths are evaluated with respect to the current source directory. Files will be installed to the given `DESTINATION` directory. For example, the command

```
install (FILES my-api.h ${CMAKE_CURRENT_BINARY_DIR}/my-config.h
         DESTINATION include)
```

Installs the file `my-api.h` from the source tree and the file `my-config.h` from the build tree into the `include` directory under the installation prefix. By default installed files are given permissions `OWNER_WRITE`, `OWNER_READ`, `GROUP_READ`, and `WORLD_READ`, but this may be overridden by specifying the `PERMISSIONS` option. Consider the case in which we want to install a global configuration file on a UNIX system that is readable only by its owner (such as root). We may accomplish this with the command

```
install (FILES my-rc DESTINATION /etc
         PERMISSIONS OWNER_WRITE OWNER_READ)
```

which installs the file `my-rc` with owner read/write permission into the absolute path `/etc`.

The `RENAME` argument specifies a name for an installed file that may be different from the original file. Renaming is allowed only when a single file is installed by the command. For example, the command

```
install(FILES version.h DESTINATION include RENAME my-version.h)
```

will install the file `version.h` from the source directory to `include/my-version.h` under the installation prefix.

Projects may also install helper programs such as shell scripts or python scripts that are not actually compiled as targets. These may be installed with the `FILES` signature using the `PERMISSIONS` option to add execute permission. However this case is common enough to justify a simpler interface. CMake provides the `PROGRAMS` signature for this purpose:

```
install (PROGRAMS files... DESTINATION <dir>
         [PERMISSIONS permissions...]
         [CONFIGURATIONS [Debug|Release|...]]
         [COMPONENT <component>]
         [RENAME <name>] [OPTIONAL])
```

The `PROGRAMS` keyword is immediately followed by a list of scripts to be installed. This command is identical to the `FILES` signature except that the default permissions additionally include `OWNER_EXECUTE`, `GROUP_EXECUTE`, and `WORLD_EXECUTE`. For example, we may install a python utility script with the command

```
install (PROGRAMS my-util.py DESTINATION bin)
```

which installs `my-util.py` to the `bin` directory under the installation prefix and gives it owner, group, and world read and execute permission plus owner write.

Projects may also provide a whole directory full of resource files such as icons or html documentation. An entire directory may be installed using the `DIRECTORY` signature:

```
install (DIRECTORY dirs... DESTINATION <dir>
         [FILE_PERMISSIONS permissions...]
         [DIRECTORY_PERMISSIONS permissions...]
         [USE_SOURCE_PERMISSIONS]
         [CONFIGURATIONS [Debug|Release|...]]
         [COMPONENT <component>]
         [[PATTERN <pattern> | REGEX <regex>]
         [EXCLUDE] [PERMISSIONS permissions...]] [...])
```

The `DIRECTORY` keyword is immediately followed by a list of directories to be installed. Relative paths are evaluated with respect to the current source directory. Each named directory is installed to the destination directory. The last component of each input directory name is appended to the destination directory as that directory is copied. For example, the command

```
install (DIRECTORY data/icons DESTINATION share/myproject)
```

will install the `data/icons` directory from the source tree into `share/myproject/icons` under the installation prefix. A trailing slash will leave the last component empty and install the contents of the input directory to the destination. The command

```
install (DIRECTORY doc/html/ DESTINATION doc/myproject)
```

installs the contents of `doc/html` from the source directory into `doc/myproject` under the installation prefix. If no input directory names are given, as in

```
install (DIRECTORY DESTINATION share/myproject/user)
```

the destination directory will be created but nothing will be installed into it.

Files installed by the `DIRECTORY` signature are given the same default permissions as the `FILES` signature. Directories installed by the `DIRECTORY` signature are given the same default permissions as the `PROGRAMS` signature. The `FILE_PERMISSIONS` and `DIRECTORY_PERMISSIONS` options may be used to override these defaults. Consider the case in which a directory full of example shell scripts is to be installed into a directory that is both owner and group writable. We may use the command

```
install (DIRECTORY data/scripts DESTINATION share/myproject
        FILE_PERMISSIONS
          OWNER_READ OWNER_EXECUTE OWNER_WRITE
          GROUP_READ GROUP_EXECUTE
          WORLD_READ WORLD_EXECUTE
        DIRECTORY_PERMISSIONS
          OWNER_READ OWNER_EXECUTE OWNER_WRITE
          GROUP_READ GROUP_EXECUTE GROUP_WRITE
          WORLD_READ WORLD_EXECUTE)
```

which installs the directory `data/scripts` into `share/myproject/scripts` and sets the desired permissions. In some cases a fully prepared input directory created by the project may have the desired permissions already set. The `USE_SOURCE_PERMISSIONS` option tells CMake to use the file and directory permissions from the input directory during installation. If in the previous example the input directory were to have already been prepared with correct permissions the following command may have been used instead.

```
install (DIRECTORY data/scripts DESTINATION share/myproject
         USE_SOURCE_PERMISSIONS)
```

If the input directory to be installed is under source management, such as CVS, there may be extra subdirectories in the input that we do not wish to install. There may also be specific files which should not be installed or be installed with different permissions while most files get the defaults. The PATTERN and REGEX options may be used for this purpose. A PATTERN option is followed first by a globbing pattern and then by an EXCLUDE or PERMISSIONS option. A REGEX option is followed first by a regular expression and then by EXCLUDE or PERMISSIONS. The EXCLUDE option skips installation of those files or directories matching the preceding pattern or expression, while the PERMISSIONS option assigns specific permissions to them.

Each input file and directory is tested against the pattern or regular expression as a full path with forward slashes. A pattern will match only complete file or directory names occurring at the end of the full path while a regular expression may match any portion. For example, the pattern "foo*" will match ".../foo.txt" but not ".../myfoo.txt" or ".../foo/bar.txt" but the regular expression "foo" will match all of them.

Returning to the above example of installing an icons directory, consider the case in which the input directory is managed by CVS and also contains some extra text files that we do not want to install. The command

```
install (DIRECTORY data/icons DESTINATION share/myproject
         PATTERN "CVS" EXCLUDE
         PATTERN "*.txt" EXCLUDE)
```

installs the icons directory while ignoring any CVS directory or text file contained. The equivalent command using the REGEX option is

```
install (DIRECTORY data/icons DESTINATION share/myproject
         REGEX "/CVS$" EXCLUDE
         REGEX "/[^/]*.txt$" EXCLUDE)
```

which uses '/' and '$' to constrain the match in the same way as the patterns. Consider a similar case in which the input directory contains shell scripts and text files that we wish to install with different permissions than the other files. The command

```
install (DIRECTORY data/other/ DESTINATION share/myproject
        PATTERN "CVS" EXCLUDE
        PATTERN "*.txt"
          PERMISSIONS OWNER_READ OWNER_WRITE
        PATTERN "*.sh"
          PERMISSIONS OWNER_READ OWNER_WRITE OWNER_EXECUTE)
```

will install the contents of `data/other` from the source directory to `share/myproject` while ignoring CVS directories and giving specific permissions to `.txt` and `.sh` files.

Project installations may need to perform tasks other than just placing files in the installation tree. Third-party packages may provide their own mechanisms to register new plugins which must be invoked during project installation. The `SCRIPT` signature is provided for this purpose:

```
install (SCRIPT <file>)
```

The `SCRIPT` keyword is immediately followed by the name of a CMake script. CMake will execute the script during installation. If the file name given is a relative path it will be evaluated with respect to the current source directory. A simple use case is printing a message during installation. We first write a `message.cmake` file containing the code

```
message ("Installing My Project")
```

and then reference this script using the command

```
install (SCRIPT message.cmake)
```

Custom installation scripts are not executed during the main CMakeLists file processing. They are executed during the installation process itself. Variables and macros defined in the code containing the `install (SCRIPT)` call will not be accessible from the script. However there are a few variables defined during the script execution which may be used to get information about the installation. The variable `CMAKE_INSTALL_PREFIX` is set to the actual installation prefix. This may be different from the corresponding cache variable value because the installation scripts may be executed by a packaging tool that uses a different prefix. An environment variable `ENV{DESTDIR}` may be set by the user or packaging tool. Its value is pre-pended to the installation prefix and to absolute installation paths to determine the location to which files are installed. In order to reference an install location on disk the custom script may use `$ENV{DESTDIR}${CMAKE_INSTALL_PREFIX}` as the top portion of the path. The variable `CMAKE_INSTALL_CONFIG_NAME` is set to the name of the build configuration currently being installed (Debug, Release, etc.). During component-specific installation the variable CMAKE_INSTALL_COMPONENT is set to the name of the current component.

Custom installation scripts as simple as the message above may be more easily created with the script code placed inline in the call to the INSTALL command. The CODE signature is provided for this purpose:

```
install (CODE "<code>")
```

The CODE keyword is immediately followed by a string containing the code to place in the installation script. An install-time message may be created using the command

```
install (CODE "MESSAGE(\"Installing My Project\")")
```

which has the same effect as the message.cmake script but contains the code inline.

4.11 Advanced Commands

There are a few commands that can be very useful but are not typically used in writing CMakeLists files. This section will discuss a few of these commands and when they are useful. First consider the add_dependencies command which creates a dependency between two targets. CMake automatically creates dependencies between targets when it can determine them. For example, CMake will automatically create a dependency for an executable target that depends on a library target. The add_dependencies command is typically used to specify inter target dependencies between targets where at least one of the targets is a custom target (see section 8.4 for more information on custom targets.)

The include_regular_expression command also relates to dependencies. This command controls the regular expression that is used for tracing source code dependencies. By default CMake will trace all the dependencies for a source file including system include files such as stdio.h. If you specify a regular expression with the include_regular_expression command that regular expression will be used to limit what include files are processed. For example; if your software project's include files all started with the prefix foo (e.g. fooMain.c fooStruct.h etc) then you could specify a regular expression of ^foo.*$ to limit the dependency checking to just the files of your project.

Occasionally you might want to get a listing of all the source files that another source file depends on. This is useful when you have a program that uses pieces of a large library but you are not sure what pieces it is using. The output_required_files command will take a source file and produce a list of all the other source files it depends on. You could then use this list to produce a reduced version of the library that only contains the necessary files for your program.

Some tools such as Rational Purify on the Sun platform are run by inserting an extra command before the final link step. So, instead of

```
CC foo.o -o foo
```

The link step would be

```
purify CC foo.o -o foo
```

It is possible to do this with CMake. To run an extra program in front of the link line change the rule variables CMAKE_CXX_LINK_EXECUTABLE, and CMAKE_C_LINK_EXECUTABLE. Rule variables are described in chapter 11. The values for these variables are contained in the file Modules/CMakeDefaultMakeRuleVariables.cmake, and they are sometimes redefined in Modules/Platform/*.cmake. Make sure it is set after the PROJECT command in the CMakeLists file. Here is a small example of using purify to link a program called foo:

```
project (foo)

set (CMAKE_CXX_LINK_EXECUTABLE
    "purify ${CMAKE_CXX_LINK_EXECUTABLE}"
    )

add_executable (foo foo.cxx)
```

Of course, for a generic CMakeLists file you should have some if checks for the correct platform. This will only work for the Makefile generators because the rule variables are not used by the IDE generators. Another option would be to use $(PURIFY) instead of plain purify. This would pass through CMake into the makefile and be a make variable. The variable could be defined on the command line like this: make PURIFY=purify. If not specified then it would just use the regular rule for linking a C++ executable as PURIFY would be expanded by make to nothing.

## Chapter 5

Packaging with CPack

CPack is a powerful, easy to use, cross-platform software packaging tool distributed with CMake since version 2.4.2. It uses the generators concept from CMake to abstract package generation on specific platforms. It can be used with or without CMake, but it may depend on some software being installed on the system. Using a simple configuration file or using a CMake module, the author of a project can package a complex project into a simple installer. This chapter will describe how to apply CPack to a CMake project.

5.1 CPack Basics

Users of your software may not always want to or be able to build the software in order to install it. The software maybe closed source, or it may take a long time to compile, or in the case of an end user application the users may have no interest in building the application. For these cases, what is needed is a way to build the software on one machine, and then move the install tree to a different machine. The most basic way to do this is to use the DESTDIR environment variable to install the software into a temporary location, and then to tar or zip up that directory and move it to the another machine. Another more powerful approach is to use the CPack tool included in CMake.

CPack is a tool included with CMake, which can be used to create installers and packages for projects. CPack can create two basic types of packages, source and binary. CPack works in much the same way as CMake does for building software. It does not aim to replace native packaging tools, but rather it provides a single interface to a variety of tools. Currently CPack supports creation of Windows installers using NullSoft installer NSIS, Mac OSX Package Maker tool, Cygwin Setup packages, Debian packages, RPMs, .tar.gz, .sh (self extracting

.tar.gz files), .zip compressed files. The implementation of CPack works in a similar way to CMake. For each type of packaging tool supported, there is a CPack generator written in C++ that is used to run the native tool and create the package. For simple tar based packages, CPack includes a library version of tar and does not require tar to be installed on the system. For many of the other installers, native tools must be present for CPack to function.

With source packages, CPack makes a copy of the source tree and creates a zip or tar file. For binary packages, the use of CPack is tied to the install commands working correctly for a project. When setting up install commands, the first step is to make sure the files go into the correct directory structure with the correct permissions. The next step is to make sure the software is relocatable and can run in an installed tree. This may require changing the software itself, and there are many techniques to do that for different environments that go beyond the scope of this book. Basically, executables should be able to find data or other files using relative paths to the location of where it is installed. CPack installs the software into a temporary directory, and copies the install tree into the format of the native packaging tool. Once the install commands have been added to a project, enabling CPack in the simplest case is done by including the CPack.cmake file into the project.

Simple Example

The most basic CPack project would look like this:

```
project(CoolStuff)
add_executable(coolstuff coolstuff.cxx)
install(TARGETS coolstuff RUNTIME DESTINATION bin)
include(CPack)
```

In the CoolStuff project, an executable is created and installed into the directory bin. Then the CPack file is included by the project. At this point project CoolStuff will have CPack enabled. To run CPack for a CoolStuff, you would first build the project as you would any other CMake project. CPack adds several targets to the generated project. These targets in makefiles are package and package_source, and PACKAGE in visual studio and Xcode. For example, to build a source and binary package for CoolStuff using a makefile generator you would run the following commands:

```
mkdir build
cd build
cmake ../CoolStuff
make
make package
make package_source
```

This would create a source zip file called CoolStuff-0.1.1-Source.zip, a NSIS installer called CoolStuff-0.1.1-win32.exe, and a binary zip file CoolStuff-0.1.1-win32.zip. The same thing could be done using the CPack command line.

```
cd build
cpack -C CPackConfig.cmake
cpack -C CPackSourceConfig.cmake
```

What happens when CPack.cmake is included

When the include(CPack) command is executed, the CPack.cmake file is included into the project. By default this will use the configure_file command to create CPackConfig.cmake and CPackSourceConfig.cmake in the binary tree of the project. These files contain a series of set commands setting variables for use when CPack is run during the packaging step. The names of the files that are configured by the CPack.cmake file can be customized with these two variables; CPACK_OUTPUT_CONFIG_FILE which defaults to CPackConfig.cmake and CPACK_SOURCE_OUTPUT_CONFIG_FILE which defaults to CPackSourceConfig.cmake.

The source for these files can be found in the Templates/CPackConfig.cmake.in. This file contains some comments, and a single variable that is set by CPack.cmake. The file contains this line of CMake code:

```
@_CPACK_OTHER_VARIABLES_@
```

If the project contains the file CPackConfig.cmake.in in the top level of the source tree, that file will be used instead of the file in the Templates directory. If the project contains the file CPackSourceConfig.cmake.in, then that file will be used for the creation of CPackSourceConfig.cmake.

The configuration files created by CPack.cmake will contain all variables that begin with "CPACK_" in the current project. This is done using the command:

```
get_cmake_property(res VARIABLES)
```

The above command gets all variables defined for the current CMake project. Some CMake code then looks for all variables starting with "CPACK_", and each variable found is then configured into the two configuration files as CMake code. For example, if you had a variable set like this in your CMake project:

```
set(CPACK_PACKAGE_NAME "CoolStuff")
```

CPackConfig.cmake and CPackSourceConfig.cmake would have the same thing in them:

```
set(CPACK_PACKAGE_NAME "CoolStuff")
```

It is important to remember that CPack is run after CMake on the project. CPack uses the same parser as CMake, but will not have the same variable values as the CMake project. It will only have the variables that start with CPACK_, and these variables will be configured into a configuration file by CMake. This can cause some errors and confusion if the values of the variables use escape characters. Since they are getting parsed twice by the CMake language, they will need double the level of escaping. For example, if you had the following in your CMake project:

```
set(CPACK_PACKAGE_NAME "Cool \"Stuff\"")
```

The resulting CPack files would have this:

```
set(CPACK_FOOBAR "Cool "Stuff"")
```

That would not be exactly what you would want or might expect. To get around this problem, there are two solutions. The first is to add an additional level of escapes to the original set command like this:

```
(CPACK_PACKAGE_NAME "Cool \\\"Stuff\\\"")
```

This would result in the correct set command which would look like this:

```
set(CPACK_FOOBAR "Cool \"Stuff\"")
```

The second solution to the escaping problem is explained in the next section.

Adding custom CPack options

To avoid the escaping problem a project specific CPack configure file can be specified. This file will be loaded by CPack after CPackConfig.cmake or CPackSourceConfig.cmake is loaded, and CPACK_GENERATOR will be set to the CPack generator being run. Variables set in this file only require one level of CMake escapes. This file can be configured or not, and contains regular CMake code. So, for the above example, you could move CPACK_FOOBAR into a file MyCPackOptions.cmake.in and configure that file into the build tree of the project. Then set the project configuration file path like this:

```
configure_file ("${PROJECT_SOURCE_DIR}/MyCPackOptions.cmake.in"
                "${PROJECT_BINARY_DIR}/MyCPackOptions.cmake"
                @ONLY)
set (CPACK_PROJECT_CONFIG_FILE
    "${PROJECT_BINARY_DIR}/CMakeCPackOptions.cmake")
```

Where MyCPackOptions.cmake.in contained:

```
(CPACK_FOOBAR "Cool \"Stuff\"")
```

The CPACK_PROJECT_CONFIG_FILE variable should contain the full path to the CPack config file for the project as seen in the above example. This has the added advantage that the cmake code can contain if statements based on the CPACK_GENERTOR value, so that packager specific values can be set for a project. For example, the CMake project sets the icon for the installer in this file:

```
set (CPACK_NSIS_MUI_ICON
    "@CMake_SOURCE_DIR@/Utilities/Release\\CMakeLogo.ico")
```

Note that the path has forward slashes except for the last part which has an escaped \ as the path separator. As of the writing of this book, NSIS needed the last part of the path to have a Windows style slash. If you do not do this, you may get the following error:

```
File: "…/Release/CMakeLogo.ico" -> no files found.
Usage: File [/nonfatal] [/a] ([/r] [/x filespec [...]]
       filespec [...] | /oname=outfile one_file_only)
```

Options added by CPack

In addition to creating the two configuration files, CPack.cmake will add some advanced options to your project. The options added depend on the environment and OS that CMake is running on, and control the default packages that are created by CPack. These options are of the form CPACK_<CPack Generator Name>. Where generator names available on each platform can be found in the following table:

Windows	Cygwin	Linux/Unix	Mac OSX
NSIS	CYGWIN_BINARY	DEB	PACKAGEMAKER
ZIP	SOURCE_CYGWIN	RPM	OSXX11
SOURCE_ZIP		STGZ	
		TBZ2	
		TZ	
		SOURCE_TGZ	
		SOURCE_TZ	

Turning these options on or off affects the packages that are created by running CPack with no options. If the option is off in the CMakeCache.txt file for the project, you can still build that package type by specifying the -G option to the CPack command line.

5.2   CPack Source Packages

Source packages in CPack simply copy the entire source tree for a project into a package file, and no install rules are used like in the case of binary packages. Out of source builds should be used to avoid having extra binary stuff polluting the source package. If you have files or directories in your source tree that are not wanted in the source package, you can use the variable CPACK_SOURCE_IGNORE_FILES to exclude things from the package. This variable contains a list of regular expressions. Any file or directory that matches a regular expression in that list will be excluded from the sources. The default setting is as follows:

```
"/CVS/;/\\\\\\\\.svn/;\\\\\\\\.swp$;\\\\\\\\.#;/#"
```

There are many levels of escapes used in the default value as this variable is parsed by CMake once and CPack again. It is important to realize that the source tree will not use any install commands, it will simply copy the entire source tree minus the files it is told to ignore into the package. To avoid the multiple levels of escape, the file referenced by CPACK_PROJECT_CONFIG_FILE should be used to set this variable. The expression is a regular expression and not a wild card statement, see section 4.4 for more information about CMake regular expressions.

5.3   CPack Installer commands

Since binary packages require CPack to interact with the install rules of the project being packaged, this section will cover some of the options CPack provides to interact with the install rules of a project. CPack can work with CMake's install scripts or with external install commands.

CPack and CMake install commands

In most CMake projects, using the cmake install rules will be sufficient to create the desired package. By default CPack will run the install rule for the current project. However, if you have a more complicated project, you can specify sub-projects and install directories with the variable CPACK_INSTALL_CMAKE_PROJECTS. This variable should hold quadruplets of install directory, install project name, install component, and install subdirectory. For example, if you had a project with a sub project called MySub that was compiled into a directory called SubProject, and you wanted to install all of its components, you would have this:

```
SET(CPACK_INSTALL_CMAKE_PROJECTS  "SubProject;MySub;ALL;/")
```

CPack and DESTDIR

By default CPack does not use the DESTDIR option during the installation phase. Instead it sets the CMAKE_INSTALL_PREFIX to the full path of the temporary directory being used by CPack to stage the install package. This can be changed by setting CPACK_SET_DESTDIR to on. If the DESTDIR option is on, CPack will use the projects cache value for CPACK_INSTALL_PREFIX, and set DESTDIR to the temporary staging area. This allows absolute paths to be installed under the temporary directory. Relative paths are installed into DESTDIR/${project's CMAKE_INSTALL_PREFIX} where DESTDIR is set to the temporary staging area.

When doing a non-DESTDIR install for packaging, which is the default, any absolute paths are installed into absolute directories, and not into the package. Therefore, projects that do not use the DESTDIR option, must not use any absolute paths in install rules. Conversely, projects that must use absolute paths, must use the DESDIR option.

One other variable can be used to control the root path into which projects are installed into. This is the CPACK_PACKAGING_INSTALL_PREFIX. By default many of the generators install into the directory /usr. That variable can be used to change that to any directory including just /.

CPack and other installed directories

It is possible to run other install rules if the project is not CMake based. This can be done by using the variables CPACK_INSTALL_COMMANDS, and CPACK_INSTALLED_DIRECTORIES. CPACK_INSTALL_COMMANDS are commands that will be run during the installation phase of the packaging. CPACK_INSTALLED_DIRECTORIES should contain pairs of directory and subdirectory. The subdirectory can be '.' to be installed in the top-level directory of the installation. The files in each directory will be copied to the corresponding sub directory of the CPack staging directory and packaged with the rest of the files.

5.4   CPack for Windows Installer NSIS

To create Windows style wizard based self extracting executables, CPack uses NSIS (NullSoft Scriptable Install System). More information about NSIS can be found at the NSIS home page: http://nsis.sourceforge.net NSIS is a powerful tool with a scripting language used to create professional Windows installers. To create Windows installers with CPack, you will need NSIS installed on your machine.

CPack uses configured template files to control NSIS. There are two files configured by CPack during the creation of a NSIS installer. Both files are found in the CMake Modules directory. `Modules/NSIS.template.in` is the template for the NSIS script, and `Modules/NSIS.InstallOptions.ini.in` is the template for the modern user interface or MUI used by NSIS. The install options file contains the information about the pages used in the install wizard. This section will describe how to configure CPack to create an NSIS install wizard.

CPack variables used by CMake for NSIS

This section will contain screen captures from the CMake NSIS install wizard. For each part of the installer that can be changed or controlled from CPack, the variables and values used will be given.

cmake-2.5.20071023-win32-x86.exe	6,290 KB	Application
cmake-2.5.20071025-win32-x86.exe	6,324 KB	Application

Figure 7 Icon for installer in Windows Explorer

The first thing that a user will see of the installer in Windows is the icon for the installer executable itself. By default the installer will have the Null Soft Installer icon as seen in Figure 7 for the 20071023 cmake installer. This icon can be changed by setting the variable `CPACK_NSIS_MUI_ICON`. The installer for 20071025 in the same figure shows the CMake icon being used for the installer.

Figure 8 Uninstall Icon for NSIS installer

The last thing a users will see of the installer in Windows is the icon for the uninstall executable as seen in Figure 8. This option can be set with the `CPACK_NSIS_MUI_UNIICON` variable. Both the install and uninstall icons must be the same size and format which must be a valid windows .ico file usable by Windows Explorer. The icons are set like this:

```
# set the install/uninstall icon used for the installer itself
set (CPACK_NSIS_MUI_ICON
     "${CMake_SOURCE_DIR}/Utilities/Release\\CMakeLogo.ico")
set (CPACK_NSIS_MUI_UNIICON
     "${CMake_SOURCE_DIR}/Utilities/Release\\CMakeLogo.ico")
```

Figure 9 First Screen of Install Wizard

When running the installer, the first screen of the wizard will look like Figure 9. In this first screen you can control the name of the project which shows up in two places on the screen. The name used for the project is controlled by the variable CPACK_PACKAGE_INSTALL_DIRECTORY. In this example, it was set to "CMake 2.5" like this:

```
set (CPACK_PACKAGE_INSTALL_DIRECTORY "CMake
     ${CMake_VERSION_MAJOR}.${CMake_VERSION_MINOR}")
```

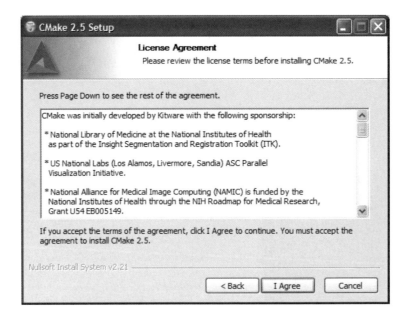

Figure 10 Second Screen of Install Wizard

The second page of the install wizard can be seen in Figure 10. This screen contains the license agreement. There are several things that can be configured on this page. The banner bitmap to the left of the "License Agreement" label is controlled by the variable CPACK_PACKAGE_ICON like this:

```
set (CPACK_PACKAGE_ICON
    "${CMake_SOURCE_DIR}/Utilities/Release\\CMakeInstall.bmp")
```

CPACK_PACKAGE_INSTALL_DIRECTORY is again used on this page everywhere you see the text "CMake 2.5". The text of the license agreement is set to the contents of the file specified in the CPACK_RESOURCE_FILE_LICENSE variable. CMake does the following:

```
set (CPACK_RESOURCE_FILE_LICENSE
    "${CMAKE_CURRENT_SOURCE_DIR}/Copyright.txt")
```

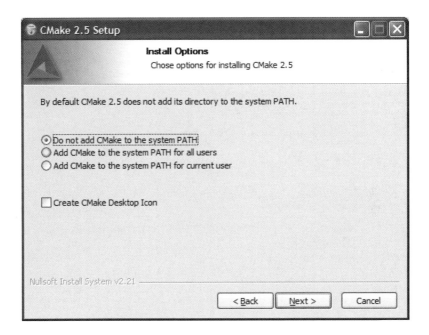

Figure 11 Third page of installer wizard

The third page of the installer can be seen in Figure 11. This page will only show up if
CPACK_NSIS_MODIFY_PATH is set to on. If you check the Create "name" Desktop Icon
button, and you put executable names in the variable CPACK_CREATE_DESKTOP_LINKS, then
a desktop icon for those executables will be created. For example, to create a desktop icon for
the CMakeSetup program of CMake, the following is done:

```
set (CPACK_CREATE_DESKTOP_LINKS CMakeSetup)
```

Multiple desktop links can be created if your application contains more than one executable.
The link will be created to the Start Menu entry, so CPACK_PACKAGE_EXECUTABLES
which is described later in this section must also contain the application in order for the a
desktop link to be created.

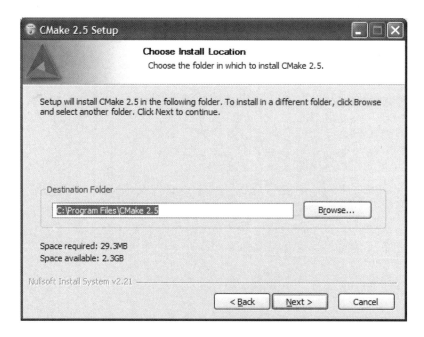

Figure 12 Fourth page of installer wizard

The fourth page of the installer seen in Figure 12 uses the variable CPACK_PACKAGE_INSTALL_DIRECTORY to specify the default destination folder in Program Files. The following cmake code was used to set that default:

```
set (CPACK_PACKAGE_INSTALL_DIRECTORY "CMake
    ${CMake_VERSION_MAJOR}.${CMake_VERSION_MINOR}")
```

The remaining pages of the installer wizard do not use any additional CPack variables, and are not included in this section. One more important option that can be set by the NSIS CPack generator is the registry key used. There are several CPack variables that control the default key used. The key is defined in the NSIS.template.in file as follows:

```
Software\@CPACK_PACKAGE_VENDOR@\@CPACK_PACKAGE_INSTALL_REGISTRY_KEY@
```

Where CPACK_PACKAGE_VENDOR defaults to Humanity, and

CPACK_PACKAGE_INSTALL_REGISTRY_KEY defaults to "${CPACK_PACKAGE_NAME} ${CPACK_PACKAGE_VERSION}"

So for CMake 2.5.20071025 the registry key would look like this:

HKEY_LOCAL_MACHINE\SOFTWARE\Kitware\CMake 2.5.20071025

Creating Windows Short Cuts in the Start Menu

There are two variables that control the short cuts that are created in the Windows Start menu by NSIS. The variables contain lists of pairs, and must have an even number of elements to work correctly. The first is CPACK_PACKAGE_EXECUTABLES and it should contain the name of the executable followed by the name of the short cut. For example in the case of CMake, the executable is called CMakeSetup, but the shortcut is just CMake. CMake does the following to create that short cut:

```
set (CPACK_PACKAGE_EXECUTABLES "CMakeSetup" "CMake" )
```

The second is CPACK_NSIS_MENU_LINKS. This variable contains arbitrary links into the install tree or to external web pages. The first of the pair is always the existing source file or location, and the second is the name that will show up in the Start menu. To add a link to the help file for CMakeSetup and a link to the CMake web page the following is done:

```
set (CPACK_NSIS_MENU_LINKS
     "doc/cmake-${VERSION_MAJOR}.${VERSION_MINOR}/CMakeSetup.html"
     "CMakeSetup Help" "http://www.cmake.org" "CMake Web Site")
```

Advanced NSIS CPack Options

In addition to the variables already discussed, CPack provides a few variables that are directly configured into the NSIS script file. These can be used to add NSIS script fragments to the final NSIS script used to create the installer. They are as follows:

CPACK_NSIS_EXTRA_INSTALL_COMMANDS

Extra commands used during install.

CPACK_NSIS_EXTRA_UNINSTALL_COMMANDS

Extra commands used during uninstall.

CPACK_NSIS_CREATE_ICONS_EXTRA

Extra NSIS commands in the icon section of the script.

CPACK_NSIS_DELETE_ICONS_EXTRA

Extra NSIS commands in the delete icons section of the script.

When using these variables the NSIS documentation should be referenced, and the user should look at the NSIS.template.in file for the exact placement of the above variables.

Setting file extension associations with NSIS

One example of a useful thing to do with the extra install commands is to create associations from file extensions to the installed application. For example, if you had an application CoolStuff that could open files with the extension .cool, you would set the following extra install and uninstall commands:

```
set (CPACK_NSIS_EXTRA_INSTALL_COMMANDS "
    WriteRegStr HKCR '.cool' '' 'CoolFile'
    WriteRegStr HKCR 'CoolFile' '' 'Cool Stuff File'
    WriteRegStr HKCR 'CoolFile\\shell' '' 'open'
    WriteRegStr HKCR 'CoolFile\\DefaultIcon' \\
                    '' '$INSTDIR\\bin\\coolstuff.exe,0'
    WriteRegStr HKCR 'CoolFile\\shell\\open\\command' \\
                    '' '$INSTDIR\\bin\\coolstuff.exe \"%1\"'
    WriteRegStr HKCR \"CoolFile\\shell\\edit' \\
                    '' 'Edit Cool File'
    WriteRegStr HKCR 'CoolFile\\shell\\edit\\command' \\
                    '' '$INSTDIR\\bin\\coolstuff.exe \"%1\"'
    System::Call \\
      'Shell32::SHChangeNotify(i 0x8000000, i 0, i 0, i 0)'
    ")

set (CPACK_NSIS_EXTRA_UNINSTALL_COMMANDS "
    DeleteRegKey HKCR '.cool'
    DeleteRegKey HKCR 'CoolFile'
    ")
```

This creates a windows file association to all files ending in .cool, so that when a user double clicks on a .cool file coolstuff.exe is run with the full path to the file as an argument. This also sets up an association for editing the file from the windows right click menu to the same coolstuff.exe program. The Windows explorer icon for the file is set to the icon found in the coolstuff.exe executable. When it is uninstalled, the registry keys are removed. Since all the double quotes and Windows path separators must be escaped, it is best put this code into the CPACK_PROJECT_CONFIG_FILE for the project.

```
configure_file(
  ${CoolStuff_SOURCE_DIR}/CoolStuffCPackOptions.cmake.in
  ${CoolStuff_BINARY_DIR}/CoolStuffCPackOptions.cmake @ONLY)
```

```
set (CPACK_PROJECT_CONFIG_FILE
  ${CoolStuff_BINARY_DIR}/CoolStuffCPackOptions.cmake)
include (CPack)
```

Installing Microsoft run time libraries

Although not strictly an NSIS CPack command, if you are creating applications on windows with the Microsoft compiler, you will most likely want to distribute the run time libraries from Microsoft along side your project. In CMake, all you need to do is the following:

```
include (InstallRequiredSystemLibraries)
```

This will add the compiler run time libraries as install files that will go into the bin directory for your application. If you do not want the libraries to go into the bin directory, you would do this:

```
set CMAKE_INSTALL_SYSTEM_RUNTIME_LIBS_SKIP TRUE)
include InstallRequiredSystemLibraries)
install PROGRAMS ${CMAKE_INSTALL_SYSTEM_RUNTIME_LIBS}
        DESTINATION mydir)
```

It is important to note, that the run time libraries must be right next to the executables for your package in order for Windows to find them. As of Visual Studio 2005, side by side manifest files are also required to be installed with your application when distributing the run time libraries. If you want to package a debug version of your software you will need to set CMAKE_INSTALL_DEBUG_LIBRARIES to ON prior to the include.

5.5   CPack for Cygwin Setup

Cygwin (http://www.cygwin.com/) is a Linux-like environment for Windows that consists of a run time dll and a collection of tools. To add tools to the official cygwin the cygwin setup program is used. The setup tool has very specific layouts for the source and binary trees that are to be included. CPack can create the source and binary tar files correctly bzip'ed that can be uploaded to the cygwin mirror sites. You must of course have your package accepted by the cygwin community before that is done. Since the layout of the package is more restrictive than other packaging tools, you may have to change some of the install options for your project.

The cygwin setup program requires that all files be installed into /usr/bin, /usr/share/project-version, /usr/share/man and /usr/share/doc/package-version. The cygwin CPack generator will automatically add the /usr to the install directory for the project. The project must install things into /share and /bin, and CPack will add the /usr prefix automatically.

Cygwin also requires that you provide a shell script that can be used to create the package from the sources. Any cygwin specific patches that are required for the package are also required to be provided in a diff file. CMake's configure_file command can be used to create both of these files for a project. Since CMake is a cygwin package, the CMake code used to configure CMake for the cygwin CPack generators is as follows:

```
set (CPACK_PACKAGE_NAME cmake)

# setup the name of the package for cygwin cmake-2.4.3
set (CPACK_PACKAGE_FILE_NAME
    "${CPACK_PACKAGE_NAME}-2.2.${CPACK_PACKAGE_VERSION_PATCH}")

# the source has the same name as the binary
set (CPACK_SOURCE_PACKAGE_FILE_NAME ${CPACK_PACKAGE_FILE_NAME})

# Create a cygwin version number in case there are changes
# for cygwin that are not reflected upstream in CMake
set (CPACK_CYGWIN_PATCH_NUMBER 1)

# if we are on cygwin and have cpack, then force the
# doc, data and man dirs to conform to cygwin style directories
set (CMAKE_DOC_DIR "/share/doc/${CPACK_PACKAGE_FILE_NAME}")
set (CMAKE_DATA_DIR "/share/${CPACK_PACKAGE_FILE_NAME}")
set (CMAKE_MAN_DIR "/share/man")

# These files are required by the cmCPackCygwinSourceGenerator and
# the files put into the release tar files.
set (CPACK_CYGWIN_BUILD_SCRIPT
    "${CMake_BINARY_DIR}/@CPACK_PACKAGE_FILE_NAME@-
        @CPACK_CYGWIN_PATCH_NUMBER@.sh")
set (CPACK_CYGWIN_PATCH_FILE
    "${CMake_BINARY_DIR}/@CPACK_PACKAGE_FILE_NAME@-
        @CPACK_CYGWIN_PATCH_NUMBER@.patch")

# include the sub directory for cygwin releases
include (Utilities/Release/Cygwin/CMakeLists.txt)

# when packaging source make sure to exclude the .build directory
set (CPACK_SOURCE_IGNORE_FILES
  "/CVS/" "/\\\\.build/" "/\\\\.svn/" "\\\\.swp$" "\\\\.#" "/#" "~$")
```

Utilities/Release/Cygwin/CMakeLists.txt:

```
# create the setup.hint file for cygwin
configure_file (
 "${CMake_SOURCE_DIR}/Utilities/Release/Cygwin/cygwin-setup.hint.in"
 "${CMake_BINARY_DIR}/setup.hint")

configure_file (
 "${CMake_SOURCE_DIR}/Utilities/Release/Cygwin/README.cygwin.in"
 "${CMake_BINARY_DIR}/Docs/@CPACK_PACKAGE_FILE_NAME@-
    @CPACK_CYGWIN_PATCH_NUMBER@.README")

install_files (/share/doc/Cygwin FILES
   ${CMake_BINARY_DIR}/Docs/@CPACK_PACKAGE_FILE_NAME@-
       @CPACK_CYGWIN_PATCH_NUMBER@.README)

# create the shell script that can build the project
configure_file (
 "${CMake_SOURCE_DIR}/Utilities/Release/Cygwin/cygwin-package.sh.in"
  ${CPACK_CYGWIN_BUILD_SCRIPT})

# Create the patch required for cygwin for the project
configure_file (
 "${CMake_SOURCE_DIR}/Utilities/Release/Cygwin/cygwin-patch.diff.in"
  ${CPACK_CYGWIN_PATCH_FILE})
```

The file Utilities/Release/Cygwin/cygwin-package.sh.in, can be found in the CMake source tree. It is a shell script that can be used to re-create the cygwin package from source. For other projects, there is a template install script that can be found in Templates/cygwin-package.sh.in. This script should be able to configure and package any cygwin based CPack project, and it is required for all official cygwin packages.

Another important file for cygwin binaries is share/doc/Cygwin/project-version.README. This file should contain the information required by cygwin about the project. In the case of CMake, the file is configured so that it can contain the correct version information. For example part of that file for CMake looks like this:

```
Build instructions:
  unpack cmake-2.5.20071029-1-src.tar.bz2
    if you use setup to install this src package, it will be
        unpacked under /usr/src automatically
  cd /usr/src
  ./cmake-2.5.20071029-1.sh all
This will create:
  /usr/src/cmake-2.5.20071029.tar.bz2
  /usr/src/cmake-2.5.20071029-1-src.tar.bz2
```

5.6   CPack for Apple OSX PackageMaker

On the Apple OSX operating system, CPack provides the ability to use the system Package Maker tool. This section will show the CMake application install screens users will see when installing the CMake package on OSX. The CPack variables set to change the text in the installer will be given for each screen of the installer.

Figure 13 Mac Package inside .dmg

In Figure 13, the .pkg file found inside the .dmg disk image created by the CPack package maker for Mac OS X is seen. The name of this file is controlled by the CPACK_PACKAGE_FILE_NAME variable. If this is not set CPack will use a default name based on the package name and version settings.

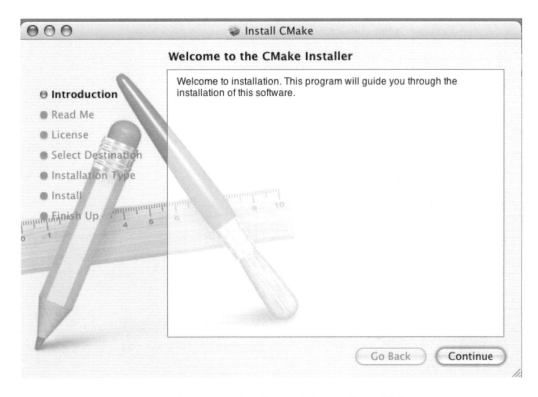

Figure 14 Introduction Screen Mac Package Maker

When the .pkg file is run, the package wizard starts with the screen seen in Figure 14. The text in this window is controlled by the file pointed to by the CPACK_RESOURCE_FILE_WELCOME variable.

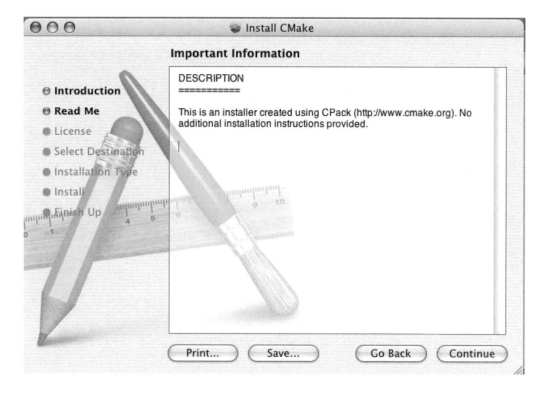

Figure 15 Readme section of Mac package wizard

Figure 15 shows the read me section of the package wizard. The text for this window is customized by using the CPACK_RESOURCE_FILE_README variable. It should contain a path to the file containing the text that should be displayed on this screen.

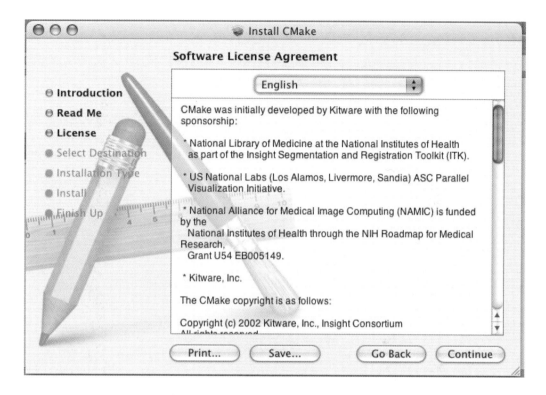

Figure 16 License screen Mac packager

Figure 16 contains the license text for the package. Users must accept the license for the installation process to continue. The text for the license comes from the file pointed to by the CPACK_RESOURCE_FILE_LICENSE variable.

The other screens in the installation process are not customizable from CPack. To change more advanced features of this installer, there are two template files used by CPack that you can modify. Modules/CPack.Info.plist.in and Modules/CPack.Description.plist.in. These files can be replaced by using the CMAKE_MODULE_PATH variable to point to a directory in your project containing a modified copy of CPackInfo.plist.in.

5.7   CPack for OSX X11 applications

CPack also includes an OSX X11 package maker generator. This can be used to package X11 based applications, and make them act more like native OSX applications. CPack not only packages them, but wraps them with a script that will allow users to run them as they would any native OSX application. Much like the OSX PackageMaker generator, the OSX X11 generator creates a disk image .dmg file. In this example, an X11 application called KWPolygonalObjectViewerExample is packaged with the OSX X11 CPack generator.

Figure 17 OSX X11 package disk image

Figure 17 shows the disk image created. In this case the CPACK_PACKAGE_NAME was set to KWPolygonalObjectViewerExample, and the version information was left with the CPack default of 0.1.1. The variable CPACK_PACKAGE_EXECUTABLES was set to the pair KWPolygonalObjectViewerExample and KWPolygonalObjectViewerExample, the installed X11 application is called KWPolygonalObjectViewerExample.

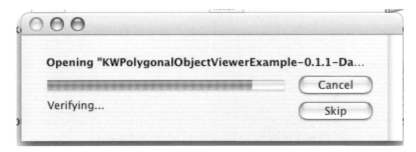

Figure 18 Opening OSX X11 disk image

Figure 18 shows what a user would see after clicking on the .dmg file created by CPack. OSX is mounting this disk image as a disk

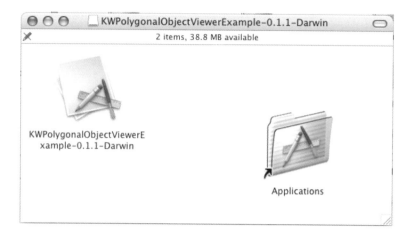

Figure 19 Mounted .dmg disk image

Figure 19 shows the mounted disk image. It will contain a symbolic link to the /Applications directory for the system, and it will contain an application bundle for each executable found in CPACK_PACKAGE_EXECUTABLES. The users can then drag and drop the applications into the Applications folder as seen in Figure 20.

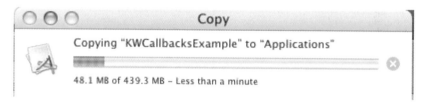

Figure 20 Drag and drop application to Applications

CPack actually provides a c++ based executable that can run an X11 applications via the Apple scripting language. The application bundle installed will run that forwarding application when the user double clicks on KWPolygonalObjectViewerExample. This script will make sure that the X11 server is started. The script that is run can be found in CMake/Modules/CPack.RuntimeScript.in. The source for the script launcher c++ program can be found in Source/CPack/OSXScriptLauncher.cxx.

5.8   CPack for Debian packages

A Debian package .deb is simply an "ar" archive. CPack includes the code for the BSD style ar that is required by Debian packages. The Debian packager used the standard set of CPack variables to initialize a set of Debian specific variables. These can be overridden in the

CPACK_PROJECT_CONFIG_FILE, the name of the generator is "DEB". The variables used
by the DEB generator are as follows:

CPACK_DEBIAN_PACKAGE_NAME

> defaults to lower case of CPACK_PACKAGE_NAME.

CPACK_DEBIAN_PACKAGE_ARCHITECTURE

> defaults to i386.

CPACK_DEBIAN_PACKAGE_DEPENDS

> Must be set to other packages that this package depends on, and if empty a warning
> is emitted.

CPACK_DEBIAN_PACKAGE_MAINTAINER

> defaults to CPACK_PACKAGE_CONTACT

CPACK_DEBIAN_PACKAGE_DESCRIPTION

> defaults to CPACK_PACKAGE_DESCRIPTION_SUMMARY

CPACK_DEBIAN_PACKAGE_SECTION

> defaults to devl

CPACK_DEBIAN_PACKAGE_PRIORITY

> defaults to optional

5.9   CPack for RPM

CPack has support for creating Linux RPM files. The name of the generator as set in
CPACK_GENERATOR is "RPM". The RPM package capability requires that rpmbuild is
installed on the machine and is in PATH. The RPM packager uses the standard set of CPack
variables to initialize RPM specific variables. The RPM specific variables are as follows:

CPACK_RPM_PACKAGE_SUMMARY

> defaults to ${CPACK_PACKAGE_DESCRIPTION_SUMMARY}

CPACK_RPM_PACKAGE_NAME

> defaults to tolower ${CPACK_PACKAGE_NAME}

CPACK_RPM_PACKAGE_VERSION

> defaults to ${CPACK_PACKAGE_VERSION}.

CPACK_RPM_PACKAGE_ARCHITECTURE

> defaults to i386

CPACK_RPM_PACKAGE_RELEASE

> defaults to 1. This is the version of the RPM file, and not the version of the software being packaged.

CPACK_RPM_PACKAGE_GROUP

> defaults to none.

CPACK_RPM_PACKAGE_VENDOR

> defaults to ${CPACK_PACKAGE_VENDOR}

5.10 CPack files

There are a number of files that are used by CPack and can be useful for learning more about how CPack works and what options you can set. These files can also be used as the starting point for other generators for CPack. These files can mostly be found in the Modules and Templates directories of CMake and typically start with the prefix CPack.

## Chapter 6

Converting Existing Systems to CMake

For many people the first thing they will do with CMake is to convert an existing project from using an older build system to use CMake. In many cases this can be a fairly easy process but there are a few issues to consider. This section will address those issues and provide some suggestions for effectively converting a project over to CMake. The first issue to consider when converting to CMake is the project's directory structure.

6.1   Source Code Directory Structures

Most small projects will have their source code in either the top level directory or in one directory named `src` or `source`. Even if the source code is all in a subdirectory we highly recommend creating a CMakeLists file for the top level directory. There are two reasons for this. First it can be confusing to some people that they must run CMake on the subdirectory of the project instead of the main directory. Second, you may want to install documentation or other support files from the other directories. By having a CMakeLists file at the top of the project you can use the `add_subdirectory` command to step down into the documentation directory where its CMakeLists file can install the documentation (you can have a CMakeLists file for a documentation directory with no targets or source code).

For projects that have source code in multiple directories there are a few options. One option that many makefile based projects use is to have a single makefile at the top level directory that lists all the source files to compile with their subdirectories. For example:

```
SOURCES=\
   subdir1/foo.cxx \
   subdir1/foo2.cxx \
   subdir2/gah.cxx \
   subdir2/bar.cxx
```

This approach works just as well with CMake using a similar syntax:

```
set (SOURCES
   subdir1/foo.cxx
   subdir1/foo2.cxx
   subdir1/gah.cxx
   subdir2/bar.cxx
   )
```

Another option is to have each subdirectory build a library or libraries that can then be linked into the executables. In that case each subdirectory would define its own list of source files and add the appropriate targets. A third option is a mix of the first two. Each subdirectory can have a CMakeLists file that lists its sources but the top level CMakeLists file will not use the `add_subdirectory` command to step into the subdirectories. Instead the top level CMakeLists file will use the `include` command to include the subdirectories' CMakeLists files. For example, a top level CMakeLists file might include the following code:

```
# collect the files for subdir1

include (subdir1/CMakeLists.txt)
foreach (FILE ${FILES})
   set (subdir1Files ${subdir1Files} subdir1/${FILE})
endforeach (FILE)

# collect the files for subdir2
include (subdir2/CMakeLists.txt)
foreach (FILE ${FILES})
   set (subdir2Files ${subdir2Files} subdir2/${FILE})
endforeach (FILE)

# add the source files to the executable
add_executable (foo ${subdir1Files} ${subdir2Files})
```

While the subdirectories' CMakeLists files might look like the following:

```
# list the source files for this directory
set (FILES
  foo1.cxx
  foo2.cxx
  )
```

Which approach you use is entirely up to you. For large projects, having multiple shared libraries can certainly improve build times when changes are made. For smaller projects the other two approaches have their advantages. The main suggestion here is to pick a strategy and stick with it.

6.2   Build Directories

The next issue to consider is where to put the resulting object files, libraries, and executables. There are a few different approaches commonly used and some work better with CMake than others. Probably the most common approach is to produce the binary files in the same directory as the source files. For some Windows generators such as Visual Studio they are actually kept in a subdirectory matching the selected configuration, e.g. debug, release, etc. CMake supports this approach by default. A closely related approach is to put the binary files into a separate tree that has the same structure as the source tree. For example if the source tree looked like the following:

```
foo/
  subdir1
  subdir2
```

the binary tree might look like:

```
foobin/
  subdir1
  subdir2
```

CMake also supports this structure by default. Switching between in-source builds and out-of-source builds is simply a matter of changing the binary directory in CMake (see How to Run CMake? on page 11). If you need to support multiple architectures from one source tree we highly recommend a directory structure like the following:

```
projectfoo/
   foo/
      subdir1
      subdir2
   foo-linux/
      subdir1
      subdir2
   foo-solaris/
      subdir1
      subdir2
   foo-hpux/
      subdir1
      subdir2
```

That way each architecture has its own build directory which will not interfere with any other architecture. Recall that not only are the object files kept in the binary directories but also any configured files are typically written to the binary tree. Another tree structure found primarily on UNIX projects is one where the binary files for different architectures are kept in subdirectories of the source tree. (see below) CMake doesn't work well with this structure so we recommend switching to the separate build tree structure shown above.

```
foo/
   subdir1/
      linux
      solaris
      hpux
   subdir2/
      linux
      solaris
      hpux
```

CMake provides two variables for controlling where binary targets are written. They are the EXECUTABLE_OUTPUT_PATH and LIBRARY_OUTPUT_PATH variables. These variables control where the resulting libraries and executables will be written respectively. Setting these enables a project to place all the libraries and executables into a single directory. For projects with many subdirectories this can be a real time saver. A typical implementation is listed below:

```
# Setup output directories.
set (LIBRARY_OUTPUT_PATH
  ${PROJECT_BINARY_DIR}/bin
  CACHE PATH
  "Single directory for all libraries."
  )

set ( EXECUTABLE_OUTPUT_PATH
  ${PROJECT_BINARY_DIR}/bin
  CACHE PATH
  "Single directory for all executables."
  )

mark_as_advanced (
  LIBRARY_OUTPUT_PATH
  EXECUTABLE_OUTPUT_PATH
  )
```

The two variables are set to the `bin` subdirectory of the project's binary tree. (in this example the bin subdirectory could just as easily be named "binaries", etc) These variables are cached so that they will impact the entire project. And finally they are marked as advanced for two reasons; first to reduce the number of choices the average user will see when running CMake, and second to reduce the chances of someone changing them to another value. Setting these variables is very useful for projects that make use of shared libraries (dlls) since it collects all of the shared libraries into one directory. If the executables are also placed in the same directory then the executables can find the required shared libraries more easily when run.

One final note on directory structures: with CMake it is perfectly acceptable to have a project within a project. For example, within the Visualization Toolkit's source tree is a directory that contains a complete copy of the zlib compression library. In writing the CMakeLists file for that library we use the PROJECT command to create a project named VTKZLIB even though it is within the VTK source tree and project. This has no real impact on VTK but it does allow us to build zlib independently from VTK without having to modify its CMakeLists file.

6.3   Useful CMake Commands when Converting Projects

There are a few CMake commands that can make the job of converting an existing project easier and faster. The `file` command with the `GLOB` argument allows you to quickly set a variable containing a list of all the files that match the glob expression. For example:

```
# collect up the source files
file (GLOB SRC_FILES *.cxx)

# create the executable
add_executable (foo ${SRC_FILES})
```

will set the SRC_FILES variable to a list of all the ".cxx" files in the current source directory. Then it will create an executable using those source files. Windows developers should be warned that glob matches are case sensitive.

Two other useful commands are make_directory and exec_program. By default CMake will create all the output directories it needs for the object files, libraries, and executables. With existing projects there may be some part of the build process that creates directories that CMake would not normally create. In these cases the make_directory command can be used. As soon as CMake executes that command it will create the directory specified if it doesn't already exist. The EXEC_PROGRAM command will execute a program when it is encountered by CMake. This is useful if you want to quickly convert a UNIX autoconf configured header file to CMake. Instead of doing the full conversion to CMake you could run configure from an exec_program command to generate the configured header file (on UNIX only of course).

6.4   Converting UNIX Makefiles

If your project is currently based on standard UNIX makefiles (not autoconf and Makefile.in or imake) then their conversion to CMake may be fairly straightforward. Essentially for every directory in your project that has a makefile you will create a matching CMakeLists file. How you handle multiple makefiles in a directory really depends on their function. If the additional makefiles (or makefile type files) are simply included into the main makefile then you can create matching CMake syntax files and include them into your main CMakeLists file in a similar manner. If the different makefiles are meant to be invoked on the command line for different situations then you should consider creating a main CMakeLists file that uses some logic to pick which one to include based on a CMake option.

Converting the makefile syntax to CMake is fairly easy. Frequently makefiles have a list of object files to compile. These can be converted to CMake variables as follows:

```
OBJS= \
  foo1.o \
  foo2.o \
  foo3.o
```

becomes

```
set (SOURCES
  foo1.c
  foo2.c
  foo3.c
)
```

While the object files are typically listed in a makefile, in CMake the focus is on the source files. If you used conditional statements in your makefiles they can be converted over to CMake `if` commands. Since CMake handles generating dependencies, most dependencies or rules to generate dependencies can be eliminated. Where you have rules to build libraries or executables replace them with `add_library` or `add_executable` commands. Some UNIX build systems (and source code) make heavy use of the system architecture to determine what files to compile or what flags to use. Typically this information is stored in a makefile variable called `ARCH` or `UNAME`.

The first choice in these cases is to try to replace the architecture specific code with a more generic test. For example, instead of switching your handling of byte order based on operating system, make the decision based on the results of a byte order test such as `CheckBigEndian.cmake`. With some software packages, there is too much architecture specific code for such a change to be reasonable, or you may want to make decisions based on architecture for other reasons. In those cases you can use the variables defined in the `CMakeDetermineSystem` module. They provide fairly detailed information on the operating system and version of the host computer.

6.5   Converting Autoconf Based Projects

Autoconf based projects primarily consist of three key pieces. The first is the configure.in file that drives the process. The second is Makefile.in which will become the resulting makefile and the third piece is the remaining configured files that result from running configure. In converting an autoconf based project to CMake you will start with the configure.in and Makefile.in files.

The Makefile.in file can be converted to CMake syntax as explained in the preceding section on converting UNIX makefiles. Once this has been done you need to convert the configure.in file into CMake syntax. Most functions (macros) in autoconf have corresponding commands in CMake. A short table of some of the basic conversions is listed below:

AC_ARG_WITH

        use the `option` command

AC_CHECK_HEADER

>   use the `CHECK_INCLUDE_FILE` macro from the `CheckIncludeFile` module

AC_MSG_CHECKING

>   use the `message` command with the `STATUS` argument

AC_SUBST

>   done automatically when using the `configure_file` command

AC_CHECK_LIB

>   use the `CHECK_LIBRARY_EXISTS` macro from the `CheckLibraryExists` module

AC_CONFIG_SUBDIRS

>   use the `add_subdirectory` command

AC_OUTPUT

>   use the `configure_file` command

AC_TRY_COMPILE

>   use the `try_compile` command

If your configure script performs test compilations using `AC_TRY_COMPILE` you can use the same code for CMake. You can either put it directly into your CMakeLists file if it is short, or preferably put it into a source code file for your project. We typically put such files into a CMake subdirectory for large projects that require such testing.

Where you are relying on autoconf to configure files you can use CMake's `configure_file` command. The basic approach is the same and we typically name input files to be configured with a `.in` extension just as autoconf does. This command replaces any variables in the input file referenced as `${VAR}` or `@VAR@` with their values as determined by CMake. If a variable is not defined, it will be replaced with nothing. Optionally, only variables of the form `@VAR@` will be replaced and `${VAR}` will be ignored. This is useful for configuring files for languages that use `${VAR}` as a syntax for evaluating variables. You can also conditionally define variables using the C pre processor by using `#cmakedefine VAR`. If the variable is defined then `configure_file` will convert the `#cmakedefine` into a `#define`. If it is not defined it will become a commented out `#undef`. For example:

```
/* what byte order is this system */
#cmakedefine CMAKE_WORDS_BIGENDIAN

/* what size is an INT */
#cmakedefine SIZEOF_INT @SIZEOF_INT@
```

6.6 Converting Windows Based Workspaces

To convert a Visual Studio workspace (or solution for Visual Studio .Net) to CMake involves a few steps. First you will need to create a CMakeLists file at the top of your source code directory. This file should start with a `project` command that defines the name of the project. This will become the name of the resulting workspace (or solution for Visual Studio .Net). Next you will need to add all of your source files into CMake variables. For large projects that have multiple directories you can create a CMakeLists file in each directory as described previously in the section on source directory structures (page 95). Next you will add your libraries and executables using `add_library` and `add_executable`. By default `add_executable` assumes that your executable is a console application. Adding the `WIN32` argument to `add_executable` indicates that it is a Windows application (using WinMain instead of main).

There are a couple of nice features that Visual Studio supports that CMake can take advantage of. One is support for class browsing. Typically in CMake only source files are added to a target, not header files. If you do add header files to a target, they will show up in the workspace and then you will be able to browse them as usual. Visual Studio also supports the notion of groups of files. By default CMake creates groups for source files and header files. Using the `source_group` command you can create your own groups and assign files to them. If you have any custom build steps in your workspace, these can be added to your CMakeLists files using the `add_custom_command` command. Custom targets (Utility Targets) in Visual Studio can be added with the `add_custom_target` command.

## Chapter 7

System Inspection

This chapter will describe how you can use CMake to inspect the environment of the system on which the software is being built. This is a critical factor in creating cross-platform applications or libraries. It covers how to find and use system and user installed header files and libraries. It also covers some of the more advanced features of CMake including the `try_compile` and `try_run` commands. These commands are extremely powerful tools for determining the capabilities of the system and compiler that is hosting your software. This chapter also describes how to generate configured files and how to cross compile with CMake. Finally, the steps required to enable a project for the `find_package` command are covered explaining how to create a `PackageConfig.cmake` file and other required files.

7.1   Using Header Files and Libraries

Many C and C++ programs depend on external libraries. However, when it comes to the practical aspects of compiling and linking a project, taking advantage of existing libraries can be difficult for both the developers and users. Problems usually show up as soon as the software is built on a system other than that on which it was developed. Assumptions regarding where libraries and header files are located become obvious when they are not installed in the same place on the new computer and the build system is unable to find them. CMake has many features to aid developers in the integration of external software libraries into a project.

The CMake commands that are most relevant to this type of integration are the `find_file`, `find_library`, `find_path`, `find_program`, and `find_package` commands. For most C and C++ libraries, a combination of `find_library` and `find_path` will be enough to compile and link with an installed library. `find_library` can be used to locate, or allow a user to locate a library, and `find_path` can be used to find the path to a representative include file from the project. For example, if you wanted to link to the tiff library, you could use the following commands in your CMakeLists.txt file:

```
# find libtiff, looking in some standard places
find_library (TIFF_LIBRARY
              NAMES tiff tiff2
              PATHS /usr/local/lib /usr/lib
              )

# find tiff.h looking in some standard places
find_path (TIFF_INCLUDES tiff.h
          /usr/local/include
          /usr/include
          )

include_directories (${TIFF_INCLUDES})

add_executable (mytiff mytiff.c )

target_link_libraries (myprogram ${TIFF_LIBRARY})
```

The first command used is `find_library` which in this case will look for a library with the name tiff or tiff2. The `find_library` command only requires the library's base name without any platform specific prefixes or suffixes such as lib and .dll. The appropriate prefixes and suffixes for the system running CMake will be added to the library name automatically when CMake attempts to find it. All the `FIND_*` commands will look in the `PATH` environment variable. In addition, the commands allow the specification of additional search paths as arguments listed after the `PATHS` marker argument. As well as supporting standard paths, windows registry entries and environment variables can also be used to construct search paths. The syntax for registry entries is the following:

```
[HKEY_CURRENT_USER\\Software\\Kitware\\Path;Build1]
```

Because software can be installed in many different places, it is impossible for CMake to find the library every time, but most standard installations should be covered. The `find_*` commands automatically create a cache variable so that users can override or specify the location from the CMake GUI. This way if CMake is unable to locate the files for which it is looking, users will still have an opportunity to specify them from the GUI. If CMake does not find a file, the value is set to `VAR-NOTFOUND`. This value tells CMake that it should continue looking each time CMake's configure step is run. Note that in `if` statements, values of VAR-NOTFOUND will evaluate as false.

The next command used is `find_path`. This is a general purpose command that, in this example, is used to locate a header file from the library. Often header files and libraries are not installed in the same location, but both locations are required to compile and link programs that use them. `find_path` is similar to `find_library`, although it only supports one name. It does support a list of search paths.

The next part of the CMakeLists file uses the variables created by the FIND_* commands. The variables can be used without checking for valid values as CMake will print an error message notifying the user if any required variables have not been set. The user can then set the cache values and reconfigure until the message goes away. Optionally, a CMakeLists file could use the `if` command to use alternative libraries or options to build the project without the library if it can not be found.

From the above example you should be able to see how using the FIND_* commands can help your software to compile on a wide variety of systems. It is worth noting that the find_* commands all search for a match starting with the first argument and first path. So when listing paths and library names you should list your preferred names and paths first. So if a library comes in multiple versions, and you would prefer tiff over tiff2, make sure you list them in that order.

7.2   System Properties

Although it is a common practice in C and C++ code to add platform-specific code inside preprocessor `ifdef` directives, for maximum portability this should be avoided. Software should not be tuned to specific platforms with `ifdefs`, but rather to a canonical system consisting of a set of features. Coding to specific systems makes the software less portable, because systems and the features they support change with time, and even from system to system. A feature that may not have worked on a platform in the past may be a required feature for the platform in the future. The following code fragments illustrate the difference between coding to a canonical system and a specific system:

```
// coding to a feature
#ifdef HAS_FOOBAR_CALL
  foobar();
#else
  myfoobar();
#endif
```

```
// coding to specific platforms
#if defined(SUN) && defined(HPUX) && !defined(GNUC)
  foobar();
#else
  myfoobar();
#endif
```

The problem with the second approach is that the code will have to be modified for each new platform on which the software is compiled. Also, some future version of SUN may no longer have the foobar call. With the HAS_FOOBAR_CALL approach, the software will work as long as HAS_FOOBAR_CALL is defined correctly. This is where CMake can help. CMake can be used to define HAS_FOOBAR_CALL correctly and automatically by making use of the try_compile and try_run commands. These commands can be used to compile and run small test programs during the CMake configure step. The test programs will be sent to the compiler that will be used to build the project, and if errors occur the feature can be disabled. These commands require that you write a small C or C++ program to test the feature. For example, to test if the foobar call is provided on the system, try compiling a simple program that uses foobar. First write the simple test program (testNeedFoobar.c in this example) and then add the CMake calls to the CMakeLists file to try compiling that code. If the compilation works then HAS_FOOBAR_CALL will be set to true.

```
--- testNeedFoobar.c -----

#include <foobar.h>
main()
{
  foobar();
}
```

```
--- testNeedFoobar.cmake ---

try_compile (HAS_FOOBAR_CALL
  ${CMAKE_BINARY_DIR}
  ${PROJECT_SOURCE_DIR}/testNeedFoobar.c
  )
```

Now that `HAS_FOOBAR_CALL` is set correctly in CMake you can use it in your source code through either the `add_definitions` command or by configuring a header file. We recommend configuring a header file as that file can be used by other projects that depend on your library. This is discussed in section 7.5.

Sometimes, just compiling a test program is not enough. In some cases, you may actually want to compile and run a program to get its output. A good example of this is testing the byte order of a machine. The following example shows how you can write a small program that CMake will compile and then run to determine the byte order of a machine.

```
---- TestByteOrder.c ------

int main () {
  /* Are we most significant byte first or last */
  union
  {
    long l;
    char c[sizeof (long)];
  } u;
  u.l = 1;
  exit (u.c[sizeof (long) - 1] == 1);
}
```

```
----- TestByteOrder.cmake-----

try_run (RUN_RESULT_VAR
  COMPILE_RESULT_VAR
  ${CMAKE_BINARY_DIR}
  ${PROJECT_SOURCE_DIR}/Modules/TestByteOrder.c
  OUTPUT_VARIABLE OUTPUT
  )
```

The return result of the run will go into `RUN_RESULT_VAR` and the result of the compile will go into `COMPILE_RESULT_VAR`, and any output from the run will go into `OUTPUT`. You can use these variables to report debug information to users of your project.

For small test programs the `FILE` command with the `WRITE` option can be used to create the source file from the CMakeLists file. The following example tests the C compiler to verify that it can be run.

```
file (WRITE
  ${CMAKE_BINARY_DIR}/CMakeTmp/testCCompiler.c
  "int main(){return 0;}"
  )

try_compile (CMAKE_C_COMPILER_WORKS
  ${CMAKE_BINARY_DIR}
  ${CMAKE_BINARY_DIR}/CMakeTmp/testCCompiler.c
  OUTPUT_VARIABLE OUTPUT
  )
```

There are several predefined try-run and try-compile macros in the CMake/Modules directory some of which are listed below. These macros allow some common checks to be done without having to create a source file for each test. For detailed documentation or to see how these macros work look at the implementation files for them in the CMake/Modules directory of your CMake installation. Many of these macros will look at the current value of the CMAKE_REQUIRED_FLAGS and CMAKE_REQUIRED_LIBRARIES variables to add additional compile flags or link libraries to the test.

CheckFunctionExists.cmake

Checks to see if a C function is on a system. This macro takes two arguments, the first is the name of the function to check for. The second is the variable to store the result into. This macro does use CMAKE_REQUIRED_FLAGS and CMAKE_REQUIRED_LIBRARIES if they are set.

CheckIncludeFile.cmake:

Checks for an include file on a system. This macro takes two arguments. The first is the include file to look for and the second is the variable to store the result into. Additional CFlags can be passed in as a third argument or by setting CMAKE_REQUIRED_FLAGS.

CheckIncludeFileCXX.cmake

Check for an include file in a C++ program. This macro takes two arguments. The first is the include file to look for and the second is the variable to store the result into. Additional CFlags can be passed in as a third argument.

CheckIncludeFiles.cmake

Check for a group of include files. This macro takes two arguments. The first is the include files to look for and the second is the variable to store the result into. This macro does use CMAKE_REQUIRED_FLAGS if it is set. This macro is useful when a header file you are interested in checking for is dependent on including another header file first.

CheckLibraryExists.cmake

> Check to see if a library exists. This macro takes four arguments; the first is the name of the library to check for. The second is the name of a function that should be in that library. The third argument is the location of where the library should be found. The fourth argument is a variable to store the result into. This macro uses CMAKE_REQUIRED_FLAGS and CMAKE_REQUIRED_LIBRARIES if they are set.

CheckSymbolExists.cmake

> Check to see if a symbol is defined in a header file. This macro takes three arguments. The first argument is the symbol to look for. The second argument is a list of header files to try including. The third argument is where the result is stored. This macro uses CMAKE_REQUIRED_FLAGS and CMAKE_REQUIRED_LIBRARIES if they are set.

CheckTypeSize.cmake

> Determines the size in bytes of a variable type. This macro takes two arguments. The first argument is the type to evaluate. The second argument is where the result is stored. Both CMAKE_REQUIRED_FLAGS and CMAKE_REQUIRED_LIBRARIES are used if they are set.

CheckVariableExists.cmake

> Checks to see if a global variable exists. This macro takes two arguments. The first argument is the variable to look for. The second argument is the variable to store the result in. This macro will prototype the named variable and then try to use it. If the test program compiles then the variable exists. This will only work for C variables. This macro uses CMAKE_REQUIRED_FLAGS and CMAKE_REQUIRED_LIBRARIES if they are set.

Consider the following example that shows a variety of these modules being used to compute properties of the platform. At the beginning of the example four modules are loaded from CMake. The remainder of the example uses the macros defined in those modules to test for header files, libraries, symbols, and type sizes respectively.

```
# Include all the necessary files for macros
include (CheckIncludeFiles)
include (CheckLibraryExists)
include (CheckSymbolExists)
include (CheckTypeSize)

# Check for header files
set (INCLUDES "")
CHECK_INCLUDE_FILES ("${INCLUDES};winsock.h" HAVE_WINSOCK_H)
```

```
if (HAVE_WINSOCK_H)
  set (INCLUDES ${INCLUDES} winsock.h)
endif (HAVE_WINSOCK_H)

CHECK_INCLUDE_FILES ("${INCLUDES};io.h" HAVE_IO_H)
if (HAVE_IO_H)
  set (INCLUDES ${INCLUDES} io.h)
endif (HAVE_IO_H)

# Check for all needed libraries
set (LIBS "")
CHECK_LIBRARY_EXISTS ("dl;${LIBS}" dlopen "" HAVE_LIBDL)
if (HAVE_LIBDL)
  set (LIBS ${LIBS} dl)
endif (HAVE_LIBDL)

CHECK_LIBRARY_EXISTS ("ucb;${LIBS}" gethostname "" HAVE_LIBUCB)
if (HAVE_LIBUCB)
  set (LIBS ${LIBS} ucb)
endif (HAVE_LIBUCB)

# Add the libraries we found to the libraries to use when
# looking for symbols with the CHECK_SYMBOL_EXISTS macro
set (CMAKE_REQUIRED_LIBRARIES ${LIBS})

# Check for some functions that are used
CHECK_SYMBOL_EXISTS (socket    "${INCLUDES}" HAVE_SOCKET)
CHECK_SYMBOL_EXISTS (poll      "${INCLUDES}" HAVE_POLL)

# Various type sizes
CHECK_TYPE_SIZE (int     SIZEOF_INT)
CHECK_TYPE_SIZE (size_t  SIZEOF_SIZE_T)
```

For more advanced `try_compile` and `try_run` operations, it may be desirable to pass flags to the compiler, or to CMake. Both commands support the optional arguments `CMAKE_FLAGS` and `COMPILE_DEFINITIONS`. `CMAKE_FLAGS` can be used to pass -D`VAR`:`TYPE`=`VALUE` flags to CMake. The value of `COMPILE_DEFINITIONS` is passed directly to the compiler command line.

7.3 Built-in Find Modules

CMake has many predefined modules that can be found in the Modules subdirectory of CMake. The modules can find many common software packages. The following Find modules are a sample of what is in CMake.

FindAVIFile	FindMatlab
FindASPELL	FindMotif
FindAVIFile	FindOpenAL
FindBZip2	FindOpenGL
FindBoost	FindOpenSSL
FindCABLE	FindPHP4
FindCURL	FindPNG
FindCups	FindPerl
FindCurses	FindPerlLibs
FindCygwin	FindPhysFS
FindDCMTK	FindPike
FindDoxygen	FindPkgConfig
FindEXPAT	FindPythonInterp
FindFLTK	FindPythonLibs
FindGCCXML	FindQt
FindGLU	FindQt3
FindGLUT	FindQt4
FindGTK	FindRuby
FindGettext	FindSDL
FindGnuplot	FindSDL_mixer
FindHSPELL	FindSDL_sound
FindHTMLHelp	FindSWIG
FindITK	FindSelfPackers
FindImageMagick	FindSubversion
FindJNI	FindTCL
FindJPEG	FindTIFF
FindJasper	FindTclsh
FindJava	FindThreads
FindKDE	FindUnixCommands
FindKDE3	FindVTK
FindKDE4	FindWget
FindLATEX	FindWish
FindLibXml2	FindX11
FindLibXslt	FindXMLRPC
FindMFC	FindZLIB
FindMPEG	FindwxWidgets
FindMPEG2	FindwxWindows
FindMPI	

Each `Find<XX>.cmake` module defines a set of variables that ill allow a project to use the software package once it is found. Those variables all start with the name of the software being found <XX>. With CMake we have tried to establish a convention for naming these variables but you should read the comments at the top of the module for a more definitive answer. The following variables are used by convention when needed:

<XX>_INCLUDE_DIRS

Where to find the package's header files, typically <XX>.h, etc.

<XX>_LIBRARIES

The libraries to link against to use <XX>. These include full paths.

<XX>_DEFINITIONS

Preprocessor definitions to use when compiling code that uses <XX>.

<XX>_EXECUTABLE

Where to find the <XX> tool that is part of the package.

<XX>_<YY>_EXECUTABLE

Where to find the <YY> tool that comes with <XX>.

<XX>_ROOT_DIR

Where to find the base directory of the installation of <XX>. This is useful for large packages where you want to reference many files relative to a common base (or root) directory.

<XX>_VERSION_<YY>

Version <YY> of the package was found if true. Authors of find modules should make sure at most one of these is ever true. For example TCL_VERSION_84

<XX>_<YY>_FOUND

If False, then the optional <YY> part of <XX> package is not available.

<XX>_FOUND

Set to false, or undefined, if we haven't found or don't want to use <XX>.

Not all of the variables may be present in each of the `FindXX.cmake` files. However, the `<XX>_FOUND` should exist under most circumstances. If <XX> is a library, then `<XX>_LIBRARIES` should also be defined, and `<XX>_INCLUDE_DIR` should usually be defined.

Modules can be included in a project either with the `include` command or the `find_package` command.

```
find_package(OpenGL)
```

is equivalent to

```
include(${CMAKE_ROOT}/Modules/FindOpenGL.cmake)
```

and

```
include(FindOpenGL)
```

If the project converts over to CMake for its build system, then the `find_package` will still work if the package provides a <XX>`Config.cmake` file. How to create a CMake package is described in section 7.6.

7.4 How to Pass Parameters to a Compilation?

Once you have determined all the features of the system in which you are interested, it is time to configure the software based on what has been found. There are two common ways to pass this information to the compiler. For very small projects this can be done with the command line -D flags passed to the compiler. The flags are passed to the compiler from a CMakeLists file with the `add_definitions` command. For example, a common practice in C code is to have the ability to selectively compile in/out debug statements.

```
#ifdef DEBUG_BUILD
  printf("the value of v is %d", v);
#endif
```

A CMake variable could be used to turn on or off debug builds using the `OPTION` command:

```
option (DEBUG_BUILD
        "Build with extra debug print messages.")

if (DEBUG_BUILD)
  add_definitions (-DDEBUG_BUILD)
endif (DEBUG_BUILD)
```

Another example would be to tell the compiler the result of the previous `HAS_FOOBAR_CALL` test that was discussed earlier in this chapter. You could do this with the following:

```
if (HAS_FOOBAR_CALL)
  add_definitions (-DHAS_FOOBAR_CALL)
endif (HAS_FOOBAR_CALL)
```

However, for maximum portability of a toolkit, it is recommended that `-D` options are not required for the compiler command line. Instead of command line options, CMake can be used to configure a header file that applications can include. The header file will include all of the `#define` macros needed to build the project. The problem with using compile line definitions can be seen when building an application that in turn uses a library. If building the library correctly relies on compile line definitions, then chances are that an application that uses the library will also require the exact same set of compile line definitions. This puts a large burden on the application writer to make sure they add the correct flags to match the library. If instead the library's build process configures a header file with all of the required definitions, then any application that uses the library will automatically get the correct definitions when that header file is included. Often times a definition can change the size of a structure or class, and if the macros are not exactly the same during the build process of the library and the application linking to the library, the application may reference the "wrong part" of a class or struct and crash unexpectedly.

7.5   How to Configure a Header File

Hopefully we have convinced you that configured header files are the right choice for most software projects. To configure a file with CMake the `configure_file` command is used. This command requires an input file that is parsed by CMake which then produces an output file with all variables expanded or replaced. There are three ways to specify a variable in an input file for `configure_file`.

```
#cmakedefine VARIABLE
```

If VARIABLE is true, then the result will be:

```
#define VARIABLE
```

If VARIABLE is false, then the result will be:

```
/* #undef VARIABLE */
```

${VARIABLE}

　　This is simply replaced by the value of VARIABLE.

@VARIABLE@

　　This is simply replaced by the value of VARIABLE.

Since the `${}` syntax is commonly used by other languages, there is a way to tell the `configure_file` command to only expand variables using the `@var@` syntax. This is done by passing the `@ONLY` option to the command. This is useful if you are configuring a script that may contain `${var}` strings that you want to preserve. This is important because CMake will replace all occurrences of `${var}` with the empty string if `var` is not defined in CMake.

The following example configures a .h file for a project that contains preprocessor variables. The first definition indicates if the FOOBAR call exists in the library, and the next one contains the path to the build tree.

```
---- CMakeLists.txt file-----

# Configure a file from the source tree
# called projectConfigure.h.in and put
# the resulting configured file in the build
# tree and call it projectConfigure.h
configure_file (
  ${PROJECT_SOURCE_DIR}/projectConfigure.h.in
  ${PROJECT_BINARY_DIR}/projectConfigure.h)
```

```
-----projectConfigure.h.in file------
/* define a variable to tell the code if the */
/* foobar call is available on this system */
#cmakedefine HAS_FOOBAR_CALL

/* define a variable with the path to the */
/* build directory  */
#define PROJECT_BINARY_DIR "${PROJECT_BINARY_DIR}"
```

It is important to configure files into the binary tree not the source tree. A single source tree may be shared by multiple build trees or platforms. By configuring files into the binary tree the differences between builds or platforms will be kept isolated into the build tree where it will not corrupt other builds. This means that you will need to include the directory of the build tree where you configured the header file into the project's list of include directories using the `include_directories` command.

7.6   Creating a <Package>Config.cmake File

Many software projects consist of sets of libraries meant to be used as foundational building blocks for other applications. The applications are often developed by different people than the ones that developed the project. The integration of the project into the application is often a complicated process prone to error. An application must be built with certain compiler and linker options to properly use the project's libraries.

On UNIX, many projects ship with a shell script that produces command line arguments for the compiler and linker that can be used inside a makefile to generate the correct flags for the compiler. For Windows, there is no standard way to do this. The result is that no two applications using the same project use it the same way. When used correctly, CMake can help with many of these problems, making applications that use a project much easier to write and maintain.

If a project uses CMake for its build system, the project can provide a simple CMake interface to applications that want to use it. With only a few lines of CMake code, user applications will be able to find the project and link to its libraries. This section will start by describing how to do this for a fairly modest sized project. Then it will go into more detail on how this can be accomplished for large complex projects.

If you are writing a library, there are certain pieces of information an application must have to make use of your library. This includes information regarding library names, library directories, include directories, required compiler flags, version information, and other optional settings in the project. When writing your library you can add a CMake file that provides this information to any application that wants to use your library. To understand this let us consider how the application will find and use this information. Earlier in this chapter we discussed using `Find` modules from CMake to find and set parameters for using common system tools and libraries. The same idea applies to using CMake created libraries.

As with other `Find` modules, the first step is for an application to include the module file. The `find_package` command takes the name of a package as an argument and then looks first in the Modules directory of CMake for a file called `Find<Package>.cmake` (where `<Package>` is the name of the package as passed to the `find_package` command). If that is found, it will be included. Any directory listed in the `CMAKE_MODULE_PATH` variable is also searched so projects may have a directory with their own modules. This is how all the existing built in modules are found such as OpenGL etc. The key to the `find_package` command is that if the `Find<Package>.cmake` file is not found, the command then looks for the file `<Package>Config.cmake` in several standard places. It also creates a cache variable called `<Package>_DIR` that points to the directory containing the `<Package>Config.cmake` file if one was found.

This means that if your library includes a `<Package>Config.cmake` file in it, then people can use it just like any of the existing `Find` modules in CMake. For example, if your library was named Gromit, then in their application's CMakeLists file they would add:

```
find_package(Gromit)
```

And then they would use the variables you provide in your `GromitConfig.cmake` file just like the variables that are typically set in a `Find` module. The motivation behind the `<Package>_DIR` cache variable is so that users can specify the location where they built or installed your library so that CMake can then find and load the `<Package>Config.cmake` file. That way if CMake can not automatically find the package, the user can set it in the CMake cache. Typically you will want to create the `<Package>Config.cmake` file as part of the configuration process for your library and write it into the binary directory. It should also be installed as part of the installation process for your library. A possible GromitConfig.cmake.in file might look like the following:

```
# Find the GROMIT includes and library
#
# GROMIT_INCLUDE_DIR - where to find gromit.h
# GROMIT_LIBRARIES
#   - List of fully qualified libraries to link against
# GROMIT_FOUND - set to 1 if found

set (GROMIT_FOUND 1)

set (GROMIT_INCLUDE_DIR "@GROMIT_INCLUDE@")

set (GROMIT_LIBRARIES "@GROMIT_LIBRARY@")
```

The commands to configure this file would look like:

```
get_target_property (GROMIT_LIBRARY Gromit LOCATION)

set (GROMIT_INCLUDE ${PROJECT_BINARY_DIR}/include)

configure_file (
  "${PROJECT_SOURCE_DIR}/GromitConfig.cmake.in"
  "${PROJECT_BINARY_DIR}/GromitConfig.cmake" )
```

This will work for a build of the Gromit project, but the file locations are not correct for an installation. To do this you need to configure the file with a different set of values that is then used for the installation. For example:

```
# get the filename of the library
get_filename_component (GROMIT_INSTALL_LIBRARY
  GROMIT_LIBRARY NAME
  )

# add the install path to the library name
set (GROMIT_LIBRARY
  ${CMAKE_INSTALL_PREFIX}/lib/${GROMIT_INSTALL_LIBRARY})
set (GROMIT_INCLUDE ${CMAKE_INSTALL_PREFIX}/include)

# configure the file for the installed version of gromit
configure_file (
  "${PROJECT_SOURCE_DIR}/GromitConfig.cmake.in"
  "${PROJECT_BINARY_DIR}/InstallFiles/GromitConfig.cmake"
  )

# add the install rule to install the GromitConfig.cmake file
install_files (/lib FILES
  "${PROJECT_BINARY_DIR}/InstallFiles/GromitConfig.cmake"
  )
```

This configures the same input file but with a set of values that are correct for an installed version of Gromit. Then we add an install rule to install this version of the GromitConfig.cmake file when Gromit is installed. That is the basic process for supporting CMake's inter-project packaging commands. For more complicated projects there are more parameters that you would need to provide to the application. We will expand the Gromit example to handle all these other issues in the following example. In these more complex cases the project might provide a Use file. The idea behind a Use file is that it takes the settings from find_package and actually applies them to your project by calling commands such as add_definitions or include_directories. An application that used the Gromit libraries would create a CMake file that looked like this:

```
find_package(Gromit)

if (Gromit_FOUND)
  include (${Gromit_USE_FILE})
  add_executable (testGromit testGromit.cxx)
  target_link_libraries(testGromit gromit)
endif(Gromit_FOUND)
```

By calling the `find_package` command, no build settings are changed, but variables describing the package will be defined. In this case, Gromit defines the variable `Gromit_USE_FILE` that specifies a CMake source file that can be included to configure a project to use Gromit. If Gromit is not found, `find_package` will automatically produce an error telling the user what to do.

To support the `find_package` command the Gromit project will have to create several files during the configure step of CMake using code as in the following example:

```
project (Gromit)

# Build the gromit library.
add_library (gromit gromit.c)

# Install the library and header files.
install (TARGETS gromit DESTINATION lib)
install_files (FILES /include .h gromit)

# Configure the file describing how to use Gromit.
configure_file (
  ${Gromit_SOURCE_DIR}/GromitConfig.cmake.in
  ${Gromit_BINARY_DIR}/GromitConfig.cmake
  @ONLY
  )

# Export our build settings and library dependencies
include (CMakeExportBuildSettings)

cmake_export_build_settings (
  ${Gromit_BINARY_DIR}/GromitBuildSettings.cmake
  )

export_library_dependencies (
  ${Gromit_BINARY_DIR}/GromitLibraryDepends.cmake
  )

# Install the packaging files for use by find_package (Gromit)
install (FILES
  ${Gromit_SOURCE_DIR}/GromitUse.cmake
  ${Gromit_BINARY_DIR}/GromitConfig.cmake
  ${Gromit_BINARY_DIR}/GromitBuildSettings.cmake
  ${Gromit_BINARY_DIR}/GromitLibraryDepends.cmake
  DESTINATION lib/gromit
  )
```

The `GromitBuildSettings.cmake` file contains the set of C and C++ flag variables currently used by CMake. This is required so that projects using Gromit can verify that it is built with compatible flags.

The `GromitLibraryDepends.cmake` file contains all of the library interdependency information for the Gromit project. CMake keeps track of each library's dependent libraries as specified by the `target_link_libraries` and `link_libraries` commands. This is a very useful feature because it allows user code to link only to the libraries they think they need, and CMake will give them all the libraries they actually need.

The `GromitConfig.cmake` is created with the `configure_file` command and requires a `GromitConfig.cmake.in` file for input. The input file should look like this:

```
# Tell the user project where to find our headers
# and libraries.
set (Gromit_INCLUDE_DIRS
  "@CMAKE_INSTALL_PREFIX@/include"
  )

set (Gromit_LIBRARY_DIRS "@CMAKE_INSTALL_PREFIX@/lib")

# Tell the user project where to find our build
# settings and library dependencies.
set (Gromit_BUILD_SETTINGS_FILE
  "@CMAKE_INSTALL_PREFIX@/lib/gromit/GromitBuildSettings.cmake"
  )

include (
  "@CMAKE_INSTALL_PREFIX@/lib/gromit/GromitLibraryDepends.cmake"
  )

# Tell the user project where to find the "USE" file.
# This file uses the above settings to configure the
# user project.
set (Gromit_USE_FILE
  "@CMAKE_INSTALL_PREFIX@/lib/gromit/GromitUse.cmake"
  )
```

The `GromitUse.cmake` file can be included by user projects through the `Gromit_USE_FILE` variable to automatically add include and library directories. It also imports Gromit's build settings automatically to ensure that the user project will build with Gromit. The file looks like this:

```
# Import gromit's build settings.
include (CMakeImportBuildSettings)

cmake_import_build_settings (${Gromit_BUILD_SETTINGS_FILE})

# Tell the compiler where to find gromit's header files.
include_directories (${Gromit_INCLUDE_DIRS})

# Tell the linker where to find gromit's libraries.
link_directories (${Gromit_LIBRARY_DIRS})
```

Note that the above example only supports creation of GromitConfig.cmake for an installation. More logic would be required to configure the file for the build tree as well. This is only required if you want your project to be used in both build and installed configurations.

## Chapter 8

Custom Commands and Targets

Frequently the build process for a software project goes beyond simply compiling libraries and executables. In many cases additional tasks may be required during or after the build process. Common examples include: compiling documentation using a documentation package, generating source files by running another executable, generating files using tools for which CMake doesn't have rules (such as lexx, and yacc), moving the resulting executables, post processing the executable, etc. CMake supports these additional tasks using custom commands and custom targets. This chapter will describe how to use custom commands and targets to perform complex tasks that CMake doesn't inherently support.

8.1 Portable Custom Commands

Before going into detail on how to use custom commands, we will discuss how to deal with some of their portability issues. Custom commands typically involve running programs with files as inputs or outputs. Even a simple command such as copying a file can be tricky to do in a cross-platform setting. For example, copying a file on UNIX is done with the cp command while on windows it is done with the copy command. To make matters worse, frequently the names of the files will change on different platforms. Executables on Windows end with .exe while on UNIX they do not. Even between UNIX implementations there are differences such as what extensions are used for shared libraries; .so, .sl, .dylib, etc.

CMake provides two main tools for handling these differences. The first is the -E option (short for execute) to `cmake`. When the `cmake` executable is passed the -E option it acts as a general purpose cross-platform utility command. The arguments following the -E option indicate what `cmake` should do. Some of the options include:

chdir dir command args

>   Changes the current directory to `dir` and then execute the command with the provided arguments.

copy file destination

>   Copies a file from one directory or filename to another.

copy_if_different in-file out-file

>   copy_if_different first checks to see if the files are different before copying them. copy_if_different is critical in many rules since the build process is based on file modification times. If the copied file is used as the input to another build rule then copy_if_different can eliminate unnecessary recompilations.

copy_directory source destination

>   This option copies the source directory including any subdirectories to the destination directory.

remove file1 file2 ...

>   Removes the listed files from the disk.

echo string

>   Echos a string to the console. This is useful for providing output during the build process.

time command args

>   Runs the command and times its execution.

These options provide a platform independent way to perform a few common tasks. The cmake executable can be referenced by using the CMAKE_COMMAND variable in your CMakeLists files as later examples will show.

The second tool CMake provides to address portability issues is a number of variables describing the characteristics of the platform. While most of these are covered in Appendix A - Variables, some are particularly useful for custom commands.

EXE_EXTENSION

>   This is the file extension for executables. Typically nothing on UNIX and .exe on MS Windows

CMAKE_CFG_INTDIR

>   Development environments such as Visual Studio and Xcode use subdirectories based on the build type selected, such as Release or Debug. When performing a

custom command on a library, executable or object file you will typically need the full path to the file. CMAKE_CFG_INTDIR on UNIX will typically be "./" while for VisualStudio it will be set to "$(INTDIR)/" which at build time will be replaced by the selected configuration.

CMAKE_CURRENT_BINARY_DIR

This is the full path to the output directory associated with the current CMakeLists file. This may be different from PROJECT_BINARY_DIR which is the full path to the top of the current project's binary tree.

CMAKE_CURRENT_SOURCE_DIR

This is the full path to the source directory associated with the current CMakeLists file. This may be different from PROJECT_SOURCE_DIR which is the full path to the top of the current project's source tree.

EXECUTABLE_OUTPUT_PATH

Some projects specify a directory into which all the executables should be built. This variable, if defined, holds the full path to that directory.

LIBRARY_OUTPUT_PATH

Some projects specify a directory into which all the libraries should be built. This variable, if defined, should hold the full path to that directory.

There are also a series of variables such as CMAKE_SHARED_MODULE_PREFIX and ...SUFFIX that describe the current platform's prefix and suffix for that type of file. These variables are defined for SHARED_MODULE, SHARED_LIBRARY, and LIBRARY. Using these variables, you can typically construct the full path to any CMake generated file that you need to. For libraries and executable targets you can also use GET_TARGET_PROPERTY with the LOCATION argument to get the full path to the target.

CMake doesn't limit you to using cmake -E in all your commands. You can use any command that you like, you just need to think about portability issues when doing it. A common practice is to use find_program to find an executable (say perl for example) and then use that executable in your custom commands.

8.2 Using add_custom_command on a Target

Now we will consider the signature for add_custom_command. In makefile terminology add_custom_command adds a rule to a makefile. For those more familiar with Visual Studio, it adds a custom build step to a file. add_custom_command has two main signatures, one for adding a custom command to a target and one for adding a custom command to build a file. When adding a custom command to a target the signature is as follows:

```
add_custom_command (
  TARGET target
  PRE_BUILD | PRE_LINK | POST_BUILD
  COMMAND command [ARGS arg1 arg2 arg3 …]
  [COMMAND command [ARGS arg1 arg2 arg3 …] …]
  [COMMENT comment]
  )
```

The target is the name of a CMake target (executable, library, or custom) to which you want
to add the custom command. Next there is a choice of when the custom command should be
executed. PRE_BUILD indicates that the command should be executed before any other
dependencies for the target are built. PRE_LINK indicates that the command should be
executed after the dependencies are all built, but before the actual link command.
POST_BUILD indicates that the custom command should be executed after the target has been
built. The COMMAND argument is the command (executable) to run and ARGS provides an
optional list of arguments to the command. Finally the COMMENT argument can be used to
provide a quoted string to be used as output when this custom command is run. This is useful
if you want to provide some feedback or documentation on what is happening during the
build. You can specify as many commands as you want for a custom command. They will be
executed in the order specified.

How to Copy an Executable Once it is Built?

Now let us consider a simple custom command for copying an executable once it has been
built.

```
# first define the executable target as usual
add_executable (Foo bar.c)

# get where the executable will be located
get_target_property (EXE_LOC Foo LOCATION)

# then add the custom command to copy it
add_custom_command (
  TARGET Foo
  POST_BUILD
  COMMAND ${CMAKE_COMMAND}
  ARGS -E copy ${EXE_LOC} /testing_department/files
  )
```

The first command in this example is the standard command for creating an executable from a
list of source files. In this case an executable named Foo is created from the source file
bar.c. The next command is get_target_property which will set the variable called

EXE_LOC to where the executable will be built. Next is the add_custom_command invocation. In this case the target is simply Foo and we are adding a post build command. The command to execute is cmake which has its full path specified in the CMAKE_COMMAND variable. Its arguments are "-E copy" and the source and destination locations. In this case it will copy the Foo executable from where it was built into the /testing_department/files directory. Note that the TARGET parameter accepts a CMake target (Foo in this example) but most commands such as cmake -E copy will require the full path to the executable which can be retrieved using GET_TARGET_PROPERTY.

8.3   Using add_custom_command to Generate a File

The second use for add_custom_command is to add a rule for how to build an output file. In this case the rule provided will replace any current rules for building that file. This signature is as follows:

```
add_custom_command(OUTPUT output1 [output2 ...]
  COMMAND command [ARGS [args...]]
  [COMMAND command [ARGS arg1 arg2 arg3 ...] ...]
  [MAIN_DEPENDENCY depend]
  [DEPENDS [depends...]]
  [COMMENT comment]
  )
```

The OUTPUT is the file or files that will result from running this custom command, the COMMAND and ARGS parameters are the command to execute and the arguments to pass it. As with the prior signature you can have as many commands as you wish. The DEPENDS are files or executables on which this custom command depends. If any of these dependencies change this custom command will re-execute. The MAIN_DEPENDENCY is an optional argument that acts as a regular dependency and under Visual Studio it provides a suggestion for what file to hang this custom command onto. If the MAIN_DEPENDENCY is not specified then one will be created automatically by CMake. The MAIN_DEPENDENCY should not be a regular .c or .cxx file since the custom command will override the default build rule for the file. Finally the optional COMMENT is a comment that may be used by some generators to provide additional information during the build process.

Using an Executable to Build a Source File

Sometimes a software project builds an executable which is then used for generating source files which are then used to build other executables or libraries. This may sound like an odd case but it occurs fairly frequently. One example is the build process for the TIFF library which creates an executable that is then run to generate a source file that has system specific information in it. This file is then used as a source file in building the main TIFF library. Another example is the Visualization Toolkit that builds an executable called vtkWrapTcl that wraps C++ classes into Tcl. The executable is built and then used to create more source files for the build process.

```
######################################################
# Test using a compiled program to create a file
######################################################

# add the executable that will create the file
# build creator executable from creator.cxx
add_executable (creator creator.cxx)

get_target_property (creator EXE_LOC LOCATION)

# add the custom command to produce created.c
add_custom_command(
  OUTPUT ${PROJECT_BINARY_DIR}/created.c
  DEPENDS creator
  COMMAND ${EXE_LOC}
  ARGS ${PROJECT_BINARY_DIR}/created.c
  )

# add an executable that uses created.c
add_executable (Foo ${PROJECT_BINARY_DIR}/created.c)
```

The first part of this example produces the `creator` executable from the source file `creator.cxx`. The custom command then sets up a rule for producing the source file `created.c` by running the executable `creator`. The custom command depends on the `creator` target and writes its result into the output tree (`PROJECT_BINARY_DIR`). Finally, an executable target called `Foo` is added that is built using the `created.c` source file. CMake will create all the required rules in the Makefile (or Visual Studio workspace) such that when you build the project, first the `creator` executable will be built, then it will be run to create `created.c`, which will then be used to build the `Foo` executable.

8.4   Adding a Custom Target

In the discussion so far CMake targets have generally referred to executables and libraries. CMake does support a more general notion of targets called custom targets that can be used whenever you want the notion of a target but the end product will not be a library or executable. Examples of custom targets include targets to build documentation, run tests, or update web pages. To add a custom target you use the `add_custom_target` command with the following signature:

```
add_custom_target ( name [ALL]
  [command arg arg arg ... ]
  [DEPENDS depend depend depend ... ]
  )
```

The name specified will be the name given to the target. You can use that name to specifically build that target with makefiles (make name) or Visual Studio (right click on the target and then select Build). If the optional ALL argument is specified then this target will be included in the ALL_BUILD target and will automatically be built whenever the makefile or Project is built. The command and arguments are optional and if specified will be added to the target as a post build command. For custom targets that will only execute a command this is all you will need. More complex custom targets may depend on other files, in these cases the DEPENDS arguments are used to list what files this target depends on. We will consider examples of both cases. First let us look at a custom target that has no dependencies:

```
add_custom_target ( FooJAR ALL
  ${JAR} -cvf "\"${PROJECT_BINARY_DIR}/Foo.jar\""
            "\"${PROJECT_SOURCE_DIR}/Java\""
  )
```

With the above definition, whenever the FooJAR target is built it will run Java's Archiver (jar) to create the Foo.jar file from java classes in the ${PROJECT_SOURCE_DIR}/Java directory. In essence this type of custom target allows the developer to tie a command onto a target so that it can be conveniently invoked during the build process. Now let us consider a more complicated example that roughly models generation of pdf files from LaTeX. In this case the custom target depends on other generated files (mainly the end product .pdf files):

```
# Add the rule to build the .dvi file from the .tex
# file. This relies on LATEX being set correctly
#
add_custom_command(
  OUTPUT   ${PROJECT_BINARY_DIR}/doc1.dvi
  DEPENDS  ${PROJECT_SOURCE_DIR}/doc1.tex
  COMMAND  ${LATEX}
  ARGS     ${PROJECT_SOURCE_DIR}/doc1.tex
  )

# Add the rule to produce the .pdf file from the .dvi
# file. This relies on DVIPDF being set correctly
#
add_custom_command(
  OUTPUT   ${PROJECT_BINARY_DIR}/doc1.pdf
```

```
  DEPENDS ${PROJECT_BINARY_DIR}/doc1.dvi
  COMMAND ${DVIPDF}
  ARGS    ${PROJECT_BINARY_DIR}/doc1.dvi
  )


# finally add the custom target that when invoked
# will cause the generation of the pdf file
#
add_custom_target ( TDocument ALL
  DEPENDS ${PROJECT_BINARY_DIR}/doc1.pdf
  )
```

This example makes use of both `add_custom_command` and `add_custom_target`. The two `add_custom_command` invocations are used to specify the rules for producing a .pdf file from a .tex file. In this case there are two steps and two custom commands. First a .dvi file is produced from the .tex file by running LaTeX, then the .dvi file is processed to produce the desired .pdf file. Finally the custom target is added called TDocument. Its command simply echoes out what it is doing while the real work is done by the two custom commands. The DEPENDS argument sets up a dependency between the custom target and the custom commands. When TDocument is built it will first look to see if all of its dependencies are built. If any are not built it will invoke the appropriate custom commands to build them. This example can be shortened by combining the two custom commands into one custom command as in the following example:

```
# Add the rule to build the .pdf file from the .tex
# file. This relies on LATEX and DVIPDF being set correctly
#
add_custom_command(
  OUTPUT  ${PROJECT_BINARY_DIR}/doc1.pdf
  DEPENDS ${PROJECT_SOURCE_DIR}/doc1.tex
  COMMAND ${LATEX}
  ARGS    ${PROJECT_SOURCE_DIR}/doc1.tex
  COMMAND ${DVIPDF}
  ARGS    ${PROJECT_BINARY_DIR}/doc1.dvi
  )


# finally add the custom target that when invoked
# will cause the generation of the pdf file
#
add_custom_target ( TDocument ALL
  DEPENDS ${PROJECT_BINARY_DIR}/doc1.pdf
  )
```

Now consider the case in which the documentation consists of multiple files. The above example can be modified to handle many files using a list of inputs and a foreach loop. For example:

```
# set the list of documents to process
set (DOCS doc1 doc2 doc3)

# add the custom commands for each document
foreach (DOC ${DOCS})

  add_custom_command (
    OUTPUT   ${PROJECT_BINARY_DIR}/${DOC}.pdf
    DEPENDS ${PROJECT_SOURCE_DIR}/${DOC}.tex
    COMMAND ${LATEX}
    ARGS     ${PROJECT_SOURCE_DIR}/${DOC}.tex
    COMMAND ${DVIPDF}
    ARGS     ${PROJECT_BINARY_DIR}/${DOC}.dvi
    )

  # build a list of all the results
  set (DOC_RESULTS ${DOC_RESULTS}
    ${PROJECT_BINARY_DIR}/${DOC}.pdf
    )

endforeach (DOC)

# finally add the custom target that when invoked
# will cause the generation of the pdf file
#
add_custom_target ( TDocument ALL
  DEPENDS ${DOC_RESULTS}
  )
```

In this example building the custom target TDocument will cause all of the specified .pdf files to be generated. Adding a new document to the list is simply a matter of adding its filename to the DOCS variable at the top of the example.

8.5   Specifying Dependencies and Outputs

When using custom commands and custom targets you will often be specifying dependencies. When you specify a dependency or output for a custom command you should always specify the full path. For example, if the command produces foo.h in the binary tree then its output should be something like ${PROJECT_BINARY_DIR}/foo.h. While CMake will try to determine the correct path for the file if it is not specified, complex projects frequently end up using files in both the source and build trees which can eventually lead to errors if the full paths are not specified.

When specifying a target as a dependency you can leave off the full path and executable extension and reference it simply by its name. Consider the specification of the generator target as an add_custom_command dependency in the example on page 130. CMake recognizes creator as matching an existing target and properly handles the dependencies.

8.6   When There Isn't One Rule for One Output

There are a couple of unusual cases that can arise when using custom commands that warrant some explanation. The first is a case where one command (or executable) can create multiple outputs and the second is the case where multiple commands can be used to create a single output.

A Single Command Producing Multiple Outputs

In CMake a custom command can produce multiple outputs simply by listing multiple outputs after the OUTPUT keyword. CMake will create the correct rules for your build system so that no matter which output is required for a target the right rules will be run. If the executable happens to produce a few outputs but the build process is only using one of them then you can simply ignore the other outputs when creating your custom command. Say that the executable produces a source file that is used in the build process and also an execution log that isn't used. The custom command should specify the source file as the output and ignore the fact that a log file is also generated.

Another case of having one command with multiple outputs is the case where the command is the same but the arguments to it change. This is effectively the same as having a different command and each case should have its own custom command. An example of this was the documentation example on page 133 where a custom command is added for each .tex file. The command is the same but the arguments passed to it are changing each time.

Having One Output That Can Be Generated By Different Commands

In rare cases you may find that you have more than one command that you can use to generate an output. Most build systems such as make and Visual Studio do not support this and likewise CMake does not. There are two common approaches to resolving this. If you truly have two different commands that produce the same output, and no other significant outputs then you can simply pick one of them and create a custom command for that one.

In the more complex case there are multiple commands with multiple outputs. For example:

```
Command1 produces foo.h and bar.h
Command2 produces widget.h and bar.h
```

There are a few approaches that can be used in this case. In some cases you might just combine both commands and all three outputs into a single custom command so that whenever one output is required all three are built at the same time. You could also create three custom commands, one for each unique output. The custom command for `foo.h` would invoke Command1 while the one for `widget.h` would invoke Command2. When specifying the custom command for `bar.h` you could choose either Command1 or Command2.

## Chapter 9

Cross compiling with CMake

Cross compiling means that software is built on one system but intended to run on a different system, which usually runs a different operating system (or none at all) and/or runs on different hardware. The typical use case is software development for embedded devices like network switches, mobile phones or engine control units. In these cases the target platform doesn't have or is not able to run the required software development environment.

Starting with CMake 2.6.0 cross compiling is fully supported by CMake, ranging from cross compiling from Linux to Windows over cross compiling for supercomputers to cross compiling for small embedded devices without operating system.

Cross compiling has several consequences for CMake;

- CMake can't automatically detect the target platform

- CMake can't find libraries and headers in the default system directories

- executables built during cross compiling can't be executed

Cross compiling support doesn't mean that all CMake-based projects can be magically cross compiled out-of-the-box (some are), but that CMake separates between information about the build platform and target platform and gives the user mechanisms to solve cross compiling issues without fancy additional requirements like e.g. running virtual machines etc.

To support cross compiling for a specific software project, CMake has to be told about the target platform via a so called toolchain file, CMakeLists.txt may have to be adjusted so they are aware that the build platform may have different properties than the target platform and it has to be dealt with the cases where a compiled executable is tried to execute on the build host.

9.1   Toolchain files

In order to use CMake for cross compiling, a CMake file which describes the target platform has to be created, called the "toolchain file". This file tells CMake everything it needs to know about the target platform. Here is an example for using the MinGW cross compiler for Windows under Linux:

```
# the name of the target operating system
set (CMAKE_SYSTEM_NAME Windows)

# which compilers to use for C and C++
set (CMAKE_C_COMPILER   i586-mingw32msvc-gcc )
set (CMAKE_CXX_COMPILER i586-mingw32msvc-g++ )

# where is the target environment located
set (CMAKE_FIND_ROOT_PATH  /usr/i586-mingw32msvc
     /home/alex/mingw-install )

# adjust the default behavior of the FIND_XXX() commands:
# search programs in the host environment
set (CMAKE_FIND_ROOT_PATH_MODE_PROGRAM NEVER)

# search headers and libraries in the target environment
set (CMAKE_FIND_ROOT_PATH_MODE_LIBRARY ONLY)
set (CMAKE_FIND_ROOT_PATH_MODE_INCLUDE ONLY)
```

If this file is saved as TC-mingw.cmake in your home directory, then you use this file as follows:

```
~/src$ cd build
~/src/build$ cmake -DCMAKE_TOOLCHAIN_FILE=~/TC-mingw.cmake ..
...
```

CMAKE_TOOLCHAIN_FILE has to be specified only on the first CMake run, after that the results are reused from the CMake cache. The toolchain file doesn't have to be written for every piece of software you want to build. The toolchain files are per target platform, i.e. if you are building several software packages all for the same target platform, you have to write only one toolchain file and you can use this for all packages. What do the settings in the toolchain file mean? We'll examine them one by one. Since CMake cannot guess the target system, you have to preset the following CMake variables:

CMAKE_SYSTEM_NAME

> This one is mandatory; it sets the name of the target system, i.e. to the same value as CMAKE_SYSTEM_NAME would have if CMake would run on the target system. Typical examples are "Linux" and "Windows". This variable is used for constructing the file names of the platform files like Linux.cmake or Windows-gcc.cmake. If your target is an embedded system without OS then set CMAKE_SYSTEM_NAME to "Generic". If CMAKE_SYSTEM_NAME is preset this way instead of being detected automatically, then the CMake variable CMAKE_CROSSCOMPILING is automatically set to TRUE, so this can be used for testing in the CMake files.

CMAKE_SYSTEM_VERSION

> This one is optional. It sets the version of your target system. CMake does not use CMAKE_SYSTEM_VERSION currently.

CMAKE_SYSTEM_PROCESSOR

> This one is optional. It sets the processor or hardware name of the target system. This variable is used in CMake for only one purpose, it is used to load the

```
${CMAKE_SYSTEM_NAME}-COMPILER_ID-${CMAKE_SYSTEM_PROCESSOR}.cmake
```

> file. This file can be used to modify settings like compiler flags etc. for the target. You probably only have to set this one if you are using a cross compiler where every target hardware needs special build settings. The value can be chosen freely, so it could be e.g. i386 or IntelPXA255 or also MyControlBoardRev42.

In CMake code the CMAKE_SYSTEM_XXX variables always describe the target platform. The same is true for the short WIN32, UNIX, APPLE etc. variables. By using these variables properties of the target system can be tested. If it is required to test the host system, there is a corresponding set of variables: CMAKE_HOST_SYSTEM_NAME, CMAKE_HOST_SYSTEM, CMAKE_HOST_SYSTEM_VERSION, CMAKE_HOST_SYSTEM_PROCESSOR and also the short forms CMAKE_HOST_WIN32, CMAKE_HOST_UNIX and CMAKE_HOST_APPLE.

Since CMake cannot guess the target system, it also cannot guess which compiler it should use. Setting the following variables defines what compilers to use for the target system.

CMAKE_C_COMPILER

> This specifies the C compiler executable as either a full path or just the filename. If it is specified with full path, then this path will be preferred when searching the C++

compiler and the other tools (binutils, linker, etc.). If this compiler is a GNU cross compiler with a prefixed name (e.g. "arm-elf-gcc") CMake will detect this and automatically find the corresponding C++ compiler (i.e. "arm-elf-c++"). This may also work for MS cross compilers. The compiler can also be preset via the CC environment variables.

CMAKE_CXX_COMPILER

This specifies the C++ compiler executable as either a full path or just the filename. It is handled the same way as CMAKE_C_COMPILER. If the toolchain is a GNU toolchain, you only need to set one of them.

Once the system and the compiler are determined by CMake, it loads the corresponding files in the order as described in section 11.2, The Enable Language Process.

Finding external libraries, programs and other files

Most non-trivial projects make use of external libraries or tools. CMake offers the find_program, find_library, find_file, find_path, and find_package commands for this purpose. They search the file system in common places for these files and return the results. find_package is a bit different in that it actually doesn't search itself, but only executes Find<*>.cmake modules, which in turn usually call the find_program, find_library, find_file and find_path commands.

When cross compiling these commands become more complicated. For example, when cross compiling to Windows on a Linux system, getting /usr/lib/libjpeg.so as the result of a find_package(JPEG) wouldn't be much of a help, since this would be the JPEG library for the host system not the target. In some cases you want to find files that are meant for the target platform, in other cases you will want to find files for the host platform. The following variables are designed to give you the flexibility to change how the typical find commands in CMake work so that you can find both host, and or target files as needed.

The toolchain will come with its own set of libraries and headers for the target platform which are usually installed under a common prefix. Additionally it is a good idea to set up a directory where all the software which is built for the target will be installed so that this doesn't get mixed up with the libraries coming from the toolchain.

The find_program command is in most cases used to find a program which will then be executed during the build, so this should still search in the host file system, not in the environment of the target platform. find_library is in most cases used to find a library which is then used for linking, so this command should search in the target environment only. For find_path and find_file it's not so obvious, in many cases they are used to search for headers, so by default they should also search only in the target environment. The following CMake variables can be set to adjust the behavior of the find commands for cross compiling.

CMAKE_FIND_ROOT_PATH

This is a list of the directories which contain the target environment. Each of the directories listed here will be prepended to each of the search directories of every find command. So if your target environment is installed under /opt/eldk/ppc_74xx and your own installation for that target platform goes to ~/install-eldk-ppc74xx, set CMAKE_FIND_ROOT_PATH to these two directories. Then `find_library` (JPEG_LIB jpeg) will search in /opt/eldk/ppc_74xx/lib, /opt/eldk/ppc_74xx/usr/lib, /lib, /usr/lib and give /opt/eldk/ppc_74xx/usr/lib/libjpeg.so as result.

By default CMAKE_FIND_ROOT_PATH is empty. If set, at first the directories prefixed with the directories given in CMAKE_FIND_ROOT_PATH will be searched and after that the unprefixed versions of the same directories will be searched.

So by setting this variable you are basically adding a new set of search prefixes to all the find commands in CMake. But, for some find commands you may not want to search the target or host directories. You can control how each find command invocation works by passing in one of the three following options NO_CMAKE_FIND_ROOT_PATH, ONLY_CMAKE_FIND_ROOT_PATH or CMAKE_FIND_ROOT_PATH_BOTH when you call it. You can also control how the find commands work using the following three variables.

CMAKE_FIND_ROOT_PATH_MODE_PROGRAM

This sets the default behavior for the `find_program` command. It can be set to NEVER, ONLY or BOTH. The default setting is BOTH. When set to NEVER, CMAKE_FIND_ROOT_PATH will not be used for `find_program` calls except where it is enabled explicitly. If set to ONLY, only the search directories with the prefixes coming from CMAKE_FIND_ROOT_PATH will be used in `find_program`. The default is BOTH, which means that at first the prefixed directories and after that the unprefixed directories will be searched.

In most cases `find_program` is used to search for an executable which will then be executed e.g. using `execute_process` or `add_custom_command`. So in most cases an executable from the build host is required, so usually set CMAKE_FIND_ROOT_PATH_MODE_PROGRAM to NEVER.

CMAKE_FIND_ROOT_PATH_MODE_LIBRARY

This is the same as above, but for the `find_library` command. In most cases this is used to find a library which will then be used for linking, so a library for the target is required. So in the common case, set it to ONLY.

CMAKE_FIND_ROOT_PATH_MODE_INCLUDE

This is the same as above and used for both `find_path` and `find_file`. In many cases this is used for finding include directories, so the target environment should be searched. So in the common case, set it to ONLY. You may have to adjust this behavior for some of the find_path or find_file calls using the NO_CMAKE_FIND_ROOT_PATH, ONLY_CMAKE_FIND_ROOT_PATH and CMAKE_FIND_ROOT_PATH_BOTH options.

With a toolchain file set up that way CMake now knows how to handle the target platform and the cross compiler, so we are now able to build software for the target platform. For complex projects some more issues have to be taken care of.

9.2   System inspection

Most portable software projects have a set of system inspection tests for finding out properties of the (target) system. The simplest way to check for a system feature with CMake is by testing variables. For this purpose CMake has provided the variables UNIX, WIN32 and APPLE. When cross compiling these variables apply to the target platform, for testing the host platform corresponding variables CMAKE_HOST_UNIX, CMAKE_HOST_WINDOWS and CMAKE_HOST_APPLE have been added.

If this granularity is too coarse, the variables CMAKE_SYSTEM_NAME, CMAKE_SYSTEM, CMAKE_SYSTEM_VERSION and CMAKE_SYSTEM_PROCESSOR can be tested along with their HOST counterparts.

```
if (CMAKE_SYSTEM MATCHES Windows)
   message (STATUS "Target system is Windows")
endif (CMAKE_SYSTEM MATCHES Windows)

if (CMAKE_HOST_SYSTEM MATCHES Linux)
   message (STATUS "Build host runs Linux")
endif (CMAKE_HOST_SYSTEM MATCHES Linux)
```

Using compile checks

In CMake there are macros such as CHECK_INCLUDE_FILES and CHECK_C_SOURCE_RUNS that are used to test properties of the platform. Most of these macros internally use either the try_compile or the try_run commands. The try_compile command works as expected when cross compiling, it tries to compile the piece of code with the cross compiling toolchain, which will give the expected result.

All tests using try_run cannot work since the created executables in general cannot run on the build host. While in some cases this could be possible, e.g. using virtual machines, emulation layers like Wine or interfaces to the actual target, CMake doesn't depend on such mechanisms. Depending on emulators during the build process would introduce a new set of potential problems, they may have a different view on the file system, use other line endings, require special hardware or software, etc.

If you invoke `try_run` when cross compiling, at first it will try to compile the software, which will work the same way as when cross compiling. If this succeeds, it will check the variable `CMAKE_CROSSCOMPILING` to determine whether the resulting executable can be executed or not. If it cannot, it will create two cache variables, which then have to be set by the user or via the CMake cache. Let's say the command looks like this:

```
try_run (SHARED_LIBRARY_PATH_TYPE
         SHARED_LIBRARY_PATH_INFO_COMPILED
         ${PROJECT_BINARY_DIR}/CMakeTmp
         ${PROJECT_SOURCE_DIR}/CMake/SharedLibraryPathInfo.cxx
         OUTPUT_VARIABLE OUTPUT
         ARGS "LDPATH")
```

The variable `SHARED_LIBRARY_PATH_INFO_COMPILED` will be set to the result of the build, e.g. `TRUE` or `FALSE`. CMake will create a cache variable `SHARED_LIBRARY_PATH_TYPE` and preset it to `PLEASE_FILL_OUT-FAILED_TO_RUN`. This variable has to be set to the exit code of the executable if it would have been executed on the target. It will also create a cache variable `SHARED_LIBRARY_PATH_TYPE__TRYRUN_OUTPUT` and preset it to `PLEASE_FILL_OUT-NOTFOUND`. This variable has to be set to the output the executable prints to stdout and stderr if it is executed on the target. This variable is only created if the `try_run` command was used with the `RUN_OUTPUT_VARIABLE` or the `OUTPUT_VARIABLE` argument. You have to fill in appropriate values for these variables. To help you with this CMake tries its best to give you useful information. To do so CMake creates a file `${CMAKE_BINARY_DIR}/TryRunResults.cmake`, which you can see here:

```
# SHARED_LIBRARY_PATH_TYPE
#   indicates whether the executable would have been able to run
#   on its target platform. If so, set SHARED_LIBRARY_PATH_TYPE
#   to the exit code (in many cases 0 for success), otherwise
#   enter "FAILED_TO_RUN".
# SHARED_LIBRARY_PATH_TYPE__TRYRUN_OUTPUT
#   contains the text the executable would have printed on
#   stdout and stderr. If the executable would not have been
#   able to run, set SHARED_LIBRARY_PATH_TYPE__TRYRUN_OUTPUT
#   empty. Otherwise check if the output is evaluated by the
#   calling CMake code. If so, check what the source file would
#   have printed when called with the given arguments.
# The SHARED_LIBRARY_PATH_INFO_COMPILED variable holds the build
# result for this TRY_RUN().
#
```

```
# Source file: ~/src/SharedLibraryPathInfo.cxx
# Executable : ~/build/cmTryCompileExec-SHARED_LIBRARY_PATH_TYPE
# Run arguments:  LDPATH
#     Called from: [1]   ~/src/CMakeLists.cmake

set (SHARED_LIBRARY_PATH_TYPE
     "0"
     CACHE STRING "Result from TRY_RUN" FORCE)

set (SHARED_LIBRARY_PATH_TYPE__TRYRUN_OUTPUT
     ""
     CACHE STRING "Output from TRY_RUN" FORCE)
```

You can find all the variables which CMake could not determine, from which CMake file they were called, the source file, the arguments for the executable and the path to the executable. CMake will also copy the executables to the build directory, they have the names `cmTryCompileExec-<name of the variable>`, e.g. in this case `cmTryCompileExec-SHARED_LIBRARY_PATH_TYPE`. You can then try to run this executable manually on the actual target platform and check the results.

Once you have these results, they have to get into the CMake cache. This can be done by using ccmake/CMakeSetup/"make edit_cache" and editing the variables directly in the cache, but then it is not possible to reuse these changes in another build directory or if CMakeCache.txt is removed.

The second option is to use the TryRunResults.cmake file. Copy it to a safe location (i.e. where it is not deleted if you delete the build dir) and give it a useful name, e.g. TryRunResults-MyProject-eldk-ppc.cmake. Then edit it so that the set commands set the required values. You can the use this file to preload the CMake cache by using the -C option of cmake:

```
src/build/ $ cmake -C ~/TryRunResults-MyProject-eldk-ppc.cmake .
```

You don't have to use the other CMake options again, they are now already in the cache. This way you can use MyProjectTryRunResults-eldk-ppc.cmake in multiple build trees and it could also be distributed with your project so it gets easier for other users who want to compile it.

9.3   Running executables built in the project itself

In some cases it is necessary that during a build an executable is invoked which has been built earlier in the same build, this is usually the case for code generators or similar tools. This doesn't work when cross compiling, since the executables are built for the target platform and cannot run on the build host (without the use of virtual machines, compatibility layers, emulators etc.). With CMake these program are created using `add_executable` and then used with `add_custom_command` or `add_custom_target`. The following three options can be used to support these executables with CMake. The old version of the cmake code looks something like this:

```
add_executable (mygen gen.c)
get_target_property (mygenLocation mygen LOCATION)
add_custom_command (
  OUTPUT "${CMAKE_CURRENT_BINARY_DIR}/generated.h"
  COMMAND ${mygenLocation}
       -o "${CMAKE_CURRENT_BINARY_DIR}/generated.h" )
```

There are two ways how this can be converted so that it works with cross compiling. The idea is that the executable is only built when doing a native build and then exported to a script file. This file is then used when cross compiling. `add_custom_command` recognizes target names as executables so no special measures are required there:

```
if (CMAKE_CROSSCOMPILING)
   find_package (MyGen)
endif (CMAKE_CROSSCOMPILING)

if (NOT CMAKE_CROSSCOMPILING)
   add_executable (mygen gen.c)
   export (TARGETS mygen FILE
          "${CMAKE_BINARY_DIR}/MyGenConfig.cmake")
endif (NOT CMAKE_CROSSCOMPILING)

add_custom_command (
  OUTPUT "${CMAKE_CURRENT_BINARY_DIR}/generated.h"
  COMMAND mygen -o "${CMAKE_CURRENT_BINARY_DIR}/generated.h" )
```

This code works, but CMake versions prior to 2.6 will not be able to process it. A compatible version which still works with CMake 2.4 looks like this:

```
if (CMAKE_CROSSCOMPILING)
   find_package (MyGen)
endif (CMAKE_CROSSCOMPILING)

if (NOT CMAKE_CROSSCOMPILING)
   add_executable (mygen gen.c)
```

```
  if (COMMAND EXPORT)
    export (TARGETS mygen FILE
           "${CMAKE_BINARY_DIR}/MyGenConfig.cmake")
  endif (COMMAND EXPORT)
endif (NOT CMAKE_CROSSCOMPILING)

get_target_property (mygenLocation mygen LOCATION)
add_custom_command (
  OUTPUT "${CMAKE_CURRENT_BINARY_DIR}/generated.h"
  COMMAND ${mygenLocation}
    -o "${CMAKE_CURRENT_BINARY_DIR}/generated.h" )
```

Here the target is only exported if the export command exists and the location of the executable is retrieved using the LOCATION target property. To actually build the project then at first a native build has to be done and then the build directory of the native build has to be given to the cross compiling build as location of the MyGen package:

```
mkdir build-native; cd build-native
cmake ..
make
cd ..
mkdir build-cross; cd build-cross
cmake -DCMAKE_TOOLCHAIN_FILE=MyToolchain.cmake \
      -DMyGen_DIR=~/src/build-native/ ..
make
```

The "old" CMake code could also be using the utility_source command:

```
subdirs (mygen)
utility_source (MYGEN_LOCATION mygen mygen gen.c)
add_custom_command (
   OUTPUT "${CMAKE_CURRENT_BINARY_DIR}/generated.h"
   COMMAND ${MYGEN_LOCATION}
      -o "${CMAKE_CURRENT_BINARY_DIR}/generated.h" )
```

In this case the CMake script doesn't have to be changed, but the invocation of CMake is more complicated, since each executable location has to be specified manually:

```
mkdir build-native; cd build-native
cmake ..
make
cd ..
mkdir build-cross; cd build-cross
cmake -DCMAKE_TOOLCHAIN_FILE=MyToolchain.cmake
      -DMYGEN_LOCATION=~/src/build-native/bin/mygen ..
make
```

9.4   Cross compiling Hello world

Now let's actually start with the cross compiling. The first step is to install a cross compiling toolchain. If this is already installed, you can skip the next paragraph.

There are many different approaches and projects which deal with cross compiling for Linux, ranging from free software projects working on Linux based PDAs to commercial embedded Linux vendors. Most of these projects come with their own way how to build and use the respective toolchain. For use with CMake any of these toolchains can be used, the only requirement is that it works within the normal file system and doesn't expect a "sandboxed" environment like the Scratchbox project does for example.

An easy to use toolchain with a relatively complete target environment is the Embedded Linux Development Toolkit (http://www.denx.de/wiki/DULG/ELDK), which supports ARM, PowerPC and MIPS as target platforms. ELDK can be downloaded from ftp://ftp.sunet.se/pub/Linux/distributions/eldk/. The easiest way is to download the ISOs, mount them and then install them:

```
mkdir mount-iso/
sudo mount -tiso9660 mips-2007-01-21.iso mount-iso/ -o loop
cd mount-iso/
./install -d /home/alex/eldk-mips/
...
Preparing...
######################################### [100%]
    1:appWeb-mips_4KCle
######################################### [100%]
Done
ls /opt/eldk-mips/
bin  eldk_init  etc  mips_4KC  mips_4KCle  usr  var  version
```

ELDK (and other toolchains) can be installed anywhere, either in the home directory or system wide if there are more users working with them. In this example the toolchain will now be located in /home/alex/eldk-mips/usr/bin/ and the target environment is in /home/alex/eldk-mips/mips_4KC/.

Now that a cross compiling toolchain is installed, CMake has to be set up to use it. As already laid out, this is done via creating a Toolchain-file for CMake. For this example the toolchain file will look like this:

```
# the name of the target operating system
set (CMAKE_SYSTEM_NAME Linux)

# which C and C++ compiler to use
set (CMAKE_C_COMPILER /home/alex/eldk-mips/usr/bin/mips_4KC-gcc)
set (CMAKE_CXX_COMPILER
     /home/alex/eldk-mips/usr/bin/mips_4KC-g++)

# here is the target environment located
set (CMAKE_FIND_ROOT_PATH /home/alex/eldk-mips/mips_4KC
                          /home/alex/eldk-mips-extra-install )

# adjust the default behavior of the FIND_XXX() commands:
# search headers and libraries in the target environment, search
# programs in the host environment
set (CMAKE_FIND_ROOT_PATH_MODE_PROGRAM NEVER)
set (CMAKE_FIND_ROOT_PATH_MODE_LIBRARY ONLY)
set (CMAKE_FIND_ROOT_PATH_MODE_INCLUDE ONLY)
```

The toolchain file can be located anywhere, it is a good idea to put them in a central place so they can be easily reused for multiple projects, so we will save this file as ~/Toolchains/Toolchain-eldk-mips4K.cmake. All the variables mentioned above are set here: CMAKE_SYSTEM_NAME, the C/C++ compilers, CMAKE_FIND_ROOT_PATH to specify where libraries and headers for the target environment are located and the find modes are set up so that libraries and headers are only searched in the target environment and programs are searched in the host environment. Now we will cross compile the hello world project from Chapter 2:

```
project (Hello)
add_executable (Hello Hello.c)
```

Then run CMake, and this time tell it to use the toolchain file from above:

```
mkdir Hello-eldk-mips
cd Hello-eldk-mips
cmake -DCMAKE_TOOLCHAIN_FILE=~/Toolchains/Toolchain-eldk-
mips4K.cmake ..
make VERBOSE=1
```

This should give you an executable which can run on the target platform and thanks to the VERBOSE=1 option you should see that really the cross compiler is used. Now we'll make the example a bit more sophisticated by adding system inspection and install rules. We will build and install a shared library named Tools and then build the Hello application which links to the Tools library.

```
include (CheckIncludeFiles)
check_include_files (stdio.h HAVE_STDIO_H)

set (VERSION_MAJOR 2)
set (VERSION_MINOR 6)
set (VERSION_PATCH 0)

configure_file (config.h.in ${CMAKE_BINARY_DIR}/config.h)

add_library (Tools  SHARED  tools.cxx)
set_target_properties (Tools PROPERTIES
    VERSION ${VERSION_MAJOR}.${VERSION_MINOR}.${VERSION_PATCH}
    SOVERSION ${VERSION_MAJOR})

install (FILES tools.h DESTINATION include)
install (TARGETS Tools DESTINATION lib)
```

There is no difference here to a normal CMakeLists.txt, no special prerequisites are required for cross compiling here. The Tools library checks that the header stdio.h is available and sets its version number. Both are configured into config.h, which is then used in tools.cxx. The version number is also used for setting up the version number of the library, which is installed to ${CMAKE_INSTALL_PREFIX}/lib and ${CMAKE_INSTALL_PREFIX}/include. Running CMake should give this result:

```
mkdir build-eldk-mips
cd build-eldk-mips
cmake -DCMAKE_TOOLCHAIN_FILE=~/Toolchains/Toolchain-eldk-
mips4K.cmake -DCMAKE_INSTALL_PREFIX=~/eldk-mips-extra-install ..
-- The C compiler identification is GNU
-- The CXX compiler identification is GNU
```

```
-- Check for working C compiler: /home/alex/eldk-
mips/usr/bin/mips_4KC-gcc
-- Check for working C compiler: /home/alex/eldk-
mips/usr/bin/mips_4KC-gcc -- works
-- Check size of void*
-- Check size of void* - done
-- Check for working CXX compiler: /home/alex/eldk-
mips/usr/bin/mips_4KC-g++
-- Check for working CXX compiler: /home/alex/eldk-
mips/usr/bin/mips_4KC-g++ -- works
-- Looking for include files HAVE_STDIO_H
-- Looking for include files HAVE_STDIO_H - found
-- Configuring done
-- Generating done
-- Build files have been written to:
/home/alex/src/tests/Tools/build-mips
make install
Scanning dependencies of target Tools
[100%] Building CXX object CMakeFiles/Tools.dir/tools.o
Linking CXX shared library libTools.so
[100%] Built target Tools
Install the project...
-- Install configuration: ""
-- Installing /home/alex/eldk-mips-extra-install/include/tools.h
-- Installing /home/alex/eldk-mips-extra-install/lib/libTools.so
```

CMake detected the correct compiler and also found the stdio.h header for the target platform. make then successfully built and installed the library in the specified installation directory. Now we can build an executable which uses the Tools library and does some system inspection:

```
project (HelloTools)

find_package (ZLIB REQUIRED)

find_library (TOOLS_LIBRARY Tools)
find_path (TOOLS_INCLUDE_DIR tools.h)

if (NOT TOOLS_LIBRARY OR NOT TOOLS_INCLUDE_DIR)
  message (FATAL_ERROR "Tools library not found")
endif (NOT TOOLS_LIBRARY OR NOT TOOLS_INCLUDE_DIR)

set (CMAKE_INCLUDE_CURRENT_DIR TRUE)
set (CMAKE_INCLUDE_DIRECTORIES_PROJECT_BEFORE TRUE)
```

```
include_directories ("${TOOLS_INCLUDE_DIR}"
                     "${ZLIB_INCLUDE_DIR}")

add_executable (HelloTools main.cpp)
target_link_libraries (HelloTools ${TOOLS_LIBRARY}
                       ${ZLIB_LIBRARIES})
set_target_properties (HelloTools PROPERTIES
                       INSTALL_RPATH_USE_LINK_PATH TRUE)

install (TARGETS HelloTools DESTINATION bin)
```

Building works just the same way as with the library, the toolchain file has to be used again and then it should just work:

```
cmake -DCMAKE_TOOLCHAIN_FILE=~/Toolchains/Toolchain-eldk-
mips4K.cmake -DCMAKE_INSTALL_PREFIX=~/eldk-mips-extra-install ..
-- The C compiler identification is GNU
-- The CXX compiler identification is GNU
-- Check for working C compiler: /home/alex/denx-
mips/usr/bin/mips_4KC-gcc
-- Check for working C compiler: /home/alex/denx-
mips/usr/bin/mips_4KC-gcc -- works
-- Check size of void*
-- Check size of void* - done
-- Check for working CXX compiler: /home/alex/denx-
mips/usr/bin/mips_4KC-g++
-- Check for working CXX compiler: /home/alex/denx-
mips/usr/bin/mips_4KC-g++ -- works
-- Found ZLIB: /home/alex/denx-mips/mips_4KC/usr/lib/libz.so
-- Found Tools library: /home/alex/denx-mips-extra-
install/lib/libTools.so
-- Configuring done
-- Generating done
-- Build files have been written to:
/home/alex/src/tests/HelloTools/build-eldk-mips
make
[100%] Building CXX object CMakeFiles/HelloTools.dir/main.o
Linking CXX executable HelloTools
[100%] Built target HelloTools
```

Obviously CMake found the correct zlib and also libTools.so which was installed in the previous step.

9.5   Cross compiling for a microcontroller

CMake can not only be used for cross compiling to targets with actual operating systems, but also for development for deeply embedded devices with small microcontrollers and no operating system at all. As an example we'll use the Small Devices C Compiler (http://sdcc.sourceforge.net), which runs e.g. under Windows, Linux and Mac OSX and which supports 8 and 16 Bit microcontrollers. For driving the build we will use MS nmake under Windows. Again the first step is to write a toolchain file so that CMake knows about the target platform. For sdcc it should look something like this:

```
set (CMAKE_SYSTEM_NAME Generic)
set (CMAKE_C_COMPILER "c:/Program Files/SDCC/bin/sdcc.exe")
```

The system name for targets which don't have an operating system "Generic" should be used as CMAKE_SYSTEM_NAME. The CMake platform file for "Generic" doesn't set up any specific features. All that it assumes is that the target platform doesn't support shared libraries. Therefore all properties will depend on the compiler and CMAKE_SYSTEM_PROCESSOR. The toolchain file above doesn't set the FIND-related variables. As long as none of the find commands is used in the CMake commands, this is ok. For many projects for small microcontrollers this will be the case. The CMakeLists.txt should look like the following:

```
project (Blink C)

add_library (blink blink.c)

add_executable (hello main.c)
target_link_libraries (hello blink)
```

There are no principal differences to other CMakeLists.txt files. One important point is that the language "C" is enabled explicitly using the PROJECT command. If this is not done, CMake also tries to enable support for C++, which will fail since sdcc supports only C. Running CMake and building the project should work as usual:

```
cmake -G"NMake Makefiles"
  -DCMAKE_TOOLCHAIN_FILE=c:/Toolchains/Toolchain-sdcc.cmake ..
-- The C compiler identification is SDCC
-- Check for working C compiler: c:/program
files/sdcc/bin/sdcc.exe
-- Check for working C compiler: c:/program
files/sdcc/bin/sdcc.exe -- works
-- Check size of void*
-- Check size of void* - done
```

```
-- Configuring done
-- Generating done
-- Build files have been written to: C:/src/tests/blink/build

nmake
Microsoft (R) Program Maintenance Utility Version 7.10.3077
Copyright (C) Microsoft Corporation.  All rights reserved.

Scanning dependencies of target blink
[ 50%] Building C object CMakeFiles/blink.dir/blink.rel
Linking C static library blink.lib
[ 50%] Built target blink
Scanning dependencies of target hello
[100%] Building C object CMakeFiles/hello.dir/main.rel
Linking C executable hello.ihx
[100%] Built target hello
```

So this was a simple example using nmake with sdcc with the default settings of sdcc. Of course more sophisticated project layouts are possible. Also for this kind of project it is a good idea to setup an install directory where reusable libraries will be installed, so it is easier in use them in multiple projects. And of course usually it is necessary to choose the correct target platform for sdcc, not everybody uses i8051, which is the default for sdcc. The recommended way to do this is via setting CMAKE_SYSTEM_PROCESSOR.

This will cause CMake to search for and load the platform file Platform/Generic-SDCC-C-${CMAKE_SYSTEM_PROCESSOR}.cmake. Since this happens directly before loading Platform/Generic-SDCC-C.cmake, it can be used to setup compiler and linker flags for the specific target hardware and project. Therefore a slightly more complex toolchain file is required:

```
get_filename_component (_ownDir
                        "${CMAKE_CURRENT_LIST_FILE}" PATH)
set (CMAKE_MODULE_PATH "${_ownDir}/Modules"
${CMAKE_MODULE_PATH})

set (CMAKE_SYSTEM_NAME Generic)
set (CMAKE_C_COMPILER "c:/Program Files/SDCC/bin/sdcc.exe")
set (CMAKE_SYSTEM_PROCESSOR "Test_DS80C400_Rev_1")

# here is the target environment located
set (CMAKE_FIND_ROOT_PATH  "c:/Program Files/SDCC"
                           "c:/ds80c400-install" )
```

```
# adjust the default behavior of the FIND_XXX() commands:
# search headers and libraries in the target environment, search
# programs in the host environment
set (CMAKE_FIND_ROOT_PATH_MODE_PROGRAM NEVER)
set (CMAKE_FIND_ROOT_PATH_MODE_LIBRARY ONLY)
set (CMAKE_FIND_ROOT_PATH_MODE_INCLUDE ONLY)
```

This toolchain file contains some new settings, it is also about the most complicated toolchain file you should ever need. CMAKE_SYSTEM_PROCESSOR is set to Test_DS80C400_Rev_1, which is just an identifier for the specific target hardware. This has the effect that CMake will try to load Platform/Generic-SDCC-C-Test_DS80C400_Rev_1.cmake. Since this file doesn't exist in the CMake system module directory, the CMake variable CMAKE_MODULE_PATH has to be adjusted so that this file can be found. If this toolchain file is saved as c:/Toolchains/sdcc-ds400.cmake, the hardware specific file should be saved in c:/Toolchains/Modules/Platform/. It will look as you can see below:

```
set (CMAKE_C_FLAGS_INIT "-mds390 --use-accelerator")
set (CMAKE_EXE_LINKER_FLAGS_INIT "")
```

This will select the DS80C390 as target platform and add the --use-accelerator argument to the default compile flags. In this example the "NMake Makefiles" generator has been used. In the same way e.g. the "MinGW Makefiles" generator can be used if GNU make from MinGW or another Windows version of GNU make are available, at least version 3.78 is required, or the "Unix Makefiles" generator under Unix. Also all Makefile-based IDE-project generators can be used, e.g. the Eclipse generators or the KDevelop3 generator.

9.6   Cross compiling an existing project

Existing CMake based projects may need some work so that they can be cross compiled, other projects may work without any modifications. One such project is FLTK, the Fast Lightweight Toolkit. We will compile fltk on a Linux machine using the MinGW cross compiler for Windows.

The first step is to install the MinGW cross compiler. For some distributions there are ready-to-use binary packages, for Debian distributions the name is mingw32. Once this is installed you need to setup a toolchain for this as described above. It should look more or less this way:

```
# the name of the target operating system
set (CMAKE_SYSTEM_NAME Windows)

# which compiler to use
set (CMAKE_C_COMPILER i586-mingw32msvc-gcc)
set (CMAKE_CXX_COMPILER i586-mingw32msvc-g++)

# where are the target libraries and headers installed ?
set(CMAKE_FIND_ROOT_PATH /usr/i586-mingw32msvc
                         /home/alex/mingw-install )

# find_program() should by default NEVER search in the target
tree
# adjust the default behavior of the FIND_XXX() commands:
# search headers and libraries in the target environment, search
# programs in the host environment
set (CMAKE_FIND_ROOT_MODE_PROGRAM NEVER)
set (CMAKE_FIND_ROOT_MODE_LIBRARY ONLY)
set (CMAKE_FIND_ROOT_MODE_INCLUDE ONLY)
```

Once this is working, just run CMake with the appropriate options on fltk:

```
mkdir build-mingw
cd build-mingw
cmake -DCMAKE_TOOLCHAIN_FILE=~/Toolchains/Toolchain-
mingw32.cmake -DCMAKE_INSTALL_PREFIX=~/mingw-install ..
-- The C compiler identification is GNU
-- The CXX compiler identification is GNU
-- Check for working C compiler: /usr/bin/i586-mingw32msvc-gcc
-- Check for working C compiler: /usr/bin/i586-mingw32msvc-gcc -
- works
...
```

UTILITY_SOURCE is used in cross compiling mode for FLUID_COMMAND. If your intention is to run this executable, you need to preload the cache with the full path to a version of that program, which runs on the build machine.

```
-- Configuring done
-- Generating done
-- Build files have been written to: /home/alex/src/fltk-1.1.x-
r5940/build-mingw
```

Here CMake prints a warning about the use of UTILITY_SOURCE. To find out more CMake offers the --debug-output argument:

```
rm -rf *
cmake -DCMAKE_TOOLCHAIN_FILE=~/Toolchains/Toolchain-
mingw32.cmake -DCMAKE_INSTALL_PREFIX=~/mingw-install .. --debug-
output
...
UTILITY_SOURCE is used in cross compiling mode for
FLUID_COMMAND. If your intention is to run this executable, you
need to preload the cache with the full path to a version of
that program, which runs on this build machine.
   Called from: [1]      /home/alex/src/fltk-1.1.x-
r5940/CMakeLists.txt
...
```

This tells us that UTILITY_SOURCE has been called from /home/alex/src/fltk-1.1.x-r5940/CMakeLists.txt, then CMake processed some more directories and finally it created the makefiles in all subdirectories. A look at the top level CMakeLists.txt shows the following:

```
# Set the fluid executable path
utility_source (FLUID_COMMAND fluid fluid fluid.cxx)
set (FLUID_COMMAND "${FLUID_COMMAND}" CACHE INTERNAL "" FORCE)
```

Apparently FLUID_COMMAND is used to hold the path for the executable fluid, which is built within the project. Fluid is used during the build to generate code, so the cross compiled executable will not work but instead a native fluid has to be used:

```
cmake . -DFLUID_COMMAND=/home/alex/src/download/fltk-1.1.x-
r5940/build-native/bin/fluid
...
-- Configuring done
-- Generating done
make
Scanning dependencies of target fltk_zlib
[  0%] Building C object
zlib/CMakeFiles/fltk_zlib.dir/adler32.obj
[  0%] Building C object
zlib/CMakeFiles/fltk_zlib.dir/compress.obj
...
Scanning dependencies of target valuators
```

```
[100%] Building CXX object
test/CMakeFiles/valuators.dir/valuators.obj
Linking CXX executable ../bin/valuators.exe
[100%] Built target valuators
```

That's it, the executables are now in mingw-bin/ and can be run via wine or by copying them to a Windows system.

9.7   Cross compiling a complex project - VTK

Building a complex project is a multi-step process. Complex means in this case that the project uses tests which try to run executables and that it builds executables which are used later on during the build to generate code or something similar. One such project is VTK, the Visualization Toolkit. It uses several `try_run` tests and creates several code generators. When running CMake on the project, every `try_run` command will produce an error message and at the end there will be a `TryRunResults.cmake` file in the build directory. You need to go through all entries of this file and fill in appropriate values. If you are unsure about the correct result, you can also actually try to execute the test binaries on the real target platform, they are also saved in your binary directory.

The code generators, such as ProcessShader is added using `add_executable` and then `get_target_property(LOCATION)` is used to get the location of the resulting binary, which is then used in `add_custom_command` or `add_custom_target` commands. Since the cross compiled executables cannot be executed during the build, the `add_executable` calls are surrounded by `if (NOT CMAKE_CROSSCOMPILING)` commands and the executable targets are imported into the project using the `add_executable` command with the `IMPORT` option. These import statements are contained in the file VTKCompileToolsConfig.cmake, which doesn't have to be created manually, but which is created by a native build of VTK.

So in order to cross compile VTK you need

- install a toolchain and create a toolchain file for CMake

- build VTK natively for the build host

- run CMake for the target platform, complete TryRunResults.cmake, use the VTKCompileToolsConfig.cmake file from the native build and finally build

So at first, build a native VTK using the standard approach.

```
cvs -d :pserver:anonymous@public.kitware.com:/cvsroot/VTK co VTK
cd VTK
mkdir build-native; cd build-native
ccmake ..
make
```

Make sure that all required options are enabled using ccmake, e.g. if you need Python wrapping for the target platform you also need to enable Python wrapping in build-native/. Once this build has finished, there will be a VTKCompileToolsConfig.cmake file in build-native/. If this succeeded, we can continue with the cross compiling, this time for an IBM BlueGene supercomputer.

```
cd VTK
mkdir build-bgl-gcc
cd build-bgl-gcc
cmake -DCMAKE_TOOLCHAIN_FILE=~/Toolchains/Toolchain-BlueGeneL-
gcc.cmake -DVTKCompileTools_DIR=~/VTK/build-native/ ..
```

This will finish with an error message for each `try_run` and a TryRunResults.cmake file, which you now have to complete as described above. Then you should save the file to a safe location, since otherwise it will be overwritten on the next CMake run.

```
cp TryRunResults.cmake ../TryRunResults-VTK-BlueGeneL-gcc.cmake
ccmake -C ../TryRunResults-VTK-BlueGeneL-gcc.cmake .
...
make
```

Now on the second run of ccmake all the other arguments can be skipped since they are now already in the cache. It is now also possible to point CMake to the build directory which now contains a CMakeCache.txt, so CMake will figure out that this is the build directory. If everything works you will now have a working cross compiled VTK.

9.8 Some tips and tricks

Dealing with try_run tests

In order to make cross compiling your project easier, try to avoid try_run tests and use other methods to test something instead. For examples of how this can be done consider the tests for endianess in CMake/Modules/TestBigEndian.cmake and the test for the compiler id using the source file CMake/Modules/CMakeCCompilerId.c. In both try_compile is used to compile the source file into an executable, where the desired information is encoded into a text string.

Using the `COPY_FILE` option of `try_compile` this executable is copied to a temporary location and the all strings are extracted from this file using `file (STRINGS)`. The test result is then obtained by using regular expressions to get the information from the string.

If you can't avoid `try_run` tests, try to use just the exit code from the run but not the output of the process. This way it won't be necessary to set both the exit code and the stdout and stderr variables for the `try_run` test when cross compiling. This way the `OUTPUT_VARIABLE` or the `RUN_OUTPUT_VARIABLE` options for `try_run` can be omitted.

If you have done all that and you have created and completed a correct TryRunResults.cmake file for the target platform, consider adding this file to the sources of the project, so it can be reused by others. These files are per-target per-toolchain.

Target platform and toolchain issues

If your toolchain is not able to build a simple program without special arguments, like e.g. a linker script file or a memory layout file, the tests CMake does initially will fail. To make it work nevertheless, there is a CMake module CMakeForceCompiler that offers the following macros:

```
CMAKE_FORCE_SYSTEM (name version processor),
CMAKE_FORCE_C_COMPILER (compiler compiler_id sizeof_void_p)
CMAKE_FORCE_CXX_COMPILER (compiler compiler_id).
```

These macros can be used in a toolchain file so that the required variables will be preset and the CMake tests are avoided.

RPATH handling under UNIX

For native builds CMake builds executables and libraries by default with RPATH. In the build tree the RPATH is set so that the executables can be run from the build tree, i.e. the RPATH points into the build tree. When installing the project, CMake links the executables again, this time with the RPATH for the install tree, which is by default empty.

When cross compiling you probably want to set up RPATH handling differently, since the executable can't run on the build host it makes more sense to build it with the install RPATH right from the start. There are several CMake variables and target properties for adjusting RPATH handling.

```
set (CMAKE_BUILD_WITH_INSTALL_RPATH TRUE)
set (CMAKE_INSTALL_RPATH "<whatever you need>")
```

With these two settings the targets will be built with the install RPATH instead of the build RPATH, which avoids the need to link them again when installing. If you don't need RPATH, you don't need to set CMAKE_INSTALL_RPATH, it is empty by default.

Setting CMAKE_INSTALL_RPATH_USE_LINK_PATH to TRUE is useful for native builds, since it automatically collects the RPATH from all libraries against which a targets links. For cross compiling leave it at the default setting, which is FALSE, since on the target the automatically generated RPATH will in most cases be wrong, since it will have a different file system layout than the build host.

## Chapter 10

Automation & Testing with CMake

10.1 Automating and Testing with CMake and CTest

Testing is a key tool for producing and maintaining robust, valid software. This chapter will examine the variety of tools that CMake includes to support software testing. We will begin with a brief discussion of testing approaches and then discuss how to add tests to your software project using CMake. Finally we will look at additional tools that support creating centralized software status dashboards.

The tests for a software package may take a number of forms. At the most basic level there are smoke tests such as one that simply verifies that the software compiles. While this may seem like a simple test, with the wide variety of platforms and configurations available, smoke tests catch more problems than any other type of test. Another form of smoke test is to verify that a test runs without crashing. This can be handy for situations where the developer does not want to spend the time creating more complex tests, but is willing to run some simple tests. Many times these simple tests can be small example programs. Running them verifies not only that the build was successful, but that any required shared libraries can be loaded (for projects that use them) and that at least some of the code can be executed without crashing.

Moving beyond basic smoke tests leads to more specific tests such as regression, black, and white box testing. Each of these has its advantages. Regression testing verifies that the results of a test do not change over time, or platform. This is very handy when performed frequently as it provides a quick check that the behavior and results of the software have not changed. When a regression test fails a quick look at recent code changes can usually identify the culprit. Unfortunately regression tests typically require more effort to create than other tests.

White and black box testing refer to tests written to exercise units of code (at various levels of integration) with and without knowledge of how those units are implemented respectively. White box testing is designed to stress potential failure points in the code knowing how that code was written, and hence its weaknesses. As with regression testing this can take a fair amount of effort to create good tests. Black box testing typically knows little or nothing about the implementation of the software other than its public API. Black box testing can provide a lot of code coverage without too much effort in developing the tests. This is especially true for libraries of object oriented software where the APIs are well defined. A black box test can be written to go through and invoke a number of typical methods on all the classes in the software.

The final type of testing we will discuss is software standard compliance testing. While the other test types we have discussed are focused on determining if the code works properly, compliance testing tries to determine if the code adheres to the coding standards of the software project. This could be a check to verify that all classes have implemented some key method, or that all functions have a common prefix. The options for this type of test are limitless and there are a number of ways to perform such testing. There are software analysis tools that can be used or specialized test programs (maybe python scripts etc) could be written. The key point is to realize that the tests do not necessarily have to involve running some part of the software. The tests might run some other tool on the source code itself.

There are a number of reasons why it helps to have testing support integrated into the build process. First, complex software projects may have a number of configuration or platform-dependent options. The build system knows what options can be enabled and can then enable the appropriate tests for those options. For example, the Visualization Toolkit (VTK) includes support for a parallel processing library called MPI. If VTK is built with MPI support then additional tests are enabled that make use of MPI and verify that the MPI-specific code in VTK is working. Secondly, the build system knows where the executables will be placed and it has tools for finding other required executables (such as perl, python etc). The third reason is that with UNIX makefiles it is common to have a test target in the Makefile so that developers can type make test and have the test be run. In order for this to work, the build system must have some knowledge of the testing process.

10.2 How does CMake Facilitate Testing?

CMake facilitates testing your software through special testing commands and the CTest executable. First we will discuss the key testing commands in CMake. To add testing to a CMake-based project is fairly simple using the `add_test` command. The `add_test` command has a simple syntax as follows:

```
add_test (TestName ExecutableToRun arg1 arg2 arg3 ...)
```

The first argument is simply a string name for the test. This is the name that will be displayed by testing programs. The second argument is the executable to run. The executable can be built as part of the project or it can be a standalone executable such as python, perl, etc. The remaining arguments will be passed to the running executable. A typical example of testing using the `add_test` command would look like this:

```
add_executable (TestInstantiator TestInstantiator.cxx)
target_link_libraries (TestInstantiator vtkCommon)
add_test (TestInstantiator
${EXECUTABLE_OUTPUT_PATH}/TestInstantiator)
```

The `add_test` command is typically placed in the CMakeLists file for the directory that has the tests in it. For large projects there may be multiple CMakeLists files with `add_test` commands in them. Once the `add_test` commands are present in the project, the user can run the tests by simply invoking the "test" target of Makefile, or `RUN_TESTS` target of Visual Studio or Xcode. An example of running tests on a CMake using Makefile generator on Linux would be:

```
$ make test
Running tests...
Test project
    1/ 53 Testing kwsys.testSystemTools        Passed
    2/ 53 Testing kwsys.testProcess-1          Passed
    3/ 53 Testing kwsys.testProcess-2          Passed
```

10.3 Testing Using CTest

When you run the tests from your build environment what really happens is that the build environment just runs CTest. CTest is an executable that comes with CMake that handles running tests. While CTest works well with CMake, you do not need to be using CMake in order to use CTest. The main input file for CTest is called CTestTestfile.cmake. This file will be created in each directory that was processed by CMake (typically every directory with a CMakeLists file). The syntax of CTestTestfile.cmake is a regular CMake syntax with a subset of commands available. If CMake is used to generate testing files, they will list any subdirectories that need to be processed as well as any `add_test` calls. The subdirectories are those that were added by `subdirs` or `add_subdirectory` commands. CTest can then parse these files to determine what tests to run. An example of such a file is listed below:

```
# CMake generated Testfile for
#   Source directory: C:/VTK/Common/Testing/Cxx
#   Build directory: C:/VTKVC7/Common/Testing/Cxx
```

```
#
# This file replicates the SUBDIRS() and ADD_TEST()
# commands from the source tree CMakeLists.txt file,
# skipping any SUBDIRS() or ADD_TEST() commands
# that are excluded by CMake control structures,
# i.e. if () commands.

SUBDIRS(Wrapping Utilities Common Filtering)

ADD_TEST(ObjectFactory "C:/VTKVC7/bin/CxxTests" ObjectFactory)
ADD_TEST(otherArrays "C:/VTKVC7/bin/CxxTests" otherArrays)
ADD_TEST(TestCxxFeatures "C:/VTKVC7/bin/TestCxxFeatures")
ADD_TEST(TestInstantiator "C:/VTKVC7/bin/TestInstantiator")
```

When CTest parses the CTestTestfile.cmake files it will extract the list of tests from them. These tests will be run and for each test, CTest will display the name and status. Consider the following sample output:

```
$ ctest

Changing directory into c:\VTKVC7\Common\Testing\Cxx
Testing ObjectFactory                        Passed
Testing otherArrays                          Passed
Testing otherEmptyCell                       Passed
Testing TestInstantiator                     Passed
Changing directory into c:\VTKVC7\Common\Testing\Tcl
Testing otherInterp                          Passed
Testing otherPrint                           Passed
Testing PrintSelf-Common                     Passed
Testing TestSetObjectMacro-Common            Passed

100% tests passed, 0 tests failed out of 8
```

CTest is run from within your build tree. It will run all the tests found in the current directory as well as any subdirectories listed in the CTestTestfile.cmake. For each test that is run CTest will report that the test passed if it returns zero from the executable. If the test returns non-zero or if the test exits due to a segfault, bus-error, etc, then the test will fail.

The CTest executable includes some handy command line options to make testing a little easier. We will start by looking at the options you would typically use from the command line.

```
-R <regex>              Run tests matching regular expression
-E <regex>              Exclude tests matching regular expression
-C <config>             Choose the configuration to test
-V,--verbose            Enable verbose output from tests.
-N,--show-only          Disable actual execution of tests.
-I [Start,End,Stride,test#,test#|Test file]
                        Run specific tests by range and number.
-H                      Display a help message
```

The -R option is probably the most commonly used. It allows you to specify a regular expression and only the tests with names matching the regular expression will be run. Using the -R option with the name (or part of the name) of a test is a quick way to run a single test. The -E option is similar except that it excludes all tests matching the regular expression. The -C option is mainly for IDE builds where you may have multiple configurations, such as Release and Debug in the same tree. The argument following the -C determines which configuration will be tested. The –V argument is useful when you are trying to determine why a test is failing. With –V CTest will print out the command line used to run the test as well as any output from the test itself. The –V option can be used with any invocation of CTest to provide more verbose output. The –N option is useful if you want to see what tests CTest would run without actually running them.

Running the tests and making sure they all pass before committing any changes to the software is a sure fire way to improve your software quality and development process. Unfortunately, for large projects the number of tests and the time required to run them may be prohibitive. In these situations the –I option of CTest can be used. The –I option allows you to flexibly specify a subset of the tests to run. For example, the following invocation of CTest will run every seventh test.

```
ctest -I ,,7
```

While this isn't as good as running every test, it is better than not running any and it may be a more practical solution for many developers. Note that if the start and end arguments are not specified, as in this example, then they will default to the first and last tests. In another example, assume that you always want to run a few tests plus a subset of the others. In this case you can explicitly add those tests to the end of the arguments for –I. For example:

```
ctest -I ,,5,1,2,3,10
```

will run tests 1, 2, 3, and 10, plus every fifth test. You can pass as many test numbers as you want after the stride argument.

10.4 Additional Test Properties

By default a test passes if all of the following conditions are true:

1. The test executable was found

2. The test ran without exception

3. The test exited with return code 0

That said, these behaviors can be modified using the `set_tests_properties` command:

```
set_tests_properties (test1 test2 ...
                      PROPERTIES prop1 value1 prop2 value2)
```

This command will set additional properties for the specified tests. Example properties are:

WILL_FAIL

> If this option is set to true, then the test will pass if the return code is not 0 and fail if it is. This reverses the third condition of the pass requirements.

PASS_REGULAR_EXPRESSION

> If this option is specified, then the output of the test is checked against the regular expression provided (a list of regular expressions may be passed in as well). If none of the regular expressions matches, then the test will fail. If at least one of them matches, then the test will pass.

FAIL_REGULAR_EXPRESSION

> If this option is specified, then the output of the test is checked against the regular expression provided (a list of regular expressions may be passed in as well). If none of the regular expressions matches, then the test will pass. If at least one of them matches, then the test will fail.

If both `PASS_REGULAR_EXPRESSION` and `FAIL_REGULAR_EXPRESSION` are specified, then the `FAIL_REGULAR_EXPRESSION` takes precedence. The following example illustrates using the `PASS_REGULAR_EXPRESSION` and `FAIL_REGULAR_EXPRESSION`:

```
add_test (outputTest ${EXECUTABLE_OUTPUT_PATH}/outputTest)

set (passRegex "^Test passed" "^All ok")
set (failRegex "Error" "Fail")
```

```
set_tests_properties (outputTest PROPERTIES
                      PASS_REGULAR_EXPRESSION "${passRegex}"
                      FAIL_REGULAR_EXPRESSION "${failRegex}")
```

10.5 Using CTest to Drive Complex Tests

Sometimes to properly test a project you need to actually compile code during the testing phase. There are several reasons for this. First, if test programs are compiled as part of the main project, they can end up taking up a significant amount of the build time. Also, if a test fails to build, the main build should not fail as well. Finally, IDE projects can quickly become too large to load and work with. The CTest command supports a group of command line options that allow it to be used as the test executable to run. When used as the test executable, CTest can run cmake, run the compile step, and finally run a compiled test. We will now look at the command line options to CTest that support building and running tests.

```
--build-and-test   src_directory build_directory
Run cmake on the given source directory using the specified
build directory.
--test-command        Name of the program to run.
--build-target        Specify a specific target to build.
--build-nocmake       Run the build without running cmake first.
--build-run-dir       Specify directory to run programs from.
--build-two-config    Run CMake twice before the build.
--build-exe-dir       Specify the directory for the executable.
--build-generator     Specify the generator to use.
--build-project       Specify the name of the project to build.
--build-makeprogram   Specify the make program to use.
--build-noclean       Skip the make clean step.
--build-options       Add extra options to the build step.
```

For an example, consider the following ADD_TEST command taken from the CMakeLists.txt file of CMake itself. It shows how CTest can be used both to compile and run a test.

```
add_test (simple ${CMAKE_CTEST_COMMAND}
    --build-and-test "${CMake_SOURCE_DIR}/Tests/Simple"
                     "${CMake_BINARY_DIR}/Tests/Simple"
    --build-generator ${CMAKE_GENERATOR}
    --build-makeprogram ${CMAKE_MAKE_PROGRAM}
    --build-project Simple
    --test-command simple)
```

In this example, the `add_test` command is first passed the name of the test "simple". After the name of the test, the command to be run is specified. In this case, the test command to be run is CTest. The CTest command is referenced via the `CMAKE_CTEST_COMMAND` variable. This variable is always set by CMake to the CTest command that came from the CMake installation used to build the project. Next, the source and binary directories are specified. The next options to CTest are the --build-generator, and --build-makeprogram options. These are specified using the cmake variables `CMAKE_MAKE_PROGRAM` and `CMAKE_GENERATOR`. Both `CMAKE_MAKE_PROGRAM` and `CMAKE_GENERATOR` are defined by CMake. This is an important step as it makes sure that the same generator is used for running the test as was used for building the project itself. The --build-project option is passed `Simple` which corresponds to the `project` command used in the Simple test. The final argument is the --test-command which tells CTest the command to run once it gets a successful build. That should be the name of the executable that will be compiled by the test.

10.6 Handling a Large Number of Tests

When a large number of tests exist in a single project, it is cumbersome to have individual executables available for each test. That said, the developer of the project should not be required to create tests with complex argument parsing. This is why CMake provides a convenience command for creating a test driver program. This command is called `create_test_sourcelist`. A test driver is a program that links together many small tests into a single executable. This is useful when building static executables with large libraries to shrink the total required size. The signature for `create_test_sourcelist` is as follows:

```
create_test_sourcelist (SourceListName
                        DriverName
                        test1 test2 test3
                        EXTRA_INCLUDE include.h
                        FUNCTION function
                        )
```

The first argument is the variable which will contain the list of source files that must be compiled to make the test executable. The DriverName is the name of the test driver program (e.g. the name of the resulting executable). The rest of the arguments consist of a list of test source files. Each test source file should have a function in it that has the same name as the file with no extension (`foo.cxx` should have `int foo(argc, argv);`) The resulting executable will be able to invoke each of the tests by name on the command line. The `EXTRA_INCLUDE` and `FUNCTION` arguments support additional customization of the test driver program. Consider the following CMakeLists file fragment to see how this command can be used:

```
# create the testing file and list of tests
create_test_sourcelist(Tests
  CommonCxxTests.cxx
  ObjectFactory.cxx
  otherArrays.cxx
  otherEmptyCell.cxx
  TestSmartPointer.cxx
  SystemInformation.cxx
  ...
  )

# add the executable
add_executable(CommonCxxTests ${Tests})

# remove the test driver source file
set (TestsToRun ${Tests})
remove (TestsToRun CommonCxxTests.cxx)

# Add all the ADD_TEST for each test
foreach (test ${TestsToRun})
  get_filename_component(TName ${test} NAME_WE)
  add_test (${TName} CommonCxxTests ${TName})
endforeach (test)
```

The `create_test_sourcelist` command is invoked to create a test driver. In this case it creates and writes CommonCXXTests.cxx into the binary tree of the project using the rest of the arguments to determine its contents. Next the `add_executable` command is used to add that executable to the build. Then a new variable called `TestsToRun` is created with an initial value of the sources required for the test driver. The `remove` command is used to remove the driver program itself from the list. Then a `foreach` command is used to loop over the remaining sources. For each source its name without file extension is extracted and put in the variable `TName`. Then a new test is added for `TName`. The end result is that for each source file in the `create_test_sourcelist` an `add_test` command is called with the name of the test. As more tests are added to the `create_test_sourcelist` command, the `foreach` loop will automatically call `add_test` for each one.

10.7 Producing Test Dashboards

As your project's testing needs grow, keeping track of the test results can become overwhelming. This is especially true for projects that are tested nightly on a number of different platforms. In these cases we recommend using a test dashboard to summarize the test results. (see Figure 21)

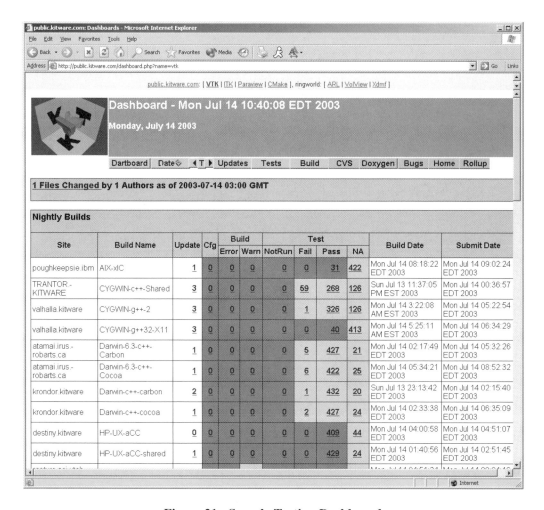

Figure 21 - Sample Testing Dashboard

A test dashboard summarizes the results for many tests on many platforms and its hyperlinks allow people to drill down into additional levels of detail quickly. The CTest executable includes support for producing test dashboards. When run with the correct options, CTest will produce XML-based output recording the build and test results and post them to a dashboard server. The dashboard server runs an open source software package called DART developed at General Electric. DART collects the XML results and produces HTML web pages from them.

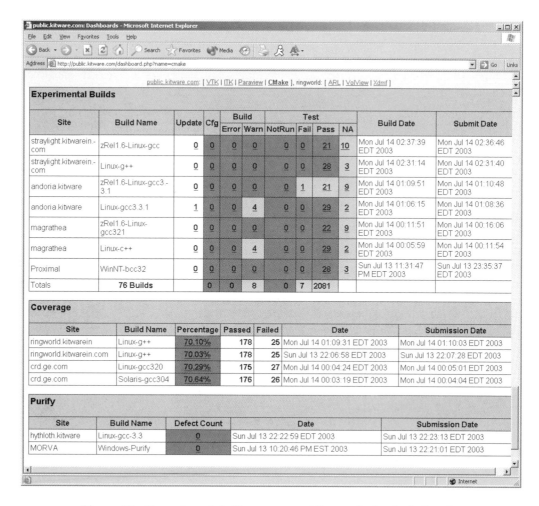

Figure 22 - Experimental, Coverage, and Dynamic Analysis Results

Before discussing how to use CTest to produce a dashboard let us consider the main parts of a testing dashboard. Each night at a specified time the dashboard server will open up a new dashboard, so each day there is a new web page showing the results of tests for that twenty-four hour period. There are links on the main page that allow you to quickly navigate through different days. Looking at the main page for a project (such as CMake's dashboard off of http://www.cmake.org) you will see that it is divided into a few main components. Near the top you will find a set of links that allow you to step to previous dashboards as well as links to the CVS, Build, and Test summaries etc.

Below that you will find results grouped according to Nightly, Experimental, Continuous, Coverage, and Dynamic Analysis (see Figure 22). The category into which a dashboard entry will be placed depends on how it was generated. The simplest are Experimental entries which represent dashboard results for someone's current copy of the project's source code. With an experimental dashboard the source code is not guaranteed to be up to date. In contrast a Nightly dashboard entry is one where CTest tries to update the source code to a specific date and time. This expected result is that all nightly dashboard entries for a given day should be based on the same source code.

A continuous dashboard entry is one that is designed to run every time new files are checked in. Depending on how frequently new files are checked in a single day's dashboard could have many continuous entries. Continuous dashboards are particularly helpful for multiplatform projects where a problem may only show up on some platforms. In those cases a developer can commit a change that works for her on her platform and then another platform running a continuous build could catch the error, allowing the developer to correct the problem promptly.

Dynamic Analysis and Coverage dashboards are designed to test the memory safety and code coverage of a project. A Dynamic Analysis dashboard entry is one where all the tests are run with a memory access/leak checking program enabled. Any resulting errors or warnings are parsed, summarized and displayed. This is important to verify that your software isn't leaking memory, reading from un-initialized memory, etc. Coverage dashboard entries are similar in that all the tests are run, but as the tests are run the lines of code executed are tracked. When all the tests have been run, a listing of how many times each line of code was executed is produced and displayed on the dashboard.

Adding DART Dashboard Support to a Project

To support dashboards in your project you need to include the CTest.cmake module. Including the CTest.cmake module is a simple process as follows.

```
# Include the standard Dart testing module
include (CTest)
```

Without specifying any additional settings, CTest will submit the results to the Public Dashboard hosted by Kitware, Inc. as a service to the community. This dashboard holds the results of several projects and does not keep history for more than a couple of days. This is why for serious testing a project specific dashboard should be used.

If you have added `add_tests` to your project, then creating a dashboard entry is as simple as running:

```
ctest -D Experimental
```

The `-D` option tells CTest to create a dashboard entry. The next argument indicates what type of dashboard entry to create. Creating a dashboard entry involves quite a few steps that can be run independently or as one command. In this example the Experimental argument will cause CTest to perform a number of different steps as one command. The different steps of creating a dashboard entry are summarized below.

Start

Prepare a new dashboard entry. This creates a Testing subdirectory in the build directory. The testing subdirectory will contain a subdirectory for the dashboard results with a name that corresponds to the dashboard time. The testing subdirectory will also contain a subdirectory for the temporary testing results called Temporary.

Update

Perform a source control update of the source code (typically used for nightlies or continuous). Currently CTest supports Concurrent Versions System (CVS) and Subversion.

Configure

Run CMake on the project to make sure the Make files or project files are up to date.

Build

Build the software using the specified generator.

Test

Run all the tests and record results.

MemoryCheck

Perform memory checks using Purify or valgrind.

Coverage

Collect source code coverage information.

Submit

Submit the testing results as a dashboard entry to the server.

Each of these steps can be run independently for a Nightly or Experimental entry using the following syntax:

```
ctest -D NightlyStart
ctest -D NightlyBuild
ctest -D NightlyCoverage -D NightlySubmit
```

or

```
ctest -D ExperimentalStart
ctest -D ExperimentalConfigure
ctest -D ExperimentalCoverage -D ExperimentalSubmit
```

etc. Or you can use shortcuts that perform the most common combinations all at once. The shortcuts that CTest has defined include:

ctest -D Experimental

> performs a start, configure, build, test, coverage, submit

ctest -D Nightly

> performs a start, update, configure, build, test, coverage, submit

ctest -D Continuous

> performs a start, update, configure, build, test, coverage, submit

ctest -D MemoryCheck

> performs a start, configure, build, memory check, coverage, submit

When first setting up a dashboard it is often useful to combine the –D option with the –V option. This will allow you to see the output of all the different stages of the dashboard process. Likewise, CTest maintains log files in the Testing/Temporary directory it creates in your binary tree. There you will find log files for the most recent build, update, test, etc. The actual dashboard results are stored in Testing as well.

Project Specific Dashboard

To let CTest know that a project specific dashboard is used, additional information needs to be provided. When using CMake to generate input files for CTest, this information is placed in a file named CTestConfig.cmake. Setting up this file is also simple although there are quite a few options. We will discuss the options that the client uses first and in section 10.10 we will cover the server options. Let us first look at an example file from CMake. As you will see this file is essentially just `set` commands that are used to initialize some variables. The first value that is set is the nightly start time. This is the time that dashboards all around the world will use for checking out their copy of the nightly source code. This time also controls how dashboard submissions will be grouped together. All submissions from the nightly start time until the next nightly start time will be included on the same "day".

```
# Dashboard is opened for submissions for a 24 hour period
# starting at the specified NIGHLY_START_TIME. Time is
# specified in 24 hour format.
set (NIGHTLY_START_TIME "21:00:00 EDT")
```

The next group of settings controls where to submit the testing results. This is the location of the DART server and it may support more than one drop method.

The DROP_METHOD specifies the method used to submit testing results. CTest currently supports four drop methods. The legacy one is FTP submission. This method uses File Transfer Protocol (FTP) to submit files to the server. Once submitted, a trigger script is called via the Hyper Text Transfer Protocol (HTTP). The triggering is the step in which the Dart server actually copies the files to the appropriate locations. The next (currently preferred) drop method is HTTP. This method uses HTTP to submit files and to do the triggering. The third method is Secure Copy (SCP). This method uses the SCP command to copy files to the appropriate locations. It does not perform the trigger step. It is up to the Dart server to actually copy the files to the appropriate locations. The final method (used by the Dart2 server) is XML Remote Procedure Call (XMLRPC). In this method, the files are submitted using XMLRPC and it is up to the server to copy them to the appropriate locations. In the example below, clients that are submitting their results using HTTP protocol use a web address as their drop site.

The DROP_SITE specifies the location of the Dart server. Build and test results generated by Dart clients are sent to this location. Which of the servers DROP_SITE refers to depends on the DROP_METHOD. The DROP_LOCATION is the directory or the HTTP script on the server where Dart clients leave their build and test reports. If the submission is via ftp, this location is relative to where the DROP_SITE_USER will log in by default. The DROP_SITE_USER specifies the ftp username the client will use on the server. For ftp submissions this user will typically be "anonymous". However, any username that can communicate with the server can be used. For ftp servers that require a password this can be stored in the DROP_SITE_PASSWORD variable. The DROP_SITE_MODE (not used in this example) is an optional variable that you can use to specify the FTP mode. Most ftp servers will handle the default passive mode but you can set the mode explicitly to active if your server does not.

Once build and test results are placed on the server, the Dart client will "trigger" the server using the value of the TRIGGER_SITE. This step is only necessary when using FTP and HTTP methods. When using SCP and XMLRPC methods, the TRIGGER_SITE option will be ignored. The TRIGGER_SITE option informs the server that new submissions are available. When "triggered" the Dart server determines whether these are valid submissions and moves them from the submission area to the Dart server area. This provides additional security for the Dart server.

```
# Dart server to submit results (used by client)
set (DROP_METHOD http)
set (DROP_SITE "public.kitware.com")
set (DROP_LOCATION "/cgi-bin/HTTPUploadDartFile.cgi")
set (TRIGGER_SITE
  "http://${DROP_SITE}/cgi-bin/Submit-proj-TestingResults.pl")
```

CTest can also be run from behind a firewall. If the firewall allows FTP and HTTP traffic, then no additional settings are required. If the firewall requires an FTP/HTTP proxy or uses a SOCKS4 or SOCKS5 type proxy, some environment variables need to be set. HTTP_PROXY and FTP_PROXY specify the servers that service HTTP and FTP proxy requests. HTTP_PROXY_PORT and FTP_PROXY_PORT specify the port on which the HTTP and FTP proxies reside. HTTP_PROXY_TYPE specifies the type of the HTTP proxy used. The three different types of proxies supported are the default, which is a generic HTTP/FTP proxy, "SOCKS4", and "SOCKS5", which specify SOCKS4 and SOCKS5 compatible proxies.

Customizing Dashboards for a Project

CTest has a few options that can be used to control how it processes a project. If, when CTest runs a dashboard it finds CTestCustom.ctest files in the binary tree, it will load these files and use the settings from them to control its behavior. The syntax of a CTestCustom file is regular CMake syntax. That said, commonly only set commands are performed. These commands specify properties that CTest will consider when performing the testing.

By default CTest has a list of regular expressions that it matches for finding the errors and warnings from the output of the build process. You can override these settings in your CTestCustom.ctest files using several variables as shown below.

```
set (CTEST_CUSTOM_WARNING_MATCH
  ${CTEST_CUSTOM_WARNING_MATCH}
  "{standard input}:[0-9][0-9]*: Warning: "
  )

set (CTEST_CUSTOM_WARNING_EXCEPTION
  ${CTEST_CUSTOM_WARNING_EXCEPTION}
  "tk8.4.5/[^/]+/[^/]+.c[:\"]"
  "xtree.[0-9]+. : warning C4702: unreachable code"
  "warning LNK4221"
  "variable .var_args[2]*. is used before its value is set"
  "jobserver unavailable"
  )
```

Another useful feature of the CTestCustom files is that you can use it to limit the tests that are run for memory checking dashboards. Memory checking using purify or valgrind is a CPU intensive process that can take twenty hours for a dashboard that normally takes one hour. To help alleviate this problem CTest allows you to exclude some of the tests from the memory checking process as follows:

```
set (CTEST_CUSTOM_MEMCHECK_IGNORE
     ${CTEST_CUSTOM_MEMCHECK_IGNORE}
  TestSetGet
  otherPrint-ParaView
  Example-vtkLocal
  Example-vtkMy
  )
```

The format for excluding tests is simply a list of test names as specified when the tests were added in your CMakeLists file with ADD_TEST.

In addition to the demonstrated settings, such as CTEST_CUSTOM_WARNING_MATCH, CTEST_CUSTOM_WARNING_EXCEPTION, and CTEST_CUSTOM_MEMCHECK_IGNORE, CTest also checks several other variables.

CTEST_CUSTOM_ERROR_MATCH

> Additional regular expressions to consider a build line as an error line

CTEST_CUSTOM_ERROR_EXCEPTION

> Additional regular expressions to consider a build line an not error line

CTEST_CUSTOM_WARNING_MATCH

> Additional regular expressions to consider a build line as a warning line

CTEST_CUSTOM_WARNING_EXCEPTION

> Additional regular expressions to consider a build line not as a warning line

CTEST_CUSTOM_MAXIMUM_NUMBER_OF_ERRORS

> Maximum number of errors before CTest stops reporting errors (default 50)

CTEST_CUSTOM_MAXIMUM_NUMBER_OF_WARNINGS

> Maximum number of warnings before CTest stops reporting warnings (default 50)

CTEST_CUSTOM_COVERAGE_EXCLUDE

> Regular expressions for files to be excluded from the coverage analysis

CTEST_CUSTOM_PRE_MEMCHECK
CTEST_CUSTOM_POST_MEMCHECK

> List of commands to execute before/after performing memory checking

CTEST_CUSTOM_MEMCHECK_IGNORE

> List of tests to exclude from the memory checking step

CTEST_CUSTOM_PRE_TEST
CTEST_CUSTOM_POST_TEST

> List of commands to execute before/after performing testing

CTEST_CUSTOM_TESTS_IGNORE

> List of tests to exclude from the testing step

CTEST_CUSTOM_MAXIMUM_PASSED_TEST_OUTPUT_SIZE

> Maximum size of test output for the passed test (default 1k)

CTEST_CUSTOM_MAXIMUM_FAILED_TEST_OUTPUT_SIZE

> Maximum size of test output for the failed test (default 300k)

Commands specified in `CTEST_CUSTOM_PRE_TEST` and `CTEST_CUSTOM_POST_TEST`, as well as the equivalent memory checking ones, are executed once per CTest run. These commands can be used for example if all tests require some initial setup and cleanup to be performed.

Adding Notes to a Dashboard

CTest and DART support adding notes to a dashboard submission. These notes will appear on the dashboard as a graphical icon that when clicked expands to the text of the notes. Using CTest you can use the –A option followed by a semicolon separated list of filenames. The contents of these files will be submitted as notes for the dashboard. For example:

```
ctest -D Continuous -A C:/MyNotes.txt;C:/OtherNotes.txt
```

Another way to submit notes with a dashboard is to copy or write the notes as files into a Notes directory under the Testing directory of your binary tree. Any files found there when CTest submits a dashboard will also be uploaded as notes.

10.8 Setting up Automated Dashboard Clients

CTest has a built-in scripting mode to help make the process of setting up dashboard clients even easier. CTest scripts will handle a number of common tasks and options that CTest –D Nightly does not. The dashboard script is written using CMake syntax and mainly involves setting up different variables or options, or creating an elaborate procedure, depending on the complexity of testing. Once you have written the script you can run the nightly dashboard on either Windows or UNIX systems as follows:

```
ctest -S myScript.cmake
```

First we will consider the most basic script you can use and then we will cover the different options you can make use of. There are four variables that you must always set in your scripts. The first two variables are the names of the source and binary directories on disk, CTEST_SOURCE_DIRECTORY and CTEST_BINARY_DIRECTORY. These should be fully specified paths. The next variable, CTEST_COMMAND, specifies which CTest command to use for running the dashboard. This may seem a bit confusing at first. The –S option of CTest is provided to do all the setup and customization for a dashboard, but the actual running of the dashboard is done with another invocation of CTest –D. Basically once CTest script has done what it needs to do to setup the dashboard, it invokes CTest –D to actually generate the results. You can adjust the value of CTEST_COMMAND to control what type of dashboard to generate (Nightly, Experimental, Continuous) as well as to pass other options to the internal CTest process such as -I ,,7 to run every 7th test. To refer to the CTest that is running the script, use the variable: CTEST_EXECUTABLE_NAME. The last required variable is CTEST_CMAKE_COMMAND which specifies the full path to the cmake executable that will be used to configure the dashboard. To refer to the CMake command that corresponds to the CTest command running the script, use the variable: CMAKE_EXECUTABLE_NAME. CTest script does an initial configuration with cmake in order to generate the CTestConfig.cmake file that CTest will use for the dashboard. The following example demonstrates the use of these four variables and is an example of the simplest script you can have.

```
# these are the source and binary directories on disk.
set (CTEST_SOURCE_DIRECTORY C:/martink/test/CMake)
set (CTEST_BINARY_DIRECTORY C:/martink/test/CMakeBin)

# which CTest command to use for running the dashboard
set (CTEST_COMMAND
  "\"${CTEST_EXECUTABLE_NAME}\" -D Nightly"
  )

# what cmake command to use for configuring this dashboard
set (CTEST_CMAKE_COMMAND
  "\"${CMAKE_EXECUTABLE_NAME}\""
  )
```

The script above really isn't that different from running CTest –D from the command line yourself. All it adds is that it verifies that the binary directory exists and creates it if it doesn't. Where CTest scripting really shines is in the optional features it supports. We will consider

these options one by one starting with one of the most commonly used options
CTEST_START_WITH_EMPTY_BINARY_DIRECTORY. When this variable is set to true it will
delete the binary directory and then recreate it as an empty directory prior to running the
dashboard. This guarantees that you are testing a clean build every time the dashboard is run.
To use this option you simply set it in your script. In the example above we would simply add
the following lines:

```
# should CTest wipe the binary tree before running
set (CTEST_START_WITH_EMPTY_BINARY_DIRECTORY TRUE)
```

Another commonly used option is the CTEST_INITIAL_CACHE variable. Whatever values
you set this to will be written into the CMakeCache file prior to running the dashboard. This
is an effective and simple way to initialize a cache with some preset values. The syntax is the
exact same as what is in the cache with the exception that you must escape any quotes.
Consider the following example:

```
# this is the initial cache to use for the binary tree, be
# careful to escape any quotes inside of this string
set (CTEST_INITIAL_CACHE "

//Command used to build entire project from the command line.
MAKECOMMAND:STRING=\"C:/PROGRA~1/MICROS~1.NET/Common7/IDE/devenv
.com\" CMake.sln /build Debug /project ALL_BUILD

//make program
CMAKE_MAKE_PROGRAM:FILEPATH=C:/PROGRA~1/MICROS~1.NET/Common7/IDE
/devenv.com

//Name of generator.
CMAKE_GENERATOR:INTERNAL=Visual Studio 7 .NET 2003

//Path to a program.
CVSCOMMAND:FILEPATH=C:/cygwin/bin/cvs.exe

//Name of the build
BUILDNAME:STRING=Win32-vs71

//Name of the computer/site where compile is being run
SITE:STRING=DASH1.kitware

")
```

Note that the above code is basically just one `set` command setting the value of `CTEST_INITIAL_CACHE` to a multiline string value. For Windows builds these are the most common cache entries that need to be set prior to running the dashboard. The first three values all control what compiler is being used to build this dashboard (Visual Studio 7.1 in this example). `CVSCOMMAND` might be found automatically, but if not it can be set here. The last two cache entries are the names that will be used to identify this dashboard submission on the dashboard.

The next two variables work together to support additional directories and projects. For example, imagine that you had a separate data directory that you needed to keep up to date with your source directory. Setting the variables `CTEST_CVS_COMMAND` and `CTEST_EXTRA_UPDATES_1` tells CTest to perform a cvs update on the specified directory, with the specified arguments prior to running the dashboard. For example:

```
# what cvs command to use for configuring this dashboard
set (CTEST_CVS_COMMAND "C:/cygwin/bin/cvs.exe")

# set any extra directories to do an update on
set (CTEST_EXTRA_UPDATES_1
    "C:/Dashboards/My Tests/VTKData" "-dAP"
   )
```

If you have more than one directory that needs to be updated you can use `CTEST_EXTRA_UPDATES_2` through `CTEST_EXTRA_UPDATES_9` in the same manner. The next variable you can set is called `CTEST_ENVIRONMENT`. This variable consolidates several set commands into a single command. Setting this variable allows you to set environment variables that will be used by the process running the dashboards. You can set as many environment variables as you want using the syntax shown below.

```
# set any extra environment variables here
set (CTEST_ENVIRONMENT
  "DISPLAY=:0"
  "USE_GCC_MALLOC=1"
)
# is the same as
set (ENV{DISPLAY} ":0")
set (ENV{USE_GCC_MALLOC} "1")
```

The final general purpose option we will discuss is CTest's support for restoring a bad dashboard. In some cases you might want to make sure that you always have a working build of the software. Or you might use the resulting executables or libraries from one dashboard in the build process of another dashboard. In these cases if the first dashboard fails it is best to drop back to the last previously working dashboard. You can do this in CTest by setting CTEST_BACKUP_AND_RESTORE to true. When this is set to true CTest will first backup the source and binary directories. It will then check out a new source directory and create a new binary directory and then run a full dashboard. If the dashboard is successful the backup directories are removed. But if for some reason the new dashboard fails, the new directories are removed and the old directories are restored. To make this work you must also set the CTEST_CVS_CHECKOUT variable. This should be set to the command required to check out your source tree. This doesn't actually have to be cvs but it must result in a source tree in the correct location. Consider the following example:

```
# do a backup and should the build fail restore,
# if this is true you must set the CTEST_CVS_CHECKOUT
# variable below.
set (CTEST_BACKUP_AND_RESTORE TRUE)

# this is the full cvs command to checkout the source dir
# this will be run from the directory above the source dir
set (CTEST_CVS_CHECKOUT
  "/usr/bin/cvs -d /cvsroot/FOO co -d FOO FOO"
)
```

Note that whatever checkout command you specify will be run from the directory above the source directory. A typical nightly dashboard client script will look like this:

```
set (CTEST_SOURCE_NAME CMake)
set (CTEST_BINARY_NAME CMake-gcc)
set (CTEST_DASHBOARD_ROOT "$ENV{HOME}/Dashboards/My Tests")
set (CTEST_SOURCE_DIRECTORY
    "${CTEST_DASHBOARD_ROOT}/${CTEST_SOURCE_NAME}")
set (CTEST_BINARY_DIRECTORY
    "${CTEST_DASHBOARD_ROOT}/${CTEST_BINARY_NAME}")

# which ctest command to use for running the dashboard
set (CTEST_COMMAND
  "\"${CTEST_EXECUTABLE_NAME}\"
  -D Nightly
  -A \"${CTEST_SCRIPT_DIRECTORY}/${CTEST_SCRIPT_NAME}\"")

# what cmake command to use for configuring this dashboard
set (CTEST_CMAKE_COMMAND "\"${CMAKE_EXECUTABLE_NAME}\"")

# should ctest wipe the binary tree before running
set (CTEST_START_WITH_EMPTY_BINARY_DIRECTORY TRUE)
```

```
# this is the initial cache to use for the binary tree
set (CTEST_INITIAL_CACHE "
SITE:STRING=midworld.kitware
BUILDNAME:STRING=DarwinG5-g++
MAKECOMMAND:STRING=make -i -j2
")

# set any extra environment variables here
set (CTEST_ENVIRONMENT
  "CC=gcc"
  "CXX=g++"
  )
```

Settings for Continuous Dashboards

The next three variables are used for setting up continuous dashboards. As mentioned earlier a continuous dashboard is designed to run continuously throughout the day providing quick feedback on the state of the software. If you are doing a continuous dashboard you can use CTEST_CONTINUOUS_DURATION and CTEST_CONTINUOUS_MINIMUM_INTERVAL to run the continuous repeatedly. The duration controls how long the script should run continuous dashboards and the minimum interval specifies the shortest allowed time between continuous dashboards. For example, say that you want to run a continuous dashboard from 9AM until 7PM and that you want no more than one dashboard every twenty minutes. To do this you would set the duration to 600 minutes (ten hours) and the minimum interval to 20 minutes. If you run the test script at 9AM it will start a continuous dashboard. When that dashboard finishes it will check to see how much time has elapsed. If less than 20 minutes has elapsed CTest will sleep until the 20 minutes are up. If 20 or more minutes have elapsed then it will immediately start another continuous dashboard. Do not be concerned that you will end up with 300 dashboards a day (10 hours * three times an hour). If there have been no changes to the source code, CTest will not bother building and submitting a dashboard. It will instead start waiting until the next interval is up and then check again. Using this feature just involves setting the following variables to the values you desire.

```
set (CTEST_CONTINUOUS_DURATION 600)
set (CTEST_CONTINUOUS_MINIMUM_INTERVAL 20)
```

Earlier we introduced the CTEST_START_WITH_EMPTY_BINARY_DIRECTORY variable that can be set to start the dashboards with an empty binary directory. If this is set to true for a continuous dashboard then every continuous where there has been a change in the source code will result in a complete build from scratch. For larger projects this can significantly limit the number of continuous dashboards that can be generated in a day while not using it can result in build errors or omissions because it is not a clean build. Fortunately there is a compromise. If you set CTEST_START_WITH_EMPTY_BINARY_DIRECTORY_ONCE to true CTest will start with a clean binary directory for the first continuous build but not subsequent ones. Based on your settings for the duration this is an easy way to start with a clean build every morning, but use existing builds for the rest of the day.

Another useful feature to use with a continuous dashboard is the –I option. A large project may have so many tests that running all the tests limits how frequently a continuous dashboard can be generated. By adding –I ,,7 (or –I ,,5 etc) to the CTEST_COMMAND value the continuous dashboard will only run every seventh test significantly reducing the time required between continuous dashboards. For example:

```
# which ctest command to use for running the dashboard
set (CTEST_COMMAND
  "\"${CTEST_EXECUTABLE_NAME}\" -D Continuous -I ,,7"
  )
```

As you can imagine there is a compromise to be made between the coverage of the continuous and the frequency of its updates. Depending on the size of your project and the compute resources at your disposal these variables can be used to fine tune a continuous dashboard to meet your needs. An example of a CTest script for a continuous dashboard looks like this:

```
# these are the names of the source and binary directories
set (CTEST_SOURCE_NAME CMake-cont)
set (CTEST_BINARY_NAME CMakeBCC-cont)
set (CTEST_DASHBOARD_ROOT "c:/Dashboards/My Tests")
set (CTEST_SOURCE_DIRECTORY
    "${CTEST_DASHBOARD_ROOT}/${CTEST_SOURCE_NAME}")
set (CTEST_BINARY_DIRECTORY
    "${CTEST_DASHBOARD_ROOT}/${CTEST_BINARY_NAME}")

# which ctest command to use for running the dashboard
set (CTEST_COMMAND
    "\"${CTEST_EXECUTABLE_NAME}\"
    -D Continuous
    -A \"${CTEST_SCRIPT_DIRECTORY}/${CTEST_SCRIPT_NAME}\"")

# what cmake command to use for configuring this dashboard
set (CTEST_CMAKE_COMMAND "\"${CMAKE_EXECUTABLE_NAME}\"")

# this is the initial cache to use for the binary tree
set (CTEST_INITIAL_CACHE "
SITE:STRING=dash14.kitware
BUILDNAME:STRING=Win32-bcc5.6
CMAKE_GENERATOR:INTERNAL=Borland Makefiles
```

```
CVSCOMMAND:FILEPATH=C:/Program Files/TortoiseCVS/cvs.exe
CMAKE_CXX_FLAGS:STRING=-w- -whid -waus -wpar -tWM
CMAKE_C_FLAGS:STRING=-w- -whid -waus -tWM
")
```

```
# set any extra environment variables here
set (ENV{PATH} "C:/Program
Files/Borland/CBuilder6/Bin\;C:/Program
Files/Borland/CBuilder6/Projects/Bpl"
  )
```

Variables Available in CTest Scripts

There are a few variables that will be set before your script executes. The first two variables are the directory the script is in, CTEST_SCRIPT_DIRECTORY, and name of the script itself CTEST_SCRIPT_NAME. These two variables can be used to make your scripts more portable. For example if you wanted to include the script itself as a note for the dashboard you could do the following:

```
set (CTEST_COMMAND
  "\"${CTEST_EXECUTABLE_NAME}\" -D Continuous
   -A \"${CTEST_SCRIPT_DIRECTORY}/${CTEST_SCRIPT_NAME}\""
  )
```

Another variable you can use is CTEST_SCRIPT_ARG. This variable can be set by providing a comma separated argument after the script name when invoking CTest -S. For example CTest -S foo.cmake,21 would result in CTEST_SCRIPT_ARG being set to 21.

10.9 Advanced CTest Scripting

CTest scripting described in 8.8 should provide support for most dashboards. That said, it has a couple limitations that advanced users may want to circumvent. This section describes how to write CTest scripts that allow the dashboard maintainer to have much more control.

Limitations of Traditional CTest Scripting

Let us start with the limitations of traditional CTest scripting. The first limitation is that the dashboard will always fail if the Configure step fails. The reason for that is that the input files for CTest are actually generated by the Configure step. To make things worse, the update step will not happen and the dashboard will be stuck. To prevent this, an additional update step is necessary. This can be achieved by adding CTEST_EXTRA_UPDATES_1 variable with "-D yesterday" or similar flag. This will update the repository prior to doing a dashboard. Since it will update to yesterday's time stamp, the actual update step of CTest will find the files that were modified since the previous day.

The second limitation of traditional CTest scripting is that it is not actually scripting. We only have control over what happens before the actual CTest run, but not what happens during or after. For example, if we want to run the testing and then move the binaries somewhere, or if we want to build the project, do some extra tasks and then run tests or something similar, we need to perform several complicated tasks, such as run CMake with –P option as a part of CTEST_COMMAND.

Extended CTest Scripting

To overcome these limitations of traditional CTest scripting, CTest provides extended scripting mode. In this mode, the dashboard maintainer has access to individual CTest handlers. By running these handlers individually, she can develop relatively elaborate testing schemes. An example of an extended CTest script would be something like this:

```
cmake_minimum_required (VERSION 2.2)

set (CTEST_SITE           "andoria.kitware")
set (CTEST_BUILD_NAME     "Linux-g++")
set (CTEST_NOTES_FILES
    "${CTEST_SCRIPT_DIRECTORY}/${CTEST_SCRIPT_NAME}")

set (CTEST_DASHBOARD_ROOT   "$ENV{HOME}/Dashboards/My Tests")
set (CTEST_SOURCE_DIRECTORY "${CTEST_DASHBOARD_ROOT}/CMake")
set (CTEST_BINARY_DIRECTORY "${CTEST_DASHBOARD_ROOT}/CMake-gcc
")
set (CTEST_UPDATE_COMMAND    "/usr/bin/cvs")
set (CTEST_CONFIGURE_COMMAND
    "\"${CTEST_SOURCE_DIRECTORY}/bootstrap\"")
set (CTEST_BUILD_COMMAND     "/usr/bin/make -j 2")


ctest_empty_binary_directory (${CTEST_BINARY_DIRECTORY})

ctest_start (Nightly)
ctest_update (SOURCE "${CTEST_SOURCE_DIRECTORY}")
ctest_configure (BUILD "${CTEST_BINARY_DIRECTORY}")
ctest_build (BUILD "${CTEST_BINARY_DIRECTORY}")
ctest_test  (BUILD "${CTEST_BINARY_DIRECTORY}")
ctest_submit ()
```

The first line is there just to make sure an appropriate version of CTest is used since the advanced scripting was introduced in CTest 2.2. Since the CMake parser is used, most commands from CMake are available. This includes the `cmake_minimum_required` command:

```
cmake_minimum_required (VERSION 2.2)
```

Overall the layout of the rest of this script is similar to the traditional one. First there are several settings that CTest will use to perform its tasks. Then, unlike in traditional CTest, there are the actual tasks that CTest will perform. Instead of providing information in the project's CMake cache, in this scripting mode, all the information is provided to CTest. For compatibility reasons we may choose to write the information to the cache, but that is up to the dashboard maintainer. The first block contains the variables about the submission.

```
set (CTEST_SITE            "andoria.kitware")
set (CTEST_BUILD_NAME      "Linux-g++")
set (CTEST_NOTES_FILES
    "${CTEST_SCRIPT_DIRECTORY}/${CTEST_SCRIPT_NAME}")
```

These variables serve the same role as the `SITE` and `BUILD_NAME` cache variables. They are used to identify the system once it submits the results to the dashboard. `CTEST_NOTES_FILES` is just a list of files that should be submitted as the notes of the dashboard submission. This variable corresponds to the –A flag of CTest.

The second block describes the information that CTest handlers will use to perform the tasks:

```
set (CTEST_DASHBOARD_ROOT    "$ENV{HOME}/Dashboards/My Tests")
set (CTEST_SOURCE_DIRECTORY "${CTEST_DASHBOARD_ROOT}/CMake")
set (CTEST_BINARY_DIRECTORY "${CTEST_DASHBOARD_ROOT}/CMake-gcc
")
set (CTEST_UPDATE_COMMAND    "/usr/bin/cvs")
set (CTEST_CONFIGURE_COMMAND
    "\"${CTEST_SOURCE_DIRECTORY}/bootstrap\"")
set (CTEST_BUILD_COMMAND     "/usr/bin/make -j 2")
```

The `CTEST_SOURCE_DIRECTORY` and `CTEST_BINARY_DIRECTORY` serve the same purpose as in the traditional CTest script. The only difference is that we will still be able to overwrite these variables later on when calling the CTest handlers. The `CTEST_UPDATE_COMMAND` is the path to the command used to update the source directory from the repository. Currently CTest supports Concurrent Versions System (CVS) and Subversion.

Both the configure and build handlers support two modes. One mode is to provide the full command that will be invoked during that stage. This is designed to support projects that do not use CMake as their configuration or build tool. In this case you specify the full command lines to configure and build your project by setting the `CTEST_CONFIGURE_COMMAND` and `CTEST_BUILD_COMMAND` variables respectively. This is similar to specifying `CTEST_CMAKE_COMMAND` in the traditional CTest scripting.

For projects that use CMake for their configuration and build steps you do not need to specify the commands lines for configuring and building your project. Instead you will specify the CMake generator to use by setting the `CTEST_CMAKE_GENERATOR` variable. This way CMake will be run with the appropriate generator. One example of this is:

```
set (CTEST_CMAKE_GENERATOR "Visual Studio 8 2005")
```

For the build step you should also set the variables `CTEST_PROJECT_NAME` and `CTEST_BUILD_CONFIGURATION` to specify how to build the project. In this case `CTEST_PROJECT_NAME` should match the top level CMake list file's `PROJECT` command. The `CTEST_BUILD_CONFIGURATION` should be one of Release, Debug, MinSizeRel, and RelWithDebInfo. Additionally `CTEST_BUILD_FLAGS` can be provided as a hint to the build command. An example of testing for a CMake based project would be:

```
set (CTEST_CMAKE_GENERATOR "Visual Studio 8 2005")
set (CTEST_PROJECT_NAME "Grommit")
set (CTEST_BUILD_CONFIGURATION "Debug")
```

The final block performs the actual testing and submission:

```
ctest_empty_binary_directory (${CTEST_BINARY_DIRECTORY})

ctest_start (Nightly)
ctest_update (SOURCE
             "${CTEST_SOURCE_DIRECTORY}" RETURN_VALUE res)
ctest_configure (BUILD
                 "${CTEST_BINARY_DIRECTORY}" RETURN_VALUE res)
ctest_build (BUILD "${CTEST_BINARY_DIRECTORY}" RETURN_VALUE res)
ctest_test (BUILD "${CTEST_BINARY_DIRECTORY}" RETURN_VALUE res)
ctest_submit (RETURN_VALUE res)
```

The `ctest_empty_binary_directory` command empties the directory and all subdirectories. Please note that this command has a safety measure built in, which is that it will only remove the directory if there is a CMakeCache.txt file in the top level directory. This is to prevent us from mistakenly removing a directory.

The rest of the block contains the calls to the actual CTest handlers. Each of them corresponds to a CTest –D option. For example, instead of:

```
ctest -D ExperimentalBuild
```

The script would contain:

```
ctest_start (Experimental)
ctest_build (BUILD "${CTEST_BINARY_DIRECTORY}" RETURN_VALUE res)
```

Each step can return a return value, which can then be used to determine if the step was successful. For example the return value of the Update stage can be used in a continuous dashboard to determine if the rest of the dashboard should be performed.

To demonstrate some advantages of using extended CTest scripting, let us examine a more advanced CTest script. This script drives testing of an application called Slicer. Slicer uses CMake internally, but it drives the build process through a series of Tcl scripts. One of the problems of this approach is that it does not support out-of-source builds. Also, on Windows, certain modules come pre-built, so they have to be copied to the build directory. To test a project like that, we would use a script like this:

```
cmake_minimum_required (VERSION 2.2)

# set the dashboard specific variables -- name and notes
set (CTEST_SITE            "dash11.kitware")
set (CTEST_BUILD_NAME      "Win32-VS71")
set (CTEST_NOTES_FILES
    "${CTEST_SCRIPT_DIRECTORY}/${CTEST_SCRIPT_NAME}")

# do not let the test run for more than 1500 seconds
set (CTEST_TIMEOUT "1500")

# set the source and binary directories
set (CTEST_SOURCE_DIRECTORY  "C:/Dashboards/MyTests/slicer2")
set (CTEST_BINARY_DIRECTORY  "${CTEST_SOURCE_DIRECTORY}-build")

set (SLICER_SUPPORT
    "//Dash11/Shared/Support/SlicerSupport/Lib")
set (TCLSH   "${SLICER_SUPPORT}/win32/bin/tclsh84.exe")
```

```
# set the complete update, configure and build commands
set (CTEST_UPDATE_COMMAND
     "C:/Program Files/TortoiseCVS/cvs.exe")
set (CTEST_CONFIGURE_COMMAND
    "\"${TCLSH}\"
    \"${CTEST_BINARY_DIRECTORY}/Scripts/genlib.tcl\"")
set (CTEST_BUILD_COMMAND
    "\"${TCLSH}\"
    \"${CTEST_BINARY_DIRECTORY}/Scripts/cmaker.tcl\"")

# clear out the binary tree
file (WRITE "${CTEST_BINARY_DIRECTORY}/CMakeCache.txt"
     "// Dummy cache just so that ctest will wipe binary dir")
ctest_empty_binary_directory (${CTEST_BINARY_DIRECTORY})

# special variables for the Slicer build process
set (ENV{MSVC6}          "0")
set (ENV{GENERATOR}      "Visual Studio 7 .NET 2003")
set (ENV{MAKE}           "devenv.exe ")
set (ENV{COMPILER_PATH}
    "C:/Program Files/Microsoft Visual Studio .NET
2003/Common7/Vc7/bin")
set (ENV{CVS}            "${CTEST_UPDATE_COMMAND}")

# start and update the dashboard
ctest_start (Nightly)
ctest_update (SOURCE "${CTEST_SOURCE_DIRECTORY}")

# define a macro to copy a directory
macro (COPY_DIR srcdir destdir)
  exec_program ("${CMAKE_EXECUTABLE_NAME}" ARGS
             "-E copy_directory \"${srcdir}\" \"${destdir}\"")
endmacro (COPY_DIR)

# Slicer does not support out of source builds so we
# first copy the source directory to the binary directory
# and then build it
copy_dir ("${CTEST_SOURCE_DIRECTORY}"
        "${CTEST_BINARY_DIRECTORY}")


# copy support libraries that slicer needs into the binary tree
copy_dir ("${SLICER_SUPPORT}"
        "${CTEST_BINARY_DIRECTORY}/Lib")
```

```
# finally do the configure, build, test and submit steps
ctest_configure (BUILD "${CTEST_BINARY_DIRECTORY}")
ctest_build (BUILD "${CTEST_BINARY_DIRECTORY}")
ctest_test (BUILD "${CTEST_BINARY_DIRECTORY}")
ctest_submit ()
```

Since with extended CTest scripting we have full control over the flow, we can perform arbitrary commands at any point. For example, after performing an update of the project, the script copies the source tree into the build directory, which allows it to do an "out-of-source" build.

10.10 Setting up a Dashboard Server

There are a few options for what to run on the server to process the dashboard results. DART has two main versions available. The older DART 1 server is based on TCL, Java, CGI scripts and XSLT. The second version of DART is based on Java and is much more self contained. Instructions for installing both versions are included in this section. The third option is to use CDash a new dashboard server based on PHP, MySQL, CSS, and XSLT which is described at the end of this section.

Dart Server Version 1 Setup

Setting up a DART server can take some time and you should have some comfort with setting up a web server (or find someone who does) before going too far ahead. You should also check the README.INSTALL file in the DART source tree for more up to date instructions. While you can setup a DART server on Windows this section will assume that you are on a UNIX server. The same basic ideas apply to the Windows case.

The first step is to obtain the Dart distribution and all prerequisites. The most basic prerequisite is a web server with CGI-BIN support. Once the web server is working, there are several scripts, programs, and CGI scripts that dart uses to perform its tasks. Dart currently requires several languages for its operations. The main ones are TCL and Java. There are several submission scripts provided that are written in Python and Perl. We recommend using the Python ones: HTTPUploadDartFile.cgi and Submit-Sample.cgi. The Submit-Sample.cgi also requires TriggerSite.py. There are also some utility scripts for rolling up dashboard entries written in Bourne Shell. These scripts are usually site specific, so you may have to write your own.

DART uses an http server for the client to drop the build and test XML reports. HTTP submission should work even for people behind firewalls. For http submissions, CTest makes use of the http PUT upload method. To setup the submission part, use the CGI-BIN script provided in the Dart source tree under /Source/Server/www/cgi-bin called HTTPUploadDartFile.cgi. This script needs to be modified to specify the target directory. By default it will put files to /dart_incoming. Also, make sure the directory where the script will store files is writable for the web server.

Make sure that the server has a checkout of your project's source code tree. This checkout of your software is needed to perform a CVS update for the server's update page. The checkout tree must be accessible (writable) from the web server, since the CVS update will be done on the web server (typically as "nobody") so that user must have permission to do a CVS update on that checkout. The best bet is to checkout the source tree from the user nobody in the first place.

At this point you should be able to create a directory (writable by the web server), that will host all the testing results. The only file required in this directory is the DartConfiguration.tcl file, that will contain the configuration of that project's server. Sample file DartConfiguration.tcl.sample from the Dart source tree can be used to write a project specific one.

Once DartConfiguration.tcl file exists, the server setup is almost complete. First you should be able to modify or write an equivalent of SampleRollup.cgi script that uses RollupDashboard.sh. These two scripts are written in Bourne shell, but they can be written by the system administrator. The scripts have to know the project's testing directory and the path to the Dart server. The SampleRollup.cgi script has to exist for each project. Once this script is customized for this project, you should be able to just run it:

```
./SampleRollup.cgi
```

At this point you should see some output and the testing structure will be created. If there were some errors, fix the appropriate settings. Usually the errors are caused by the wrong path in SampleRollup.cgi or DartConfiguration.tcl file. Also, errors may be caused by bad permissions. To make rollup stage periodic, cron jobs needs to be created. Below is a snippet of a crontab:

```
MAILTO=root@localhost

# Roll up the dashboard each hour on the hour
0 0-23 * * * /usr/lib/cgi-bin/SampleRollup.cgi > /dev/null 2>&1

# End of cron tab
```

Since rolling up the dashboard will cause all the web-pages to be created, we should be able to make appropriate symbolic links or web server aliases for the testing directory to be accessible from the web browser. Consult your web server manual on how to do this. The subdirectory that must be visible from the web browser is: Testing/HTML/TestingResults.

To finish setting up the server, we should make sure the submission is working. To do this, let us first setup the DartConfig.cmake file on the client system. In section 10.8 we setup the options that the client uses. There are a number of additional options that the server uses to control producing dashboards. Make sure the options correspond to the server you just setup. Once the DartConfig.cmake file is properly setup in the source code of the project, we should be able to run an experimental dashboard using CTest. If the dashboard is not submitted, examine the error messages of CTest.

Setting up a dashboard server can be a daunting process with many options. The Examples/dt directory in the DART source code tree contains a simple example that can be used to test your server and client configurations (localhost). Check the Examples/dt/README for more information. If you run into problems beyond that, DART has a mailing list you can join. Visit the DART homepage at http://public.kitware.com/Dart/HTML/Index.shtml for more information.

Dart Server Version 2 Setup

Dart version 2 was overhauled and rewritten from the ground up to support a more flexible environment, and at the same time be much simpler than Dart 1. It is completely written in Java, so the requirement of multiple interpreters is over. Also, it is using an SQL server to store the testing results, which makes it much faster and smaller at the same time.

Though most concepts within Dart2 stayed the same, there are some fundamental changes. First of all, various submission methods were replaced with a single one, which is XMLRPC. This one is much more flexible and since it is running through a HTTP protocol it is accessible through firewalls. As opposed to Dart1, Dart2 runs a single process that controls everything from the Web server to the database. That said, both Web server and database can be used externally.

The only prerequisite for Dart2 server is a Java interpreter. To install Dart2 server, follow the following steps:

1. Create a testing server. To perform all the tasks, Dart2 requires only one testing server. Testing server can be created by issuing the following command:

```
java -jar DartServer.jar --createserver MyServer
```

2. Creating the server will create a directory with the same name as the name of the server. You should be able to edit the file Server.xml in that directory to customize for your needs.

3. Once you are satisfied with the Server.xml file, you should initialize the server database by issuing the following command:

```
java -jar DartServer.jar --initializeserver MyServer
```

4. To be able to work with specific projects, each project needs to be created. The project is not associated with the server and the server is not associated with the project. That said, we should make sure that the same project is used by at most one server. The project can be created by issuing the following command:

```
java -jar DartServer.jar --create MyProject
```

5. Similarly to creating a server, creating the project will create a subdirectory with the same name as the project name. This directory contains a file called Project.xml. This file can be customized to correspond to the project's properties.

6. Completing all these tasks, we should be able to initialize and start the server. To do this, you should issue the following command:

```
java -jar DartServer.jar --initialize --refresh \
    --refreshServer MyServer MyProject
```

7. After a couple of seconds of initialization the server will be running and you should be able to check it out by launching the web browser and going to the location where the Dart2 server is running. By default, this will be the port 8081 on the same system:

```
http://system-name.com:8081/TestProject/Dashboard/
```

Once the Dart2 server is up and running, dashboards can be submitted to it. The DartConfig.cmake on the client side has to be modified to use Dart2 server. An example file would be:

```
set (NIGHTLY_START_TIME "21:00:00 EDT")

# Dart server to submit results
set (DROP_METHOD xmlrpc)
set (DROP_SITE "system-name.com")
set (DROP_LOCATION "MyProject")
set (COMPRESS_SUBMISSION ON)
```

If all options are specified properly, CTest will be able to submit an experimental dashboard to the given server.

CDash Server

CDash is a new dashboard server developed by Kitware that is based on the common LAMP platform. It makes use of PHP, CSS, XSL, MySQL and of course your web server such as Apache. CDash takes the dashboard submissions as XML and stores them into a MySQL database. When the web server receives requests for pages the PHP scripts extract the relevant data from the MySQL database and produce XML that is sent to XSL templates that in turn convert it into HTML. CSS is used to provide the overall look and feel for the pages.

You can get CDash off of the www.cmake.org website or you can get the latest code from SVN from the following address

```
svn co https://www.kitware.com:8443/svn/CDash/trunk CDash
```

Your web server will need to have PHP5 or later installed as well as the XSL processor for PHP (apt-get install php5-xsl). Once you have downloaded CDash you will need to edit config.php and change the value accordingly for your server. Then point your web browser to the CDash/install.php script and follow the instructions on it. For your project's CTestConfig file use the following settings:

```
SET(DROP_METHOD "http")
SET(DROP_SITE "yourserver.org")
SET(DROP_LOCATION "/CDash/submit.php?project=YourProject")
```

## Chapter 11

Porting CMake to New Platforms and Languages

In order to generate build files for a particular system, CMake needs to determine what system it is running on, and what compiler tools to use for enabled languages. To do this CMake loads a series of files containing CMake code from the Modules directory. This all has to happen before the first try-compile or try-run is executed. To avoid having to re-compute all of this information for each try-compile and for subsequent runs of CMake, the discovered values are stored in several configured files that are read each time CMake is run. These files are also copied into the try-compile and try-run directories. This chapter will describe how this process of system and tool discovery works. An understanding of the process is necessary to extend CMake to run on new platforms, and to add support for new languages.

11.1 The Determine System Process

The first thing CMake needs to do is to determine on what platform it is running and what the target platform is. Except when you are cross compiling the host platform and the target platform are always identical. The host platform is determined by loading the `CMakeDetermineSystem.cmake` file. On POSIX systems, "uname" is used to get the name of the system. `CMAKE_HOST_SYSTEM_NAME` is set to the result of uname -s, and `CMAKE_HOST_SYSTEM_VERSION` is set to the result of uname -r. On Windows systems, `CMAKE_HOST_SYSTEM_NAME` is set to Windows and `CMAKE_HOST_SYSTEM_VERSION` is set to the value returned by the system function GetVersionEx. The variable `CMAKE_HOST_SYSTEM` is set to a combination of `CMAKE_HOST_SYSTEM_NAME` and `CMAKE_HOST_SYSTEM_VERSION` as follows:

```
${CMAKE_HOST_SYSTEM_NAME}-${CMAKE_HOST_SYSTEM_VERSION}
```

Additionally CMake tries to figure out the processor of the host, on POSIX systems it uses uname -m or uname -p to retrieve this information, on Windows it uses the environment variable PROCESSOR_ARCHITECTURE. CMAKE_HOST_SYSTEM_PROCESSOR holds the value of the result.

Now that CMake has the information about the host on which it is running, it needs to find the information for the target platform. The results will be stored in the CMAKE_SYSTEM_NAME, CMAKE_SYSTEM_VERSION, CMAKE_SYSTEM and CMAKE_SYSTEM_PROCESSOR variables, corresponding to the CMAKE_HOST_SYSTEM_* variables described above. See the "Cross compiling with CMake" chapter on how this is done when cross compiling. In all other cases the CMAKE_SYSTEM_* variables will be set to the value of their corresponding CMAKE_HOST_SYSTEM_* variable.

Once the CMAKE_SYSTEM information has been determined, CMakeSystem.cmake.in is configured into ${CMAKE_BINARY_DIR}/CMakeFiles/CMakeSystem.cmake. CMake versions prior to 2.6.0 didn't support cross compiling and so only the CMAKE_SYSTEM_* set of variables was available.

11.2 The Enable Language Process

After the platform has been determined, the next step is to enable all languages specified in the project command. For each language specified CMake loads CMakeDetermine(LANG)Compiler.cmake where LANG is the name of the language specified in the PROJECT command. For example with project (f Fortran) the file is called CMakeDetermineFortranCompiler.cmake. This file discovers the compiler and tools that will be used to compile files for the particular language. Starting with version 2.6.0 CMake tries to identify the compiler for C, C++ and Fortran not only by its filename, but by compiling source code, which is named CMake(LANG)CompilerId.(LANG_SUFFIX). If this succeeds, it will return a unique id for every compiler supported by CMake. Once the compiler has been determined for a language, CMake configures the file CMake(LANG)Compiler.cmake.in into CMake(LANG)Compiler.cmake.

After the platform and compiler tools have been determined, CMake loads CMakeSystemSpecificInformation.cmake which in turn will load ${CMAKE_SYSTEM_NAME}.cmake from the platform subdirectory of modules if it exists for the platform. An example would be SunOS.cmake. This file contains OS specific information for compiler flags, creation of executables, libraries, and object files.

Next, CMake loads CMake(LANG)Information.cmake for each LANG that was enabled. This file in turn loads two files; ${CMAKE_SYSTEM_NAME}-${COMPILER_ID}-LANG-

`${CMAKE_SYSTEM_PROCESSOR}.cmake` if it exists and after that `${CMAKE_SYSTEM_NAME}-${COMPILER_ID}-LANG.cmake`. In these file names `COMPILER_ID` references the compiler identification determined as described above. The `CMake(LANG)Information.cmake` file contains default rules for creating executables, libraries, and object files on most UNIX systems. The defaults can be overridden by setting values in either `${CMAKE_SYSTEM_NAME}.cmake` or `${CMAKE_SYSTEM_NAME}-${COMPILER_ID}-LANG.cmake`.

`${CMAKE_SYSTEM_NAME}-${COMPILER_ID}-LANG-${CMAKE_SYSTEM_PROCESSOR}.cmake` is intended to be used only for cross compiling, it is loaded before `${CMAKE_SYSTEM_NAME}-${COMPILER_ID}-LANG.cmake`, so variables can be set up which can then be used in the rule variables.

In addition to the files with the `COMPILER_ID` in their name, CMake supports these files also using the `COMPILER_BASE_NAME`. `COMPILER_BASE_NAME` is the name of the compiler with no path information. For example `cl` would be the `COMPILER_BASE_NAME` for the Microsoft Windows compiler, and `Windows-cl.cmake` would be loaded. If a `COMPILER_ID` exists, it will be preferred over the `COMPILER_BASE_NAME`, since on one side the same compiler can have different names, but there can be also different compilers all with the same name. This means, if

```
${CMAKE_SYSTEM_NAME}-${COMPILER_ID}-LANG-
${CMAKE_SYSTEM_PROCESSOR}.cmake
```

wasn't found, CMake tries

```
${CMAKE_SYSTEM_NAME}-${COMPILER_BASE_NAME}.cmake
```

and if

```
${CMAKE_SYSTEM_NAME}-${COMPILER_ID}-LANG.cmake
```

wasn't found, CMake tries

```
${CMAKE_SYSTEM_NAME}-${COMPILER_BASE_NAME}.cmake.
```

`CMake(LANG)Information.cmake` and associated Platform files define special CMake variables, called rule variables. A rule variable consists of a list of commands separated by spaces. The commands are enclosed by quotes. In addition to the normal variable expansion performed by CMake, some special tag variables are expanded by the makefile generator.

Tag variables have the syntax of `<NAME>` where `NAME` is the name of the variable. An example rule variable is `CMAKE_CXX_CREATE_SHARED_LIBRARY`, and the default setting is

```
set (CMAKE_CXX_CREATE_SHARED_LIBRARY
    "<CMAKE_CXX_COMPILER> <CMAKE_SHARED_LIBRARY_CXX_FLAGS>
    <LINK_FLAGS> <CMAKE_SHARED_LIBRARY_CREATE_CXX_FLAGS>
    <CMAKE_SHARED_LIBRARY_SONAME_CXX_FLAG><TARGET_SONAME> -o
    <TARGET> <OBJECTS> <LINK_LIBRARIES>")
```

At this point, CMake has determined the system it is running on, the tools it will be using to compile the enabled languages, and the rules to use the tools. This means there is enough information for CMake to perform a try-compile. CMake now tests the detected compilers for each enabled language by loading `CMakeTest(LANG)Compiler.cmake`. This file will usually run a try-compile on a simple source file for the given language to make sure the chosen compiler actually works.

Once the platform has been determined, and the compilers have been tested, CMake loads a few more files that can be used to change some of the computed values. The first file that is loaded is `CMake(PROJECTNAME)Compatibility.cmake` where `PROJECTNAME` is the name given to the top level `PROJECT` command in the project. The project compatibility file is used to add backwards compatibility fixes into CMake. For example, if a new version of CMake fails to build a project that the previous version of CMake could build, then fixes can be added on a per project basis to CMake. The last file that is loaded is `${CMAKE_USER_MAKE_RULES_OVERRIDE}`. This file is an optionally user supplied variable, that can allow a project to make very specific platform based changes to the build rules.

11.3 Porting to a New Platform

Many common platforms are already supported by CMake. However, you may come across a compiler or platform that has not yet been used. If the compiler uses an Integrated Development Environment (IDE), then you would have to extend CMake from the C++ level. However, if the compiler supports a standard make program, then you can specify in CMake the rules to use to compile object code and build libraries by creating CMake configuration files. These files are written using the CMake language with a few special tags that are expanded when the makefiles are created by CMake. If you run CMake on your system and get a message like the following, you will want to read how to create platform specific settings.

```
System is unknown to cmake, create:
Modules/Platform/MySystem.cmake
to use this system, please send your config file to
cmake@www.cmake.org so it can be added to cmake
```

At a minimum you will need to create the `Platform/${CMAKE_SYSTEM_NAME}.cmake` file for the new platform. Depending on the tools for the platform, you may also want to create `Platform/${CMAKE_SYSTEM_NAME}-${COMPILER_BASE_NAME}.cmake`. On most systems, there is a vendor compiler and the GNU compiler. The rules for both of these compilers can be put in `Platform/${CMAKE_SYSTEM_NAME}.cmake` instead of creating separate files for each of the compilers. For most new systems or compilers, if they follow the basic UNIX compiler flags, you will only need to specify the system specific flags for shared library and module creation.

The following example is from `Platform/IRIX.cmake`. This file specifies several flags, and also one CMake rule variable. The rule variable tells how to use the IRIX CC compiler to create a static library, which is required for template instantiation to work with IRIX CC.

```
# there is no -ldl required on this system
set (CMAKE_DL_LIBS "")

# Specify the flag to create a shared c library
set (CMAKE_SHARED_LIBRARY_CREATE_C_FLAGS
    "-shared -rdata_shared")

# Specify the flag to create a shared c++ library
set (CMAKE_SHARED_LIBRARY_CREATE_CXX_FLAGS
    "-shared -rdata_shared")

# specify the flag to specify run time paths for shared
# libraries -rpath
set (CMAKE_SHARED_LIBRARY_RUNTIME_C_FLAG "-Wl,-rpath,")

# specify a separator for paths on the -rpath, if empty
# then -rpath will be repeated.
set (CMAKE_SHARED_LIBRARY_RUNTIME_C_FLAG_SEP "")

# if the compiler is not GNU, then specify the initial flags
if (NOT CMAKE_COMPILER_IS_GNUCXX)
  # use the CC compiler to create static library
  set (CMAKE_CXX_CREATE_STATIC_LIBRARY
      "<CMAKE_CXX_COMPILER> -ar -o <TARGET> <OBJECTS>")
  # initializes flags for the native compiler
  set (CMAKE_CXX_FLAGS_INIT "")
  set (CMAKE_CXX_FLAGS_DEBUG_INIT "-g")
  set (CMAKE_CXX_FLAGS_MINSIZEREL_INIT "-O3 -DNDEBUG")
  set (CMAKE_CXX_FLAGS_RELEASE_INIT "-O2 -DNDEBUG")
  set (CMAKE_CXX_FLAGS_RELWITHDEBINFO_INIT "-O2")
endif (NOT CMAKE_COMPILER_IS_GNUCXX)
```

11.4 Adding a New Language

In addition to porting CMake to new platforms a user may want to add a new language. This can be done either by the use of custom commands, or by defining a new language for CMake. Once a new language is defined, the standard `add_library` and `add_executable` commands can be used to create libraries and executables for the new languages. To add a new language, you need to create four files. The name `LANG` has to match in exact case the name used in the `PROJECT` command to enable the language. For example Fortran has the file `CMakeDeterminFortranCompiler.cmake`, and is enabled with a call like this `project (f Fortran)`. The four files are as follows:

CMakeDetermine(LANG)Compiler.cmake

> This file will find the path to the compiler for `LANG` and then configure CMake(LANG)Compiler.cmake.in

CMake(LANG)Compiler.cmake.in

> This file should be used as input to a configure file call in the CMakeDetermine(LANG)Compiler.cmake file. It is used to store compiler information and is copied down into try-compile directories so that try compiles do not need to re-determine and test the `LANG`.

CMakeTest(LANG)Compiler.cmake

> This should use a try compile command to make sure the compiler and tools are working. If the tools are working, the following variable should be set in this way:

```
set (CMAKE_(LANG)_COMPILER_WORKS 1 CACHE INTERNAL "")
```

CMake(LANG)Information.cmake

> Set values for the following rule variables for LANG:

```
CMAKE_(LANG)_CREATE_SHARED_LIBRARY
CMAKE_(LANG)_CREATE_SHARED_MODULE
CMAKE_(LANG)_CREATE_STATIC_LIBRARY
CMAKE_(LANG)_COMPILE_OBJECT
CMAKE_(LANG)_LINK_EXECUTABLE
```

11.5 Rule Variable Listing

For each language that CMake supports, the following rule variables are expanded into build makefiles at generation time. `LANG` is the name used in the `PROJECT (name LANG)` command. CMake currently supports CXX, C, Fortran, and Java as values for `LANG`.

General Tag Variables

The following set of variables will be expanded by CMake.

\<TARGET\>

>   The name of the target being built (this may be a full path).

\<TARGET_QUOTED\>

>   The name of the target being built (this may be a full path) double quoted.

\<TARGET_BASE\>

>   This is replaced by the name of the target without a suffix.

\<TARGET_SONAME\>

>   This is replaced by
>
>   CMAKE_SHARED_LIBRARY_SONAME_(LANG)_FLAG

\<OBJECTS\>

>   This is the list of object files to be linked into the target.

\<OBJECTS_QUOTED\>

>   This is the list of object files to be linked into the target double quoted.

\<OBJECT\>

>   This is the name of the object file to be built.

\<LINK_LIBRARIES\>

>   This is the list of libraries that are linked into an executable or shared object.

\<FLAGS\>

>   This is the command line flags for the linker or compiler.

\<LINK_FLAGS\>

>   This is the flags used at link time.

\<SOURCE\>

>   The source file name.

Language Specific Information

The following set of variables related to the compiler tools will also be expanded.

<CMAKE_(LANG)_COMPILER>

> This is the (LANG) compiler command.

<CMAKE_SHARED_LIBRARY_CREATE_(LANG)_FLAGS>

> This is the flags used to create a shared library for (LANG) code.

<CMAKE_SHARED_MODULE_CREATE_(LANG)_FLAGS>

> This is the flags used to create a shared module for (LANG) code.

<CMAKE_(LANG)_LINK_FLAGS>

> This is the flags used to link a (LANG) program.

<CMAKE_AR>

> This is the command to create a .a archive file.

<CMAKE_RANLIB>

> This is the command to ranlib a .a archive file.

11.6 Compiler and Platform Examples

Como Compiler

A good example to look at would be the como compiler on Linux found in Modules/Platforms/Linux-como.cmake. This compiler requires several non-standard commands when creating libraries and executables in order to instantiate C++ templates.

```
# create a shared C++ library

set (CMAKE_CXX_CREATE_SHARED_LIBRARY
    "<CMAKE_CXX_COMPILER> --prelink_objects <OBJECTS>"
    "<CMAKE_CXX_COMPILER>
<CMAKE_SHARED_LIBRARY_CREATE_CXX_FLAGS> <LINK_FLAGS> -o <TARGET>
<OBJECTS> <LINK_LIBRARIES>")

# create a C++ static library
set (CMAKE_CXX_CREATE_STATIC_LIBRARY
    "<CMAKE_CXX_COMPILER> --prelink_objects <OBJECTS>"
    "<CMAKE_AR> cr <TARGET> <LINK_FLAGS> <OBJECTS> "
    "<CMAKE_RANLIB> <TARGET> ")

set (CMAKE_CXX_LINK_EXECUTABLE
    "<CMAKE_CXX_COMPILER> --prelink_objects <OBJECTS>"
```

```
    "<CMAKE_CXX_COMPILER> <CMAKE_CXX_LINK_FLAGS> <LINK_FLAGS>
<FLAGS> <OBJECTS> -o <TARGET> <LINK_LIBRARIES>")

set (CMAKE_SHARED_LIBRARY_RUNTIME_FLAG "")
set (CMAKE_SHARED_LIBRARY_C_FLAGS "")
set (CMAKE_SHARED_LIBRARY_LINK_FLAGS "")
```

This overrides the creation of libraries (shared and static), and the linking of executable c++ programs. You can see that the linking process of executables and shared libraries requires an extra command that calls the compiler with the flag `--prelink_objects` and gets passed all of the object files.

Borland Compiler

The full Borland compiler rules can be found in Platforms/Windows-bcc32.cmake. The following code is an excerpt from that file, showing some of the features used to define rules for the Borland compiler set.

```
set (CMAKE_CXX_CREATE_SHARED_LIBRARY
     "<CMAKE_CXX_COMPILER> ${CMAKE_START_TEMP_FILE}-e<TARGET>
-tWD <LINK_FLAGS> -tWR <LINK_LIBRARIES>
<OBJECTS>${CMAKE_END_TEMP_FILE}"
 "implib -c -w <TARGET_BASE>.lib <TARGET_BASE>.dll"
)

set (CMAKE_CXX_CREATE_SHARED_MODULE
     ${CMAKE_CXX_CREATE_SHARED_LIBRARY})

# create a C shared library
set (CMAKE_C_CREATE_SHARED_LIBRARY
 "<CMAKE_C_COMPILER> ${CMAKE_START_TEMP_FILE}-e<TARGET> -tWD
<LINK_FLAGS> -tWR <LINK_LIBRARIES>
<OBJECTS>${CMAKE_END_TEMP_FILE}"
 "implib -c -w <TARGET_BASE>.lib <TARGET_BASE>.dll"
)

# create a C++ static library
set (CMAKE_CXX_CREATE_STATIC_LIBRARY  "tlib
${CMAKE_START_TEMP_FILE}/p512 <LINK_FLAGS> /a <TARGET_QUOTED>
<OBJECTS_QUOTED>${CMAKE_END_TEMP_FILE}")

# compile a C++ file into an object file
set (CMAKE_CXX_COMPILE_OBJECT
```

```
   "<CMAKE_CXX_COMPILER>   ${CMAKE_START_TEMP_FILE}-DWIN32 -P
<FLAGS>   -o<OBJECT> -c <SOURCE>${CMAKE_END_TEMP_FILE}")
```

11.7 Extending CMake

Occasionally you will come across a situation where you want to do something during your build process that CMake can't seem to handle. Examples of this include creating wrappers for C++ classes to make them available to other languages, or creating bindings for C++ classes to support runtime introspection. In these cases you may want to extend CMake by adding your own commands. CMake supports this capability through its C plugin API. Using this API a project can extend CMake to add specialized commands to handle project specific tasks.

A loaded command in CMake is essentially a C code plugin that is compiled into a shared library (a.k.a. DLL). This shared library is then loaded into the running CMake to provide the functionality of the loaded command. Creating a loaded command is a two step process. You must first write the C code and CMakeLists file for the command and place it in your source tree. Then you must modify your project's CMakeLists file to compile the loaded command and then load it. We will start by looking at writing the plugin. Before resorting to creating a loaded command you should first see if you can accomplish what you want with a macro. With the commands in CMake a macro has most of the same flexibility as a loaded command but does not require compilation or as much complexity. Almost always you can and should use a macro instead of a loaded command.

Creating a Loaded Command

While CMake itself is written in C++ we suggest that you write your plugins using only C code. This avoids a number of portability and compiler issues that can plague C++ plugins being loaded into CMake executables. The API for a plugin is defined in the header file cmCPluginAPI.h. This file defines all of the CMake functions that you can invoke from your plugin. It also defines the cmLoadedCommandInfo structure that is passed to a plugin. Before going into detail on these functions, consider the following simple plugin:

```
#include "cmCPluginAPI.h"

static int InitialPass(void *inf, void *mf,
                       int argc, char *argv[])
{
  cmLoadedCommandInfo *info = (cmLoadedCommandInfo *)inf;
  info->CAPI->AddDefinition(mf, "FOO", "BAR");

  return 1;
}
```

```
void CM_PLUGIN_EXPORT
HELLO_WORLDInit(cmLoadedCommandInfo *info)
{
  info->InitialPass = InitialPass;
  info->Name = "HELLO_WORLD";
}
```

First this plugin includes the `cmCPluginAPI.h` file to get the definitions and structures required for a plugin. Next it defines a static function called `InitialPass` that will be called whenever this loaded command is invoked. This function is always passed four parameters: the `cmLoadedCommandInfo` structure, the makefile, the number of arguments, and the list of arguments. Inside of this function we typecast the `inf` argument to its actual type and then use it to invoke the C API (CAPI) `AddDefinition` function. This function will set the variable `FOO` to the value of `BAR` in the current `cmMakefile` instance.

The second function is called `HELLO_WORLDInit` and it will be called when the plugin is loaded. The name of this function must exactly match the name of the loaded command with `Init` appended. In this example the name of the command is `HELLO_WORLD` so the function is named `HELLO_WORLDInit`. This function will be called as soon as your command is loaded. It is responsible for initializing the elements of the `cmLoadedCommandInfo` structure. In this example it sets the `InitialPass` member to the address of the `InitialPass` function defined above. Then it sets the name of the command by setting the `Name` member to `"HELLO_WORLD"`.

Using a Loaded Command

Now let us consider how to use this new `HELLO_WORLD` command in a project. The basic process is that CMake will have to compile the plugin into a shared library and then dynamically load it. To do this you first create a subdirectory in your project's source tree called CMake or CMakeCommands (by convention, any name can be used). Place the source code to your plugin in that directory. We recommend naming the file with the prefix `cm` and then the name of the command. For example, `cmHELLO_WORLD.c`. Then you must create a simple CMakeLists.txt file for this directory that includes instructions to build the shared library. Typically this will be the following:

```
project (HELLO_WORLD)

set (CMAKE_CXX_FLAGS "${CMAKE_CXX_FLAGS}"
  "${CMAKE_ANSI_CXXFLAGS}"
  )

set (CMAKE_C_FLAGS "${CMAKE_C_FLAGS}"
  "${CMAKE_ANSI_CFLAGS}"
  )
```

```
include_directories (${CMAKE_ROOT}/include
  ${CMAKE_ROOT}/Source
  )


add_library (cmHELLO_WORLD MODULE cmHELLO_WORLD.c)
```

It is critical that you name the library cm followed by the name of the command as shown in the add_library call in the above example (e.g. cmHELLO_WORLD). When CMake goes to load a command it assumes that the command is in a library named using that pattern. The next step is to modify your project's main CMakeLists file to compile and load the plugin. This can be accomplished with the following code:

```
# if the command has not been loaded, compile and load it
if (NOT COMMAND HELLO_WORLD)

  # try compiling it first
  try_compile (COMPILE_OK
    ${PROJECT_BINARY_DIR}/CMake
    ${PROJECT_SOURCE_DIR}/CMake
    HELLO_WORLD
    )

  # if it compiled OK then load it
  if (COMPILE_OK)
    load_command (HELLO_WORLD
      ${PROJECT_BINARY_DIR}/CMake
      ${PROJECT_BINARY_DIR}/CMake/Debug
      )

  # if it did not compile OK, then display an error
  else (COMPILE_OK)
    message ("error compiling HELLO_WORLD extension")
  endif (COMPILE_OK)

endif (NOT COMMAND HELLO_WORLD)
```

In the above example you would simply replace HELLO_WORLD with the name of your command and replace ${PROJECT_SOURCE_DIR}/CMake with the actual name of the subdirectory where you placed your loaded command. Now let us look at creating loaded commands in more detail. We will start by looking at the cmLoadedCommandInfo structure.

```
typedef const char* (*CM_DOC_FUNCTION)();

typedef int (*CM_INITIAL_PASS_FUNCTION)(
    void *info, void *mf, int argc, char *[]);

typedef void (*CM_FINAL_PASS_FUNCTION)(
    void *info, void *mf);
typedef void (*CM_DESTRUCTOR_FUNCTION)(void *info);

typedef struct {
    unsigned long reserved1;
    unsigned long reserved2;
    cmCAPI *CAPI;
    int m_Inherited;
    CM_INITIAL_PASS_FUNCTION InitialPass;
    CM_FINAL_PASS_FUNCTION FinalPass;
    CM_DESTRUCTOR_FUNCTION Destructor;
    CM_DOC_FUNCTION GetTerseDocumentation;
    CM_DOC_FUNCTION GetFullDocumentation;
    const char *Name;
    char *Error;
    void *ClientData;
  } cmLoadedCommandInfo;
```

The first two entries of the structure are reserved for future use. The next entry, CAPI, is a pointer to a structure containing pointers to all the CMake functions you can invoke from a plugin. The m_Inherited member only applies to CMake versions 2.0 and earlier. It can be set to indicate if this command should be inherited by subdirectories or not. If you are creating a command that will work with versions of CMake prior to 2.2 then you probably want to set this to zero. The next five members are pointers to functions that your plugin may provide. The InitialPass function must be provided and it is invoked whenever your loaded command is invoked from a CMakeLists file. The FinalPass function is optional and is invoked after configuration but before generation of the output. The Destructor function is optional and will be invoked when your command is destroyed by CMake (typically on exit). It can be used to clean up any memory that you have allocated in the InitialPass or FinalPass. The next two functions are optional and are used to provide documentation for your command. The Name member is used to store the name of your command. This is what will be compared against when parsing a CMakeLists file so it should be in all caps in keeping with CMake's conventions. The Error and ClientData members are used internally by CMake and you should not directly access them. Instead you can use CAPI functions to manipulate them.

Now let us consider some of the common CAPI functions you will use from within a loaded command. First we will consider some utility functions that are provided specifically for

loaded commands. Since loaded commands use a C interface they will receive arguments as
(int   argc,   char   *argv[])   so   for   convenience   you   can   call
GetTotalArgumentSize(argc, argv) which will return the total length of all the
arguments. Likewise some CAPI methods will return an (argc,argv) pair that you will be
responsible for freeing. The FreeArguments(argc, argv) function can be used to free
such return values. If your loaded command has a FinalPass() then you might want to pass
data from the InitialPass() to the FinalPass() invocation. This can be accomplished
using   the   SetClientData(void   *info,   void   *data)   and   void
*GetClientData(void *info) functions. Since the client data is passed as a void *
argument, any client data larger than a pointer must be allocated and then finally freed in your
Destructor() function. Be aware that CMake will create multiple instances of your loaded
command so using global variables or static variables is not recommended. If you should
encounter an error in executing your loaded command, you can call SetError(void
*info, const char *errorString) to pass an error message on to the user.

Another group of CAPI functions worth noting are the cmSourceFile functions.
cmSourceFile is a C++ object that represents information about a single file including its
full path, file extension, special compiler flags, etc. Some loaded commands will need to
either create or access cmSourceFile instances. This can be done using the void
*CreateSourceFile() and void * GetSource (void *mf, const char
*sourceName) functions. Both of these functions return a pointer to a cmSourceFile as a
void * return value. This pointer can then be passed into other functions that manipulate
cmSourceFiles such as SourceFileGetProperty() or SourceFileSetProperty().

## Chapter 12

Tutorials

This chapter provides a step by step tutorial that covers common build system issues that CMake helps address. Many of these topics have been introduced in prior chapters as separate issues but seeing how they all work together in an example project can be very helpful. This tutorial can be found in the Tests/Tutorial directory of the CMake source code tree. Each step has its own subdirectory containing a complete copy of the tutorial for that step.

12.1 A Basic Starting Point (Step 1)

The most basic project is an executable built from source code files. For simple projects a two line CMakeLists file is all that is required. This will be our starting point for this tutorial. The CMakeLists file looks like:

```
project (Tutorial)
add_executable(Tutorial tutorial.cxx)
```

Note that this example uses lower case commands in the CMakeLists file. Upper, lower, and mixed case commands are supported by CMake. The source code for `tutorial.cxx` will compute the square root of a number and the first version of it is very simple as follows:

```
// A simple program that computes the square root of a number
#include <stdio.h>
#include <math.h>
```

```
int main (int argc, char *argv[])
{
  if (argc < 2)
    {
    fprintf(stdout,"Usage: %s number\n",argv[0]);
    return 1;
    }
  double inputValue = atof(argv[1]);
  double outputValue = sqrt(inputValue);
  fprintf(stdout,"The square root of %g is %g\n",
          inputValue, outputValue);
  return 0;
}
```

Adding a Version Number and Configured Header File

The first feature we will add is to provide our executable and project with a version number. While you can do this exclusively in the source code, doing it in the CMakeLists file provides more flexibility. To add a version number we modify the CMakeLists file as follows:

```
project (Tutorial)

# The version number.
set (Tutorial_VERSION_MAJOR 1)
set (Tutorial_VERSION_MINOR 0)

# configure a header file to pass some of the CMake settings
# to the source code
configure_file (
  "${PROJECT_SOURCE_DIR}/TutorialConfig.h.in"
  "${PROJECT_BINARY_DIR}/TutorialConfig.h"
  )

# add the binary tree to the search path for include files
# so that we will find TutorialConfig.h
include_directories("${PROJECT_BINARY_DIR}")

# add the executable
add_executable(Tutorial tutorial.cxx)
```

Since the configured file will be written into the binary tree we must add that directory to the list of paths to search for include files. We then create a `TutorialConfig.h.in` file in the source tree with the following contents:

```
// the configured options and settings for Tutorial
#define Tutorial_VERSION_MAJOR @Tutorial_VERSION_MAJOR@
#define Tutorial_VERSION_MINOR @Tutorial_VERSION_MINOR@
```

When CMake configures this header file the values for `@Tutorial_VERSION_MAJOR@` and `@Tutorial_VERSION_MINOR@` will be replaced by the values from the CMakeLists file. Next we modify `tutorial.cxx` to include the configured header file and to make use of the version numbers. The resulting source code is listed below.

```
// A simple program that computes the square root of a number
#include <stdio.h>
#include <math.h>
#include "TutorialConfig.h"

int main (int argc, char *argv[])
{
  if (argc < 2)
    {
    fprintf(stdout,"%s Version %d.%d\n",
            argv[0],
            Tutorial_VERSION_MAJOR,
            Tutorial_VERSION_MINOR);
    fprintf(stdout,"Usage: %s number\n",argv[0]);
    return 1;
    }
  double inputValue = atof(argv[1]);
  double outputValue = sqrt(inputValue);
  fprintf(stdout,"The square root of %g is %g\n",
          inputValue, outputValue);
  return 0;
}
```

The main changes are the inclusion of the `TutorialConfig.h` header file and printing out a version number as part of the usage message.

12.2 Adding a Library (Step 2)

Now let us add a library to our project. We will add a library that contains our own implementation for computing the square root of a number. The executable can then use this library instead of the standard square root function provided by the compiler. For this tutorial we will put the library into a subdirectory called MathFunctions. It will have the following one line CMakeLists file:

```
add_library(MathFunctions mysqrt.cxx)
```

The source file `mysqrt.cxx` has one function called `mysqrt` that provides similar functionality to the compiler's `sqrt` function. To make use of the new library we add an `add_subdirectory` call in the top level CMakeLists file so that the library will be built. We also add another include directory so that the `MathFunctions/mysqrt.h` header file can be found for the function prototype. The last change is to add the new library to the executable. The last few lines of the top level CMakeLists file now look like:

```
include_directories ("${PROJECT_SOURCE_DIR}/MathFunctions")
add_subdirectory (MathFunctions)

# add the executable
add_executable (Tutorial tutorial.cxx)
target_link_libraries (Tutorial MathFunctions)
```

Now let us consider making the MathFunctions library optional. In this tutorial there really isn't any reason to do so but with larger libraries or libraries that rely on third party code you might want to. The first step is to add an option to the top level CMakeLists file.

```
# should we use our own math functions?
option (USE_MYMATH
        "Use tutorial provided math implementation" ON)
```

This will show up in the CMake GUI with a default value of ON that the user can then change as desired. This setting will be stored in the cache so that the user does not need to keep setting it each time they run CMake on this project. The next change is to make the build and linking of the MathFunctions library conditional. To do this we change the end of the top level CMakeLists file to look like the following:

```
# add the MathFunctions library?
#
if (USE_MYMATH)
  include_directories ("${PROJECT_SOURCE_DIR}/MathFunctions")
  add_subdirectory (MathFunctions)
  set (EXTRA_LIBS ${EXTRA_LIBS} MathFunctions)
endif (USE_MYMATH)
```

```
# add the executable
add_executable (Tutorial tutorial.cxx)
target_link_libraries (Tutorial  ${EXTRA_LIBS})
```

This uses the setting of USE_MYMATH to determine if the MathFunctions should be compiled and used. Note the use of a variable (EXTRA_LIBS in this case) to collect up any optional libraries to later be linked into the executable. This is a common approach used to keep larger projects with many optional components clean. The corresponding changes to the source code are fairly straight forward and leave us with:

```c
// A simple program that computes the square root of a number
#include <stdio.h>
#include <math.h>
#include "TutorialConfig.h"

#ifdef USE_MYMATH
#include "MathFunctions.h"
#endif

int main (int argc, char *argv[])
{
  if (argc < 2)
    {
    fprintf(stdout,"%s Version %d.%d\n", argv[0],
            Tutorial_VERSION_MAJOR,
            Tutorial_VERSION_MINOR);
    fprintf(stdout,"Usage: %s number\n",argv[0]);
    return 1;
    }

  double inputValue = atof(argv[1]);

#ifdef USE_MYMATH
  double outputValue = mysqrt(inputValue);
#else
  double outputValue = sqrt(inputValue);
#endif

  fprintf(stdout,"The square root of %g is %g\n",
          inputValue, outputValue);
  return 0;
}
```

In the source code we make use of `USE_MYMATH` as well. This is provided from CMake to the source code through the `TutorialConfig.h.in` configured file by adding the following line to it:

```
#cmakedefine USE_MYMATH
```

12.3 Installing and Testing (Step 3)

For the next step we will add install rules and testing support to our project. The install rules are fairly straight forward. For the MathFunctions library we setup the library and the header file to be installed by adding the following two lines to MathFunctions' CMakeLists file:

```
install (TARGETS MathFunctions DESTINATION bin)
install (FILES MathFunctions.h DESTINATION include)
```

For the application the following lines are added to the top level CMakeLists file to install the executable and the configured header file:

```
# add the install targets
install (TARGETS Tutorial DESTINATION bin)
install (FILES "${PROJECT_BINARY_DIR}/TutorialConfig.h"
         DESTINATION include)
```

That is all there is to it. At this point you should be able to build the tutorial and then type make install (or build the `INSTALL` target from an IDE) and it will install the appropriate header files, libraries, and executables. The CMake variable `CMAKE_INSTALL_PREFIX` is used to determine the root of where the files will be installed. Adding testing is also a fairly straight forward process. At the end of the top level CMakeLists file we can add a number of basic tests to verify that the application is working correctly.

```
# does the application run
add_test (TutorialRuns Tutorial 25)

# does it sqrt of 25
add_test (TutorialComp25 Tutorial 25)

set_tests_properties (TutorialComp25
  PROPERTIES PASS_REGULAR_EXPRESSION "25 is 5"
  )
```

```
# does it handle negative numbers
add_test (TutorialNegative Tutorial -25)
set_tests_properties (TutorialNegative
  PROPERTIES PASS_REGULAR_EXPRESSION "-25 is 0"
  )

# does it handle small numbers
add_test (TutorialSmall Tutorial 0.0001)
set_tests_properties (TutorialSmall
  PROPERTIES PASS_REGULAR_EXPRESSION "0.0001 is 0.01"
  )

# does the usage message work?
add_test (TutorialUsage Tutorial)
set_tests_properties (TutorialUsage
  PROPERTIES
  PASS_REGULAR_EXPRESSION "Usage:.*number"
  )
```

The first test simply verifies that the application runs, does not segfault or otherwise crash, and has a zero return value. This is the basic form of a ctest test. The next few tests all make use of the PASS_REGULAR_EXPRESSION test property to verify that the output of the test contains certain strings. In this case verifying that the computed square root is what it should be and that the usage message is printed when an incorrect number of arguments are provided. If you wanted to add a lot of tests to test different input values you might consider creating a macro like the following:

```
#define a macro to simplify adding tests
macro (do_test arg result)
  add_test (TutorialComp${arg} Tutorial ${arg})
  set_tests_properties (TutorialComp${arg}
    PROPERTIES PASS_REGULAR_EXPRESSION ${result}
    )
endmacro (do_test)

# do a bunch of result based tests
do_test (25 "25 is 5")
do_test (-25 "-25 is 0")
do_test (0.0001 "0.0001 is 0.01")
```

For each invocation of do_test, another test is added to the project with a name, input, and results based on the passed arguments.

12.4 Adding System Introspection (Step 4)

Next let us consider adding some code to our project that depends on features the target platform may not have. For this example we will add some code that depends on whether or not the target platform has the `log` and `exp` functions. Of course most every platform has these functions but for this tutorial assume that they are less common. If the platform has `log` then we will use that to compute the square root in the `mysqrt` function. We first test for the availability of these functions using the CheckFunctionExists.cmake macro in the top level CMakeLists file as follows:

```
# does this system provide the log and exp functions?
include (CheckFunctionExists.cmake)
check_function_exists (log HAVE_LOG)
check_function_exists (exp HAVE_EXP)
```

Next we modify the `TutorialConfig.h.in` to define those values if CMake found them on the platform as follows:

```
// does the platform provide exp and log functions?
#cmakedefine HAVE_LOG
#cmakedefine HAVE_EXP
```

It is important that the tests for `log` and `exp` are done before the `configure_file` command for `TutorialConfig.h`. The `configure_file` command immediately configures the file using the current settings in CMake. Finally in the `mysqrt` function we can provide an alternate implementation based on `log` and `exp` if they are available on the system using the following code:

```
// if we have both log and exp then use them
#if defined (HAVE_LOG) && defined (HAVE_EXP)
  result = exp(log(x)*0.5);
#else // otherwise use an iterative approach
  . . .
```

12.5 Adding a Generated File and Generator (Step 5)

In this section we will show how you can add a generated source file into the build process of an application. For this example we will create a table of precomputed square roots as part of the build process and then compile that table into our application. To accomplish this we first need a program that will generate the table. In the MathFunctions subdirectory a new source file named `MakeTable.cxx` will do just that.

```
// A simple program that builds a sqrt table
#include <stdio.h>
#include <math.h>

int main (int argc, char *argv[])
{
  int i;
  double result;

  // make sure we have enough arguments
  if (argc < 2)
    {
    return 1;
    }

  // open the output file
  FILE *fout = fopen(argv[1],"w");
  if (!fout)
    {
    return 1;
    }

  // crate a source file with a table of square roots
  fprintf(fout,"double sqrtTable[] = {\n");
  for (i = 0; i < 10; ++i)
    {
    result = sqrt(static_cast<double>(i));
    fprintf(fout,"%g,\n",result);
    }

  // close the table with a zero
  fprintf(fout,"0};\n");
  fclose(fout);
  return 0;
}
```

Note that the table is produced as valid C++ code and that the name of the file to write the output to is passed in as an argument. The next step is to add the appropriate commands to MathFunctions' CMakeLists file to build the MakeTable executable and then run it as part of the build process. There are a few commands to do this as shown below.

```
# first we add the exetuable that generates the table
add_executable(MakeTable MakeTable.cxx)

# add the command to generate the source code
add_custom_command (
  OUTPUT ${CMAKE_CURRENT_BINARY_DIR}/Table.h
  DEPENDS MakeTable
  COMMAND MakeTable
  ARGS ${CMAKE_CURRENT_BINARY_DIR}/Table.h
  )

set_source_files_properties (
  mysqrt.cxx PROPERTIES
  OBJECT_DEPENDS ${CMAKE_CURRENT_BINARY_DIR}/Table.h
  )

# add the binary tree directory to the search path for
# include files
include_directories( ${CMAKE_CURRENT_BINARY_DIR} )
```

First the executable for `MakeTable` is added as any other executable would be added. Then we add a custom command that specifies how to produce `Table.h` by running MakeTable. Next we have to let CMake know that `mysqrt.cxx` does depend on the generated file `Table.h`. This is done with by setting the `OBJECT_DEPENDS` on `mysqrt.cxx`. Finally we have to add the current binary directory to the list of include directories so that `Table.h` can be found and included by `mysqrt.cxx`.

When this project is built it will first build the `MakeTable` executable. It will then run `MakeTable` to produce `Table.h`. Then it will compile `mysqrt.cxx` which includes `Table.h` to produce the MathFunctions library.

At this point the top level CMakeLists file with all the features we have added looks like the following:

```
project (Tutorial)

# The version number.
set (Tutorial_VERSION_MAJOR 1)
set (Tutorial_VERSION_MINOR 0)

# does this system provide the log and exp functions?
include (${CMAKE_ROOT}/Modules/CheckFunctionExists.cmake)
```

```
check_function_exists (log HAVE_LOG)
check_function_exists (exp HAVE_EXP)

# should we use our own math functions
option(USE_MYMATH
  "Use tutorial provided math implementation" ON)

# configure a header file to pass some of the CMake settings
# to the source code
configure_file (
  "${PROJECT_SOURCE_DIR}/TutorialConfig.h.in"
  "${PROJECT_BINARY_DIR}/TutorialConfig.h"
  )

# add the binary tree to the search path for include files
# so that we will find TutorialConfig.h
include_directories ("${PROJECT_BINARY_DIR}")

# add the MathFunctions library?
if (USE_MYMATH)
  include_directories ("${PROJECT_SOURCE_DIR}/MathFunctions")
  add_subdirectory (MathFunctions)
  set (EXTRA_LIBS ${EXTRA_LIBS} MathFunctions)
endif (USE_MYMATH)

# add the executable
add_executable (Tutorial tutorial.cxx)
target_link_libraries (Tutorial  ${EXTRA_LIBS})

# add the install targets
install (TARGETS Tutorial DESTINATION bin)
install (FILES "${PROJECT_BINARY_DIR}/TutorialConfig.h"
         DESTINATION include)

# does the application run
add_test (TutorialRuns Tutorial 25)

# does the usage message work?
add_test (TutorialUsage Tutorial)
set_tests_properties (TutorialUsage
  PROPERTIES
  PASS_REGULAR_EXPRESSION "Usage:.*number"
  )
```

```
#define a macro to simplify adding tests
macro (do_test arg result)
  add_test (TutorialComp${arg} Tutorial ${arg})
  set_tests_properties (TutorialComp${arg}
    PROPERTIES PASS_REGULAR_EXPRESSION ${result}
    )
endmacro (do_test)

# do a bunch of result based tests
do_test (4 "4 is 2")
do_test (9 "9 is 3")
do_test (5 "5 is 2.236")
do_test (7 "7 is 2.645")
do_test (25 "25 is 5")
do_test (-25 "-25 is 0")
do_test (0.0001 "0.0001 is 0.01")
```

TutorialConfig.h looks like:

```
// the configured options and settings for Tutorial
#define Tutorial_VERSION_MAJOR @Tutorial_VERSION_MAJOR@
#define Tutorial_VERSION_MINOR @Tutorial_VERSION_MINOR@
#cmakedefine USE_MYMATH

// does the platform provide exp and log functions?
#cmakedefine HAVE_LOG
#cmakedefine HAVE_EXP
```

And the CMakeLists file for MathFunctions looks like:

```
# first we add the executable that generates the table
add_executable(MakeTable MakeTable.cxx)


# add the command to generate the source code
add_custom_command (
  OUTPUT ${CMAKE_CURRENT_BINARY_DIR}/Table.h
  DEPENDS MakeTable
  COMMAND MakeTable
  ARGS ${CMAKE_CURRENT_BINARY_DIR}/Table.h
  )

set_source_files_properties (
```

```
  mysqrt.cxx PROPERTIES
  OBJECT_DEPENDS ${CMAKE_CURRENT_BINARY_DIR}/Table.h
  )

# add the binary tree directory to the search path
# for include files
include_directories( ${CMAKE_CURRENT_BINARY_DIR} )

# add the main library
add_library(MathFunctions mysqrt.cxx)

install (TARGETS MathFunctions DESTINATION bin)
install (FILES MathFunctions.h DESTINATION include)
```

12.6 Building an Installer (Step 6)

Next suppose that we want to distribute our project to other people so that they can use it. We want to provide both binary and source distributions on a variety of platforms. This is a little different from the installing we did in section 12.3 where we were installing the binaries that we had built from the source code. In this example we will be building installation packages that support binary installations and package management features as found in cygwin, debian, RPMs etc. To accomplish this we will use CPack to create platform specific installers as described in Chapter 5. Specifically we need to add a few lines to the bottom of our toplevel CMakeLists.txt file.

```
# build a CPack driven installer package
include (InstallRequiredSystemLibraries)
set (CPACK_RESOURCE_FILE_LICENSE
    "${CMAKE_CURRENT_SOURCE_DIR}/License.txt")
set (CPACK_PACKAGE_VERSION_MAJOR "${Tutorial_VERSION_MAJOR}")
set (CPACK_PACKAGE_VERSION_MINOR "${Tutorial_VERSION_MINOR}")
include (CPack)
```

That is all there is to it. We start by including InstallRequiredSystemLibraries. This module will include any runtime libraries that are needed by the project for the current platform. Next we set some CPack variables to where we have stored the license and version information for this project. The version information makes use of the variables we set earlier in this tutorial. Finally we include the CPack module which will use these variables and some other properties of the system you are on to setup an installer.

The next step is to build the project in the usual manner and then run cpack on it. To build a binary distribution you would run:

```
cpack -C CPackConfig.cmake
```

To create a source distribution you would type

```
Cpack -C CPackSourceConfig.cmake
```

12.7 Adding Support for a Dashboard (Step 7)

Adding support for submitting our test results to a dashboard is very easy. We already defined a number of tests for our project in the earlier steps of this tutorial. We just have to run those tests and submit them to a dashboard. To include support for dashboards we include the CTest module in our toplevel CMakeLists file.

```
# enable dashboard scripting
include (CTest)
```

We also create a CTestConfig.cmake file where we specify the name of this project for the dashboard.

```
set (CTEST_PROJECT_NAME "Tutorial")
```

CTest will read in this file when it runs. Now to create a simple dashboard you can run CMake on your project, change directory to the binary tree, and then run ctest –D Experimental. The results of your dashboard will be uploaded to Kitware's public dashboard at:

```
http://public.kitware.com/Public/Dashboard/MostRecentResults-
Nightly/Dashboard.html
```

Appendix A - Variables

When CMake is run on a project, it automatically defines many variables. These variables can be used by your CMakeLists files to control what files are compiled, how header files are configured and many other aspects of the build process. This section describes each of those variables and what they represent. The list of variables is broken down according to when they are defined. If you wish to see the list of variables that are defined by CMake when running your CMakeLists file you can add the following commands to the end of your CMakeLists file. This code will create a file called `AllVariables.txt` in the binary tree that contains this information.

```
file(WRITE ${CMAKE_CURRENT_BINARY_DIR}/AllVariables.txt "")
get_cmake_property(VARS VARIABLES)
foreach (var ${VARS})
  file (APPEND ${CMAKE_CURRENT_BINARY_DIR}/AllVariables.txt
          "${var} \"${${var}}\"\n")
endforeach (var ${VARS})
```

Variables That Change Behavior

- **BUILD_SHARED_LIBS**: Global flag to cause add_library to create shared libraries if on.

  If present and true, this will cause all libraries to be built shared unless the library was explicitly added as a static library. This variable is often added to projects as an

OPTION so that each user of a project can decide if they want to build the project using shared or static libraries.

- **CMAKE_BACKWARDS_COMPATIBILITY**: Version of cmake required to build project

  From the point of view of backwards compatibility, this specifies what version of CMake should be supported. By default this value is the version number of CMake that you are running. You can set this to an older version of CMake to support deprecated commands of CMake in projects that were written to use older versions of CMake. This can be set by the user or set at the beginning of a CMakeLists file.

- **CMAKE_BUILD_TYPE**: Specifies the build type for make based generators.

  This specifies what build type will be built in this tree. Possible values are empty, Debug, Release, RelWithDebInfo and MinSizeRel. This variable is only supported for make based generators. If this variable is supported, then CMake will also provide initial values for the variables with the name CMAKE_C_FLAGS_[Debug|Release|RelWithDebInfo|MinSizeRel]. For example, if CMAKE_BUILD_TYPE is Debug, then CMAKE_C_FLAGS_DEBUG will be added to the CMAKE_C_FLAGS.

- **CMAKE_CONFIGURATION_TYPES**: Specifies the available build types.

  This specifies what build types will be available such as Debug, Release, RelWithDebInfo etc. This has reasonable defaults on most platforms. But can be extended to provide other build types. See also CMAKE_BUILD_TYPE.

- **CMAKE_CROSSCOMPILING**: Is CMake currently cross compiling.

  This variable will be set to true by CMake if CMake is cross compiling. Specifically if the build platform is different from the target platform.

- **CMAKE_FIND_LIBRARY_PREFIXES**: Prefixes to prepend when looking for libraries.

  This specifies what prefixes to add to library names when the find_library command looks for libraries. On UNIX systems this is typically lib, meaning that when trying to find the foo library it will look for libfoo.

- **CMAKE_FIND_LIBRARY_SUFFIXES**: Suffixes to append when looking for libraries.

This specifies what suffixes to add to library names when the find_library command looks for libraries. On Windows systems this is typically .lib and .dll, meaning that when trying to find the foo library it will look for foo.dll etc.

- **CMAKE_INSTALL_PREFIX**: Install directory used by install.

If "make install" is invoked or INSTALL is built, this directory is pre-pended onto all install directories. This variable defaults to /usr/local on UNIX and c:/Program Files on Windows.

- **CMAKE_MFC_FLAG**: Tell cmake to use MFC for an executable or dll.

This can be set in a CMakeLists.txt file and will enable MFC in the application. It should be set to 1 for static the static MFC library, and 2 for the shared MFC library. This is used in visual studio 6 and 7 project files. The CMakeSetup dialog uses MFC and the CMakeLists.txt looks like this:

```
add_definitions(-D_AFXDLL)
set(CMAKE_MFC_FLAG 2)
add_executable(CMakeSetup WIN32 ${SRCS})
```

- **CMAKE_MODULE_PATH**: Path to look for cmake modules to load.

Specifies a path to override the default search path for CMake modules. For example include commands will look in this path first for modules to include.

- **CMAKE_NOT_USING_CONFIG_FLAGS**: Skip _BUILD_TYPE flags if true.

This is an internal flag used by the generators in CMake to tell CMake to skip the _BUILD_TYPE flags.

- **CMAKE_USER_MAKE_RULES_OVERRIDE**: Specify a file that can change the build rule variables.

If this variable is set, it should to point to a CMakeLists.txt file that will be read in by CMake after all the system settings have been set, but before they have been used. This would allow you to override any variables that need to be changed for some special project.

Variables That Describe the System

- **APPLE**: True if running on Mac OSX.

  Set to true on Mac OSX.

- **BORLAND**: True of the Borland compiler is being used.

  This is set to true if the Borland compiler is being used.

- **CMAKE_CL_64**: Using the 64 bit compiler from Microsoft

  Set to true when using the 64 bit cl compiler from Microsoft.

- **CMAKE_COMPILER_2005**: Using the Visual Studio 2005 compiler from Microsoft

  Set to true when using the Visual Studio 2005 compiler from Microsoft.

- **CMAKE_HOST_APPLE**: True for Apple OSXoperating systems.

  Set to true when the host system is Apple OSX.

- **CMAKE_HOST_SYSTEM**: Name of system cmake is being run on.

  The same as CMAKE_SYSTEM but for the host system instead of the target system when cross compiling.

- **CMAKE_HOST_SYSTEM_NAME**: Name of the OS CMake is running on.

  The same as CMAKE_SYSTEM_NAME but for the host system instead of the target system when cross compiling.

- **CMAKE_HOST_SYSTEM_PROCESSOR**: The name of the CPU CMake is running on.

  The same as CMAKE_SYSTEM_PROCESSOR but for the host system instead of the target system when cross compiling.

- **CMAKE_HOST_SYSTEM_VERSION**: OS version CMake is running on.

The same as CMAKE_SYSTEM_VERSION but for the host system instead of the target system when cross compiling.

- **CMAKE_HOST_UNIX**: True for UNIX and UNIX like operating systems.

  Set to true when the host system is UNIX or UNIX like (i.e. APPLE and CYGWIN).

- **CMAKE_HOST_WIN32**: True on windows systems, including win64.

  Set to true when the host system is Windows and on cygwin.

- **CMAKE_SYSTEM**: Name of system cmake is compiling for.

  This variable is the composite of CMAKE_SYSTEM_NAMEand CMAKE_SYSTEM_VERSION, like this ${CMAKE_SYSTEM_NAME}-${CMAKE_SYSTEM_VERSION}. If CMAKE_SYSTEM_VERSION is not set, then CMAKE_SYSTEM is the same as CMAKE_SYSTEM_NAME.

- **CMAKE_SYSTEM_NAME**: Name of the OS CMake is building for.

  This is the name of the operating system on which CMake is targeting. On systems that have the uname command, this variable is set to the output of uname -s. Linux, Windows, and Darwin for Mac OSX are the values found on the big three operating systems.

- **CMAKE_SYSTEM_PROCESSOR**: The name of the CPU CMake is building for.

  On systems that support uname, this variable is set to the output of uname -p, on windows it is set to the value of the environment variable PROCESSOR_ARCHITECTURE

- **CMAKE_SYSTEM_VERSION**: OS version CMake is building for.

  A numeric version string for the system, on systems that support uname, this variable is set to the output of uname -r. On other systems this is set to major-minor version numbers.

- **CYGWIN**: True for cygwin.

  Set to true when using CYGWIN.

- **MSVC**: True when using Microsoft Visual C

  Set to true when the compiler is some version of Microsoft Visual C.

- **MSVC80**: True when using Microsoft Visual C 8.0

  Set to true when the compiler is version 8.0 of Microsoft Visual C.

- **MSVC_IDE**: True when using the Microsoft Visual C IDE

  Set to true when the target platform is the Microsoft Visual C IDE, as opposed to the command line compiler.

- **MSVC_VERSION**: The version of Microsoft Visual C/C++ being used if any.

  The version of Microsoft Visual C/C++ being used if any. For example 1300 is MSVC 6.0.

- **UNIX**: True for UNIX and UNIX like operating systems.

  Set to true when the target system is UNIX or UNIX like (i.e. APPLE and CYGWIN).

- **WIN32**: True on windows systems, including win64.

  Set to true when the target system is Windows and on cygwin.

Variables for Languages

- **CMAKE_<LANG>_COMPILER**: The full path to the compiler for LANG.

  This is the command that will be used as the <LANG> compiler. Once set, you can not change this variable.

- **CMAKE_<LANG>_COMPILER_ID**: An internal variable subject to change.

  This is used in determining the compiler and is subject to change.

- **CMAKE_<LANG>_COMPILE_OBJECT**: Rule variable to compile a single object file.

This is a rule variable that tells CMake how to compile a single object file for for the language <LANG>.

- **CMAKE_<LANG>_CREATE_SHARED_LIBRARY**: Rule variable to create a shared library.

  This is a rule variable that tells CMake how to create a shared library for the language <LANG>.

- **CMAKE_<LANG>_CREATE_SHARED_MODULE**: Rule variable to create a shared module.

  This is a rule variable that tells CMake how to create a shared library for the language <LANG>.

- **CMAKE_<LANG>_CREATE_STATIC_LIBRARY**: Rule variable to create a static library.

  This is a rule variable that tells CMake how to create a static library for the language <LANG>.

- **CMAKE_<LANG>_FLAGS_DEBUG**: Flags for Debug build type or configuration.

  <LANG> flags used when CMAKE_BUILD_TYPE is Debug.

- **CMAKE_<LANG>_FLAGS_MINSIZEREL**: Flags for MinSizeRel build type or configuration.

  <LANG> flags used when CMAKE_BUILD_TYPE is MinSizeRel.Short for minimum size release.

- **CMAKE_<LANG>_FLAGS_RELEASE**: Flags for Release build type or configuration.

  <LANG> flags used when CMAKE_BUILD_TYPE is Release

- **CMAKE_<LANG>_FLAGS_RELWITHDEBINFO**: Flags for RelWithDebInfo type or configuration.

  <LANG> flags used when CMAKE_BUILD_TYPE is RelWithDebInfo. Short for Release With Debug Information.

- **CMAKE_<LANG>_IGNORE_EXTENSIONS**: File extensions that should be ignored by the build.

  This is a list of file extensions that may be part of a project for a given language but are not compiled.

- **CMAKE_<LANG>_LINKER_PREFERENCE**: Determine if a language should be used for linking.

  If this is "Preferred" then if there is a mixed language shared library or executable, then this languages linker command will be used.

- **CMAKE_<LANG>_LINK_EXECUTABLE** : Rule variable to link and executable.

  Rule variable to link and executable for the given language.

- **CMAKE_<LANG>_OUTPUT_EXTENSION**: Extension for the output of a compile for a single file.

  This is the extension for an object file for the given <LANG>. For example .obj for C on Windows.

- **CMAKE_<LANG>_PLATFORM_ID**: An internal variable subject to change.

  This is used in determining the platform and is subject to change.

- **CMAKE_<LANG>_SOURCE_FILE_EXTENSIONS**: Extensions of source files for the given language.

  This is the list of extensions for a given languages source files.

- **CMAKE_COMPILER_IS_GNU<LANG>**: True if the compiler is GNU.

  If the selected <LANG> compiler is the GNU compiler then this is TRUE, if not it is FALSE.

- **CMAKE_USER_MAKE_RULES_OVERRIDE_<LANG>**: Specify a file that can change the build rule variables.

  If this variable is set, it should to point to a CMakeLists.txt file that will be read in by CMake after all the system settings have been set, but before they have been used.

This would allow you to override any variables that need to be changed for some language.

Variables that Control the Build

- **CMAKE_ARCHIVE_OUTPUT_DIRECTORY**: Where to put all the ARCHIVE targets when built.

  This variable is used to initialize the ARCHIVE_OUTPUT_DIRECTORY property on all the targets. See that target property for additional information.

- **CMAKE_BUILD_WITH_INSTALL_RPATH**: Use the install path for the RPATH

  Normally CMake uses the build tree for the RPATH when building executables etc on systems that use RPATH. When the software is installed the executables etc are relinked by CMake to have the install RPATH. If this variable is set to true then the software is always built with the install path for the RPATH and does not need to be relinked when installed.

- **CMAKE_DEBUG_POSTFIX**: A postfix to add to targets when build as debug.

  This variable is used to initialize the DEBUG_POSTFIX property on all the targets. If set the postfix will be appended to any targets built when the configuration is Debug.

- **CMAKE_EXE_LINKER_FLAGS**: Linker flags used to create executables.

  Flags used by the linker when creating an executable.

- **CMAKE_EXE_LINKER_FLAGS_[CMAKE_BUILD_TYPE]**: Flag used when linking an executable.

  Same as CMAKE_C_FLAGS_* but used by the linker when creating executables.

- **CMAKE_INSTALL_NAME_DIR**: Mac OSX directory name for installed targets.

  CMAKE_INSTALL_NAME_DIR is used to initialize the INSTALL_NAME_DIR property on all targets. See that target property for more information.

- **CMAKE_INSTALL_RPATH**: The rpath to use for installed targets.

A semicolon-separated list specifying the rpath to use in installed targets (for platforms that support it). This is used to initialize the target property INSTALL_RPATH for all targets.

- **CMAKE_INSTALL_RPATH_USE_LINK_PATH**: Add paths to linker search and installed rpath.

  CMAKE_INSTALL_RPATH_USE_LINK_PATH is a boolean that if set to true will append directories in the linker search path and outside the project to the INSTALL_RPATH. This is used to initialize the target property INSTALL_RPATH_USE_LINK_PATH for all targets.

- **CMAKE_LIBRARY_OUTPUT_DIRECTORY**: Where to put all the LIBRARY targets when built.

  This variable is used to initialize the LIBRARY_OUTPUT_DIRECTORY property on all the targets. See that target property for additional information.

- **CMAKE_LIBRARY_PATH_FLAG**: The flag used to add a library search path to a compiler.

  The flag used to specify a library directory to the compiler. On most compilers this is "-L".

- **CMAKE_LINK_DEF_FILE_FLAG** : Linker flag used to specify a .def file for dll creation.

  The flag used to add a .def file when creating a dll on Windows, this is only defined on Windows.

- **CMAKE_LINK_LIBRARY_FLAG**: Flag used to link a library into an executable.

  The flag used to specify a library to link to an executable. On most compilers this is "-l".

- **CMAKE_RUNTIME_OUTPUT_DIRECTORY**: Where to put all the RUNTIME targets when built.

  This variable is used to initialize the RUNTIME_OUTPUT_DIRECTORY property on all the targets. See that target property for additional information.

- **CMAKE_SKIP_BUILD_RPATH**: Do not include RPATHs in the build tree.

Normally CMake uses the build tree for the RPATH when building executables etc on systems that use RPATH. When the software is installed the executables etc are relinked by CMake to have the install RPATH. If this variable is set to true then the software is always built with no RPATH.

- **CMAKE_USE_RELATIVE_PATHS**: Use relative paths (May not work!).

  If this is set to TRUE, then the CMake will use relative paths between the source and binary tree. This option does not work for more complicated projects, and relative paths are used when possible. In general, it is not possible to move CMake generated makefiles to a different location regardless of the value of this variable.

- **EXECUTABLE_OUTPUT_PATH**: Location for all executables in a project.

  If set, this is the directory where all executables built during the build process will be placed.

- **LIBRARY_OUTPUT_PATH**: Location for all libraries in a project.

  If set, this is the directory where all the libraries built during the build process will be placed.

Variables that Provide Information

variables defined by cmake, that give information about the project, and cmake

- **CMAKE_AR**: Name of archiving tool for static libraries.

  This specifies name of the program that creates archive or static libraries.

- **CMAKE_BINARY_DIR**: The path to the top level of the build tree.

  This is the full path to the top level of the current CMake build tree. For an in-source build, this would be the same as CMAKE_SOURCE_DIR.

- **CMAKE_BUILD_TOOL**: Tool used for the acutal build process.

  This variable is set to the program that will be needed to build the output of CMake. If the generator selected was Visual Studio 6, the CMAKE_MAKE_PROGRAM will be set to msdev, for Unix makefiles it will be set to make or gmake, and for Visual

Studio 7 it set to devenv. For Nmake Makefiles the value is nmake. This can be useful for adding special flags and commands based on the final build environment.

- **CMAKE_CACHEFILE_DIR**: The directory with the CMakeCache.txt file.

  This is the full path to the directory that has the CMakeCache.txt file in it. This is the same as CMAKE_BINARY_DIR.

- **CMAKE_CACHE_MAJOR_VERSION**: Major version of CMake used to create the CMakeCache.txt file

  This is stores the major version of CMake used to write a CMake cache file. It is only different when a different version of CMake is run on a previously created cache file.

- **CMAKE_CACHE_MINOR_VERSION**: Minor version of CMake used to create the CMakeCache.txt file

  This is stores the minor version of CMake used to write a CMake cache file. It is only different when a different version of CMake is run on a previously created cache file.

- **CMAKE_CACHE_RELEASE_VERSION**: Release version of CMake used to create the CMakeCache.txt file

  This is stores the release version of CMake used to write a CMake cache file. It is only different when a different version of CMake is run on a previously created cache file.

- **CMAKE_CFG_INTDIR**: Build time configuration directory for project.

  This is a variable that is used to provide developers access to the intermediate directory used by Visual Studio IDE projects. For example, if building Debug all executables and libraries end up in a Debug directory. On UNIX systems this variable is set to ".". However, with Visual Studio this variable is set to $(IntDir). $(IntDir) is expanded by the IDE only. So this variable should only be used in custom commands that will be run during the build process. This variable should not be used directly in a CMake command. CMake has no way of knowing if Debug or Release will be picked by the IDE for a build type. If a program needs to know the directory it was built in, it can use CMAKE_INTDIR. CMAKE_INTDIR is a C/C++ preprocessor macro that is defined on the command line of the compiler. If it has a value, it will be the intermediate directory used to build the file. This way an executable or a library can find files that are located in the build directory.

- **CMAKE_COMMAND**: The full path to the cmake executable.

  This is the full path to the CMake executable cmake which is useful from custom commands that want to use the cmake -E option for portable system commands. (e.g. /usr/local/bin/cmake

- **CMAKE_CTEST_COMMAND**: Full path to ctest command installed with cmake.

  This is the full path to the CTest executable ctest which is useful from custom commands that want to use the cmake -E option for portable system commands.

- **CMAKE_CURRENT_BINARY_DIR**: The path to the binary directory currently being processed.

  This the full path to the build directory that is currently being processed by cmake. Each directory added by add_subdirectory will create a binary directory in the build tree, and as it is being processed this variable will be set. For in-source builds this is the current source directory being processed.

- **CMAKE_CURRENT_LIST_FILE**: Full path to the listfile currently being processed.

  As CMake processes the listfiles in your project this variable will always be set to the one currently being processed. See also CMAKE_PARENT_LIST_FILE.

- **CMAKE_CURRENT_LIST_LINE**: The line number of the current file being processed.

  This is the line number of the file currently being processed by cmake.

- **CMAKE_CURRENT_SOURCE_DIR**: The path to the source directory currently being processed.

  This the full path to the source directory that is currently being processed by cmake.

- **CMAKE_DL_LIBS**: Name of library containing dlopen and dlcose.

  The name of the library that has dlopen and dlclose in it, usually -ldl on most UNIX machines.

- **CMAKE_EDIT_COMMAND**: Full path to CMakeSetup or ccmake.

This is the full path to the CMake executable that can graphically edit the cache. For example, CMakeSetup, ccmake, or cmake -i.

- **CMAKE_EXECUTABLE_SUFFIX**: The suffix for executables on this platform.

  The suffix to use for the end of an executable if any, .exe on Windows.

- **CMAKE_GENERATOR**: The generator used to build the project.

  The name of the generator that is being used to generate the build files. (e.g. "Unix Makefiles", "Visual Studio 6", etc.)

- **CMAKE_HOME_DIRECTORY**: Path to top of source tree.

  This is the path to the top level of the source tree.

- **CMAKE_IMPORT_LIBRARY_PREFIX**: The prefix for import libraries that you link to.

  The prefix to use for the name of an import library if used on this platform.

- **CMAKE_IMPORT_LIBRARY_SUFFIX**: The suffix for import libraries that you link to.

  The suffix to use for the end of an import library if used onthis platform.

- **CMAKE_LINK_LIBRARY_SUFFIX**: The suffix for libraries that you link to.

  The suffix to use for the end of a library, .lib on Windows.

- **CMAKE_MAJOR_VERSION**: The Major version of cmake (i.e. the 2 in 2.X.X)

  This specifies the major version of the CMake executable being run.

- **CMAKE_MAKE_PROGRAM**: See CMAKE_BUILD_TOOL.

  This variable is around for backwards compatibility, see CMAKE_BUILD_TOOL.

- **CMAKE_MINOR_VERSION**: The Minor version of cmake (i.e. the 4 in X.4.X).

  This specifies the minor version of the CMake executable being run.

- **CMAKE_PARENT_LIST_FILE**: Full path to the parent listfile of the one currently being processed.

  As CMake processes the listfiles in your project this variable will always be set to the listfile that included or somehow invoked the one currently being processed. See also CMAKE_CURRENT_LIST_FILE.

- **CMAKE_PROJECT_NAME**: The name of the current project.

  This specifies name of the current project from the closest inherited PROJECT command.

- **CMAKE_RANLIB**: Name of randomizing tool for static libraries.

  This specifies name of the program that randomizes libraries on UNIX, not used on Windows, but may be present.

- **CMAKE_ROOT**: Install directory for running cmake.

  This is the install root for the running CMake and the Modules directory can be found here. This is commonly used in this format: ${CMAKE_ROOT}/Modules

- **CMAKE_SHARED_LIBRARY_PREFIX**: The prefix for shared libraries that you link to.

  The prefix to use for the name of a shared library, lib on UNIX.

- **CMAKE_SHARED_LIBRARY_SUFFIX**: The suffix for shared libraries that you link to.

  The suffix to use for the end of a shared library, .dll on Windows.

- **CMAKE_SHARED_MODULE_PREFIX**: The prefix for loadable modules that you link to.

  The prefix to use for the name of a loadable module on this platform.

- **CMAKE_SHARED_MODULE_SUFFIX**: The suffix for shared libraries that you link to.

  The suffix to use for the end of a loadable module on this platform

- **CMAKE_SIZEOF_VOID_P**: Size of a void pointer.

  This is set to the size of a pointer on the machine, and is determined by a try compile. If a 64 bit size is found, then the library search path is modified to look for 64 bit libraries first.

- **CMAKE_SKIP_RPATH**: If true, do not add run time path information.

  If this is set to TRUE, then the rpath information is not added to compiled executables. The defaultis to add rpath information if the platform supports it.This allows for easy running from the build tree.

- **CMAKE_SOURCE_DIR**: The path to the top level of the source tree.

  This is the full path to the top level of the current CMake source tree. For an in-source build, this would be the same as CMAKE_BINARY_DIR.

- **CMAKE_STANDARD_LIBRARIES**: Libraries linked into every executable and shared library.

  This is the list of libraries that are linked into all executables and libraries.

- **CMAKE_STATIC_LIBRARY_PREFIX**: The prefix for static libraries that you link to.

  The prefix to use for the name of a static library, lib on UNIX.

- **CMAKE_STATIC_LIBRARY_SUFFIX**: The suffix for static libraries that you link to.

  The suffix to use for the end of a static library, .lib on Windows.

- **CMAKE_USING_VC_FREE_TOOLS**: True if free visual studio tools being used.

  This is set to true if the compiler is Visual Studio free tools.

- **CMAKE_VERBOSE_MAKEFILE**: Create verbose makefiles if on.

  This variable defaults to false. You can set this variable to true to make CMake produce verbose makefiles that show each command line as it is used.

- **PROJECT_BINARY_DIR**: Full path to build directory for project.

  This is the binary directory of the most recent PROJECT command.

- **PROJECT_NAME**: Name of the project given to the project command.

  This is the name given to the most recent PROJECT command.

- **PROJECT_SOURCE_DIR**: Top level source directory for the current project.

  This is the source directory of the most recent PROJECT command.

- **[Project name]_BINARY_DIR**: Top level binary directory for the named project.

  A variable is created with the name used in the PROJECT command, and is the binary directory for the project. This can be useful when SUBDIR is used to connect several projects.

- **[Project name]_SOURCE_DIR**: Top level source directory for the named project.

  A variable is created with the name used in the PROJECT command, and is the source directory for the project. This can be useful when add_subdirectory is used to connect several projects.

Variables In CMakeBackwardCompatibilityC.cmake

Versions of CMake prior to version 1.4 always defined a number of variables with information about the current platform. In CMake versions 1.4 there are more powerful modules that can be used to determine these values. As a convenience these values can be determined in later versions of CMake by including the CMakeBackwardCompatibilityC.cmake module.

CMAKE_SIZEOF_INT

   Size of an int data type in bytes

CMAKE_SIZEOF_LONG

   Size of long data type in bytes

CMAKE_SIZEOF_VOID_P

> Size of void* data type in bytes

CMAKE_SIZEOF_CHAR

> Size of char data type in bytes

CMAKE_SIZEOF_SHORT

> Size of short data type in bytes

CMAKE_SIZEOF_FLOAT

> Size of float data type in bytes

CMAKE_SIZEOF_DOUBLE

> Size of double data type in bytes

CMAKE_HAVE_LIMITS_H

> True if the system header files limits.h exists on the machine.

CMAKE_HAVE_UNISTD_H

> True if the system header files unistd.h exists on the machine.

CMAKE_HAVE_SYS_PRCTL_H

> True if the system header file <sys/prctl.h> exists on the machine.

CMAKE_HAVE_PTHREAD_H

> True if the system header file pthreads.h exists on the machine.

CMAKE_WORDS_BIGENDIAN

> True if the byte order of the machine is big-endian.

CMAKE_X_CFLAGS

> Compile flags to be used with X11 programs, includes –I and –D options.

CMAKE_X_LIBS

> Libraries needed to link X11 programs.

CMAKE_HAS_X

> True if the system has X11.

CMAKE_THREAD_LIBS

> The libraries needed to link thread support into an application.

CMAKE_USE_PTHREADS

> True if the system has pthreads.

CMAKE_USE_WIN32_THREADS

> True if the system is win32 and win32 threads are in the CMAKE_THREAD_LIBS variable.

CMAKE_HP_PTHREADS

> True if the system should use HP threads.

CMAKE_USE_SPROC

> True if the system should use sproc.

Variables in CMakeBackwardCompatibilityCXX.cmake

Similar to the CMakeBackwardsCompatibilityC.cmake variables, these variables were defined in CMake versions prior to 1.4 and can still be set by including CMakeBackwardCompatibilityCXX.cmake.

CMAKE_ANSI_CXXFLAGS

> flags that when given to a c++ compiler make it compile "ANSI" c++. For example, on SGI, -LANG:std is the value for this variable.

CMAKE_NO_ANSI_STRING_STREAM

> The compiler does not support the ANSI stringstream class.

CMAKE_NO_STD_NAMESPACE

> The compiler does not support the std namespace.

CMAKE_NO_ANSI_FOR_SCOPE

> The compiler does not support the ANSI scoping of variables in for loops for C++.

CMAKE_NO_EXPLICIT_TEMPLATE_INSTANTIATION

> the compiler does not support the explicit form of template instantiation in C++.

System Environment Variables That Affect CMake

Some environment variables, if set before CMake is run, will be used to initialize cache values for the CMake. There names and functions are as follows;

CC

> The C compiler to use

CFLAGS

> If set this will initialize the CMAKE_C_FLAGS variable.

CXX

> The C++ compiler to use.

FC

> The Fortran compiler to use.

JAVA_COMPILER

> The Java compiler to use.

CXXFLAGS

> If set this will initialize the CMAKE_CXX_FLAGS variable.

LDFLAGS

> Linker flags used at link time for executables and shared libraries.

Appendix B – CMake Command Reference

CMake Command-Line Options

```
cmake [options] <path-to-source>
cmake [options] <path-to-existing-build>
```

The "cmake" executable is the CMake command-line interface. It may be used to configure projects in scripts. Project configuration settings may be specified on the command line with the -D option. The -i option will cause cmake to interactively prompt for such settings.

- **−C <initial-cache>**: Pre-load a script to populate the cache.

  When cmake is first run in an empty build tree, it creates a CMakeCache.txt file and populates it with customizable settings for the project. This option may be used to specify a file from which to load cache entries before the first pass through the project's cmake listfiles. The loaded entries take priority over the project's default values. The given file should be a CMake script containing set commands that use the CACHE option, not a cache-format file.

- **−D <var>:<type>=<value>**: Create a cmake cache entry.

When cmake is first run in an empty build tree, it creates a CMakeCache.txt file and populates it with customizable settings for the project. This option may be used to specify a setting that takes priority over the project's default value. The option may be repeated for as many cache entries as desired.

- **-U <globbing_expr>**: Remove matching entries from CMake cache.

This option may be used to remove one or more variables from the CMakeCache.txt file, globbing expressions using * and ? are supported. The option may be repeated for as many cache entries as desired. Use with care, you can break your CMakeCache.txt file.

- **-G <generator-name>**: Specify a makefile generator.

CMake may support multiple native build systems on certain platforms. A makefile generator is responsible for generating a particular build system. Possible generator names are specified in the Generators section.

- **-E**: CMake command mode.

For true platform independence, CMake provides a list of commands that can be used on all systems. Run with -E help for the usage information.

- **-i**: Run in wizard mode.

Wizard mode runs cmake interactively without a GUI. The user is prompted to answer questions about the project configuration. The answers are used to set cmake cache values.

- **-L[A][H]**: List non-advanced cached variables.

List cache variables will run CMake and list all the variables from the CMake cache that are not marked as INTERNAL or ADVANCED. This will effectively display current CMake settings, which can be then changed with -D option. Changing some of the variable may result in more variables being created. If A is specified, then it will display also advanced variables. If H is specified, it will also display help for each variable.

- **-N**: View mode only.

Only load the cache. Do not actually run configure and generate steps.

- **-P <file>**: Process script mode.

  Process the given cmake file as a script written in the CMake language. No configure or generate step is performed and the cache is not modified. If variables are defined using -D, this must be done before the -P argument.

- **--graphviz=[file]**: Generate graphviz of dependencies.

  Generate a graphviz input file that will contain all the library and executable dependencies in the project.

- **--system-information [file]**: Dump information about this system.

  Dump a wide range of information about the current system. If run from the top of a binary tree for a CMake project it will dump additional information such as the cache, log files etc.

- **--debug-trycompile**: Do not delete the try compile directories..

  Do not delete the files and directories created for try_compile calls. This is useful in debugging failed try_compiles.

- **--debug-output**: Put cmake in a debug mode.

  Print extra stuff during the cmake run like stack traces with message(send_error) calls.

- **--help-command cmd [file]**: Print help for a single command and exit.

  Full documentation specific to the given command is displayed. If a file is specified, the documentation is written into and the output format is determined depending on the filename suffix. Supported are man page, HTML and plain text.

- **--help-command-list [file]**: List available listfile commands and exit.

  The list contains all commands for which help may be obtained by using the --help-command argument followed by a command name. If a file is specified, the documentation is written into and the output format is determined depending on the filename suffix. Supported are man page, HTML and plain text.

- **--help-commands [file]**: Print help for all commands and exit.

Full documentation specific for all current command is displayed.If a file is specified, the documentation is written into and the output format is determined depending on the filename suffix. Supported are man page, HTML and plain text.

- **`--help-compatcommands [file]`**: Print help for compatibility commands.

Full documentation specific for all compatibility commands is displayed.If a file is specified, the documentation is written into and the output format is determined depending on the filename suffix. Supported are man page, HTML and plain text.

- **`--help-module module [file]`**: Print help for a single module and exit.

Full documentation specific to the given module is displayed.If a file is specified, the documentation is written into and the output format is determined depending on the filename suffix. Supported are man page, HTML and plain text.

- **`--help-module-list [file]`**: List available modules and exit.

The list contains all modules for which help may be obtained by using the --help-module argument followed by a module name. If a file is specified, the documentation is written into and the output format is determined depending on the filename suffix. Supported are man page, HTML and plain text.

- **`--help-modules [file]`**: Print help for all modules and exit.

Full documentation for all modules is displayed. If a file is specified, the documentation is written into and the output format is determined depending on the filename suffix. Supported are man page, HTML and plain text.

- **`--help-custom-modules [file]`**: Print help for all custom modules and exit.

Full documentation for all custom modules is displayed. If a file is specified, the documentation is written into and the output format is determined depending on the filename suffix. Supported are man page, HTML and plain text.

- **`--help-property prop [file]`**: Print help for a single property and exit.

Full documentation specific to the given module is displayed.If a file is specified, the documentation is written into and the output format is determined depending on the filename suffix. Supported are man page, HTML and plain text.

- **--help-property-list [file]**: List available properties and exit.

  The list contains all properties for which help may be obtained by using the --help-property argument followed by a property name. If a file is specified, the help is written into it.If a file is specified, the documentation is written into and the output format is determined depending on the filename suffix. Supported are man page, HTML and plain text.

- **--help-properties [file]**: Print help for all properties and exit.

  Full documentation for all properties is displayed.If a file is specified, the documentation is written into and the output format is determined depending on the filename suffix. Supported are man page, HTML and plain text.

- **--copyright [file]**: Print the CMake copyright and exit.

  If a file is specified, the copyright is written into it.

- **--help**: Print usage information and exit.

  Usage describes the basic command line interface and its options.

- **--help-full [file]**: Print full help and exit.

  Full help displays most of the documentation provided by the UNIX man page. It is provided for use on non-UNIX platforms, but is also convenient if the man page is not installed. If a file is specified, the help is written into it.

- **--help-html [file]**: Print full help in HTML format.

  This option is used by CMake authors to help produce web pages. If a file is specified, the help is written into it.

- **--help-man [file]**: Print full help as a UNIX man page and exit.

  This option is used by the cmake build to generate the UNIX man page. If a file is specified, the help is written into it.

- **--version [file]**: Show program name/version banner and exit.

  If a file is specified, the version is written into it.

CMake Generators

The following generators are available on this platform:

- **Borland Makefiles**: Generates Borland makefiles.
- **MSYS Makefiles**: Generates MSYS makefiles.

  The makefiles use /bin/sh as the shell. They require msys to be installed on the machine.

- **MinGW Makefiles**: Generates a make file for use with mingw32-make.

  The makefiles generated use cmd.exe as the shell. They do not require msys or a unix shell.

- **NMake Makefiles**: Generates NMake makefiles.
- **Unix Makefiles**: Generates standard UNIX makefiles.

  A hierarchy of UNIX makefiles is generated into the build tree. Any standard UNIX-style make program can build the project through the default make target. A "make install" target is also provided.

- **Visual Studio 6**: Generates Visual Studio 6 project files.
- **Visual Studio 7**: Generates Visual Studio .NET 2002 project files.
- **Visual Studio 7 .NET 2003**: Generates for Visual Studio .NET 2003.
- **Visual Studio 8 2005**: Generates Visual Studio .NET 2005 project files.
- **Visual Studio 8 2005 Win64**: Generates for VS .NET 2005 Win64.
- **Visual Studio 9 2008**: Generates Visual Studio 9 2008 project files.
- **Watcom WMake**: Generates Watcom WMake makefiles.
- **CodeBlocks - MinGW Makefiles**: Generates CodeBlocks project files.

  Project files for CodeBlocks will be created in the top directory and in every subdirectory which features a CMakeLists.txt file containing a PROJECT() call. Additionally a hierarchy of makefiles is generated into the build tree. The appropriate make program can build the project through the default make target. A "make install" target is also provided.

- **CodeBlocks - Unix Makefiles**: Generates CodeBlocks project files.

  Project files for CodeBlocks will be created in the top directory and in every subdirectory which features a CMakeLists.txt file containing a PROJECT() call.

Additionally a hierarchy of makefiles is generated into the build tree. The appropriate make program can build the project through the default make target. A "make install" target is also provided.

- **Eclipse CDT4 - MinGW Makefiles**: Generates Eclipse CDT 4.0 project files.

  Project files for Eclipse will be created in the top directory and will have a linked resource to every subdirectory which features a CMakeLists.txt file containing a PROJECT() call.Additionally a hierarchy of makefiles is generated into the build tree. The appropriate make program can build the project through the default make target. A "make install" target is also provided.

- **Eclipse CDT4 - NMake Makefiles**: Generates Eclipse CDT 4.0 project files.

  Project files for Eclipse will be created in the top directory and will have a linked resource to every subdirectory which features a CMakeLists.txt file containing a PROJECT() call.Additionally a hierarchy of makefiles is generated into the build tree. The appropriate make program can build the project through the default make target. A "make install" target is also provided.

- **Eclipse CDT4 - Unix Makefiles**: Generates Eclipse CDT 4.0 project files.

  Project files for Eclipse will be created in the top directory and will have a linked resource to every subdirectory which features a CMakeLists.txt file containing a PROJECT() call.Additionally a hierarchy of makefiles is generated into the build tree. The appropriate make program can build the project through the default make target. A "make install" target is also provided.

CTest Command-Line Options

```
ctest [options]
```

The "ctest" executable is the CMake test driver program. CMake-generated build trees created for projects that use the ENABLE_TESTING and ADD_TEST commands have testing support. This program will run the tests and report results.

- **-C <cfg>, --build-config <cfg>**: Choose configuration to test.

Some CMake-generated build trees can have multiple build configurations in the same tree. This option can be used to specify which one should be tested. Example configurations are "Debug" and "Release".

- **-V, --verbose**: Enable verbose output from tests.

  Test output is normally suppressed and only summary information is displayed. This option will show all test output.

- **-VV, --extra-verbose**: Enable more verbose output from tests.

  Test output is normally suppressed and only summary information is displayed. This option will show even more test output.

- **--debug**: Displaying more verbose internals of CTest.

  This feature will result in large number of output that is mostly useful for debugging dashboard problems.

- **-Q, --quiet**: Make ctest quiet.

  This option will suppress all the output. The output log file will still be generated if the --output-log is specified. Options such as --verbose, --extra-verbose, and --debug are ignored if --quiet is specified.

- **-O <file>, --output-log <file>**: Output to log file

  This option tells ctest to write all its output to a log file.

- **-N, --show-only**: Disable actual execution of tests.

  This option tells ctest to list the tests that would be run but not actually run them. Useful in conjunction with the -R and -E options.

- **-R <regex>, --tests-regex <regex>**: Run tests matching regular expression.

  This option tells ctest to run only the tests whose names match the given regular expression.

- **-E <regex>, --exclude-regex <regex>**: Exclude tests matching regular expression.

  This option tells ctest to NOT run the tests whose names match the given regular expression.

- **-D <dashboard>, --dashboard <dashboard>**: Execute dashboard test

  This option tells ctest to perform act as a Dart client and perform a dashboard test. All tests are <Mode><Test>, where Mode can be Experimental, Nightly, and Continuous, and Test can be Start, Update, Configure, Build, Test, Coverage, and Submit.

- **-M <model>, --test-model <model>**: Sets the model for a dashboard

  This option tells ctest to act as a Dart client where the TestModel can be Experimental, Nightly, and Continuous. Combining -M and -T is similar to -D

- **-T <action>, --test-action <action>**: Sets the dashboard action to perform

  This option tells ctest to act as a Dart client and perform some action such as start, build, test etc. Combining -M and -T is similar to -D

- **--track <track>**: Specify the track to submit dashboard to

  Submit dashboard to specified track instead of default one. By default, the dashboard is submitted to Nightly, Experimental, or Continuous track, but by specifying this option, the track can be arbitrary.

- **-S <script>, --script <script>**: Execute a dashboard for a configuration

  This option tells ctest to load in a configuration script which sets a number of parameters such as the binary and source directories. Then ctest will do what is required to create and run a dashboard. This option basically sets up a dashboard and then runs ctest -D with the appropriate options.

- **-SP <script>, --script-new-process <script>**: Execute a dashboard for a configuration

This option does the same operations as -S but it will do them in a seperate process. This is primarily useful in cases where the script may modify the environment and you do not want the modified enviroment to impact other -S scripts.

- **-A <file>, --add-notes <file>**: Add a notes file with submission

This option tells ctest to include a notes file when submitting dashboard.

- **-I [Start,End,Stride,test#,test#|Test file], --tests-information**: Run a specific number of tests by number.

This option causes ctest to run tests starting at number Start, ending at number End, and incrementing by Stride. Any additional numbers after Stride are considered individual test numbers. Start, End,or stride can be empty. Optionally a file can be given that contains the same syntax as the command line.

- **-U, --union**: Take the Union of -I and -R

When both -R and -I are specified by default the intersection of tests are run. By specifying -U the union of tests is run instead.

- **--interactive-debug-mode [0|1]**: Set the interactive mode to 0 or 1.

This option causes ctest to run tests in either an interactive mode or a non-interactive mode. On Windows this means that in non-interactive mode, all system debug pop up windows are blocked. In dashboard mode (Experimental, Nightly, Continuous), the default is non-interactive. When just running tests not for a dashboard the default is to allow popups and interactive debugging.

- **--build-and-test**: Configure, build and run a test.

This option tells ctest to configure (i.e. run cmake on), build, and or execute a test. The configure and test steps are optional. The arguments to this command line are the source and binary directories. By default this will run CMake on the Source/Bin directories specified unless --build-nocmake is specified. Both --build-makeprogram and --build-generator MUST be provided to use --built-and-test. If --test-command is specified then that will be run after the build is complete. Other options that affect this mode are --build-target --build-nocmake, --build-run-dir, --build-two-config, --build-exe-dir, --build-project,--build-noclean, --build-options

- **--build-target**: Specify a specific target to build.

This option goes with the --build-and-test option, if left out the all target is built.

- **--build-nocmake**: Run the build without running cmake first.

Skip the cmake step.

- **--build-run-dir**: Specify directory to run programs from.

Directory where programs will be after it has been compiled.

- **--build-two-config**: Run CMake twice
- **--build-exe-dir**: Specify the directory for the executable.
- **--build-generator**: Specify the generator to use.
- **--build-project**: Specify the name of the project to build.
- **--build-makeprogram**: Specify the make program to use.
- **--build-noclean**: Skip the make clean step.
- **--build-config-sample**: A sample executable to use to determine the configuration

A sample executable to use to determine the configuration that should be used. e.g. Debug/Release/etc

- **--build-options**: Add extra options to the build step.

This option must be the last option with the exception of --test-command

- **--test-command**: The test to run with the --build-and-test option.
- **--test-timeout**: The time limit in seconds, internal use only.
- **--tomorrow-tag**: Nightly or experimental starts with next day tag.

This is useful if the build will not finish in one day.

- **--ctest-config**: The configuration file used to initialize CTest state when submitting dashboards.

This option tells CTest to use different initialization file instead of DartConfiguration.tcl. This way multiple initialization files can be used for example to submit to multiple dashboards.

- **--overwrite**: Overwrite CTest configuration option.

By default ctest uses configuration options from configuration file. This option will overwrite the configuration option.

- **--extra-submit <file>[;<file>]**: Submit extra files to the dashboard.

This option will submit extra files to the dashboard.

- **--force-new-ctest-process**: Run child CTest instances as new processes

By default CTest will run child CTest instances within the same process. If this behavior is not desired, this argument will enforce new processes for child CTest processes.

- **--submit-index**: Submit individual dashboard tests with specific index

This option allows performing the same CTest action (such as test) multiple times and submit all stages to the same dashboard (Dart2 required). Each execution requires different index.

- **--copyright [file]**: Print the CMake copyright and exit.

If a file is specified, the copyright is written into it.

- **--help**: Print usage information and exit.

Usage describes the basic command line interface and its options.

- **--help-full [file]**: Print full help and exit.

Full help displays most of the documentation provided by the UNIX man page. It is provided for use on non-UNIX platforms, but is also convenient if the man page is not installed. If a file is specified, the help is written into it.

- **--help-html [file]**: Print full help in HTML format.

This option is used by CMake authors to help produce web pages. If a file is specified, the help is written into it.

- **--help-man [file]**: Print full help as a UNIX man page and exit.

This option is used by the cmake build to generate the UNIX man page. If a file is specified, the help is written into it.

- **--version [file]**: Show program name/version banner and exit.

If a file is specified, the version is written into it.

CPack Command-Line Options

```
cpack -G <generator> [options]
```

The "cpack" executable is the CMake packaging program. CMake-generated build trees created for projects that use the INSTALL_* commands have packaging support. This program will generate the package.

CMake is a cross-platform build system generator. Projects specify their build process with platform-independent CMake listfiles included in each directory of a source tree with the name CMakeLists.txt. Users build a project by using CMake to generate a build system for a native tool on their platform.

- **-G <generator>**: Use the specified generator to generate package.

CPack may support multiple native packaging systems on certain platforms. A generator is responsible for generating input files for particular system and invoking that systems. The following generators are available on this platform:

- **NSIS**: Null Soft Installer
- **STGZ**: Self extracting Tar GZip compression
- **TBZ2**: Tar BZip2 compression
- **TGZ**: Tar GZip compression
- **TZ**: Tar Compress compression
- **ZIP**: ZIP file format

- **-C <Configuration>**: Specify the project configuration

This option specifies the configuration that the project was build with, for example 'Debug', 'Release'.

- **-D <var>=<value>**: Set a CPack variable.

Set a variable that can be used by the generator.

- **`--config <config file>`**: Specify the config file.

  Specify the config file to use to create the package. By default CPackConfig.cmake in the current directory will be used.

- **`--copyright [file]`**: Print the CMake copyright and exit.

  If a file is specified, the copyright is written into it.

- **`--help`**: Print usage information and exit.

  Usage describes the basic command line interface and its options.

- **`--help-full [file]`**: Print full help and exit.

  Full help displays most of the documentation provided by the UNIX man page. It is provided for use on non-UNIX platforms, but is also convenient if the man page is not installed. If a file is specified, the help is written into it.

- **`--help-html [file]`**: Print full help in HTML format.

  This option is used by CMake authors to help produce web pages. If a file is specified, the help is written into it.

- **`--help-man [file]`**: Print full help as a UNIX man page and exit.

  This option is used by the cmake build to generate the UNIX man page. If a file is specified, the help is written into it.

- **`--version [file]`**: Show program name/version banner and exit.

  If a file is specified, the version is written into it.

Listfile Commands

The following commands are available in CMakeLists.txt code:

- **`add_custom_command`**: Add a custom build rule to the generated build system.

There are two main signatures for add_custom_command The first signature is for adding a custom command to produce an output.

```
add_custom_command(OUTPUT output1 [output2 ...]
                COMMAND command1 [ARGS] [args1...]
                [COMMAND command2 [ARGS] [args2...] ...]
                [MAIN_DEPENDENCY depend]
                [DEPENDS [depends...]]
                [IMPLICIT_DEPENDS <lang1> depend1 ...]
                [WORKING_DIRECTORY dir]
                [COMMENT comment] [VERBATIM] [APPEND])
```

This defines a new command that can be executed during the build process. The outputs named should be listed as source files in the target for which they are to be generated. Note that MAIN_DEPENDENCY is completely optional and is used as a suggestion to visual studio about where to hang the custom command. In makefile terms this creates a new target in the following form:

```
OUTPUT: MAIN_DEPENDENCY DEPENDS
        COMMAND
```

If more than one command is specified they will be executed in order. The optional ARGS argument is for backward compatibility and will be ignored.

The second signature adds a custom command to a target such as a library or executable. This is useful for performing an operation before or after building the target. The command becomes part of the target and will only execute when the target itself is built. If the target is already built, the command will not execute.

```
add_custom_command(TARGET target
                PRE_BUILD | PRE_LINK | POST_BUILD
                COMMAND command1 [ARGS] [args1...]
                [COMMAND command2 [ARGS] [args2...] ...]
                [WORKING_DIRECTORY dir]
                [COMMENT comment] [VERBATIM])
```

This defines a new command that will be associated with building the specified target. When the command will happen is determined by which of the following is specified:

```
PRE_BUILD - run before all other dependencies
PRE_LINK - run after other dependencies
POST_BUILD - run after the target has been built
```

Note that the PRE_BUILD option is only supported on Visual Studio 7 or later. For all other generators PRE_BUILD will be treated as PRE_LINK.

If WORKING_DIRECTORY is specified the command will be executed in the directory given. If COMMENT is set, the value will be displayed as a message before the commands are executed at build time. If APPEND is specified the COMMAND and DEPENDS option values are appended to the custom command for the first output specified. There must have already been a previous call to this command with the same output. The COMMENT, WORKING_DIRECTORY, and MAIN_DEPENDENCY options are currently ignored when APPEND is given, but may be used in the future.

If VERBATIM is given then all the arguments to the commands will be passed exactly as specified no matter the build tool used. Note that one level of escapes is still used by the CMake language processor before ADD_CUSTOM_TARGET even sees the arguments. Use of VERBATIM is recommended as it enables correct behavior. When VERBATIM is not given the behavior is platform specific. In the future VERBATIM may be enabled by default. The only reason it is an option is to preserve compatibility with older CMake code.

If the output of the custom command is not actually created as a file on disk it should be marked as SYMBOLIC with SET_SOURCE_FILES_PROPERTIES.

The IMPLICIT_DEPENDS option requests scanning of implicit dependencies of an input file. The language given specifies the programming language whose corresponding dependency scanner should be used. Currently only C and CXX language scanners are supported. Dependencies discovered from the scanning are added to those of the custom command at build time. Note that the IMPLICIT_DEPENDS option is currently supported only for Makefile generators and will be ignored by other generators.

If COMMAND specifies an executable target (created by ADD_EXECUTABLE) it will automatically be replaced by the location of the executable created at build time. Additionally a target-level dependency will be added so that the executable target will be built before any target using this custom command. However this does NOT add a file-level dependency that would cause the custom command to re-run whenever the executable is recompiled.

If DEPENDS specifies any target (created by an ADD_* command) a target-level dependency is created to make sure the target is built before any target using this custom command. Additionally, if the target is an executable or library a file-level dependency is created to cause the custom command to re-run whenever the target is recompiled.

- **add_custom_target**: Add a target with no output so it will always be built.

```
add_custom_target(Name [ALL] [command1 [args1...]]
                       [COMMAND command2 [args2...] ...]
                       [DEPENDS depend depend depend ... ]
                       [WORKING_DIRECTORY dir]
                       [COMMENT comment] [VERBATIM])
```

Adds a target with the given name that executes the given commands. The target has no output file and is ALWAYS CONSIDERED OUT OF DATE even if the commands try to create a file with the name of the target. Use ADD_CUSTOM_COMMAND to generate a file with dependencies. By default nothing depends on the custom target. Use ADD_DEPENDENCIES to add dependencies to or from other targets. If the ALL option is specified it indicates that this target should be added to the default build target so that it will be run every time (the command cannot be called ALL). The command and arguments are optional and if not specified an empty target will be created. If WORKING_DIRECTORY is set, then the command will be run in that directory. If COMMENT is set, the value will be displayed as a message before the commands are executed at build time. Dependencies listed with the DEPENDS argument may reference files and outputs of custom commands created with ADD_CUSTOM_COMMAND.

If VERBATIM is given then all the arguments to the commands will be passed exactly as specified no matter the build tool used. Note that one level of escapes is still used by the CMake language processor before add_custom_target even sees the arguments. Use of VERBATIM is recommended as it enables correct behavior. When VERBATIM is not given the behavior is platform specific. In the future VERBATIM may be enabled by default. The only reason it is an option is to preserve compatibility with older CMake code.

- **add_definitions**: Adds -D define flags to the command line of C and C++ compilers.

```
add_definitions(-DFOO -DBAR ...)
```

Adds flags to command line of C and C++ compilers. This command can be used to add any flag to a compile line, but the -D flag is accepted most C/C++ compilers. Other flags may not be as portable.

- **add_dependencies**: Add a dependency between top-level targets.

```
add_dependencies(target-name depend-target1
                   depend-target2 ...)
```

Make a top-level target depend on other top-level targets. A top-level target is one created by add_executable, add_library, or add_custom_target. Adding dependencies with this command can be used to make sure one target is built before another target. See the DEPENDS option of add_custom_target and add_custom_command for adding file-level dependencies in custom rules. See the OBJECT_DEPENDS option in set_source_files_properties to add file-level dependencies to object files.

- **`add_executable`**: Add an executable to the project using the specified source files.

```
add_executable(exename [WIN32] [MACOSX_BUNDLE]
               [EXCLUDE_FROM_ALL]
               source1 source2 ... sourceN)
```

This command adds an executable target to the current directory. The executable will be built from the list of source files specified.

After specifying the executable name, WIN32 and/or MACOSX_BUNDLE can be specified. WIN32 indicates that the executable (when compiled on windows) is a windows app (using WinMain) not a console app (using main). The variable CMAKE_MFC_FLAG be used if the windows app uses MFC. This variable can be set to the following values:

```
0: Use Standard Windows Libraries
1: Use MFC in a Static Library
2: Use MFC in a Shared DLL
```

MACOSX_BUNDLE indicates that when build on Mac OSX, executable should be in the bundle form. The MACOSX_BUNDLE also allows several variables to be specified:

```
MACOSX_BUNDLE_INFO_STRING
MACOSX_BUNDLE_ICON_FILE
MACOSX_BUNDLE_GUI_IDENTIFIER
MACOSX_BUNDLE_LONG_VERSION_STRING
MACOSX_BUNDLE_BUNDLE_NAME
MACOSX_BUNDLE_SHORT_VERSION_STRING
MACOSX_BUNDLE_BUNDLE_VERSION
MACOSX_BUNDLE_COPYRIGHT
```

If EXCLUDE_FROM_ALL is given the target will not be built by default. It will be built only if the user explicitly builds the target or another target that requires the target depends on it.

- **add_library**: Add a library to the project using the specified source files.

```
add_library(libname [SHARED | STATIC | MODULE]
            [EXCLUDE_FROM_ALL]
            source1 source2 ... sourceN)
```

Adds a library target. SHARED, STATIC or MODULE keywords are used to set the library type. If the keyword MODULE appears, the library type is set to MH_BUNDLE on systems which use dyld. On systems without dyld, MODULE is treated like SHARED. If no keywords appear as the second argument, the type defaults to the current value of BUILD_SHARED_LIBS. If this variable is not set, the type defaults to STATIC.

If EXCLUDE_FROM_ALL is given the target will not be built by default. It will be built only if the user explicitly builds the target or another target that requires the target depends on it.

- **add_subdirectory**: Add a subdirectory to the build.

```
add_subdirectory(source_dir [binary_dir]
                 [EXCLUDE_FROM_ALL])
```

Add a subdirectory to the build. The source_dir specifies the directory in which the source CmakeLists.txt and code files are located. If it is a relative path it will be evaluated with respect to the current directory (the typical usage), but it may also be an absolute path. The binary_dir specifies the directory in which to place the output files. If it is a relative path it will be evaluated with respect to the current output directory, but it may also be an absolute path. If binary_dir is not specified, the value of source_dir, before expanding any relative path, will be used (the typical usage). The CMakeLists.txt file in the specified source directory will be processed immediately by CMake before processing in the current input file continues beyond this command.

If the EXCLUDE_FROM_ALL argument is provided then this subdirectory will not be included in build by default. Users will have to explicitly start a build in the generated output directory. This is useful for having cmake create a build system for a set of examples in a project. One would want cmake to generate a single build system for all the examples, but one may not want the targets to show up in the main build system.

- **add_test**: Add a test to the project with the specified arguments.

```
add_test(testname Exename arg1 arg2 ...)
```

If the ENABLE_TESTING command has been run, this command adds a test target to the current directory. If ENABLE_TESTING has not been run, this command does nothing. The tests are run by the testing subsystem by executing Exename with the specified arguments. Exename can be either an executable built by this project or an arbitrary executable on the system (like tclsh). The test will be run with the current working directory set to the CMakeList.txt files corresponding directory in the binary tree.

- **`aux_source_directory`**: Find all source files in a directory.

    ```
    aux_source_directory(dir VARIABLE)
    ```

Collects the names of all the source files in the specified directory and stores the list in the variable provided. This command is intended to be used by projects that use explicit template instantiation. Template instantiation files can be stored in a "Templates" subdirectory and collected automatically using this command to avoid manually listing all instantiations.

It is tempting to use this command to avoid writing the list of source files for a library or executable target. While this seems to work, there is no way for CMake to generate a build system that knows when a new source file has been added. Normally the generated build system knows when it needs to rerun CMake because the CMakeLists.txt file is modified to add a new source. When the source is just added to the directory without modifying this file, one would have to manually rerun CMake to generate a build system incorporating the new file.

- **`build_command`**: Get the command line that will build this project.

    ```
    build_command(variable MAKECOMMAND)
    ```

Sets the given variable to a string containing the command that will build this project from the root of the build tree using the build tool given by MAKECOMMAND. MAKECOMMAND should be msdev, nmake, make or one of the end user build tools. This is useful for configuring testing systems.

- **`cmake_minimum_required`**: Set the minimum required version of cmake for a project.

    ```
    cmake_minimum_required(VERSION versionNumber
    [FATAL_ERROR])
    ```

Let cmake know that the project requires a certain version of a cmake, or newer. CMake will also try to be backwards compatible to the version of cmake specified, if a newer version of cmake is running. If FATAL_ERROR is given then failure to meet the requirements will be considered an error instead of a warning.

- **configure_file**: Copy a file to another location and modify its contents.

```
configure_file(InputFile OutputFile
                [COPYONLY] [ESCAPE_QUOTES] [@ONLY])
```

The Input and Ouput files have to have full paths. This command replaces any variables in the input file referenced as ${VAR} or @VAR@ with their values as determined by CMake. If a variable is not defined, it will be replaced with nothing. If COPYONLY is specified, then no variable expansion will take place. If ESCAPE_QUOTES is specified then any substituted quotes will be C-style escaped. The file will be configured with the current values of CMake variables. If @ONLY is specified, only variables of the form @VAR@ will be replaces and ${VAR} will be ignored. This is useful for configuring scripts that use ${VAR}. Any occurrences of #cmakedefine VAR will be replaced with either #define VAR or /* #undef VAR */ depending on the setting of VAR in CMake

- **create_test_sourcelist**: Create a test driver and source list for building test programs.

```
create_test_sourcelist(SourceListName DriverName
                        test1 test2 test3
                        EXTRA_INCLUDE include.h
                        FUNCTION function)
```

A test driver is a program that links together many small tests into a single executable. This is useful when building static executables with large libraries to shrink the total required size. The list of source files needed to build the test driver will be in SourceListName. DriverName is the name of the test driver program. The rest of the arguments consist of a list of test source files, can be semicolon separated. Each test source file should have a function in it that is the same name as the file with no extension (foo.cxx should have int foo();) DriverName will be able to call each of the tests by name on the command line. If EXTRA_INCLUDE is specified, then the next argument is included into the generated file. If FUNCTION is specified, then the next argument is taken as a function name that is passed a pointer to ac and av. This can be used to add extra command line processing to each test. The cmake variable CMAKE_TESTDRIVER_BEFORE_TESTMAIN can be set to have code that will be placed directly before calling the test main function. CMAKE_TESTDRIVER_AFTER_TESTMAIN can be set to have code that will be placed directly after the call to the test main function.

- **define_property**: Define properties used by CMake.

```
define_property(property_name scope_value
                short_description
                full_description inherit)
```

Define a property for a scope. scope_value is either GLOBAL, DIRECTORY, TARGET, TEST, SOURCE_FILE, VARIABLE or CACHED_VARIABLE. The short and full descriptions are used to document the property. If inherit is TRUE, it will inherit its value from the next more global property if it hasn't been set at the specified scope. This means that e.g. a TARGET property inherits it's value from the DIRECTORY property with the same name if it hasn't been set for the target, and then from GLOBAL if it hasn't been set for the directory.

- **else**: Starts the else portion of an if block.

```
else(expression)
```

See the if command.

- **elseif**: Starts the elseif portion of an if block.

```
elseif(expression)
```

See the if command.

- **enable_language**: Enable a language (CXX/C/Fortran/etc)

```
enable_language(languageName [OPTIONAL] )
```

This command enables support for the named language in CMake. This is the same as the project command but does not create any of the extra varaibles that are created by the project command. Example languages are CXX, C, Fortran.

If OPTIONAL is used, use the CMAKE_<languageName>_COMPILER_WORKS variable to check whether the language has been enabled successfully.

- **enable_testing**: Enable testing for current directory and below.

```
enable_testing()
```

Enables testing for this directory and below. See also the add_test command. Note that ctest expects to find a test file in the build directory root. Therefore, this command should be in the source directory root.

- **endforeach**: Ends a list of commands in a FOREACH block.

  ```
  endforeach(expression)
  ```

  See the FOREACH command.

- **endif**: Ends a list of commands in an if block.

  ```
  endif(expression)
  ```

  See the if command.

- **endmacro**: Ends a list of commands in a macro block.

  ```
  endmacro(expression)
  ```

  See the macro command.

- **endwhile**: Ends a list of commands in a while block.

  ```
  endwhile(expression)
  ```

  See the while command.

- **execute_process**: Execute one or more child processes.

  ```
  execute_process(COMMAND <cmd1> [args1...]]
                  [COMMAND <cmd2> [args2...] [...]]
                  [WORKING_DIRECTORY <directory>]
                  [TIMEOUT <seconds>]
                  [RESULT_VARIABLE <variable>]
                  [OUTPUT_VARIABLE <variable>]
                  [ERROR_VARIABLE <variable>]
                  [INPUT_FILE <file>]
                  [OUTPUT_FILE <file>]
                  [ERROR_FILE <file>]
                  [OUTPUT_QUIET]
                  [ERROR_QUIET]
  ```

```
[OUTPUT_STRIP_TRAILING_WHITESPACE]
[ERROR_STRIP_TRAILING_WHITESPACE])
```

Runs the given sequence of one or more commands with the standard output of each process piped to the standard input of the next. A single standard error pipe is used for all processes. If WORKING_DIRECTORY is given the named directory will be set as the current working directory of the child processes. If TIMEOUT is given the child processes will be terminated if they do not finish in the specified number of seconds (fractions are allowed). If RESULT_VARIABLE is given the variable will be set to contain the result of running the processes. This will be an integer return code from the last child or a string describing an error condition. If OUTPUT_VARIABLE or ERROR_VARIABLE are given the variable named will be set with the contents of the standard output and standard error pipes respectively. If the same variable is named for both pipes their output will be merged in the order produced. If INPUT_FILE, OUTPUT_FILE, or ERROR_FILE is given the file named will be attached to the standard input of the first process, standard output of the last process, or standard error of all processes respectively. If OUTPUT_QUIET or ERROR_QUIET is given then the standard output or standard error results will be quietly ignored. If more than one OUTPUT_* or ERROR_* option is given for the same pipe the precedence is not specified. If no OUTPUT_* or ERROR_* options are given the output will be shared with the corresponding pipes of the CMake process itself.

The execute_process command is a newer more powerful version of exec_program, but the old command has been kept for compatibility.

- **export**: Write out the dependency information for all targets of a project.

  ```
  export(TARGETS tgt1 tgt2 ...  [PREFIX <prefix>]
         FILE <filename> [APPEND])
  ```

  Create a file that can be included into a CMake listfile with the INCLUDE command. The file will contain a number of SET commands that will set all the variables needed for library dependency information. This should be the last command in the top level CMakeLists.txt file of the project. If the APPEND option is specified, the SET commands will be appended to the given file instead of replacing it.

- **export_library_dependencies**: Write out the dependency information for all targets of a project.

  ```
  export_library_dependencies(FILE [APPEND])
  ```

Create a file that can be included into a CMake listfile with the INCLUDE command. The file will contain a number of SET commands that will set all the variables needed for library dependency information. This should be the last command in the top level CMakeLists.txt file of the project. If the APPEND option is specified, the SET commands will be appended to the given file instead of replacing it.

- **file**: File manipulation command.

```
file(WRITE filename "message to write"... )
file(APPEND filename "message to write"... )
file(READ filename variable [LIMIT numBytes])
file(STRINGS filename variable [LIMIT_COUNT num]
     [LIMIT_INPUT numBytes] [LIMIT_OUTPUT numBytes]
     [LENGTH_MINIMUM numBytes]
     [LENGTH_MAXIMUM numBytes]
     [NEWLINE_CONSUME] [REGEX regex]
     [NO_HEX_CONVERSION])
file(GLOB variable [RELATIVE path]
     [globbing expressions]...)
file(GLOB_RECURSE variable [RELATIVE path]
     [globbing expressions]...)
file(REMOVE [file1 ...])
file(REMOVE_RECURSE [file1 ...])
file(MAKE_DIRECTORY [directory1 directory2 ...])
file(RELATIVE_PATH variable directory file)
file(TO_CMAKE_PATH path result)
file(TO_NATIVE_PATH path result)
```

WRITE will write a message into a file called 'filename'. It overwrites the file if it already exists, and creates the file if it does not exist.

APPEND will write a message into a file same as WRITE, except it will append it to the end of the file

NOTE: When using file WRITE and file APPEND, the produced file cannot be used as an input to CMake (configure_file, source file ...) because it will lead to an infinite loop. Use configure_file if you want to generate input files to CMake.

READ will read the content of a file and store it into the variable.

STRINGS will parse a list of ASCII strings from a file and store it in a variable. Binary data in the file are ignored. Carriage return (CR) characters are ignored. It

works also for Intel Hex and Motorola S-record files, which are automatically
converted to binary format when reading them. Disable this using
NO_HEX_CONVERSION.

LIMIT_COUNT sets the maximum number of strings to return. LIMIT_INPUT sets
the maximum number of bytes to read from the input file. LIMIT_OUTPUT sets the
maximum number of bytes to store in the output variable. LENGTH_MINIMUM
sets the minimum length of a string to return. Shorter strings are ignored.
LENGTH_MAXIMUM sets the maximum length of a string to return. Longer
strings are split into strings no longer than the maximum length.
NEWLINE_CONSUME allows newlines to be included in strings instead of
terminating them.

REGEX specifies a regular expression that a string must match to be returned.
Typical usage

```
file(STRINGS myfile.txt myfile)
```

stores a list in the variable "myfile" in which each item is a line from the input file.

GLOB will generate a list of all files that match the globbing expressions and store it
into the variable. Globbing expressions are similar to regular expressions, but much
simpler. If RELATIVE flag is specified for an expression, the results will be returned
as a relative path to the given path.

Examples of globbing expressions include:

```
*.cxx     - match all files with extension cxx
*.vt?     - match all files with extension vta,...,vtz
f[3-5].txt - match files f3.txt, f4.txt, f5.txt
```

GLOB_RECURSE will generate similar list as the regular GLOB, except it will
traverse all the subdirectories of the matched directory and match the files.

Examples of recursive globbing include:

```
/dir/*.py  - match all python files in /dir and
subdirectories
```

MAKE_DIRECTORY will create the given directories, also if their parent
directories don't exist yet

REMOVE will remove the given files, also in subdirectories

REMOVE_RECURSE will remove the given files and directories, also non-empty directories

RELATIVE_PATH will determine relative path from directory to the given file.

TO_CMAKE_PATH will convert path into a cmake style path with unix /. The input can be a single path or a system path like "$ENV{PATH}". Note the double quotes around the ENV call TO_CMAKE_PATH only takes one argument.

TO_NATIVE_PATH works just like TO_CMAKE_PATH, but will convert from a cmake style path into the native path style \ for windows and / for UNIX.

- **find_file**: Find the full path to a file.

```
find_path(<VAR> name1 path1 path2 ...)
```

This is the short-hand signature for the command that is sufficient in many cases. It is the same as find_path(<VAR> name1 PATHS path2 path2 ...)

```
find_path(
          <VAR>
          name | NAMES name1 [name2 ...]
          PATHS path1 [path2 ... ENV var]
          [PATH_SUFFIXES suffix1 [suffix2 ...]]
          [DOC "cache documentation string"]
          [NO_DEFAULT_PATH]
          [NO_CMAKE_ENVIRONMENT_PATH]
          [NO_CMAKE_PATH]
          [NO_SYSTEM_ENVIRONMENT_PATH]
          [NO_CMAKE_SYSTEM_PATH]
          [CMAKE_FIND_ROOT_PATH_BOTH |
            ONLY_CMAKE_FIND_ROOT_PATH |
            NO_CMAKE_FIND_ROOT_PATH ]
        )
```

This command is used to find a full path to named file. A cache entry named by <VAR> is created to store the result of this command. If the full path to a file is found the result is stored in the variable and the search will not be repeated unless the variable is cleared. If nothing is found, the result will be <VAR>-NOTFOUND, and the search will be attempted again the next time find_path is invoked with the same variable. The name of the full path to a file that is searched for is specified by the names listed after the NAMES argument. Additional search locations can be specified after the PATHS argument. If ENV var is found in the PATHS section the environment variable var will be read and converted from a system environment variable to a cmake style list of paths. For example ENV PATH would be a way to list the system path variable. The argument after DOC will be used for the documentation string in the cache. PATH_SUFFIXES can be used to give sub directories that will be appended to the search paths.

If NO_DEFAULT_PATH is specified, then no additional paths are added to the search. If NO_DEFAULT_PATH is not specified, the search process is as follows:

1. Search cmake specific environment variables. This can be skipped if NO_CMAKE_ENVIRONMENT_PATH is passed.

```
CMAKE_FRAMEWORK_PATH
CMAKE_APPBUNDLE_PATH
CMAKE_INCLUDE_PATH
```

2. Search cmake variables with the same names as the cmake specific environment variables. These are intended to be used on the command line with a -DVAR=value. This can be skipped if NO_CMAKE_PATH is passed.

```
CMAKE_FRAMEWORK_PATH
CMAKE_APPBUNDLE_PATH
CMAKE_INCLUDE_PATH
```

3. Search the standard system environment variables. This can be skipped if NO_SYSTEM_ENVIRONMENT_PATH is an argument.

```
PATH
INCLUDE
```

4. Search cmake variables defined in the Platform files for the current system. This can be skipped if NO_CMAKE_SYSTEM_PATH is passed.

```
CMAKE_SYSTEM_FRAMEWORK_PATH
CMAKE_SYSTEM_APPBUNDLE_PATH
CMAKE_SYSTEM_INCLUDE_PATH
```

5. Search the paths specified after PATHS or in the short-hand version of the command.

On Darwin or systems supporting OSX Frameworks, the cmake variable CMAKE_FIND_FRAMEWORK can be set to empty or one of the following:

```
"FIRST"   - Try to find frameworks before standard
            libraries or headers. This is the default
            on Darwin.
"LAST"    - Try to find frameworks after standard
            libraries or headers.
"ONLY"    - Only try to find frameworks.
"NEVER".  - Never try to find frameworks.
```

On Darwin or systems supporting OSX Application Bundles, the cmake variable CMAKE_FIND_APPBUNDLE can be set to empty or one of the following:

```
"FIRST"   - Try to find application bundles before
            Standard programs. This is the default
            on Darwin.
"LAST"    - Try to find application bundles after
            standard programs.
"ONLY"    - Only try to find application bundles.
"NEVER".  - Never try to find application bundles.
```

The CMake variable CMAKE_FIND_ROOT_PATH specifies one or more directories which will be prefixed to all of the search directories. By default it is empty. It is especially useful when cross-compiling to point to the root directory of the target environment and CMake will search there too. By default at first the directories listed in CMAKE_FIND_ROOT_PATH and then the non-prefixed directories will be searched. The default behavior can be adjusted by setting CMAKE_FIND_ROOT_PATH_MODE_INCLUDE. This behavior can be manually overridden on a per-call basis. By using CMAKE_FIND_ROOT_PATH_BOTH the search order will be as described above. If NO_CMAKE_FIND_ROOT_PATH is used then CMAKE_FIND_ROOT_PATH will not be used. If ONLY_CMAKE_FIND_ROOT_PATH is used then only the prefixed directories will be searched.

The reason the paths listed in the call to the command are searched last is that most users of CMake would expect things to be found first in the locations specified by their environment. Projects may override this behavior by simply calling the command twice:

```
find_path(<VAR> NAMES name PATHS paths
          NO_DEFAULT_PATH)
find_path(<VAR> NAMES name)
```

Once one of these calls succeeds the result variable will be set and stored in the cache so that neither call will search again.

- **find_library**: Find a library.

  ```
  find_library(<VAR> name1 path1 path2 ...)
  ```

This is the short-hand signature for the command that is sufficient in many cases. It is the same as find_library(<VAR> name1 PATHS path2 path2 ...)

```
find_library(
        <VAR>
        name | NAMES name1 [name2 ...]
        PATHS path1 [path2 ... ENV var]
        [PATH_SUFFIXES suffix1 [suffix2 ...]]
        [DOC "cache documentation string"]
        [NO_DEFAULT_PATH]
        [NO_CMAKE_ENVIRONMENT_PATH]
        [NO_CMAKE_PATH]
        [NO_SYSTEM_ENVIRONMENT_PATH]
        [NO_CMAKE_SYSTEM_PATH]
        [CMAKE_FIND_ROOT_PATH_BOTH |
          ONLY_CMAKE_FIND_ROOT_PATH |
          NO_CMAKE_FIND_ROOT_PATH ]
      )
```

This command is used to find a library. A cache entry named by <VAR> is created to store the result of this command. If the library is found the result is stored in the variable and the search will not be repeated unless the variable is cleared. If nothing is found, the result will be <VAR>-NOTFOUND, and the search will be attempted again the next time find_library is invoked with the same variable. The name of the library that is searched for is specified by the names listed after the NAMES argument. Additional search locations can be specified after the PATHS argument. If ENV var is found in the PATHS section the environment variable var will be read and converted from a system environment variable to a cmake style list of paths. For example ENV PATH would be a way to list the system path variable. The argument after DOC will be used for the documentation string in the cache. PATH_SUFFIXES can be used to give sub directories that will be appended to the search paths.

If NO_DEFAULT_PATH is specified, then no additional paths are added to the search. If NO_DEFAULT_PATH is not specified, the search process is as follows:

1. Search cmake specific environment variables. This can be skipped if NO_CMAKE_ENVIRONMENT_PATH is passed.

```
CMAKE_FRAMEWORK_PATH
CMAKE_APPBUNDLE_PATH
CMAKE_LIBRARY_PATH
```

2. Search cmake variables with the same names as the cmake specific environment variables. These are intended to be used on the command line with a -DVAR=value. This can be skipped if NO_CMAKE_PATH is passed.

```
CMAKE_FRAMEWORK_PATH
CMAKE_APPBUNDLE_PATH
CMAKE_LIBRARY_PATH
```

3. Search the standard system environment variables. This can be skipped if NO_SYSTEM_ENVIRONMENT_PATH is an argument.

```
PATH
LIB
```

4. Search cmake variables defined in the Platform files for the current system. This can be skipped if NO_CMAKE_SYSTEM_PATH is passed.

```
CMAKE_SYSTEM_FRAMEWORK_PATH
CMAKE_SYSTEM_APPBUNDLE_PATH
CMAKE_SYSTEM_LIBRARY_PATH
```

5. Search the paths specified after PATHS or in the short-hand version of the command.

On Darwin or systems supporting OSX Frameworks, the cmake variable CMAKE_FIND_FRAMEWORK can be set to empty or one of the following:

```
"FIRST"   - Try to find frameworks before standard
            libraries or headers. This is the default
            on Darwin.
"LAST"    - Try to find frameworks after standard
            libraries or headers.
"ONLY"    - Only try to find frameworks.
"NEVER".  - Never try to find frameworks.
```

On Darwin or systems supporting OSX Application Bundles, the cmake variable CMAKE_FIND_APPBUNDLE can be set to empty or one of the following:

```
"FIRST"   - Try to find application bundles before
```

```
              Standard programs. This is the default
              on Darwin.
    "LAST"    - Try to find application bundles after
              standard programs.
    "ONLY"    - Only try to find application bundles.
    "NEVER".  - Never try to find application bundles.
```

The CMake variable CMAKE_FIND_ROOT_PATH specifies one or more directories which will be prefixed to all of the search directories. By default it is empty. It is especially useful when cross-compiling to point to the root directory of the target environment and CMake will search there too. By default at first the directories listed in CMAKE_FIND_ROOT_PATH and then the non-prefixed directories will be searched. The default behavior can be adjusted by setting CMAKE_FIND_ROOT_PATH_MODE_LIBRARY. This behavior can be manually overridden on a per-call basis. By using CMAKE_FIND_ROOT_PATH_BOTH the search order will be as described above. If NO_CMAKE_FIND_ROOT_PATH is used then CMAKE_FIND_ROOT_PATH will not be used. If ONLY_CMAKE_FIND_ROOT_PATH is used then only the prefixed directories will be searched.

The reason the paths listed in the call to the command are searched last is that most users of CMake would expect things to be found first in the locations specified by their environment. Projects may override this behavior by simply calling the command twice:

```
    find_library(<VAR> NAMES name PATHS paths
                 NO_DEFAULT_PATH)
    find_library(<VAR> NAMES name)
```

Once one of these calls succeeds the result variable will be set and stored in the cache so that neither call will search again.

If the library found is a framework, then VAR will be set to the full path to the framework <fullPath>/A.framework. When a full path to a framework is used as a library, CMake will use a -framework A, and a -F<fullPath> to link the framework to the target.

• **find_package**: Load settings for an external project.

```
    find_package(<name> [major.minor] [QUIET] [NO_MODULE]
                 [[REQUIRED|COMPONENTS] [components...]])
```

Finds and loads settings from an external project. <name>_FOUND will be set to indicate whether the package was found. Settings that can be used when <name>_FOUND is true are package-specific. The package is found through several steps. Directories listed in CMAKE_MODULE_PATH are searched for files called "Find<name>.cmake". If such a file is found, it is read and processed by CMake, and is responsible for finding the package. This first step may be skipped by using the NO_MODULE option. If no such file is found, it is expected that the package is another project built by CMake that has a "<name>Config.cmake" file. A cache entry called <name>_DIR is created and is expected to be set to the directory containing this file. If the file is found, it is read and processed by CMake to load the settings of the package. If <name>_DIR has not been set during a configure step, the command will generate an error describing the problem unless the QUIET argument is specified. If <name>_DIR has been set to a directory not containing a "<name>Config.cmake" file, an error is always generated. If REQUIRED is specified and the package is not found, a FATAL_ERROR is generated and the configure step stops executing. A package-specific list of components may be listed after the REQUIRED option, or after the COMPONENTS option if no REQUIRED option is given.

- **find_path**: Find the directory containing a file.

```
find_path(<VAR> name1 path1 path2 ...)
```

This is the short-hand signature for the command that is sufficient in many cases. It is the same as find_path(<VAR> name1 PATHS path2 path2 ...)

```
find_path(
          <VAR>
          name | NAMES name1 [name2 ...]
          PATHS path1 [path2 ... ENV var]
          [PATH_SUFFIXES suffix1 [suffix2 ...]]
          [DOC "cache documentation string"]
          [NO_DEFAULT_PATH]
          [NO_CMAKE_ENVIRONMENT_PATH]
          [NO_CMAKE_PATH]
          [NO_SYSTEM_ENVIRONMENT_PATH]
          [NO_CMAKE_SYSTEM_PATH]
          [CMAKE_FIND_ROOT_PATH_BOTH |
            ONLY_CMAKE_FIND_ROOT_PATH |
            NO_CMAKE_FIND_ROOT_PATH ]
          )
```

This command is used to find a directory containing the named file. A cache entry named by <VAR> is created to store the result of this command. If the file in a directory is found the result is stored in the variable and the search will not be repeated unless the variable is cleared. If nothing is found, the result will be <VAR>-NOTFOUND, and the search will be attempted again the next time find_path is invoked with the same variable. The name of the file in a directory that is searched for is specified by the names listed after the NAMES argument. Additional search locations can be specified after the PATHS argument. If ENV var is found in the PATHS section the environment variable var will be read and converted from a system environment variable to a cmake style list of paths. For example ENV PATH would be a way to list the system path variable. The argument after DOC will be used for the documentation string in the cache. PATH_SUFFIXES can be used to give sub directories that will be appended to the search paths.

If NO_DEFAULT_PATH is specified, then no additional paths are added to the search. If NO_DEFAULT_PATH is not specified, the search process is as follows:

1. Search cmake specific environment variables. This can be skipped if NO_CMAKE_ENVIRONMENT_PATH is passed.

```
CMAKE_FRAMEWORK_PATH
CMAKE_APPBUNDLE_PATH
CMAKE_INCLUDE_PATH
```

2. Search cmake variables with the same names as the cmake specific environment variables. These are intended to be used on the command line with a -DVAR=value. This can be skipped if NO_CMAKE_PATH is passed.

```
CMAKE_FRAMEWORK_PATH
CMAKE_APPBUNDLE_PATH
CMAKE_INCLUDE_PATH
```

3. Search the standard system environment variables. This can be skipped if NO_SYSTEM_ENVIRONMENT_PATH is an argument.

```
PATH
INCLUDE
```

4. Search cmake variables defined in the Platform files for the current system. This can be skipped if NO_CMAKE_SYSTEM_PATH is passed.

```
CMAKE_SYSTEM_FRAMEWORK_PATH
CMAKE_SYSTEM_APPBUNDLE_PATH
CMAKE_SYSTEM_INCLUDE_PATH
```

5. Search the paths specified after PATHS or in the short-hand version of the command.

On Darwin or systems supporting OSX Frameworks, the cmake variable CMAKE_FIND_FRAMEWORK can be set to empty or one of the following:

```
"FIRST"    - Try to find frameworks before standard
             libraries or headers. This is the default
             on Darwin.
"LAST"     - Try to find frameworks after standard
             libraries or headers.
"ONLY"     - Only try to find frameworks.
"NEVER".   - Never try to find frameworks.
```

On Darwin or systems supporting OSX Application Bundles, the cmake variable CMAKE_FIND_APPBUNDLE can be set to empty or one of the following:

```
"FIRST"    - Try to find application bundles before
             Standard programs. This is the default
             on Darwin.
"LAST"     - Try to find application bundles after
             standard programs.
"ONLY"     - Only try to find application bundles.
"NEVER".   - Never try to find application bundles.
```

The CMake variable CMAKE_FIND_ROOT_PATH specifies one or more directories which will be prefixed to all of the search directories. By default it is empty. It is especially useful when cross-compiling to point to the root directory of the target environment and CMake will search there too. By default at first the directories listed in CMAKE_FIND_ROOT_PATH and then the non-prefixed directories will be searched. The default behavior can be adjusted by setting CMAKE_FIND_ROOT_PATH_MODE_INCLUDE. This behavior can be manually overridden on a per-call basis. By using CMAKE_FIND_ROOT_PATH_BOTH the search order will be as described above. If NO_CMAKE_FIND_ROOT_PATH is used then CMAKE_FIND_ROOT_PATH will not be used. If ONLY_CMAKE_FIND_ROOT_PATH is used then only the prefixed directories will be searched.

The reason the paths listed in the call to the command are searched last is that most users of CMake would expect things to be found first in the locations specified by their environment. Projects may override this behavior by simply calling the command twice:

```
find_path(<VAR> NAMES name PATHS paths
          NO_DEFAULT_PATH)
find_path(<VAR> NAMES name)
```

Once one of these calls succeeds the result variable will be set and stored in the cache so that neither call will search again.

When searching for frameworks, if the file is specified as A/b.h, then the framework search will look for A.framework/Headers/b.h. If that is found the path will be set to the path to the framework. CMake will convert this to the correct -F option to include the file.

- **find_program**: Find an executable program.

  ```
  find_program(<VAR> name1 path1 path2 ...)
  ```

This is the short-hand signature for the command that is sufficient in many cases. It is the same as find_program(<VAR> name1 PATHS path2 path2 ...)

```
find_program(
        <VAR>
        name | NAMES name1 [name2 ...]
        PATHS path1 [path2 ... ENV var]
        [PATH_SUFFIXES suffix1 [suffix2 ...]]
        [DOC "cache documentation string"]
        [NO_DEFAULT_PATH]
        [NO_CMAKE_ENVIRONMENT_PATH]
        [NO_CMAKE_PATH]
        [NO_SYSTEM_ENVIRONMENT_PATH]
        [NO_CMAKE_SYSTEM_PATH]
        [CMAKE_FIND_ROOT_PATH_BOTH |
          ONLY_CMAKE_FIND_ROOT_PATH |
          NO_CMAKE_FIND_ROOT_PATH ]
        )
```

This command is used to find a program. A cache entry named by <VAR> is created to store the result of this command. If the program is found the result is stored in the variable and the search will not be repeated unless the variable is cleared. If nothing is found, the result will be <VAR>-NOTFOUND, and the search will be attempted again the next time find_program is invoked with the same variable. The name of the program that is searched for is specified by the names listed after the NAMES argument. Additional search locations can be specified after the PATHS argument. If ENV var is found in the PATHS section the environment variable var will be read and converted from a system environment variable to a cmake style list of paths. For example ENV PATH would be a way to list the system path variable. The argument after DOC will be used for the documentation string in the cache. PATH_SUFFIXES can be used to give sub directories that will be appended to the search paths.

If NO_DEFAULT_PATH is specified, then no additional paths are added to the search. If NO_DEFAULT_PATH is not specified, the search process is as follows:

1. Search cmake specific environment variables. This can be skipped if NO_CMAKE_ENVIRONMENT_PATH is passed.

```
CMAKE_FRAMEWORK_PATH
CMAKE_APPBUNDLE_PATH
CMAKE_PROGRAM_PATH
```

2. Search cmake variables with the same names as the cmake specific environment variables. These are intended to be used on the command line with a -DVAR=value. This can be skipped if NO_CMAKE_PATH is passed.

```
CMAKE_FRAMEWORK_PATH
CMAKE_APPBUNDLE_PATH
CMAKE_PROGRAM_PATH
```

3. Search the standard system environment variables. This can be skipped if NO_SYSTEM_ENVIRONMENT_PATH is an argument.

```
PATH
```

4. Search cmake variables defined in the Platform files for the current system. This can be skipped if NO_CMAKE_SYSTEM_PATH is passed.

```
CMAKE_SYSTEM_FRAMEWORK_PATH
CMAKE_SYSTEM_APPBUNDLE_PATH
CMAKE_SYSTEM_PROGRAM_PATH
```

5. Search the paths specified after PATHS or in the short-hand version of the command.

On Darwin or systems supporting OSX Frameworks, the cmake variable CMAKE_FIND_FRAMEWORK can be set to empty or one of the following:

```
"FIRST"    - Try to find frameworks before standard
             libraries or headers. This is the default
             on Darwin.
"LAST"     - Try to find frameworks after standard
             libraries or headers.
"ONLY"     - Only try to find frameworks.
"NEVER".   - Never try to find frameworks.
```

On Darwin or systems supporting OSX Application Bundles, the cmake variable
CMAKE_FIND_APPBUNDLE can be set to empty or one of the following:

```
"FIRST"    - Try to find application bundles before
             Standard programs. This is the default
             on Darwin.
"LAST"     - Try to find application bundles after
             standard programs.
"ONLY"     - Only try to find application bundles.
"NEVER".   - Never try to find application bundles.
```

The CMake variable CMAKE_FIND_ROOT_PATH specifies one or more
directories which will be prefixed to all of the search directories. By default it is
empty. It is especially useful when cross-compiling to point to the root directory of
the target environment and CMake will search there too. By default at first the
directories listed in CMAKE_FIND_ROOT_PATH and then the non-prefixed
directories will be searched. The default behavior can be adjusted by setting
CMAKE_FIND_ROOT_PATH_MODE_PROGRAM. This behavior can be
manually overridden on a per-call basis. By using
CMAKE_FIND_ROOT_PATH_BOTH the search order will be as described above.
If NO_CMAKE_FIND_ROOT_PATH is used then CMAKE_FIND_ROOT_PATH
will not be used. If ONLY_CMAKE_FIND_ROOT_PATH is used then only the
prefixed directories will be searched.

The reason the paths listed in the call to the command are searched last is that most
users of CMake would expect things to be found first in the locations specified by
their environment. Projects may override this behavior by simply calling the
command twice:

```
find_program(<VAR> NAMES name PATHS paths
             NO_DEFAULT_PATH)
find_program(<VAR> NAMES name)
```

Once one of these calls succeeds the result variable will be set and stored in the
cache so that neither call will search again.

- **fltk_wrap_ui**: Create FLTK user interfaces Wrappers.

```
fltk_wrap_ui(resultingLibraryName source1
             source2 ... sourceN )
```

Produce .h and .cxx files for all the .fl and .fld files listed. The resulting .h and .cxx files will be added to a variable named resultingLibraryName_FLTK_UI_SRCS which should be added to your library.

- **foreach**: Evaluate a group of commands for each value in a list.

```
foreach(loop_var arg1 arg2 ...)
  COMMAND1(ARGS ...)
  COMMAND2(ARGS ...)
  ...
endforeach(loop_var)
foreach(loop_var RANGE total)
foreach(loop_var RANGE start stop [step])
```

All commands between foreach and the matching endforeach are recorded without being invoked. Once the endforeach is evaluated, the recorded list of commands is invoked once for each argument listed in the original foreach command. Before each iteration of the loop "${loop_var}" will be set as a variable with the current value in the list.

Foreach can also iterate over a generated range of numbers. There are three types of this iteration:

* When specifying single number, the range will have elements 0 to "total".

* When specifying two numbers, the range will have elements from the first number to the second number.

* The third optional number is the increment used to iterate from the first number to the second number.

- **get_cmake_property**: Get a property of the CMake instance.

```
get_cmake_property(VAR property)
```

Get a property from the CMake instance. The value of the property is stored in the variable VAR. If the property is not found, CMake will report an error. Some supported properties include: VARIABLES, CACHE_VARIABLES, COMMANDS, and MACROS.

- **get_directory_property**: Get a property of the directory.

```
get_directory_property(VAR [DIRECTORY dir] property)
```

Get a property from the Directory. The value of the property is stored in the variable VAR. If the property is not found, CMake will report an error. The properties include: VARIABLES, CACHE_VARIABLES, COMMANDS, MACROS, INCLUDE_DIRECTORIES, LINK_DIRECTORIES, DEFINITIONS, INCLUDE_REGULAR_EXPRESSION, LISTFILE_STACK, PARENT_DIRECTORY, and DEFINITION varname. If the DIRECTORY argument is provided then the property of the provided directory will be retrieved instead of the current directory. You can only get properties of a directory during or after it has been traversed by cmake.

- **get_filename_component**: Get a specific component of a full filename.

```
get_filename_component(VarName FileName
                       PATH|ABSOLUTE|NAME|EXT|NAME_WE
                       [CACHE])
```

Set VarName to be the path (PATH), file name (NAME), file extension (EXT), file name without extension (NAME_WE) of FileName, or the full absolute (ABSOLUTE) file name without symlinks. Note that the path is converted to Unix slashes format and has no trailing slashes. The longest file extension is always considered. If the optional CACHE argument is specified, the result variable is added to the cache.

```
get_filename_component(VarName FileName
                       PROGRAM [PROGRAM_ARGS ArgVar]
                       [CACHE])
```

The program in FileName will be found in the system search path or left as a full path. If PROGRAM_ARGS is present with PROGRAM, then any command-line arguments present in the FileName string are split from the program name and stored in ArgVar. This is used to separate a program name from its arguments in a command line string.

- **get_property**: Get a property.

```
get_property(VAR scope_value property)
```

Get a property from cmake. The scope_value is either GLOBAL, DIRECTORY dir_name, TARGET tgt_name, SOURCE_FILE src_name, or TEST test_name. The resulting value is stored in the variable VAR. If the property is not found, CMake will report an error.

- **get_source_file_property**: Get a property for a source file.

```
get_source_file_property(VAR file property)
```

Get a property from a source file. The value of the property is stored in the variable VAR. If the property is not found, VAR will be set to "NOTFOUND". Use set_source_files_properties to set property values. Source file properties usually control how the file is built. One property that is always there is LOCATION

- **get_target_property**: Get a property from a target.

```
get_target_property(VAR target property)
```

Get a property from a target. The value of the property is stored in the variable VAR. If the property is not found, VAR will be set to "NOTFOUND". Use set_target_properties to set property values. Properties are usually used to control how a target is built.

The read-only property "<CONFIG>_LOCATION" provides the full path to the file on disk that will be created for the target when building under configuration <CONFIG> (in upper-case, such as "DEBUG_LOCATION"). The read-only property "LOCATION" specifies the full path to the file on disk that will be created for the target. The path may contain a build-system-specific portion that is replaced at build time with the configuration getting built (such as "$(ConfigurationName)" in VS). This is very useful for executable targets to get the path to the executable file for use in a custom command.

The read-only property "TYPE" returns which type the specified target has (EXECUTABLE, STATIC_LIBRARY, SHARED_LIBRARY, MODULE_LIBRARY, UTILITY, INSTALL_FILES or INSTALL_PROGRAMS). This command can get properties for any target so far created. The targets do not need to be in the current CMakeLists.txt file.

- **get_test_property**: Get a property of the test.

```
get_test_property(test VAR property)
```

Get a property from the Test. The value of the property is stored in the variable VAR. If the property is not found, CMake will report an error. For a list of standard properties you can type cmake --help-property-list

- **if**: Conditionally execute a group of commands.

```
if(expression)
  # then section.
  COMMAND1(ARGS ...)
  COMMAND2(ARGS ...)
  ...
elseif(expression2)
  # elseif section.
  COMMAND1(ARGS ...)
  COMMAND2(ARGS ...)
  ...
else(expression)
  # else section.
  COMMAND1(ARGS ...)
  COMMAND2(ARGS ...)
  ...
endif(expression)
```

Evaluates the given expression. If the result is true, the commands in the then section are invoked. Otherwise, the commands in the else section are invoked. The elseif and else sections are optional. You may have multiple elseif clauses. Note that the same expression must be given to if, and endif. Long expressions can be used and the order or precedence is that the EXISTS, COMMAND, and DEFINED operators will be evaluated first. Then any EQUAL, LESS, GREATER, STRLESS, STRGREATER, STREQUAL, MATCHES will be evaluated. Then NOT operators and finally AND, OR operators will be evaluated. Possible expressions are:

```
if(variable)
```

True if the variable's value is not empty, 0, N, NO, OFF, FALSE, NOTFOUND, or <variable>-NOTFOUND.

```
if(NOT variable)
```

True if the variable's value is empty, 0, N, NO, OFF, FALSE, NOTFOUND, or <variable>-NOTFOUND.

```
if(variable1 AND variable2)
```

True if both variables would be considered true individually.

```
if(variable1 OR variable2)
```

True if either variable would be considered true individually.

```
if(COMMAND command-name)
```

True if the given name is a command that can be invoked.

```
if(EXISTS file-name)
if(EXISTS directory-name)
```

True if the named file or directory exists. Behavior is well-defined only for full paths.

```
if(file1 IS_NEWER_THAN file2)
```

True if file1 is newer than file2 or if one of the two files doesn't exist. Behavior is well-defined only for full paths.

```
if(IS_DIRECTORY directory-name)
```

True if the given name is a directory. Behavior is well-defined only for full paths.

```
if(IS_ABSOLUTE path)
```

True if the given path is an absolute path.

```
if(variable MATCHES regex)
if(string MATCHES regex)
```

True if the given string or variable's value matches the given regular expression.

```
if(variable LESS number)
if(string LESS number)
if(variable GREATER number)
if(string GREATER number)
if(variable EQUAL number)
if(string EQUAL number)
```

True if the given string or variable's value is a valid number and the inequality or equality is true.

```
if(variable STRLESS string)
if(string STRLESS string)
if(variable STRGREATER string)
if(string STRGREATER string)
if(variable STREQUAL string)
if(string STREQUAL string)
```

True if the given string or variable's value is lexicographically less (or greater, or equal) than the string on the right.

```
if(DEFINED variable)
```

True if the given variable is defined. It does not matter if the variable is true or false just if it has been set.

- **include**: Read CMake listfile code from the given file.

```
include(file1 [OPTIONAL] [RESULT_VARIABLE <VAR>])
include(module [OPTIONAL] [RESULT_VARIABLE <VAR>])
```

Reads CMake listfile code from the given file. Commands in the file are processed immediately as if they were written in place of the include command. If OPTIONAL is present, then no error is raised if the file does not exist. If RESULT_VARIABLE is given the variable will be set to the full filename which has been included or NOTFOUND if it failed.

If a module is specified instead of a file, the file with name <modulename>.cmake is searched in the CMAKE_MODULE_PATH.

- **include_directories**: Add include directories to the build.

```
include_directories([AFTER|BEFORE] [SYSTEM] dir1 dir2
...)
```

Add the given directories to those searched by the compiler for include files. By default the directories are appended onto the current list of directories. This default behavior can be changed by setting CMAKE_include_directories_BEFORE to ON. By using BEFORE or AFTER you can select between appending and prepending, independent from the default. If the SYSTEM option is given the compiler will be told that the directories are meant as system include directories on some platforms.

- **include_external_msproject**: Include an external Microsoft project file in a workspace.

```
include_external_msproject(projectname location
                           dep1 dep2 ...)
```

Includes an external Microsoft project in the generated workspace file. Currently does nothing on UNIX.

- **include_regular_expression**: Set the regular expression used for dependency checking.

```
include_regular_expression(regex_match
                           [regex_complain])
```

Set the regular expressions used in dependency checking. Only files matching regex_match will be traced as dependencies. Only files matching regex_complain will generate warnings if they cannot be found (standard header paths are not searched). The defaults are:

```
regex_match    = "^.*$" (match everything)
regex_complain = "^$" (match empty string only)
```

- **install**: Specify rules to run at install time.

This command generates installation rules for a project. Rules specified by calls to this command within a source directory are executed in order during installation. The order across directories is not defined.

There are multiple signatures for this command. Some of them define installation properties for files and targets. Properties common to multiple signatures are covered here but they are valid only for signatures that specify them.

DESTINATION arguments specify the directory on disk to which a file will be installed. If a full path (with a leading slash or drive letter) is given it is used directly. If a relative path is given it is interpreted relative to the value of CMAKE_INSTALL_PREFIX.

PERMISSIONS arguments specify permissions for installed files. Valid permissions are OWNER_READ, OWNER_WRITE, OWNER_EXECUTE, GROUP_READ, GROUP_WRITE, GROUP_EXECUTE, WORLD_READ, WORLD_WRITE, WORLD_EXECUTE, SETUID, and SETGID. Permissions that do not make sense on certain platforms are ignored on those platforms.

The CONFIGURATIONS argument specifies a list of build configurations for which the install rule applies (Debug, Release, etc.).

The COMPONENT argument specifies an installation component name with which the install rule is associated, such as "runtime" or "development". During component-specific installation only install rules associated with the given component name will be executed. During a full installation all components are installed.

The RENAME argument specifies a name for an installed file that may be different from the original file. Renaming is allowed only when a single file is installed by the command.

The OPTIONAL argument specifies that it is not an error if the file to be installed does not exist.

The TARGETS signature:

```
install(TARGETS targets...
        [[ARCHIVE|LIBRARY|RUNTIME]
         [DESTINATION <dir>]
         [PERMISSIONS permissions...]
         [CONFIGURATIONS [Debug|Release|...]]
         [COMPONENT <component>]
         [OPTIONAL]
        ] [...])
```

The TARGETS form specifies rules for installing targets from a project. There are three kinds of target files that may be installed: archive, library, and runtime. Executables are always treated as runtime targets. Static libraries are always treated as archive targets. Module libraries are always treated as library targets. For non-DLL platforms shared libraries are treated as library targets. For DLL platforms the DLL part of a shared library is treated as a runtime target and the corresponding import library is treated as an archive target. All Windows-based systems including Cygwin are DLL platforms. The ARCHIVE, LIBRARY, and RUNTIME arguments change the type of target to which the subsequent properties apply. If none is given the installation properties apply to all target types. If only one is given then only targets of that type will be installed (which can be used to install just a DLL or just an import library).

One or more groups of properties may be specified in a single call to the TARGETS form of this command. A target may be installed more than once to different locations. Consider hypothetical targets "myExe", "mySharedLib", and "myStaticLib". The code

```
install(TARGETS myExe mySharedLib myStaticLib
        RUNTIME DESTINATION bin
        LIBRARY DESTINATION lib
        ARCHIVE DESTINATION lib/static)
install(TARGETS mySharedLib
        DESTINATION /some/full/path)
```

will install myExe to <prefix>/bin and myStaticLib to <prefix>/lib/static. On non-DLL platforms mySharedLib will be installed to <prefix>/lib and /some/full/path. On DLL platforms the mySharedLib DLL will be installed to <prefix>/bin and /some/full/path and its import library will be installed to <prefix>/lib/static and /some/full/path. On non-DLL platforms mySharedLib will be installed to <prefix>/lib and /some/full/path.

Installing a target with EXCLUDE_FROM_ALL set to true has undefined behavior.

The FILES signature:

```
install(FILES files... DESTINATION <dir>
        [PERMISSIONS permissions...]
        [CONFIGURATIONS [Debug|Release|...]]
        [COMPONENT <component>]
        [RENAME <name>] [OPTIONAL])
```

The FILES form specifies rules for installing files for a project. File names given as relative paths are interpreted with respect to the current source directory. Files installed by this form are by default given permissions OWNER_WRITE, OWNER_READ, GROUP_READ, and WORLD_READ if no PERMISSIONS argument is given.

The PROGRAMS signature:

```
install(PROGRAMS files... DESTINATION <dir>
        [PERMISSIONS permissions...]
        [CONFIGURATIONS [Debug|Release|...]]
```

```
       [COMPONENT <component>]
       [RENAME <name>] [OPTIONAL])
```

The PROGRAMS form is identical to the FILES form except that the default permissions for the installed file also include OWNER_EXECUTE, GROUP_EXECUTE, and WORLD_EXECUTE. This form is intended to install programs that are not targets, such as shell scripts. Use the TARGETS form to install targets built within the project.

The DIRECTORY signature:

```
  install(DIRECTORY dirs... DESTINATION <dir>
          [FILE_PERMISSIONS permissions...]
          [DIRECTORY_PERMISSIONS permissions...]
          [USE_SOURCE_PERMISSIONS]
          [CONFIGURATIONS [Debug|Release|...]]
          [COMPONENT <component>]
          [[PATTERN <pattern> | REGEX <regex>]
           [EXCLUDE] [PERMISSIONS permissions...]]
          [...])
```

The DIRECTORY form installs contents of one or more directories to a given destination. The directory structure is copied verbatim to the destination. The last component of each directory name is appended to the destination directory but a trailing slash may be used to avoid this because it leaves the last component empty. Directory names given as relative paths are interpreted with respect to the current source directory. If no input directory names are given the destination directory will be created but nothing will be installed into it. The FILE_PERMISSIONS and DIRECTORY_PERMISSIONS options specify permissions given to files and directories in the destination. If USE_SOURCE_PERMISSIONS is specified and FILE_PERMISSIONS is not, file permissions will be copied from the source directory structure. If no permissions are specified files will be given the default permissions specified in the FILES form of the command, and the directories will be given the default permissions specified in the PROGRAMS form of the command. The PATTERN and REGEX options specify a globbing pattern or regular expression to match directories or files encountered during traversal of an input directory. The full path to an input file or directory (with forward slashes) is matched against the expression. A PATTERN will match only complete file names: the portion of the full path matching the pattern must occur at the end of the file name and be preceded by a slash. A REGEX will match any portion of the full path but it may use '/' and '$' to simulate the PATTERN behavior. Options following one of these matching expressions are applied only to files or directories matching them. The EXCLUDE option will skip the matched file or directory. The PERMISSIONS option overrides the permissions setting for the matched file or directory. For example the code

```
install(DIRECTORY icons scripts/
        DESTINATION share/myproj
        PATTERN "CVS" EXCLUDE
        PATTERN "scripts/*"
        PERMISSIONS OWNER_EXECUTE
                    OWNER_WRITE OWNER_READ
                    GROUP_EXECUTE GROUP_READ)
```

will install the icons directory to share/myproj/icons and the scripts directory to share/myproj. The icons will get default file permissions, the scripts will be given specific permissions, and any CVS directories will be excluded.

The SCRIPT and CODE signature:

```
install([[SCRIPT <file>] [CODE <code>]] [...])
```

The SCRIPT form will invoke the given CMake script files during installation. If the script file name is a relative path it will be interpreted with respect to the current source directory. The CODE form will invoke the given CMake code during installation. Code is specified as a single argument inside a double-quoted string. For example, the code

```
install(CODE "MESSAGE(\"Sample install message.\")")
```

will print a message during installation.

NOTE: This command supercedes the INSTALL_TARGETS command and the target properties PRE_INSTALL_SCRIPT and POST_INSTALL_SCRIPT. It also replaces the FILES forms of the INSTALL_FILES and INSTALL_PROGRAMS commands. The processing order of these install rules relative to those generated by INSTALL_TARGETS, INSTALL_FILES, and INSTALL_PROGRAMS commands is not defined.

- **link_directories**: Specify directories in which to search for libraries.

  ```
  link_directories(directory1 directory2 ...)
  ```

Specify the paths in which the linker should search for libraries.

- **list**: List operations.

```
list(LENGTH <list> <output variable>)
list(GET <list> <element index> [<element index> ...]
     <output variable>)
list(APPEND <list> <element> [<element> ...])
list(FIND <list> <value> <output variable>)
list(INSERT <list> <element_index> <element>
     [<element> ...])
list(REMOVE_ITEM <list> <value> [<value> ...])
list(REMOVE_AT <list> <index> [<index> ...])
list(REVERSE <list>)
list(SORT <list>)
```

LENGTH will return a given list's length.

GET will return list of elements specified by indices from the list.

APPEND will append elements to the list.

FIND will return the index of the element specified in the list or -1 if it wasn't found.

INSERT will insert elements to the list to the specified location.

When specifying an index, negative value corresponds to index from the end of the list.

REMOVE_AT and REMOVE_ITEM will remove items from the list. The difference is that REMOVE_ITEM will remove the given items, while REMOVE_AT will remove the items at the given indices.

REVERSE reverses the contents of the list in-place.

SORT sorts the list in-place alphabetically.

* **load_cache**: Load in the values from another project's CMake cache.

```
load_cache(pathToCacheFile READ_WITH_PREFIX
           prefix entry1...)
```

Read the cache and store the requested entries in variables with their name prefixed with the given prefix. This only reads the values, and does not create entries in the local project's cache.

```
load_cache(pathToCacheFile [EXCLUDE entry1...]
           [INCLUDE_INTERNALS entry1...])
```

Load in the values from another cache and store them in the local project's cache as internal entries. This is useful for a project that depends on another project built in a different tree. EXCLUDE option can be used to provide a list of entries to be excluded. INCLUDE_INTERNALS can be used to provide a list of internal entries to be included. Normally, no internal entries are brought in. Use of this form of the command is strongly discouraged, but it is provided for backward compatibility.

- **load_command**: Load a command into a running CMake.

```
load_command(COMMAND_NAME <loc1> [loc2 ...])
```

The given locations are searched for a library whose name is cmCOMMAND_NAME. If found, it is loaded as a module and the command is added to the set of available CMake commands. Usually, try_compile is used before this command to compile the module. If the command is successfully loaded a variable named

```
CMAKE_LOADED_COMMAND_<COMMAND_NAME>
```

will be set to the full path of the module that was loaded. Otherwise the variable will not be set.

- **macro**: Start recording a macro for later invocation as a command.

```
macro(<name> [arg1 [arg2 [arg3 ...]]])
  COMMAND1(ARGS ...)
  COMMAND2(ARGS ...)
  ...
endmacro(<name>)
```

Define a macro named <name> that takes arguments named arg1 arg2 arg3 (...). Commands listed after macro, but before the matching endmacro, are not invoked until the macro is invoked. When it is invoked, the commands recorded in the macro are first modified by replacing formal parameters (${arg1}) with the arguments passed, and then invoked as normal commands. In addition to referencing the formal parameters you can reference the variable ARGC which will be set to the number of arguments passed into the function as well as ARGV0 ARGV1 ARGV2 ... which will have the actual values of the arguments passed in. This facilitates creating macros with optional arguments. Additionally ARGV holds the list of all arguments given to the macro and ARGN holds the list of argument pass the last expected argument.

- **mark_as_advanced**: Mark cmake cached variables as advanced.

  ```
  mark_as_advanced([CLEAR|FORCE] VAR VAR2 VAR...)
  ```

  Mark the named cached variables as advanced. An advanced variable will not be displayed in any of the cmake GUIs unless the show advanced option is on. If CLEAR is the first argument advanced variables are changed back to unadvanced. If FORCE is the first argument, then the variable is made advanced. If neither FORCE nor CLEAR is specified, new values will be marked as advanced, but if the variable already has an advanced/non-advanced state, it will not be changed.

  It does nothing in script mode.

- **math**: Mathematical expressions.

  ```
  math(EXPR <output variable> <math expression>)
  ```

  EXPR evaluates mathematical expression and return result in the output variable. Example mathematical expression is '5 * (10 + 13)'. Supported operators are + - * / % | & ^ ~ << >> * / %. They have the same meaning as they do in c code.

- **message**: Display a message to the user.

  ```
  message([SEND_ERROR | STATUS | FATAL_ERROR]
          "message to display" ...)
  ```

  By default the message is displayed in a pop up window (CMakeSetup), or in the stdout of cmake, or the error section of ccmake. If the first argument is SEND_ERROR then an error is raised, and the generate phase will be skipped. If the first argument is FATAL_ERROR, all processing is halted. If the first argument is STATUS then the message is displayed in the progress line for the GUI, or with a -- in the command line cmake.

- **option**: Provides an option that the user can optionally select.

  ```
  option(OPTION_VAR "help string describing option"
         [initial value])
  ```

Provide an option for the user to select as ON or OFF. If no initial value is provided, OFF is used.

- **output_required_files**: Output a list of required source files for a specified source file.

  ```
  output_required_files(srcfile outputfile)
  ```

  Outputs a list of all the source files that are required by the specified srcfile. This list is written into outputfile. This is similar to writing out the dependencies for srcfile except that it jumps from .h files into .cxx, .c and .cpp files if possible.

- **project**: Set a name for the entire project.

  ```
  project(projectname [CXX] [C] [Java])
  ```

  Sets the name of the project. This creates the variables projectname_BINARY_DIR and projectname_SOURCE_DIR. Optionally you can specify which languages your project supports. By default all languages are supported. If you do not have a C++ compiler, but want to build a c program with cmake, then use this option.

- **qt_wrap_cpp**: Create QT Wrappers.

  ```
  qt_wrap_cpp(resultingLibraryName DestName
              SourceLists ...)
  ```

  Produce moc files for all the .h files listed in the SourceLists. The moc files will be added to the library using the DestName source list.

- **qt_wrap_ui**: Create QT user interfaces Wrappers.

  ```
  qt_wrap_ui(resultingLibraryName HeadersDestName
             SourcesDestName SourceLists ...)
  ```

  Produce .h and .cxx files for all the .ui files listed in the SourceLists. The .h files will be added to the library using the HeadersDestNamesource list. The .cxx files will be added to the library using the SourcesDestNamesource list.

- **remove_definitions**: Removes -D define flags to the command line of C and C++ compilers.

  ```
  remove_definitions(-DFOO -DBAR ...)
  ```

Removes flags from command line of C and C++ compilers. This command can be used to remove any flag from a compile line, but the -D flag is accepted by most C/C++ compilers. Other flags may not be as portable.

- **separate_arguments**: Split space separated arguments into a semi-colon separated list.

```
separate_arguments(VARIABLE)
```

Convert the value of VARIABLE to a semi-colon separated list. All spaces are replaced with ';'. This helps with generating command lines.

- **set**: Set a CMAKE variable to a given value.

```
set(VAR [VALUE] [CACHE TYPE DOCSTRING [FORCE]])
```

Within CMake sets VAR to the value VALUE. VALUE is expanded before VAR is set to it. If CACHE is present, then the VAR is put in the cache. TYPE and DOCSTRING are required. TYPE is used by the CMake GUI to choose a widget with which the user sets a value. The value for TYPE may be one of

```
FILEPATH = File chooser dialog.
PATH     = Directory chooser dialog.
STRING   = Arbitrary string.
BOOL     = Boolean ON/OFF checkbox.
INTERNAL = No GUI entry (for persistent variables).
```

If TYPE is INTERNAL, then the VALUE is always written into the cache, replacing any values existing in the cache. If it is not a cache variable, then this always writes into the current makefile. The FORCE option will overwrite the cache value removing any changes by the user.

```
set(VAR VALUE1 ... VALUEN).
```

In this case VAR is set to a semicolon separated list of values.

VAR can be an environment variable such as:

```
set( ENV{PATH} /home/martink )
```

in which case the environment variable will be set.

- **set_directory_properties**: Set a property of the directory.

```
set_directory_properties(PROPERTIES prop1 value1
                         prop2 value2)
```

Set a property for the current directory and subdirectories. If the property is not found, CMake will report an error. The properties include: INCLUDE_DIRECTORIES, LINK_DIRECTORIES, INCLUDE_REGULAR_EXPRESSION, and ADDITIONAL_MAKE_CLEAN_FILES. ADDITIONAL_MAKE_CLEAN_FILES is a list of files that will be cleaned as a part of "make clean" stage.

- **set_properties**: Set properties used by CMake.

```
set_properties(scope_value
               PROPERTIES prop1 value1
               prop2 value2 ...)
```

Set properties on something. The scope_value is either GLOBAL, DIRECTORY dir_name, TARGET tgt_name, SOURCE_FILE src_name, or TEST test_name.

- **set_source_files_properties**: Source files can have properties that affect how they are built.

```
set_source_files_properties(file1 file2 ...
                            PROPERTIES prop1 value1
                            prop2 value2 ...)
```

Set properties on a file. The syntax for the command is to list all the files you want to change, and then provide the values you want to set next. You can make up your own properties as well. The following are used by CMake. The ABSTRACT flag (boolean) is used by some class wrapping commands. If WRAP_EXCLUDE (boolean) is true then many wrapping commands will ignore this file. If GENERATED (boolean) is true then it is not an error if this source file does not exist when it is added to a target. Obviously, it must be created (presumably by a custom command) before the target is built. If the HEADER_FILE_ONLY (boolean) property is true then dependency information is not created for that file (this is set automatically, based on the file's name's extension and is probably only used by Makefiles). OBJECT_DEPENDS (string) adds dependencies to the object file. COMPILE_FLAGS (string) is passed to the compiler as additional command line arguments when the source file is compiled. LANGUAGE (string) CXX|C will change the default compiler used to compile the source file. The languages used need to be enabled in the PROJECT command. If SYMBOLIC (boolean) is set to true the build system will be informed that the source file is not actually created on disk but instead used as a symbolic name for a build rule.

- **set_target_properties**: Targets can have properties that affect how they are built.

```
set_target_properties(target1 target2 ...
                      PROPERTIES prop1 value1
                      prop2 value2 ...)
```

Set properties on a target. The syntax for the command is to list all the files you want to change, and then provide the values you want to set next. You can use any prop value pair you want and extract it later with the GET_TARGET_PROPERTY command.

Properties that affect the name of a target's output file are as follows. The PREFIX and SUFFIX properties override the default target name prefix (such as "lib") and suffix (such as ".so"). IMPORT_PREFIX and IMPORT_SUFFIX are the equivalent properties for the import library corresponding to a DLL (for SHARED library targets). OUTPUT_NAME sets the real name of a target when it is built and can be used to help create two targets of the same name even though CMake requires unique logical target names. There is also a <CONFIG>_OUTPUT_NAME that can set the output name on a per-configuration basis. <CONFIG>_POSTFIX sets a postfix for the real name of the target when it is built under the configuration named by <CONFIG> (in upper-case, such as "DEBUG_POSTFIX"). The value of this property is initialized when the target is created to the value of the variable CMAKE_<CONFIG>_POSTFIX (except for executable targets because earlier CMake versions which did not use this variable for executables).

The LINK_FLAGS property can be used to add extra flags to the link step of a target. LINK_FLAGS_<CONFIG> will add to the configuration <CONFIG>, for example, DEBUG, RELEASE, MINSIZEREL, RELWITHDEBINFO. DEFINE_SYMBOL sets the name of the preprocessor symbol defined when compiling sources in a shared library. If not set here then it is set to target_EXPORTS by default (with some substitutions if the target is not a valid C identifier). This is useful for headers to know whether they are being included from inside their library our outside to properly setup dllexport/dllimport decorations. The COMPILE_FLAGS property sets additional compiler flags used to build sources within the target. It may also be used to pass additional preprocessor definitions.

The LINKER_LANGUAGE property is used to change the tool used to link an executable or shared library. The default is set the language to match the files in the library. CXX and C are common values for this property.

For shared libraries VERSION and SOVERSION can be used to specify the build version and api version respectively. When building or installing appropriate symlinks are created if the platform supports symlinks and the linker supports so-names. If only one of both is specified the missing is assumed to have the same version number. For executables VERSION can be used to specify the build version. When building or installing appropriate symlinks are created if the platform supports symlinks. For shared libraries and executables on Windows the VERSION attribute is parsed to extract a "major.minor" version number. These numbers are used as the image version of the binary.

There are a few properties used to specify RPATH rules. INSTALL_RPATH is a semicolon-separated list specifying the rpath to use in installed targets (for platforms that support it). INSTALL_RPATH_USE_LINK_PATH is a boolean that if set to true will append directories in the linker search path and outside the project to the INSTALL_RPATH. SKIP_BUILD_RPATH is a boolean specifying whether to skip automatic generation of an rpath allowing the target to run from the build tree. BUILD_WITH_INSTALL_RPATH is a boolean specifying whether to link the target in the build tree with the INSTALL_RPATH. This takes precedence over SKIP_BUILD_RPATH and avoids the need for relinking before installation. INSTALL_NAME_DIR is a string specifying the directory portion of the "install_name" field of shared libraries on Mac OSX to use in the installed targets. When the target is created the values of the variables CMAKE_INSTALL_RPATH, CMAKE_INSTALL_RPATH_USE_LINK_PATH, CMAKE_SKIP_BUILD_RPATH, CMAKE_BUILD_WITH_INSTALL_RPATH, and CMAKE_INSTALL_NAME_DIR are used to initialize these properties.

PROJECT_LABEL can be used to change the name of the target in an IDE like visual studio. VS_KEYWORD can be set to change the visual studio keyword, for example QT integration works better if this is set to Qt4VSv1.0.

When a library is built CMake by default generates code to remove any existing library using all possible names. This is needed to support libraries that switch between STATIC and SHARED by a user option. However when using OUTPUT_NAME to build a static and shared library of the same name using different logical target names the two targets will remove each other's files. This can be prevented by setting the CLEAN_DIRECT_OUTPUT property to 1.

The PRE_INSTALL_SCRIPT and POST_INSTALL_SCRIPT properties are the old way to specify CMake scripts to run before and after installing a target. They are used only when the old INSTALL_TARGETS command is used to install the target. Use the INSTALL command instead.

The EXCLUDE_FROM_DEFAULT_BUILD property is used by the visual studio generators. If it is set to 1 the target will not be part of the default build when you select "Build Solution".

- **set_tests_properties**: Set a property of the tests.

  ```
  set_tests_properties(test1 [test2...] PROPERTIES prop1
  value1 prop2 value2)
  ```

  Set a property for the tests. If the property is not found, CMake will report an error. The properties include:

  WILL_FAIL: If set to true, this will invert the pass/fail flag of the test.

  PASS_REGULAR_EXPRESSION: If set, the test output will be checked against the specified regular expressions and at least one of the regular expressions has to match, otherwise the test will fail.

  ```
  Example: PASS_REGULAR_EXPRESSION "TestPassed;All ok"
  ```

  FAIL_REGULAR_EXPRESSION: If set, if the output will match to one of specified regular expressions, the test will fail.

  ```
  Example: PASS_REGULAR_EXPRESSION
                  "[^a-z]Error;ERROR;Failed"
  ```

  Both PASS_REGULAR_EXPRESSION and FAIL_REGULAR_EXPRESSION expect a list of regular expressions.

- **site_name**: Set the given variable to the name of the computer.

  ```
  site_name(variable)
  ```

- **source_group**: Define a grouping for sources in the makefile.

  ```
  source_group(name [REGULAR_EXPRESSION regex] [FILES
  src1 src2 ...])
  ```

  Defines a group into which sources will be placed in project files. This is mainly used to setup file tabs in Visual Studio. Any file whose name is listed or matches the regular expression will be placed in this group. If a file matches multiple groups, the LAST group that explicitly lists the file will be favored, if any. If no group explicitly lists the file, the LAST group whose regular expression matches the file will be favored.

The name of the group may contain backslashes to specify subgroups:

```
source_group(outer\\inner ...)
```

For backwards compatibility, this command is also supports the format:

```
source_group(name regex)
```

- **string**: String operations.

```
string(REGEX MATCH <regular_expression>
       <output variable> <input> [<input>...])
string(REGEX MATCHALL <regular_expression>
       <output variable> <input> [<input>...])
string(REGEX REPLACE <regular_expression>
       <replace_expression> <output variable>
       <input> [<input>...])
string(REPLACE <match_string>
       <replace_string> <output variable>
       <input> [<input>...])
string(COMPARE EQUAL <string1> <string2>
       <output variable>)
string(COMPARE NOTEQUAL <string1> <string2>
       <output variable>)
string(COMPARE LESS <string1> <string2>
       <output variable>)
string(COMPARE GREATER <string1> <string2>
       <output variable>)
string(ASCII <number> [<number> ...]
       <output variable>)
string(CONFIGURE <string1> <output variable>
       [@ONLY] [ESCAPE_QUOTES])
string(TOUPPER <string1> <output variable>)
string(TOLOWER <string1> <output variable>)
string(LENGTH <string> <output variable>)
string(SUBSTRING <string> <begin> <length>
       <output variable>)
string(STRIP <string> <output variable>)
string(RANDOM [LENGTH <length>] [ALPHABET <alphabet>]
       <output variable>)
```

REGEX MATCH will match the regular expression once and store the match in the output variable.

REGEX MATCHALL will match the regular expression as many times as possible and store the matches in the output variable as a list.

REGEX REPLACE will match the regular expression as many times as possible and substitute the replacement expression for the match in the output. The replace expression may refer to paren-delimited subexpressions of the match using \1, \2, ..., \9. Note that two backslashes (\\1) are required in CMake code to get a backslash through argument parsing.

REPLACE will replace all occurences of match_string in the input with replace_string and store the result in the output.

COMPARE EQUAL/NOTEQUAL/LESS/GREATER will compare the strings and store true or false in the output variable.

ASCII will convert all numbers into corresponding ASCII characters.

CONFIGURE will transform a string like CONFIGURE_FILE transforms a file.

TOUPPER/TOLOWER will convert string to upper/lower characters.

LENGTH will return a given string's length.

SUBSTRING will return a substring of a given string.

STRIP will return a substring of a given string with leading and trailing spaces removed.

RANDOM will return a random string of given length consisting of characters from the given alphabet. Default length is 5 characters and default alphabet is all numbers and upper and lower case letters.

The following characters have special meaning in regular expressions:

```
    ^       Matches at beginning of a line
    $       Matches at end of a line
    .       Matches any single character
    [ ]     Matches any character(s) inside the brackets
    [^ ]    Matches any character(s) not inside the
```

```
            brackets
     -      Matches any character in range on either side
            of a dash
     *      Matches preceding pattern zero or more times
     +      Matches preceding pattern one or more times
     ?      Matches preceding pattern zero or once only
     |      Matches a pattern on either side of the |
     ()     Saves a matched subexpression, which can be
referenced in the REGEX REPLACE operation. Additionally
it is saved in the special CMake variables
CMAKE_MATCH_(0..9).
```

- **target_link_libraries**: Link a target to given libraries.

```
target_link_libraries(target library1
                      <debug | optimized | general>
                      library2
                      ...)
```

Specify a list of libraries to be linked into the specified target. The debug and optimized strings may be used to indicate that the next library listed is to be used only for that specific type of build. general indicates it is used for all build types and is assumed if not specified.

- **try_compile**: Try compiling some code.

```
try_compile(RESULT_VAR bindir srcdir
            projectName <targetname>
            [CMAKE_FLAGS <Flags>]
            [OUTPUT_VARIABLE var])
```

Try compiling a program. In this form, srcdir should contain a complete CMake project with a CMakeLists.txt file and all sources. The bindir and srcdir will not be deleted after this command is run. If <target name> is specified then build just that target otherwise the all or ALL_BUILD target is built.

```
try_compile(RESULT_VAR bindir srcfile
            [CMAKE_FLAGS <Flags>]
            [COMPILE_DEFINITIONS <flags> ...]
            [OUTPUT_VARIABLE var]
            [COPY_FILE <filename> )
```

Try compiling a srcfile. In this case, the user need only supply a source file. CMake will create the appropriate CMakeLists.txt file to build the source. If COPY_FILE is used, the compiled file will becopied to the given file.

In this version all files in bindir/CMakeFiles/CMakeTmp, will be cleaned automatically, for debugging a --debug-trycompile can be passed to cmake to avoid the clean. Some extra flags that can be included are, INCLUDE_DIRECTORIES, LINK_DIRECTORIES, and LINK_LIBRARIES. COMPILE_DEFINITIONS are -Ddefinition that will be passed to the compile line. try_compile creates a CMakeList.txt file on the fly that looks like this:

```
add_definitions( <expanded COMPILE_DEFINITIONS>)
include_directories(${INCLUDE_DIRECTORIES})
link_directories(${LINK_DIRECTORIES})
add_executable(cmTryCompileExec sources)
target_link_libraries(cmTryCompileExec
                      ${LINK_LIBRARIES})
```

In both versions of the command, if OUTPUT_VARIABLE is specified, then the output from the build process is stored in the given variable. Return the success or failure in RESULT_VAR. CMAKE_FLAGS can be used to pass -DVAR:TYPE=VALUE flags to the cmake that is run during the build.

- **try_run**: Try compiling and then running some code.

```
try_run(RUN_RESULT_VAR COMPILE_RESULT_VAR
        bindir srcfile [CMAKE_FLAGS <Flags>]
        [COMPILE_DEFINITIONS <flags>]
        [COMPILE_OUTPUT_VARIABLE comp]
        [RUN_OUTPUT_VARIABLE run]
        [OUTPUT_VARIABLE var]
        [ARGS <arg1> <arg2>...])
```

Try compiling a srcfile. Return TRUE or FALSE for success or failure in COMPILE_RESULT_VAR. Then if the compile succeeded, run the executable and return its exit code in RUN_RESULT_VAR. If the executable was built, but failed to run, then RUN_RESULT_VAR will be set to FAILED_TO_RUN. COMPILE_OUTPUT_VARIABLE specifies the variable where the output from the compile step goes. RUN_OUTPUT_VARIABLE specifies the variable where the output from the running executable goes.

For compatibility reasons OUTPUT_VARIABLE is still supported, which gives you the output from the compile and run step combined.

Cross compiling issues

When cross compiling, the executable compiled in the first step usually cannot be run on the build host. try_run() checks the CMAKE_CROSSCOMPILING variable to detect whether CMake is in crosscompiling mode. If that's the case, it will still try to compile the executable, but it will not try to run the executable. Instead it will create cache variables which must be filled by the user or by presetting them in some CMake script file to the values the executable would have produced if it would have been run on its actual target platform. These variables are RUN_RESULT_VAR (explanation see above) and if RUN_OUTPUT_VARIABLE (or OUTPUT_VARIABLE) was used, an additional cache variable RUN_RESULT_VAR__COMPILE_RESULT_VAR__TRYRUN_OUTPUT.This is intended to hold stdout and stderr from the executable.

In order to make cross compiling your project easier, use try_run only if really required. If you use try_run, use RUN_OUTPUT_VARIABLE (or OUTPUT_VARIABLE) only if really required. Using them will require that when crosscompiling, the cache variables will have to be set manually to the output of the executable. You can also "guard" the calls to try_run with if(CMAKE_CROSSCOMPILING) and provide an easy-to-preset alternative for this case.

- **variable_watch**: Watch the CMake variable for change.

```
variable_watch(<variable name> [<command to execute>])
```

If the specified variable changes, the message will be printed about the variable being changed. If the command is spceified, the command will be executed. The command will receive the following arguments: COMMAND(<variable> <access> <value> <current list file> <stack>)

- **while**: Evaluate a group of commands while a condition is true

```
while(condition)
  COMMAND1(ARGS ...)
  COMMAND2(ARGS ...)
  ...
endwhile(condition)
```

All commands between while and the matching endwhile are recorded without being invoked. Once the endwhile is evaluated, the recorded list of commands is invoked as long as the condition is true. The condition is evaulated using the same logic as the if command.

Extra CTest Listfile Commands

- **ctest_build**: Builds the repository.

  ```
  ctest_build([BUILD build_dir] [RETURN_VALUE res])
  ```

  Builds the given build directory and stores results in Build.xml.

- **ctest_configure**: Configures the repository.

  ```
  ctest_configure(BUILD build_dir RETURN_VALUE res)
  ```

  Configures the given build directory and stores results in Configure.xml. The second argument is a variable that will hold return value.

- **ctest_coverage**: Tests the repository.

  ```
  ctest_coverage([BUILD build_dir] [RETURN_VALUE res])
  ```

  Perform the coverage of the given build directory and stores results in Coverage.xml. The second argument is a variable that will hold value.

- **ctest_empty_binary_directory**: empties the binary directory

  ```
  ctest_empty_binary_directory( directory )
  ```

  Removes a binary directory. This command will perform some checks prior to deleting the directory in an attempt to avoid malicious or accidental directory deletion.

- **ctest_memcheck**: Tests the repository.

  ```
  ctest_memcheck([BUILD build_dir] [RETURN_VALUE res])
  ```

  Performs a memory checking of tests in the given build directory and stores results in MemCheck.xml. The second argument is a variable that will hold value.

- **ctest_read_custom_files**: read CTestCustom files.

  ```
  ctest_read_custom_files( directory ... )
  ```

Read all the CTestCustom.ctest or CTestCustom.cmake files from the given directory.

- **ctest_run_script**: runs a ctest -S script

```
ctest_run_script([NEW_PROCESS] script_file_name
                 script_file_name1
                 script_file_name2 ...)
```

Runs a script or scripts much like if it was run from ctest -S. If no argument is provided then the current script is run using the current settings of the variables. If NEW_PROCESS is specified then each script will be run in a seperate process.

- **ctest_sleep**: sleeps for some amount of time

```
ctest_sleep( seconds )
ctest_sleep( time1 duration time2 )
```

With one argument it will sleep for a given number of seconds. With three arguments it will wait for time2 - time1 - duration seconds.

- **ctest_start**: Starts the testing for a given model

```
ctest_start(Model [TRACK <track>] [source [binary]])
```

Starts the testing for a given model. The command should be called after the binary directory is initialized. If the 'source' and 'binary' directory are not specified, it reads the CTEST_SOURCE_DIRECTORY and CTEST_BINARY_DIRECTORY. If the track is specified, the submissions will go to the specified track.

- **ctest_submit**: Submits the repository.

```
ctest_submit([RETURN_VALUE res])
```

Submits the test results for the project.

- **ctest_test**: Tests the repository.

```
ctest_test([BUILD build_dir] [RETURN_VALUE res])
```

Tests the given build directory and stores results in Test.xml. The second argument is a variable that will hold value.

- **`ctest_update`**: Updates the repository.

  ```
  ctest_update([SOURCE source] [RETURN_VALUE res])
  ```

  Updates the given source directory and stores results in Update.xml. The second argument is a variable that will hold the number of files modified. If there is a problem, the variable will be -1.

Compatibility Listfile Commands

The following commands are deprecated but still available in CMakeLists.txt code:

- **`build_name`**: Deprecated. Use ${CMAKE_SYSTEM} and ${CMAKE_CXX_COMPILER} instead.

  ```
  build_name(variable)
  ```

  Sets the specified variable to a string representing the platform and compiler settings. These values are now available through the CMAKE_SYSTEM and CMAKE_CXX_COMPILER variables.

- **`exec_program`**: Deprecated. Use the execute_process() command instead.

  Run an executable program during the processing of the CMakeList.txt file.

  ```
  exec_program(Executable [directory in which to run]
               [ARGS <arguments to executable>]
               [OUTPUT_VARIABLE <var>]
               [RETURN_VALUE <var>])
  ```

  The executable is run in the optionally specified directory. The executable can include arguments if it is double quoted, but it is better to use the optional ARGS argument to specify arguments to the program. This is because cmake will then be able to escape spaces in the executable path. An optional argument OUTPUT_VARIABLE specifies a variable in which to store the output. To capture the return value of the execution, provide a RETURN_VALUE. If OUTPUT_VARIABLE is specified, then no output will go to the stdout/stderr of the console running cmake.

- **`install_files`**: Deprecated. Use the install(FILES) command instead.

This command has been superceded by the install command. It is provided for compatibility with older CMake code. The FILES form is directly replaced by the FILES form of the install command. The regexp form can be expressed more clearly using the GLOB form of the file command.

```
install_files(<dir> extension file file ...)
```

Create rules to install the listed files with the given extension into the given directory. Only files existing in the current source tree or its corresponding location in the binary tree may be listed. If a file specified already has an extension, that extension will be removed first. This is useful for providing lists of source files such as foo.cxx when you want the corresponding foo.h to be installed. A typical extension is '.h'.

```
install_files(<dir> regexp)
```

Any files in the current source directory that match the regular expression will be installed.

```
install_files(<dir> FILES file file ...)
```

Any files listed after the FILES keyword will be installed explicitly from the names given. Full paths are allowed in this form.

The directory <dir> is relative to the installation prefix, which is stored in the variable CMAKE_INSTALL_PREFIX.

• **install_programs**: Deprecated. Use the install(PROGRAMS) command instead.

This command has been superceded by the install command. It is provided for compatibility with older CMake code. The FILES form is directly replaced by the PROGRAMS form of the INSTALL command. The regexp form can be expressed more clearly using the GLOB form of the FILE command.

```
install_programs(<dir> file1 file2 [file3 ...])
install_programs(<dir> FILES file1 [file2 ...])
```

Create rules to install the listed programs into the given directory. Use the FILES argument to guarantee that the file list version of the command will be used even when there is only one argument.

```
install_programs(<dir> regexp)
```

In the second form any program in the current source directory that matches the regular expression will be installed.

This command is intended to install programs that are not built by cmake, such as shell scripts. See the TARGETS form of the INSTALL command to create installation rules for targets built by cmake.

The directory <dir> is relative to the installation prefix, which is stored in the variable CMAKE_INSTALL_PREFIX.

- **install_targets**: Deprecated. Use the install(TARGETS) command instead.

This command has been superceded by the install command. It is provided for compatibility with older CMake code.

```
install_targets(<dir> [RUNTIME_DIRECTORY dir] target
target)
```

Create rules to install the listed targets into the given directory. The directory <dir> is relative to the installation prefix, which is stored in the variable CMAKE_INSTALL_PREFIX. If RUNTIME_DIRECTORY is specified, then on systems with special runtime files (Windows DLL), the files will be copied to that directory.

- **link_libraries**: Deprecated. Use the target_link_libraries() command instead.

Link libraries to all targets added later.

```
link_libraries(library1 <debug | optimized> library2
...)
```

Specify a list of libraries to be linked into any following targets (typically added with the add_executable or add_library calls). This command is passed down to all subdirectories. The debug and optimized strings may be used to indicate that the next library listed is to be used only for that specific type of build.

- **make_directory**: Deprecated. Use the file(MAKE_DIRECTORY) command instead.

```
make_directory(directory)
```

Creates the specified directory. Full paths should be given. Any parent directories that do not exist will also be created. Use with care.

- **remove**: Deprecated. Use the list(REMOVE_ITEM) command instead.

```
remove(VAR VALUE VALUE ...)
```

Removes VALUE from the variable VAR. This is typically used to remove entries from a vector (e.g. semicolon separated list). VALUE is expanded.

- **subdir_depends**: Deprecated. Does nothing.

```
subdir_depends(subdir dep1 dep2 ...)
```

Does not do anything. This command used to help projects order parallel builds correctly. This functionality is now automatic.

- **subdirs**: Deprecated. Use the add_subdirectory() command instead.

Add a list of subdirectories to the build.

```
subdirs(dir1 dir2 ...[EXCLUDE_FROM_ALL exclude_dir1
exclude_dir2 ...] [PREORDER] )
```

Add a list of subdirectories to the build. The add_subdirectory command should be used instead of subdirs although subdirs will still work. This will cause any CMakeLists.txt files in the sub directories to be processed by CMake. Any directories after the PREORDER flag are traversed first by makefile builds, the PREORDER flag has no effect on IDE projects. Any directories after the EXCLUDE_FROM_ALL marker will not be included in the top level makefile or project file. This is useful for having CMake create makefiles or projects for a set of examples in a project. You would want CMake to generate makefiles or project files for all the examples at the same time, but you would not want them to show up in the top level project or be built each time make is run from the top.

- **use_mangled_mesa**: Copy mesa headers for use in combination with system GL.

```
use_mangled_mesa(PATH_TO_MESA OUTPUT_DIRECTORY)
```

The path to mesa includes, should contain gl_mangle.h. The mesa headers are copied to the specified output directory. This allows mangled mesa headers to override other GL headers by being added to the include directory path earlier.

- **utility_source**: Specify the source tree of a third-party utility.

```
utility_source(cache_entry executable_name
               path_to_source [file1 file2 ...])
```

When a third-party utility's source is included in the distribution, this command specifies its location and name. The cache entry will not be set unless the path_to_source and all listed files exist. It is assumed that the source tree of the utility will have been built before it is needed.

When cross compiling CMake will print a warning if a utility_source() command is executed, because in many cases it is used to build an executable which is executed later on. This doesn't work when cross compiling, since the executable can run only on their target platform. So in this case the cache entry has to be adjusted manually so it points to an executable which is runnable on the build host.

- **variable_requires**: Deprecated. Use the if() command instead.

Assert satisfaction of an option's required variables.

```
variable_requires(TEST_VARIABLE RESULT_VARIABLE
                  REQUIRED_VARIABLE1
                  REQUIRED_VARIABLE2 ...)
```

The first argument (TEST_VARIABLE) is the name of the variable to be tested, if that variable is false nothing else is done. If TEST_VARIABLE is true, then the next argument (RESULT_VARIABLE) is a variable that is set to true if all the required variables are set. The rest of the arguments are variables that must be true or not set to NOTFOUND to avoid an error. If any are not true, an error is reported.

- **write_file**: Deprecated. Use the file(WRITE) command instead.

```
write_file(filename "message to write"... [APPEND])
```

The first argument is the file name, the rest of the arguments are messages to write. If the argument APPEND is specified, then the message will be appended.

NOTE 1: file(WRITE ... and file(APPEND ... do exactly the same as this one but add some more functionality.

NOTE 2: When using write_file the produced file cannot be used as an input to CMake (CONFIGURE_FILE, source file ...) because it will lead to an infinite loop. Use configure_file if you want to generate input files to CMake.

Appendix C – CMake Modules

Standard CMake Modules

The following modules are provided with CMake. They can be used with

```
include(ModuleName)
```

- **AddFileDependencies**:

  ADD_FILE_DEPENDENCIES(source_file depend_files...)

  Adds the given files as dependencies to source_file

- **CheckCCompilerFlag**: Check whether the C compiler supports a given flag.

  CHECK_C_COMPILER_FLAG(FLAG VARIABLE)

  ```
  FLAG - the compiler flag
  VARIABLE - variable to store the result
  ```

- **CheckCSourceCompiles**: macro which checks if the source code compiles

  CHECK_C_SOURCE_COMPILES(SOURCE VAR)

```
SOURCE - source code to try to compile
VAR    - variable to store whether the source code
         Compiled
```

The following variables may be set before calling this macro to modify the way the check is run:

```
CMAKE_REQUIRED_FLAGS       = string of compile command
                             line flags
CMAKE_REQUIRED_DEFINITIONS = list of macros to define
                                  (-DFOO=bar)
CMAKE_REQUIRED_INCLUDES  = list of include directories
CMAKE_REQUIRED_LIBRARIES = list of libraries to link
```

- **CheckCSourceRuns**: macro which checks if the source code runs

CHECK_C_SOURCE_RUNS(SOURCE VAR)

```
SOURCE    - source code to try to compile
VAR       - variable to store the result, 1 for
            success, empty for failure
```

The following variables may be set before calling this macro to modify the way the check is run:

```
CMAKE_REQUIRED_FLAGS = string of compile command
                       line flags
CMAKE_REQUIRED_DEFINITIONS = list of macros to define
                                  (-DFOO=bar)
CMAKE_REQUIRED_INCLUDES = list of include directories
CMAKE_REQUIRED_LIBRARIES = list of libraries to link
```

- **CheckCXXCompilerFlag**: Check whether the CXX compiler supports a given flag.

CHECK_CXX_COMPILER_FLAG(FLAG VARIABLE)

```
FLAG - the compiler flag
VARIABLE - variable to store the result
```

- **CheckCXXSourceCompiles**: macro which checks if the source code compiles

CHECK_CXX_SOURCE_COMPILES(SOURCE VAR)

```
SOURCE - source code to try to compile
VAR    - variable to store whether the source
         code compiled
```

The following variables may be set before calling this macro to modify the way the check is run:

```
CMAKE_REQUIRED_FLAGS = string of compile command
                       line flags
CMAKE_REQUIRED_DEFINITIONS = list of macros to define
                             (-DFOO=bar)
CMAKE_REQUIRED_INCLUDES = list of include directories
CMAKE_REQUIRED_LIBRARIES = list of libraries to link
```

- **CheckCXXSourceRuns**: macro which checks if the source code compiles

CHECK_CXX_SOURCE_RUNS(SOURCE VAR)

```
SOURCE - source code to try to compile
VAR    - variable to store the result, 1 for success,
         empty for failure
```

The following variables may be set before calling this macro to modify the way the check is run:

```
CMAKE_REQUIRED_FLAGS = string of compile command line
                       flags
CMAKE_REQUIRED_DEFINITIONS = list of macros to define
                             (-DFOO=bar)
CMAKE_REQUIRED_INCLUDES = list of include directories
CMAKE_REQUIRED_LIBRARIES = list of libraries to link
```

- **CheckFunctionExists**: macro which checks if the function exists

CHECK_FUNCTION_EXISTS(FUNCTION VARIABLE)

```
FUNCTION - the name of the function
VARIABLE - variable to store the result
```

The following variables may be set before calling this macro to modify the way the check is run:

```
CMAKE_REQUIRED_FLAGS = string of compile command line
                       flags
CMAKE_REQUIRED_DEFINITIONS = list of macros to define
                             (-DFOO=bar)
CMAKE_REQUIRED_INCLUDES = list of include directories
CMAKE_REQUIRED_LIBRARIES = list of libraries to link
```

- **CheckIncludeFile**: macro which checks the include file exists.

  CHECK_INCLUDE_FILE(INCLUDE VARIABLE)

  ```
  INCLUDE  - name of include file
  VARIABLE - variable to return result
  ```

an optional third argument is the CFlags to add to the compile line or you can use CMAKE_REQUIRED_FLAGS. The following variables may be set before calling this macro to modify the way the check is run:

```
CMAKE_REQUIRED_FLAGS = string of compile command line
                       flags
CMAKE_REQUIRED_DEFINITIONS = list of macros to define
                             (-DFOO=bar)
CMAKE_REQUIRED_INCLUDES = list of include directories
```

- **CheckIncludeFileCXX**: Check if the include file exists.

  CHECK_INCLUDE_FILE_CXX(INCLUDE VARIABLE)

  ```
  INCLUDE  - name of include file
  VARIABLE - variable to return result
  ```

An optional third argument is the CFlags to add to the compile line or you can use CMAKE_REQUIRED_FLAGS. The following variables may be set before calling this macro to modify the way the check is run:

```
CMAKE_REQUIRED_FLAGS = string of compile command line
                              flags
CMAKE_REQUIRED_DEFINITIONS = list of macros to define
                              (-DFOO=bar)
CMAKE_REQUIRED_INCLUDES = list of include directories
```

- **CheckIncludeFiles**: Check if the files can be included

CHECK_INCLUDE_FILES(INCLUDE VARIABLE)

```
INCLUDE  - list of files to include
VARIABLE - variable to return result
```

The following variables may be set before calling this macro to modify the way the check is run:

```
CMAKE_REQUIRED_FLAGS = string of compile command line
                              flags
CMAKE_REQUIRED_DEFINITIONS = list of macros to define
                              (-DFOO=bar)
CMAKE_REQUIRED_INCLUDES = list of include directories
```

- **CheckLibraryExists**: Check if the function exists.

CHECK_LIBRARY_EXISTS (LIBRARY FUNCTION LOCATION VARIABLE)

```
LIBRARY  - the name of the library you are looking for
FUNCTION - the name of the function
LOCATION - location where the library should be found
VARIABLE - variable to store the result
```

The following variables may be set before calling this macro to modify the way the check is run:

```
CMAKE_REQUIRED_FLAGS = string of compile command line
                              flags
CMAKE_REQUIRED_DEFINITIONS = list of macros to define
                              (-DFOO=bar)
CMAKE_REQUIRED_LIBRARIES = list of libraries to link
```

- **CheckStructHasMember**: Check if the given struct or class has the specified member variable

  CHECK_STRUCT_HAS_MEMBER (STRUCT MEMBER HEADER VARIABLE)

  ```
  STRUCT  - the name of the struct or class you are
            interested in
  MEMBER  - the member which existence you want to check
  HEADER  - the header(s) where the prototype should be
            declared
  VARIABLE - variable to store the result
  ```

  The following variables may be set before calling this macro to modify the way the check is run:

  ```
  CMAKE_REQUIRED_FLAGS = string of compile command line
                         flags
  CMAKE_REQUIRED_DEFINITIONS = list of macros to define
                               (-DFOO=bar)
  CMAKE_REQUIRED_INCLUDES = list of include directories
  ```

  Example:

  ```
  CHECK_STRUCT_HAS_MEMBER("struct timeval" tv_sec sys/select.h
                  HAVE_TIMEVAL_TV_SEC)
  ```

- **CheckSymbolExists**: Check if the symbol exists in include files

  CHECK_SYMBOL_EXISTS(SYMBOL FILES VARIABLE)

  ```
  SYMBOL   - symbol
  FILES    - include files to check
  VARIABLE - variable to return result
  ```

  The following variables may be set before calling this macro to modify the way the check is run:

  ```
  CMAKE_REQUIRED_FLAGS = string of compile command line
                         flags
  CMAKE_REQUIRED_DEFINITIONS = list of macros to define
  ```

```
                                         (-DFOO=bar)
   CMAKE_REQUIRED_INCLUDES = list of include directories
   CMAKE_REQUIRED_LIBRARIES = list of libraries to link
```

- **CheckTypeSize**: Check sizeof a type

```
   CHECK_TYPE_SIZE(TYPE VARIABLE)
```

Check if the type exists and determine size of type. if the type exists, the size will be stored to the variable.

```
   VARIABLE - variable to store size if the type exists.
   HAVE_${VARIABLE} - does the variable exists or not
```

The following variables may be set before calling this macro to modify the way the check is run:

```
   CMAKE_REQUIRED_FLAGS = string of compile command line
                          flags
   CMAKE_REQUIRED_DEFINITIONS = list of macros to define
                          (-DFOO=bar)
   CMAKE_REQUIRED_INCLUDES = list of include directories
   CMAKE_REQUIRED_LIBRARIES = list of libraries to link
```

- **CheckVariableExists**: Check if the variable exists.

```
   CHECK_VARIABLE_EXISTS(VAR VARIABLE)

   VAR      - the name of the variable
   VARIABLE - variable to store the result
```

This macro is only for C variables. The following variables may be set before calling this macro to modify the way the check is run:

```
   CMAKE_REQUIRED_FLAGS = string of compile command line
                          flags
   CMAKE_REQUIRED_DEFINITIONS = list of macros to define
                          (-DFOO=bar)
   CMAKE_REQUIRED_LIBRARIES = list of libraries to link
```

- **CMakeBackwardCompatibilityCXX**: define a bunch of backwards compatibility variables

```
CMAKE_ANSI_CXXFLAGS - flag for ansi c++
CMAKE_HAS_ANSI_STRING_STREAM - has <strstream>
INCLUDE(TestForANSIStreamHeaders)
INCLUDE(CheckIncludeFileCXX)
INCLUDE(TestForSTDNamespace)
INCLUDE(TestForANSIForScope)
```

- **CMakeDependentOption**: Macro to provide an option dependent on other options.

  This macro presents an option to the user only if a set of other conditions are true. When the option is not presented a default value is used, but any value set by the user is preserved for when the option is presented again. Example invocation:

```
CMAKE_DEPENDENT_OPTION(USE_FOO "Use Foo" ON
                       "USE_BAR;NOT USE_ZOT" OFF)
```

  If USE_BAR is true and USE_ZOT is false, this provides an option called USE_FOO that defaults to ON. Otherwise, it sets USE_FOO to OFF. If the status of USE_BAR or USE_ZOT ever changes, any value for the USE_FOO option is saved so that when the option is re-enabled it retains its old value.

- **CMakeDetermineASM-ATTCompiler**:

  determine the compiler to use for ASM using AT&T syntax

- **CMakeDetermineASMCompiler**:

  determine the compiler to use for ASM programs

- **CMakeExportBuildSettings**: export build settings from a project.

```
CMAKE_EXPORT_BUILD_SETTINGS(SETTINGS_FILE)
```

  macro defined to export the build settings for use by another project.

```
SETTINGS_FILE - the file into which the settings are
                to be stored.
```

- **CMakeFindFrameworks**: helper module to find OSX frameworks

- **CMakeImportBuildSettings**: import build settings from another project

  ```
  CMAKE_IMPORT_BUILD_SETTINGS(SETTINGS_FILE)
  ```

  macro defined to import the build settings from another project. SETTINGS_FILE is a file created by the other project's call to the CMAKE_EXPORT_BUILD_SETTINGS macro, see CMakeExportBuildSettings.

- **CMakeJavaInformation**:

  This should be included before the _INIT variables are used to initialize the cache. Since the rule variables have if blocks on them, users can still define them here. But, it should still be after the platform file so changes can be made to those values.

- **CMakePrintSystemInformation**: print system information

  This file can be used for diagnostic purposes just include it in a project to see various internal CMake variables.

- **CPack**:

  Default output files will be CPackConfig.cmake and CPackSourceConfig.cmake. This can be overwritten with CPACK_OUTPUT_CONFIG_FILE and CPACK_SOURCE_OUTPUT_CONFIG_FILE.

- **CPackRPM**:

  CPack script for creating RPM package Author: Eric Noulard with the help of Alexander Neundorf

- **CTest**: Configure a project for testing with CTest/Dart

  This file configures a project to use the CTest testing and dashboard process. This module should be included in the CMakeLists.txt file at the top of a project. Typical usage:

  ```
  INCLUDE(CTest)
  IF(BUILD_TESTING)
    # ... testing related CMake code ...
  ENDIF(BUILD_TESTING)
  ```

The BUILD_TESTING option is created by the CTest module to determine whether testing support should be enabled. The default is ON.

- **Documentation**: DocumentationVTK.cmake

  This file provides support for the VTK documentation framework. It relies on several tools (Doxygen, Perl, etc).

- **FeatureSummary**: Macros for generating a summary of enabled/disabled features

  ```
  PRINT_ENABLED_FEATURES()
  ```

  Print a summary of all enabled features. By default all successful FIND_PACKAGE() calls will appear here, except the ones which used the QUIET keyword. Additional features can be added by appending an entry to the global ENABLED_FEATURES property. If SET_FEATURE_INFO() is used for that feature, the output will be much more informative.

  ```
  PRINT_DISABLED_FEATURES()
  ```

  Same as PRINT_ENABLED_FEATURES(), but for disabled features. It can be extended the same way by adding to the global property DISABLED_FEATURES.

  ```
  SET_FEATURE_INFO(NAME DESCRIPTION [URL [COMMENT] ] )
  ```

  Use this macro to set up information about the named feature, which will then be displayed by PRINT_ENABLED / DISABLED_FEATURES(). Example: SET_FEATURE_INFO(LibXml2 "XML processing library." "http://xmlsoft.org/")

- **FindASPELL**: Try to find ASPELL

  Once done this will define

  ```
  ASPELL_FOUND - system has ASPELL
  ASPELL_INCLUDE_DIR - the ASPELL include directory
  ASPELL_LIBRARIES  - The libraries needed to use ASPELL
  ASPELL_DEFINITIONS - Compiler switches required for
                       using ASPELL
  ```

- **FindAVIFile**: Locate AVIFILE library and include paths

AVIFILE (http://avifile.sourceforge.net/)is a set of libraries for i386 machines to use various AVI codecs. Support is limited beyond Linux. Windows provides native AVI support, and so doesn't need this library. This module defines

```
AVIFILE_INCLUDE_DIR, where to find avifile.h , etc.
AVIFILE_LIBRARIES, the libraries to link against
AVIFILE_DEFINITIONS, definitions to use when compiling
AVIFILE_FOUND, If false, don't try to use AVIFILE
```

- **FindBoost**: Find the Boost includes and libraries.

The following variables are set if Boost is found. If Boost is not found, Boost_FOUND is set to false.

```
Boost_FOUND          - True when the Boost include
                       directory is found.
Boost_INCLUDE_DIRS - the path to where the boost
                       include files are.
Boost_LIBRARY_DIRS - The path to where the boost
                       library files are.
Boost_LIB_DIAGNOSTIC_DEFINITIONS - Only set if using
                                   Windows.
```

- **FindBZip2**: Try to find BZip2

Once done this will define

```
BZIP2_FOUND - system has BZip2
BZIP2_INCLUDE_DIR - the BZip2 include directory
BZIP2_LIBRARIES - Link these to use BZip2
BZIP2_DEFINITIONS - Compiler switches required for
                    using BZip2
BZIP2_NEED_PREFIX - this is set if the functions are
                    prefixed with BZ2_
```

- **FindCABLE**: Find CABLE

This module finds if CABLE is installed and determines where the include files and libraries are. This code sets the following variables:

```
CABLE              the path to the cable executable
CABLE_TCL_LIBRARY the path to the Tcl wrapper library
CABLE_INCLUDE_DIR the path to the include directory
```

To build Tcl wrappers, you should add shared library and link it to ${CABLE_TCL_LIBRARY}. You should also add ${CABLE_INCLUDE_DIR} as an include directory.

- **FindCups**: Try to find the Cups printing system

Once done this will define

```
CUPS_FOUND - system has Cups
CUPS_INCLUDE_DIR - the Cups include directory
CUPS_LIBRARIES - Libraries needed to use Cups
```

Set CUPS_REQUIRE_IPP_DELETE_ATTRIBUTE to TRUE if you need a version which features this function (i.e. at least 1.1.19)

- **FindCURL**: Find curl

Find the native CURL headers and libraries.

```
CURL_INCLUDE_DIRS - where to find curl/curl.h, etc.
CURL_LIBRARIES    - List of libraries when using curl.
CURL_FOUND        - True if curl found.
```

- **FindCurses**: Find the curses include file and library

```
CURSES_FOUND - system has Curses
CURSES_INCLUDE_DIR - the Curses include directory
CURSES_LIBRARIES - The libraries needed to use Curses
CURSES_HAVE_CURSES_H - true if curses.h is available
CURSES_HAVE_NCURSES_H - true if ncurses.h is available
CURSES_HAVE_NCURSES_NCURSES_H - true if
                       ncurses/ncurses.h is available
CURSES_HAVE_NCURSES_CURSES_H - true if
                       ncurses/curses.h is available
```

Set CURSES_NEED_NCURSES to TRUE before the FIND_PACKAGE() command if NCurses functionality is required.

- **FindCygwin**: this module looks for Cygwin

- **FindDCMTK**: find DCMTK libraries

- **FindDoxygen**: This module looks for Doxygen and the path to Graphviz's dot

  Doxygen is a documentation generation tool see http://www.doxygen.org With the OS X GUI version, it likes to be installed to /Applications and it contains the doxygen executable in the bundle. In the versions I've seen, it is located in Resources, but in general, more often binaries are located in MacOS. This code sets the following variables:

  ```
  DOXYGEN_EXECUTABLE   = The path to the doxygen command.
  DOXYGEN_DOT_EXECUTABLE = The path to the dot program
                           used by doxygen.
  DOXYGEN_DOT_PATH     = The path to dot not including
                           the executable
  DOXYGEN = same as DOXYGEN_EXECUTABLE for backwards
            compatibility
  DOT     = same as DOXYGEN_DOT_EXECUTABLE for backwards
            compatibility
  ```

- **FindEXPAT**: Find expat

  Find the native EXPAT headers and libraries.

  ```
  EXPAT_INCLUDE_DIRS - where to find expat.h, etc.
  EXPAT_LIBRARIES  - List of libraries when using expat.
  EXPAT_FOUND      - True if expat found.
  ```

- **FindFLTK**: Find the native FLTK includes and library

  The following settings are defined

  ```
  FLTK_FLUID_EXECUTABLE, where to find the Fluid tool
  FLTK_WRAP_UI, This enables the FLTK_WRAP_UI command
  FLTK_INCLUDE_DIR, where to find include files
  ```

```
FLTK_LIBRARIES, list of fltk libraries
FLTK_FOUND, Don't use FLTK if false.
```

The following settings should not be used in general.

```
FLTK_BASE_LIBRARY   = the full path to fltk.lib
FLTK_GL_LIBRARY     = the full path to fltk_gl.lib
FLTK_FORMS_LIBRARY  = the full path to fltk_forms.lib
FLTK_IMAGES_LIBRARY = the full path to fltk_images.lib
```

- **FindGCCXML**: Find the GCC-XML front-end executable.

- **FindGettext**: Find GNU gettext tools

  This module looks for the GNU gettext tools. This module defines the following values:

  ```
  GETTEXT_MSGMERGE_EXECUTABLE: the full path to the
                                     msgmerge tool.
  GETTEXT_MSGFMT_EXECUTABLE: the full path to the msgfmt
                                  tool.
  GETTEXT_FOUND: True if gettext has been found.
  ```

  Additionally it provides the following macro:

  ```
  GETTEXT_CREATE_TRANSLATIONS (outputFile [ALL] file1 .. fileN)
  ```

  This will create a target "translations" which will convert the given input po files into the binary output mo file. If the ALL option is used, the translations will also be created when building the default target.

- **FindGLUT**: try to find glut library and include files

  ```
  GLUT_INCLUDE_DIR, where to find GL/glut.h, etc.
  GLUT_LIBRARIES, the libraries to link against
  GLUT_FOUND, If false, do not try to use GLUT.
  ```

  Also defined, but not for general use are:

```
GLUT_glut_LIBRARY = the full path to the glut library.
GLUT_Xmu_LIBRARY  = the full path to the Xmu library.
GLUT_Xi_LIBRARY   = the full path to the Xi Library.
```

- **FindGnuplot**: this module looks for gnuplot

  Once done this will define

  ```
  GNUPLOT_FOUND - system has Gnuplot
  GNUPLOT_EXECUTABLE - the Gnuplot executable
  ```

- **FindGTK**: try to find GTK (and glib) and GTKGLArea

  ```
  GTK_INCLUDE_DIR    - Directories to include to use GTK
  GTK_LIBRARIES      - Files to link against to use GTK
  GTK_FOUND          - GTK was found
  GTK_GL_FOUND       - GTK's GL features were found
  ```

- **FindHSPELL**: Try to find HSPELL

  Once done this will define

  ```
  HSPELL_FOUND - system has HSPELL
  HSPELL_INCLUDE_DIR - the HSPELL include directory
  HSPELL_LIBRARIES - The libraries needed to use HSPELL
  HSPELL_DEFINITIONS - Compiler switches required for
                       using HSPELL
  ```

- **FindHTMLHelp**: This module looks for Microsoft HTML Help Compiler

  It defines:

  ```
  HTML_HELP_COMPILER     : full path to the Compiler
                           (hhc.exe)
  HTML_HELP_INCLUDE_PATH : include path to the API
                           (htmlhelp.h)
  HTML_HELP_LIBRARY      : full path to the library
                           (htmlhelp.lib)
  ```

- **FindImageMagick**: Find Image Magick

This module finds if ImageMagick tools are installed and determines where the executables are. This code sets the following variables:

```
IMAGEMAGICK_CONVERT_EXECUTABLE    =
    the full path to the 'convert' utility
IMAGEMAGICK_MOGRIFY_EXECUTABLE    =
    the full path to the 'mogrify' utility
IMAGEMAGICK_IMPORT_EXECUTABLE     =
    the full path to the 'import'  utility
IMAGEMAGICK_MONTAGE_EXECUTABLE    =
    the full path to the 'montage' utility
IMAGEMAGICK_COMPOSITE_EXECUTABLE =
    the full path to the 'composite' utility
```

- **FindITK**: Find an ITK installation or build tree.

- **FindJasper**: Try to find the Jasper JPEG2000 library

  Once done this will define

  ```
  JASPER_FOUND - system has Jasper
  JASPER_INCLUDE_DIR - the Jasper include directory
  JASPER_LIBRARIES - The libraries needed to use Jasper
  ```

- **FindJava**: Find Java

  This module finds if Java is installed and determines where the include files and libraries are. This code sets the following variables:

  ```
  JAVA_RUNTIME    = the full path to the Java runtime
  JAVA_COMPILE    = the full path to the Java compiler
  JAVA_ARCHIVE    = the full path to the Java archiver
  ```

- **FindJNI**: Find JNI java libraries.

  This module finds if Java is installed and determines where the include files and libraries are. It also determines what the name of the library is. This code sets the following variables:

```
JAVA_AWT_LIB_PATH     = the path to the jawt library
JAVA_JVM_LIB_PATH     = the path to the jvm library
JAVA_INCLUDE_PATH     = the include path to jni.h
JAVA_INCLUDE_PATH2    = the include path to jni_md.h
JAVA_AWT_INCLUDE_PATH = the include path to jawt.h
```

- **FindJPEG**: Find JPEG

  Find the native JPEG includes and library This module defines

  ```
  JPEG_INCLUDE_DIR, where to find jpeglib.h, etc.
  JPEG_LIBRARIES, the libraries needed to use JPEG.
  JPEG_FOUND, If false, do not try to use JPEG.
  ```

  also defined, but not for general use are

  ```
  JPEG_LIBRARY, where to find the JPEG library.
  ```

- **FindKDE3**: Find the KDE3 include and library dirs, KDE preprocessors and define a some macros

  This module defines the following variables:

  ```
  KDE3_DEFINITIONS    - compiler definitions required for
                        compiling KDE software
  KDE3_INCLUDE_DIR    - the KDE include directory
  KDE3_INCLUDE_DIRS   - the KDE and the Qt include
                        directory, for use with
                        include_directories()
  KDE3_LIB_DIR        - the directory where the KDE
                        libraries are installed, for use
                        with link_directories()
  QT_AND_KDECORE_LIBS - this contains both the Qt and
                         the kdecore library
  KDE3_DCOPIDL_EXECUTABLE - the dcopidl executable
  KDE3_DCOPIDL2CPP_EXECUTABLE - the dcopidl2cpp
                               executable
  KDE3_KCFGC_EXECUTABLE - the kconfig_compiler
                          executable
  KDE3_FOUND          - set to TRUE if all of the above
                        has been found
  ```

The following user adjustable options are provided:

```
KDE3_BUILD_TESTS - enable this to build KDE testcases
```

It also adds the following macros (from KDE3Macros.cmake) SRCS_VAR is always the variable which contains the list of source files for your application or library.

KDE3_AUTOMOC(file1 ... fileN)

Call this if you want to have automatic moc file handling. This means if you include "foo.moc" in the source file foo.cpp a moc file for the header foo.h will be created automatically. You can set the property SKIP_AUTOMAKE using SET_SOURCE_FILES_PROPERTIES() to exclude some files in the list from being processed.

```
KDE3_ADD_MOC_FILES(SRCS_VAR file1 ... fileN )
```

If you don't use the KDE3_AUTOMOC() macro, for the files listed here moc files will be created (named "foo.moc.cpp")

KDE3_ADD_DCOP_SKELS(SRCS_VAR header1.h ... headerN.h)

Use this to generate DCOP skeletions from the listed headers.

KDE3_ADD_DCOP_STUBS(SRCS_VAR header1.h ... headerN.h)

Use this to generate DCOP stubs from the listed headers.

KDE3_ADD_UI_FILES(SRCS_VAR file1.ui ... fileN.ui)

Use this to add the Qt designer ui files to your application/library.

KDE3_ADD_KCFG_FILES(SRCS_VAR file1.kcfgc ... fileN.kcfgc)

Use this to add KDE kconfig compiler files to your application/library.

KDE3_INSTALL_LIBTOOL_FILE(target)

This will create and install a simple libtool file for the given target.

KDE3_ADD_EXECUTABLE(name file1 ... fileN)

Currently identical to ADD_EXECUTABLE(), may provide some advanced features in the future.

KDE3_ADD_KPART(name [WITH_PREFIX] file1 ... fileN)

Create a KDE plugin (KPart, kioslave, etc.) from the given source files. If WITH_PREFIX is given, the resulting plugin will have the prefix "lib", otherwise it won't. It creates and installs an appropriate libtool la-file.

KDE3_ADD_KDEINIT_EXECUTABLE(name file1 ... fileN)

Create a KDE application in the form of a module loadable via kdeinit. A library named kdeinit_<name> will be created and a small executable which links to it.

The option KDE3_ENABLE_FINAL to enable all-in-one compilation is no longer supported.

Author: Alexander Neundorf <neundorf@kde.org>

- **FindKDE4**:

  Find KDE4 and provide all necessary variables and macros to compile software for it. It looks for KDE 4 in the following directories in the given order:

  ```
  CMAKE_INSTALL_PREFIX
  KDEDIRS
  /opt/kde4
  ```

  Please look in FindKDE4Internal.cmake and KDE4Macros.cmake for more information. They are installed with the KDE 4 libraries in $KDEDIRS/share/apps/cmake/modules/.

  Author: Alexander Neundorf <neundorf@kde.org>

- **FindLATEX**: Find Latex

  This module finds if Latex is installed and determines where the executables are. This code sets the following variables:

  ```
  LATEX_COMPILER:        path to the LaTeX compiler
  ```

```
PDFLATEX_COMPILER:      path to the PdfLaTeX compiler
BIBTEX_COMPILER:        path to the BibTeX compiler
MAKEINDEX_COMPILER:     path to the MakeIndex compiler
DVIPS_CONVERTER:        path to the DVIPS converter
PS2PDF_CONVERTER:       path to the PS2PDF converter
LATEX2HTML_CONVERTER:   path to the LaTeX2Html converter
```

- **FindLibXml2**: Try to find LibXml2

  Once done this will define

  ```
  LIBXML2_FOUND - system has LibXml2
  LIBXML2_INCLUDE_DIR - the LibXml2 include directory
  LIBXML2_LIBRARIES - the libraries needed to use
                       LibXml2
  LIBXML2_DEFINITIONS - Compiler switches required for
                       using LibXml2
  ```

- **FindLibXslt**: Try to find LibXslt

  Once done this will define

  ```
  LIBXSLT_FOUND - system has LibXslt
  LIBXSLT_INCLUDE_DIR - the LibXslt include directory
  LIBXSLT_LIBRARIES - Link these to LibXslt
  LIBXSLT_DEFINITIONS - Compiler switches required for
                       using LibXslt
  ```

- **FindMatlab**: this module looks for Matlab

  Defines:

  ```
  MATLAB_INCLUDE_DIR: include path for mex.h, engine.h
  MATLAB_LIBRARIES:   required libraries: libmex, etc
  MATLAB_MEX_LIBRARY: path to libmex.lib
  MATLAB_MX_LIBRARY:  path to libmx.lib
  MATLAB_ENG_LIBRARY: path to libeng.lib
  ```

- **FindMFC**: Find MFC on Windows

  Find the native MFC - i.e. decide if this is an MS VC box.

```
MFC_FOUND - Was MFC support found
```

You don't need to include anything or link anything to use it.

- **FindMotif**: Try to find Motif (or lesstif)

  Once done this will define:

  ```
  MOTIF_FOUND          - system has MOTIF
  MOTIF_INCLUDE_DIR    - incude paths to use Motif
  MOTIF_LIBRARIES      - Link these to use Motif
  ```

- **FindMPEG**: Find the native MPEG includes and library

  This module defines

  ```
  MPEG_INCLUDE_DIR, where to find MPEG.h, etc.
  MPEG_LIBRARIES, the libraries required to use MPEG.
  MPEG_FOUND, If false, do not try to use MPEG.
  ```

  also defined, but not for general use are

  ```
  MPEG_mpeg2_LIBRARY, where to find the MPEG library.
  MPEG_vo_LIBRARY, where to find the vo library.
  ```

- **FindMPEG2**: Find the native MPEG2 includes and library

  This module defines

  ```
  MPEG2_INCLUDE_DIR, path to mpeg2dec/mpeg2.h, etc.
  MPEG2_LIBRARIES, the libraries required to use MPEG2.
  MPEG2_FOUND, If false, do not try to use MPEG2.
  ```

  also defined, but not for general use are

  ```
  MPEG2_mpeg2_LIBRARY, where to find the MPEG2 library.
  MPEG2_vo_LIBRARY, where to find the vo library.
  ```

- **FindMPI**: Find MPI

This module looks for MPI (Message Passing Interface) support it will define the following values

```
MPI_INCLUDE_PATH = where mpi.h can be found
MPI_LIBRARY = the library to link in (mpi mpich etc)
```

- **FindOpenAL**: Locate OpenAL

This module defines

```
OPENAL_LIBRARY
OPENAL_FOUND, if false, do not try to link to OpenAL
OPENAL_INCLUDE_DIR, where to find the headers
```

$OPENALDIR is an environment variable that would correspond to the ./configure --prefix=$OPENALDIR used in building OpenAL.

Created by Eric Wing. This was influenced by the FindSDL.cmake module. On OSX, this will prefer the Framework version (if found) over others. People will have to manually change the cache values of OPENAL_LIBRARY to override this selection. Tiger will include OpenAL as part of the System. But for now, we have to look around. Other (Unix) systems should be able to utilize the non-framework paths.

- **FindOpenGL**: Try to find OpenGL

Once done this will define

```
OPENGL_FOUND          - system has OpenGL
OPENGL_XMESA_FOUND    - system has XMESA
OPENGL_GLU_FOUND      - system has GLU
OPENGL_INCLUDE_DIR    - the GL include directory
OPENGL_LIBRARIES      - Link these to use OpenGL and GLU
```

If you want to use just GL you can use these values

```
OPENGL_gl_LIBRARY    - Path to OpenGL Library
OPENGL_glu_LIBRARY   - Path to GLU Library
```

On OSX default to using the framework version of opengl People will have to change the cache values of OPENGL_glu_LIBRARY and OPENGL_gl_LIBRARY to use OpenGL with X11 on OSX

- **FindOpenSSL**: Try to find the OpenSSL encryption library

  Once done this will define

  ```
  OPENSSL_FOUND - system has the OpenSSL library
  OPENSSL_INCLUDE_DIR - the OpenSSL include directory
  OPENSSL_LIBRARIES - The libraries needed to use
                      OpenSSL
  ```

- **FindPackageHandleStandardArgs**:

  FIND_PACKAGE_HANDLE_STANDARD_ARGS(NAME (DEFAULT_MSG|"Custom failure message") VAR1 ...)

  This macro is intended to be used in FindXXX.cmake modules files. It handles the REQUIRED and QUIET argument to FIND_PACKAGE() and it also sets the <UPPERCASED_NAME>_FOUND variable. The package is found if all variables listed are TRUE. Example:

  ```
  FIND_PACKAGE_HANDLE_STANDARD_ARGS(LibXml2 DEFAULT_MSG
                                    LIBXML2_LIBRARIES
                                    LIBXML2_INCLUDE_DIR)
  ```

  LibXml2 is considered to be found, if both LIBXML2_LIBRARIES and LIBXML2_INCLUDE_DIR are valid. Then also LIBXML2_FOUND is set to TRUE. If it is not found and REQUIRED was used, it fails with FATAL_ERROR, independent whether QUIET was used or not. If it is found, the location is reported using the VAR1 argument, so here a message "Found LibXml2: /usr/lib/libxml2.so" will be printed out. If the second argument is DEFAULT_MSG, the message in the failure case will be "Could NOT find LibXml2", if you don't like this message you can specify your own custom failure message there.

- **FindPerl**: Find perl

  this module looks for Perl

```
PERL_EXECUTABLE  - the full path to perl
PERL_FOUND       - If false, don't attempt to use perl.
```

- **FindPerlLibs**: Find Perl libraries

  This module finds if PERL is installed and determines where the include files and libraries are. It also determines what the name of the library is. This code sets the following variables:

  ```
  PERL_INCLUDE_PATH = path to where perl.h is found
  PERL_EXECUTABLE   = full path to the perl binary
  ```

- **FindPHP4**: Find PHP4

  This module finds if PHP4 is installed and determines where the include files and libraries are. It also determines what the name of the library is. This code sets the following variables:

  ```
  PHP4_INCLUDE_PATH  = path to where php.h can be found
  PHP4_EXECUTABLE    = full path to the php4 binary
  ```

- **FindPhysFS**: Locate PhysFS library

  This module defines

  ```
  PHYSFS_LIBRARY, the name of the library to link with
  PHYSFS_FOUND, if false, do not try to link to PHYSFS
  PHYSFS_INCLUDE_DIR, where to find PHYSFS/PHYSFS.h
  ```

  $PHYSFSDIR is an environment variable that would correspond to the ./configure --prefix=$PHYSFSDIR used in building PHYSFS.

  Created by Eric Wing. This was influenced by the FindSDL.cmake module, but with modifications to recognize OS X frameworks.

- **FindPike**: Find Pike

  This module finds if PIKE is installed and determines where the include files and libraries are. It also determines what the name of the library is. This code sets the following variables:

```
PIKE_INCLUDE_PATH   = path to where program.h is found
PIKE_EXECUTABLE     = full path to the pike binary
```

- **FindPkgConfig**: a pkg-config module for CMake

Usage:

```
pkg_check_modules(<PREFIX> [REQUIRED] <MODULE>
                    [<MODULE>]*)
  checks for all the given modules

pkg_search_module(<PREFIX> [REQUIRED] <MODULE>
                    [<MODULE>]*)
  checks for the given modules and uses the first
  working one
```

When the 'REQUIRED' argument was set, macros will fail with an error when module(s) could not be found It sets the following variables:

```
PKG_CONFIG_FOUND      = true if pkg-config works on
                        the system
PKG_CONFIG_EXECUTABLE = pathname of the pkg-config
                        program
<PREFIX>_FOUND = set to 1 if module(s) exist
```

For the following variables two sets of values exist; first one is the common one and has the given PREFIX. The second set contains flags which are given out when pkgconfig was called with the '--static' option.

```
<XPREFIX>_LIBRARIES    = only the libraries
                         (w/o the '-l')
<XPREFIX>_LIBRARY_DIRS = the paths of the libraries
                         (w/o the '-L')
<XPREFIX>_LDFLAGS = all required linker flags
<XPREFIX>_LDFLAGS_OTHERS = all other linker flags
<XPREFIX>_INCLUDE_DIRS = the '-I' preprocessor flags
                         (w/o the '-I')
<XPREFIX>_CFLAGS       = all required cflags
<XPREFIX>_CFLAGS_OTHERS = the other compiler flags
```

```
<XPREFIX> = <PREFIX>          for common case
<XPREFIX> = <PREFIX>_STATIC for static linking
```

There are some special variables whose prefix depends on the count of given modules. When there is only one module, <PREFIX> stays unchanged. When there are multiple modules, the prefix will be changed to <PREFIX>_<MODNAME>:

```
<XPREFIX>_VERSION = version of the module
<XPREFIX>_PREFIX  = prefix-directory of the module
<XPREFIX>_INCLUDEDIR = include-dir of the module
<XPREFIX>_LIBDIR     = lib-dir of the module



<XPREFIX> = <PREFIX>  when |MODULES| == 1, else
<XPREFIX> = <PREFIX>_<MODNAME>
```

A <MODULE> parameter can have the following formats:

```
{MODNAME}                 = matches any version
{MODNAME}>={VERSION} = at least version <VERSION> is
                            required
{MODNAME}={VERSION}  = exactly version <VERSION> is
                            required
{MODNAME}<={VERSION} = modules must not be newer than
                            <VERSION>
```

Examples

```
pkg_check_modules (GLIB2   glib-2.0)

pkg_check_modules (GLIB2   glib-2.0>=2.10)
  requires at least version 2.10 of glib2 and defines
  e.g. GLIB2_VERSION=2.10.3

pkg_check_modules (FOO     glib-2.0>=2.10 gtk+-2.0)
  requires both glib2 and gtk2, and defines e.g.
    FOO_glib-2.0_VERSION=2.10.3
    FOO_gtk+-2.0_VERSION=2.8.20
```

```
pkg_search_module (BAR libxml-2.0 libxml2 libxml>=2)
```

- **FindPNG**: Find the native PNG includes and library

This module defines

```
PNG_INCLUDE_DIR - where to find png.h, etc.
PNG_LIBRARIES   - the libraries to link against to use
                  PNG.
PNG_DEFINITIONS - You should
                  add_definitons(${PNG_DEFINITIONS})
                  before compiling code that includes
                  png library files.
PNG_FOUND       - If false, do not try to use PNG.
```

also defined, but not for general use are

```
PNG_LIBRARY - where to find the PNG library.
```

None of the above will be defined unles zlib can be found. PNG depends on Zlib

- **FindPythonInterp**: Find python interpreter

This module finds if Python interpreter is installed and determines where the executables are. This code sets the following variables:

```
PYTHONINTERP_FOUND - Was the Python executable found
PYTHON_EXECUTABLE  - path to the Python interpreter
```

- **FindPythonLibs**: Find python libraries

This module finds if Python is installed and determines where the include files and libraries are. It also determines what the name of the library is. This code sets the following variables:

```
PYTHONLIBS_FOUND      = have the Python libs been found
PYTHON_LIBRARIES      = path to the python library
PYTHON_INCLUDE_PATH   = path to where Python.h is found
PYTHON_DEBUG_LIBRARIES = path to the debug library
```

- **FindQt**: Searches for all installed versions of QT.

  This should only be used if your project can work with multiple versions of QT. If not, you should just directly use FindQt4 or FindQt3. If multiple versions of QT are found on the machine, then The user must set the option DESIRED_QT_VERSION to the version they want to use. If only one version of qt is found on the machine, then the DESIRED_QT_VERSION is set to that version and the matching FindQt3 or FindQt4 module is included. Once the user sets DESIRED_QT_VERSION, then the FindQt3 or FindQt4 module is included.

  ```
  QT_REQUIRED if this is set to TRUE then if CMake can
              not find QT4 or QT3 an error is raised
              and a message is sent to the user.

  DESIRED_QT_VERSION OPTION is created
  QT4_INSTALLED is set to TRUE if qt4 is found.
  QT3_INSTALLED is set to TRUE if qt3 is found.
  ```

- **FindQt3**: Locate Qt include paths and libraries

  This module defines:

  ```
  QT_INCLUDE_DIR - where to find qt.h, etc.
  QT_LIBRARIES   - the libraries to link against to use
                   Qt.
  QT_DEFINITIONS - definitions to use when
                   compiling code that uses Qt.
  QT_FOUND       - If false, don't try to use Qt.
  ```

  If you need the multithreaded version of Qt, set QT_MT_REQUIRED to TRUE Also defined, but not for general use are:

  ```
  QT_MOC_EXECUTABLE, where to find the moc tool.
  QT_UIC_EXECUTABLE, where to find the uic tool.
  QT_QT_LIBRARY, where to find the Qt library.
  QT_QTMAIN_LIBRARY, where to find the qtmain library.
                This is only required by Qt3 on Windows.
  ```

- **FindQt4**: Find QT 4

  This module can be used to find Qt4. The most important issue is that the Qt4 qmake is available via the system path. This qmake is then used to detect basically

everything else. This module defines a number of key variables and macros. First is
QT_USE_FILE which is the path to a CMake file that can be included to compile Qt
4 applications and libraries. By default, the QtCore and QtGui libraries are loaded.
This behavior can be changed by setting one or more of the following variables to
true:

```
QT_DONT_USE_QTCORE
QT_DONT_USE_QTGUI
QT_USE_QT3SUPPORT
QT_USE_QTASSISTANT
QT_USE_QTDESIGNER
QT_USE_QTMOTIF
QT_USE_QTMAIN
QT_USE_QTNETWORK
QT_USE_QTNSPLUGIN
QT_USE_QTOPENGL
QT_USE_QTSQL
QT_USE_QTXML
QT_USE_QTSVG
QT_USE_QTTEST
QT_USE_QTUITOOLS
QT_USE_QTDBUS
QT_USE_QTSCRIPT
```

All the libraries required are stored in a variable called QT_LIBRARIES. Add this
variable to your TARGET_LINK_LIBRARIES.

```
macro QT4_WRAP_CPP(outfiles inputfile ... )
macro QT4_WRAP_UI(outfiles inputfile ... )
macro QT4_ADD_RESOURCES(outfiles inputfile ... )
macro QT4_AUTOMOC(inputfile ... )
macro QT4_GENERATE_MOC(inputfile outputfile )

macro QT4_ADD_DBUS_INTERFACE(outfiles interface
                               basename)
```

create a the interface header and implementation files with the given basename from
the given interface xml file and add it to the list of sources

```
macro QT4_ADD_DBUS_INTERFACES(outfiles inputfile ... )
```

create the interface header and implementation files for all listed interface xml files
the name will be automatically determined from the name of the xml file

```
macro QT4_ADD_DBUS_ADAPTOR(outfiles xmlfile
                          parentheader
                          parentclassname [basename]
                          )
```

create a dbus adaptor (header and implementation file) from the xml file describing
the interface, and add it to the list of sources. The adaptor forwards the calls to a
parent class, defined in parentheader and named parentclassname. The name of the
generated files will be <basename>adaptor.{cpp,h} where basename is the basename
of the xml file.

```
macro QT4_GENERATE_DBUS_INTERFACE(header
                                  [interfacename] )
```

generate the xml interface file from the given header. If the optional argument
interfacename is omitted, the name of the interface file is constructed from the
basename of the header with the suffix .xml appended.

```
QT_FOUND              If false, don't try to use Qt.
QT4_FOUND             If false, don't try to use Qt 4.
QT_EDITION            Set to the edition of Qt
                      (e.g. DesktopLight)
QT_EDITION_DESKTOPLIGHT True if
                        QT_EDITION == DesktopLight
QT_QTCORE_FOUND         True if QtCore was found.
QT_QTGUI_FOUND          True if QtGui was found.
QT_QT3SUPPORT_FOUND     True if Qt3Support was found.
QT_QTASSISTANT_FOUND    True if QtAssistant was found.
QT_QTDBUS_FOUND         True if QtDBus was found.
QT_QTDESIGNER_FOUND     True if QtDesigner was found.
QT_QTDESIGNERCOMPONENTS True if QtDesignerComponents
                        was found.
QT_QTMOTIF_FOUND        True if QtMotif was found.
QT_QTNETWORK_FOUND      True if QtNetwork was found.
QT_QTNSPLUGIN_FOUND     True if QtNsPlugin was found.
QT_QTOPENGL_FOUND       True if QtOpenGL was found.
QT_QTSQL_FOUND          True if QtSql was found.
QT_QTXML_FOUND          True if QtXml was found.
QT_QTSVG_FOUND          True if QtSvg was found.
```

```
QT_QTSCRIPT_FOUND           True if QtScript was found.
QT_QTTEST_FOUND             True if QtTest was found.
QT_QTUITOOLS_FOUND          True if QtUiTools was found.

QT_DEFINITIONS - Definitions to use when compiling
                 code that uses Qt.

QT_INCLUDES - List of paths to all include directories
              of Qt4 QT_INCLUDE_DIR and
              QT_QTCORE_INCLUDE_DIR are always in this
              variable even if NOTFOUND, all other
              INCLUDE_DIRS are only added if they are
              found.

QT_INCLUDE_DIR                     Path to "include" of Qt4
QT_QT_INCLUDE_DIR                  Path to "include/Qt"
QT_QT3SUPPORT_INCLUDE_DIR          Path to
                                   "include/Qt3Support"
QT_QTASSISTANT_INCLUDE_DIR         Path to
                                   "include/QtAssistant"
QT_QTCORE_INCLUDE_DIR              Path to "include/QtCore"
QT_QTDESIGNER_INCLUDE_DIR          Path to
                                   "include/QtDesigner"
QT_QTDESIGNERCOMPONENTS_INCLUDE_DIR Path to
                                   "include/QtDesigner"
QT_QTDBUS_INCLUDE_DIR              Path to "include/QtDBus"
QT_QTGUI_INCLUDE_DIR               Path to "include/QtGui"
QT_QTMOTIF_INCLUDE_DIR             Path to "include/QtMotif"
QT_QTNETWORK_INCLUDE_DIR           Path to
                                   "include/QtNetwork"
QT_QTNSPLUGIN_INCLUDE_DIR          Path to
                                   "include/QtNsPlugin"
QT_QTOPENGL_INCLUDE_DIR            Path to "include/QtOpenGL"
QT_QTSQL_INCLUDE_DIR               Path to "include/QtSql"
QT_QTXML_INCLUDE_DIR               Path to "include/QtXml"
QT_QTSVG_INCLUDE_DIR               Path to "include/QtSvg"
QT_QTSCRIPT_INCLUDE_DIR            Path to "include/QtScript"
QT_QTTEST_INCLUDE_DIR              Path to "include/QtTest"

QT_LIBRARY_DIR                     Path to "lib" of Qt4
QT_PLUGINS_DIR                     Path to "plugins" for Qt4
```

For every library of Qt there are three variables:

```
QT_QTFOO_LIBRARY_RELEASE - which contains the full
                            path to the release version
QT_QTFOO_LIBRARY_DEBUG - which contains the full path
                          to the debug version
QT_QTFOO_LIBRARY - the full path to the release
                    version if available, otherwise to
                    the debug version
```

So there are the following variables for the Qt3Support library:

```
QT_QT3SUPPORT_LIBRARY
QT_QT3SUPPORT_LIBRARY_RELEASE
QT_QT3SUPPORT_DEBUG
```

The same idea applies to:

```
QT_QTASSISTANT_LIBRARY
QT_QTCORE_LIBRARY
QT_QTDBUS_LIBRARY
QT_QTDESIGNER_LIBRARY
QT_QTDESIGNERCOMPONENTS_LIBRARY
QT_QTGUI_LIBRARY
QT_QTMOTIF_LIBRARY
QT_QTNETWORK_LIBRARY
QT_QTNSPLUGIN_LIBRARY
QT_QTOPENGL_LIBRARY
QT_QTSQL_LIBRARY
QT_QTXML_LIBRARY
QT_QTSVG_LIBRARY
QT_QTSCRIPT_LIBRARY
QT_QTTEST_LIBRARY
QT_QTMAIN_LIBRARY
QT_QTUITOOLS_LIBRARY
```

also defined, but NOT for general use are

```
QT_MOC_EXECUTABLE          Where to find the moc tool.
QT_UIC_EXECUTABLE          Where to find the uic tool.
QT_UIC3_EXECUTABLE         Where to find the uic3 tool.
QT_RCC_EXECUTABLE          Where to find the rcc tool
QT_DBUSCPP2XML_EXECUTABLE  Where to find the
```

	qdbuscpp2xml tool.
QT_DBUSXML2CPP_EXECUTABLE	Where to find the qdbusxml2cpp tool.
QT_DOC_DIR	Path to "doc" of Qt4
QT_MKSPECS_DIR	Path to "mkspecs" of Qt4

These are around for backwards compatibility they will be set

```
QT_WRAP_CPP   Set true if QT_MOC_EXECUTABLE is found
QT_WRAP_UI    Set true if QT_UIC_EXECUTABLE is found
```

These variables do _NOT_ have any effect anymore (compared to FindQt.cmake)

```
QT_MT_REQUIRED          Qt4 is now always multithreaded
```

These variables are set to "" Because Qt structure changed (They make no sense in Qt4)

```
QT_QT_LIBRARY           Qt-Library is now split
```

- **FindRuby**: Find Ruby

This module finds if Ruby is installed and determines where the include files and libraries are. It also determines what the name of the library is. This code sets the following variables:

```
RUBY_INCLUDE_PATH = path to where ruby.h can be found
RUBY_EXECUTABLE   = full path to the ruby binary
```

- **FindSDL**: Locate the SDL library

This module defines

```
SDL_LIBRARY, the library to link against
SDL_FOUND, if false, do not try to link to SDL
SDL_INCLUDE_DIR, where to find SDL.h
```

Don't forget to include SDLmain.h and SDLmain.m your project for the OS X framework based version. (Other versions link to -lSDLmain which this module will try to find on your behalf.) Also for OS X, this module will automatically add the -framework Cocoa on your behalf. $SDLDIR is an environment variable that would correspond to the ./configure --prefix=$SDLDIR used in building SDL. i.e.galup 9-20-02

Modified by Eric Wing. Added new modifications to recognize OS X frameworks and additional Unix paths (FreeBSD, etc). Also corrected the header search path to follow "proper" SDL guidelines. Added a search for SDLmain which is needed by some platforms. Added a search for threads which is needed by some platforms. Added needed compile switches for MinGW.

On OSX, this will prefer the Framework version (if found) over others. People will have to manually change the cache values of SDL_LIBRARY to override this selection.

Note that the header path has changed from SDL/SDL.h to just SDL.h This needed to change because "proper" SDL convention is #include "SDL.h", not <SDL/SDL.h>. This is done for portability reasons because not all systems place things in SDL/ (see FreeBSD).

- **FindSDL_image**: Locate SDL_image library

This module defines

```
SDLIMAGE_LIBRARY, the library to link against
SDLIMAGE_FOUND, if false, do not try to link to SDL
SDLIMAGE_INCLUDE_DIR, where to find SDL/SDL.h
```

$SDLDIR is an environment variable that would correspond to the ./configure --prefix=$SDLDIR used in building SDL.

Created by Eric Wing. This was influenced by the FindSDL.cmake module, but with modifications to recognize OS X frameworks and additional Unix paths (FreeBSD, etc).

- **FindSDL_mixer**: Locate the SDL_mixer library

This module defines

```
SDLMIXER_LIBRARY, library to link against
SDLMIXER_FOUND, if false, do not try to link to SDL
SDLMIXER_INCLUDE_DIR, where to find SDL/SDL.h
```

$SDLDIR is an environment variable that would correspond to the ./configure --prefix=$SDLDIR used in building SDL.

Created by Eric Wing. This was influenced by the FindSDL.cmake module, but with modifications to recognize OS X frameworks and additional Unix paths (FreeBSD, etc).

- **FindSDL_net**: Locate the SDL_net library

This module defines

```
SDLNET_LIBRARY, the library to link against
SDLNET_FOUND, if false, do not try to link against
SDLNET_INCLUDE_DIR, where to find the headers
```

$SDLDIR is an environment variable that would correspond to the ./configure --prefix=$SDLDIR used in building SDL.

Created by Eric Wing. This was influenced by the FindSDL.cmake module, but with modifications to recognize OS X frameworks and additional Unix paths (FreeBSD, etc). On OSX, this will prefer the Framework version (if found) over others. People will have to manually change the cache values of SDLNET_LIBRARY to override this selection.

- **FindSDL_sound**: Locates the SDL_sound library

This module depends on SDL being found and must be called AFTER FindSDL.cmake is called.

This module defines SDL_SOUND_INCLUDE_DIR, where to find SDL_sound.h SDL_SOUND_FOUND, if false, do not try to link to SDL SDL_SOUND_LIBRARIES, this contains the list of libraries that you need to link against. This is a read-only variable and is marked INTERNAL. SDL_SOUND_EXTRAS, this is an optional variable for you to add your own flags to SDL_SOUND_LIBRARIES. This is prepended to SDL_SOUND_LIBRARIES. This is available mostly for cases this module failed to anticipate for and you must add additional flags. This is marked as ADVANCED.

This module also defines (but you shouldn't need to use directly) SDL_SOUND_LIBRARY, the name of just the SDL_sound library you would link against. Use SDL_SOUND_LIBRARIES for you link instructions and not this one. And might define the following as needed

```
MIKMOD_LIBRARY
MODPLUG_LIBRARY
OGG_LIBRARY
VORBIS_LIBRARY
SMPEG_LIBRARY
FLAC_LIBRARY
SPEEX_LIBRARY
```

Typically, you should not use these variables directly, and you should use SDL_SOUND_LIBRARIES which contains SDL_SOUND_LIBRARY and the other audio libraries (if needed) to successfully compile on your system .

Created by Eric Wing.

This module is a bit more complicated than the other FindSDL* family modules. The reason is that SDL_sound can be compiled in a large variety of different ways which are independent of platform. SDL_sound may dynamically link against other 3rd party libraries to get additional codec support, such as Ogg Vorbis, SMPEG, ModPlug, MikMod, FLAC, Speex, and potentially others. Under some circumstances which I don't fully understand, there seems to be a requirement that dependent libraries of libraries you use must also be explicitly linked against in order to successfully compile. SDL_sound does not currently have any system in place to know how it was compiled. So this CMake module does the hard work in trying to discover which 3rd party libraries are required for building (if any).

This module uses a brute force approach to create a test program that uses SDL_sound, and then tries to build it. If the build fails, it parses the error output for known symbol names to figure out which libraries are needed. Responds to the $SDLDIR and $SDLSOUNDDIR environmental variable that would correspond to the ./configure --prefix=$SDLDIR used in building SDL.

On OSX, this will prefer the Framework version (if found) over others. People will have to manually change the cache values of SDL_LIBRARY to override this selection.

- **FindSDL_ttf**: Locate SDL_ttf library

This module defines

```
SDLTTF_LIBRARY, the library to link against
SDLTTF_FOUND, if false, do not try to link to SDL
SDLTTF_INCLUDE_DIR, where to find SDL/SDL.h
```

$SDLDIR is an environment variable that would correspond to the ./configure --prefix=$SDLDIR used in building SDL. Created by Eric Wing. This was influenced by the FindSDL.cmake module, but with modifications to recognize OS X frameworks and additional Unix paths (FreeBSD, etc). On OSX, this will prefer the Framework version (if found) over others. People will have to manually change the cache values of SDLTTF_LIBRARY to override this selection.

- **FindSelfPackers**: Find upx

This module looks for some executable packers (i.e. softwares that compress executables or shared libs into on-the-fly self-extracting executables or shared libs). Examples:

```
UPX: http://wildsau.idv.uni-linz.ac.at/mfx/upx.html
```

- **FindSubversion**: Extract information from a subversion working copy

The module defines the following variables:

```
Subversion_SVN_EXECUTABLE - path to svn command line
                            client
Subversion_VERSION_SVN - version of svn command line
                         client
Subversion_FOUND - true if the command line client was
                   found
```

If the command line client executable is found the macro

```
Subversion_WC_INFO(<dir> <var-prefix>)
```

is defined to extract information of a subversion working copy at a given location. The macro defines the following variables:

```
<var-prefix>_WC_URL - url of the repository (at <dir>)
<var-prefix>_WC_ROOT - root url of the repository
```

```
<var-prefix>_WC_REVISION - current revision
<var-prefix>_WC_LAST_CHANGED_AUTHOR
        - author of last commit
<var-prefix>_WC_LAST_CHANGED_DATE
        - date of last commit
<var-prefix>_WC_LAST_CHANGED_REV
        - revision of last commit
<var-prefix>_WC_LAST_CHANGED_LOG
        - last log of base revision
<var-prefix>_WC_INFO
        - output of command `svn info <dir>'
```

Example usage:

```
FIND_PACKAGE(Subversion)
IF(Subversion_FOUND)
  Subversion_WC_INFO(${PROJECT_SOURCE_DIR} Project)
  MESSAGE("Current revision is
${Project_WC_REVISION}")
  ENDIF(Subversion_FOUND)
```

- **FindSWIG**: Find SWIG

This module finds an installed SWIG. It sets the following variables:

```
SWIG_FOUND - set to true if SWIG is found
SWIG_DIR - the directory where swig is installed
SWIG_EXECUTABLE - the path to the swig executable
```

- **FindTCL**: Find Tcl includes and libraries.

This module finds if TCL is installed and determines where the include files and libraries are. It also determines what the name of the library is. This code sets the following variables:

```
TCL_FOUND              = Tcl was found
TK_FOUND               = Tk was found
TCLTK_FOUND            = Tcl and Tk were found
TCL_LIBRARY            = path to Tcl library (tcl tcl80)
TCL_LIBRARY_DEBUG      = path to Tcl library (debug)
TCL_STUB_LIBRARY       = path to Tcl stub library
TCL_STUB_LIBRARY_DEBUG = path to debug stub library
TCL_INCLUDE_PATH       = path to where tcl.h can be found
```

```
TCL_TCLSH           = path to tclsh binary (tcl tcl80)
TK_LIBRARY          = path to Tk library (tk tk80 etc)
TK_LIBRARY_DEBUG    = path to Tk library (debug)
TK_STUB_LIBRARY     = path to Tk stub library
TK_STUB_LIBRARY_DEBUG = path to debug Tk stub library
TK_INCLUDE_PATH     = path to where tk.h can be found
TK_INTERNAL_PATH    = path to where tkWinInt.h is found
TK_WISH             = full path to the wish executable
```

- **FindTclsh**: Find tclsh

This module finds if TCL is installed and determines where the include files and libraries are. It also determines what the name of the library is. This code sets the following variables:

```
TCLSH_FOUND = TRUE if tclsh has been found
TCL_TCLSH = the path to the tclsh executable
```

In cygwin, look for the cygwin version first. Don't look for it later to avoid finding the cygwin version on a Win32 build.

- **FindThreads**: This module determines the thread library of the system.

The following variables are set

```
CMAKE_THREAD_LIBS_INIT      - the thread library
CMAKE_USE_SPROC_INIT        - are we using sproc?
CMAKE_USE_WIN32_THREADS_INIT - using WIN32 threads?
CMAKE_USE_PTHREADS_INIT     - are we using pthreads
CMAKE_HP_PTHREADS_INIT      - are we using hp pthreads
```

- **FindTIFF**: Find TIFF library

Find the native TIFF includes and library This module defines

```
TIFF_INCLUDE_DIR, where to find tiff.h, etc.
TIFF_LIBRARIES, libraries to link against to use TIFF.
TIFF_FOUND, If false, do not try to use TIFF.
```

also defined, but not for general use are

```
TIFF_LIBRARY, where to find the TIFF library.
```

- **FindUnixCommands**: Find unix commands from cygwin

  This module looks for some usual Unix commands.

- **FindVTK**: Find a VTK installation or build tree.

  The following variables are set if VTK is found. If VTK is not found, VTK_FOUND is set to false.

  ```
  VTK_FOUND           - Set to true when VTK is found.
  VTK_USE_FILE        - CMake file to use VTK.
  VTK_MAJOR_VERSION   - The VTK major version number.
  VTK_MINOR_VERSION   - The VTK minor version number
                        (odd non-release).
  VTK_BUILD_VERSION   - The VTK patch level
                        (meaningless for odd minor).
  VTK_INCLUDE_DIRS    - Include directories for VTK
  VTK_LIBRARY_DIRS    - Link directories for VTK libraries
  VTK_KITS            - List of VTK kits, in CAPS
                        (COMMON,IO,) etc.
  VTK_LANGUAGES       - List of wrapped languages, in CAPS
                        (TCL, PYHTON,) etc.
  ```

  The following cache entries must be set by the user to locate VTK:

  ```
  VTK_DIR   - The directory containing VTKConfig.cmake.
              This is either the root of the build tree,
              or the lib/vtk directory.  This is the
              only cache entry.
  ```

  The following variables are set for backward compatibility and should not be used in new code:

  ```
  USE_VTK_FILE - The full path to the UseVTK.cmake file.
                 This is provided for backward
                 compatibility.  Use VTK_USE_FILE
                 instead.
  ```

- **FindWget**: Find wget

This module looks for wget. This module defines the following values:

```
WGET_EXECUTABLE: the full path to the wget tool.
WGET_FOUND: True if wget has been found.
```

- **FindWish**: Find wish installation

This module finds if TCL is installed and determines where the include files and libraries are. It also determines what the name of the library is. This code sets the following variables:

```
TK_WISH = the path to the wish executable
```

if UNIX is defined, then it will look for the cygwin version first

- **FindwxWidgets**: Find a wxWidgets (a.k.a., wxWindows) installation.

This module finds if wxWidgets is installed and selects a default configuration to use. The following variables are searched for and set to defaults in case of multiple choices. Change them if the defaults are not desired:

```
wxWidgets_ROOT_DIR        - Base wxWidgets directory
                             (e.g., C:/wxWidgets-2.6.3).
wxWidgets_LIB_DIR         - Path to wxWidgets libraries
                 (e.g., C:/wxWidgets-2.6.3/lib/vc_lib).
wxWidgets_CONFIGURATION - Configuration to use
                 (e.g., msw, mswd, mswu, mswunivud, etc.)
wxWidgets_USE_LIBS        - Libraries to use besides the
                 common required ones; set to base and
                 core by default. You could also list
                 them in FIND_PACKAGE(wxWidgets REQUIRED
                                      <components>)
```

The following are set after configuration is done:

```
wxWidgets_FOUND   - Set to TRUE if wxWidgets was found.
wxWidgets_INCLUDE_DIRS - Include directories for WIN32
                         i.e., where to find "wx/wx.h"
                         and "wx/setup.h"; possibly
```

```
                                    empty for unices.
wxWidgets_LIBRARIES - Path to the wxWidgets libraries.
wxWidgets_LIBRARY_DIRS - compile time link dirs,
                                    useful for rpath on UNIX.
                                    Typically an empty string
                                    in WIN32 environment.
wxWidgets_DEFINITIONS  - Contains defines required to
                                    compile/link against WX, e.g.
                                    -DWXUSINGDLL
wxWidgets_CXX_FLAGS    - Include dirs and compiler
                                    flags For unices, empty on
                                    WIN32.
wxWidgets_USE_FILE     - convenience include file
```

Sample usage:

```
set (wxWidgets_USE_LIBS base core gl net)
find_package (wxWidgets)
if (wxWidgets_FOUND)
  include (${wxWidgets_USE_FILE})
  target_link_libraries(<YourTarget>
                             ${wxWidgets_LIBRARIES})
endif(wxWidgets_FOUND)
```

Sample usage with monolithic wx build:

```
set(wxWidgets_USE_LIBS msw26 expat jpeg gl
    png regex tiff zlib)
...
```

- **FindwxWindows**: Find wxWindows (wxWidgets) installation

This module finds if wxWindows/wxWidgets is installed and determines where the include files and libraries are. It also determines what the name of the library is. Please note this file is DEPRECATED and replaced by FindwxWidgets.cmake. This code sets the following variables:

```
WXWINDOWS_FOUND     = system has WxWindows
WXWINDOWS_LIBRARIES = path to the wxWindows libraries
                      on Unix/Linux with additional
                      linker flags from
```

```
                                 "wx-config --libs"
CMAKE_WXWINDOWS_CXX_FLAGS =
     Compiler flags for wxWindows, essentially
     "`wx-config --cxxflags`" on Linux
WXWINDOWS_INCLUDE_DIR =
     where to find "wx/wx.h" and "wx/setup.h"
WXWINDOWS_LINK_DIRECTORIES =
     link directories, useful for rpath on Unix
WXWINDOWS_DEFINITIONS       = extra defines
```

OPTIONS If you need OpenGL support please

```
SET(WXWINDOWS_USE_GL 1)
```

in your CMakeLists.txt *before* you include this file.

```
HAVE_ISYSTEM =
   true required to replace -I by -isystem on g++
```

For convenience include Use_wxWindows.cmake in your project's CMakeLists.txt using include(Use_wxWindows).

USAGE

```
set(WXWINDOWS_USE_GL 1)
find_package(wxWindows)
```

NOTES wxWidgets 2.6.x is supported for monolithic builds e.g. compiled in wx/build/msw dir as:

```
  nmake -f makefile.vc BUILD=debug SHARED=0 USE_OPENGL=1
MONOLITHIC=1
```

DEPRECATED

```
CMAKE_WX_CAN_COMPILE
WXWINDOWS_LIBRARY
CMAKE_WX_CXX_FLAGS
WXWINDOWS_INCLUDE_PATH
```

AUTHOR Jan Woetzel <http://www.mip.informatik.uni-kiel.de/~jw> (07/2003-01/2006)

- **FindX11**: Find X11 installation

Try to find X11 on UNIX systems. The following values are defined

```
X11_FOUND          - True if X11 is available
X11_INCLUDE_DIR    - include directories to use X11
X11_LIBRARIES      - link against these to use X11
```

it also defines the following more fine grained variables:

```
X11_ICE_INCLUDE_PATH,
X11_ICE_LIB
X11_ICE_FOUND
X11_Xaccessrules_INCLUDE_PATH
X11_Xaccess_FOUND
X11_Xaccessstr_INCLUDE_PATH
X11_Xaccess_FOUND
X11_Xau_INCLUDE_PATH
X11_Xau_LIB
X11_Xau_FOUND
X11_Xcomposite_INCLUDE_PATH
X11_Xcomposite_LIB
X11_Xcomposite_FOUND
X11_Xcursor_INCLUDE_PATH
X11_Xcursor_LIB
X11_Xcursor_FOUND
X11_Xdamage_INCLUDE_PATH
X11_Xdamage_LIB
X11_Xdamage_FOUND
X11_Xdmcp_INCLUDE_PATH
X11_Xdmcp_LIB
X11_Xdmcp_FOUND
X11_Xext_LIB
X11_Xext_FOUND
X11_dpms_INCLUDE_PATH          (in X11_Xext_LIB),
X11_dpms_FOUND
X11_XShm_INCLUDE_PATH          (in X11_Xext_LIB),
X11_XShm_FOUND
```

```
X11_Xshape_INCLUDE_PATH        (in X11_Xext_LIB),
X11_Xshape_FOUND
X11_Xf86misc_INCLUDE_PATH
X11_Xxf86misc_LIB
X11_Xf86misc_FOUND
X11_xf86vmode_INCLUDE_PATH
X11_Xf86vmode_FOUND
X11_Xfixes_INCLUDE_PATH
X11_Xfixes_LIB
X11_Xfixes_FOUND
X11_Xft_INCLUDE_PATH
X11_Xft_LIB
X11_Xft_FOUND
X11_Xinerama_INCLUDE_PATH
X11_Xinerama_LIB
X11_Xinerama_FOUND
X11_Xinput_INCLUDE_PATH
X11_Xinput_LIB
X11_Xinput_FOUND
X11_Xkb_INCLUDE_PATH
X11_Xkb_FOUND
X11_Xkblib_INCLUDE_PATH
X11_Xkb_FOUND
X11_Xpm_INCLUDE_PATH
X11_Xpm_LIB
X11_Xpm_FOUND
X11_XTest_INCLUDE_PATH
X11_XTest_LIB
X11_XTest_FOUND
X11_Xrandr_INCLUDE_PATH
X11_Xrandr_LIB
X11_Xrandr_FOUND
X11_Xrender_INCLUDE_PATH
X11_Xrender_LIB
X11_Xrender_FOUND
X11_Xscreensaver_INCLUDE_PATH
X11_Xscreensaver_LIB
X11_Xscreensaver_FOUND
X11_Xt_INCLUDE_PATH
X11_Xt_LIB
X11_Xt_FOUND
X11_Xutil_INCLUDE_PATH
X11_Xutil_FOUND
X11_Xv_INCLUDE_PATH
```

```
X11_Xv_LIB
X11_Xv_FOUND
```

- **FindXMLRPC**: Find xmlrpc

  Find the native XMLRPC headers and libraries.

  ```
  XMLRPC_INCLUDE_DIRS   - where to find xmlrpc.h, etc.
  XMLRPC_LIBRARIES      - libraries when using xmlrpc.
  XMLRPC_FOUND          - True if xmlrpc found.
  ```

  XMLRPC modules may be specified as components for this find module. Modules may be listed by running "xmlrpc-c-config". Modules include:

  ```
  c++             C++ wrapper code
  libwww-client   libwww-based client
  cgi-server      CGI-based server
  abyss-server    ABYSS-based server
  ```

  Typical usage:

  ```
  find_package(XMLRPC REQUIRED libwww-client)
  ```

- **FindZLIB**: Find zlib

  Find the native ZLIB includes and library

  ```
  ZLIB_INCLUDE_DIR - where to find zlib.h, etc.
  ZLIB_LIBRARIES   - List of libraries when using zlib.
  ZLIB_FOUND       - True if zlib found.
  ```

- **InstallRequiredSystemLibraries**:

  By including this file, all files in the CMAKE_INSTALL_DEBUG_LIBRARIES, will be installed with INSTALL_PROGRAMS into /bin for WIN32 and /lib for non-win32. If it is the MSVC compiler, then the microsoft run time libraries will be found add automatically added to the CMAKE_INSTALL_DEBUG_LIBRARIES, and installed. If CMAKE_INSTALL_DEBUG_LIBRARIES is set and it is the MSVC compiler, then the debug libraries are installed when available. If CMAKE_INSTALL_MFC_LIBRARIES is set then the MFC run time libraries are installed as well as the CRT run time libraries.

- **TestBigEndian**: Define macro to determine endian type

  Check if the system is big endian or little endian

  ```
  TEST_BIG_ENDIAN(VARIABLE)
  VARIABLE - variable to store the result to
  ```

- **TestCXXAcceptsFlag**: Test CXX compiler for a flag

  Check if the CXX compiler accepts a flag

  ```
  Macro CHECK_CXX_ACCEPTS_FLAG(FLAGS VARIABLE) -
     checks if the function exists
  FLAGS - the flags to try
  VARIABLE - variable to store the result
  ```

- **TestForANSIForScope**: Check for ANSI for scope support

  Check if the compiler supports std:: on stl classes.

  ```
  CMAKE_NO_STD_NAMESPACE - holds result
  ```

- **TestForANSIStreamHeaders**: Test for compiler support of ANSI stream headers iostream, etc.

  check if we they have the standard ansi stream files (without the .h)

  ```
  CMAKE_NO_ANSI_STREAM_HEADERS - defined by the results
  ```

- **TestForSSTREAM**:

  Test for std:: namespace support check if the compiler supports std:: on stl classes

  ```
  CMAKE_NO_ANSI_STRING_STREAM - defined by the results
  ```

- **TestForSTDNamespace**: Test for std:: namespace support

  check if the compiler supports std:: on stl classes

  ```
  CMAKE_NO_STD_NAMESPACE - defined by the results
  ```

- **UseEcos**: This module defines variables and macros required to build eCos application. This file contains the following macros:

  ECOS_ADD_INCLUDE_DIRECTORIES() - add the eCos include dirs

  ECOS_ADD_EXECUTABLE(name source1 ... sourceN) - create an eCos executable

  ECOS_ADJUST_DIRECTORY(VAR source1 ... sourceN) - adjusts the path of the source files and puts the result into VAR

  Macros for selecting the toolchain:

  ECOS_USE_ARM_ELF_TOOLS() - enable the ARM ELF toolchain for the directory where it is called

  ECOS_USE_I386_ELF_TOOLS() - enable the i386 ELF toolchain for the directory where it is called

  ECOS_USE_PPC_EABI_TOOLS() - enable the PowerPC toolchain for the directory where it is called

  It contains the following variables:

  ECOS_DEFINITIONS

  ECOSCONFIG_EXECUTABLE

  ECOS_CONFIG_FILE - defaults to ecos.ecc, if your eCos configuration file has a different name, adjust this variable for internal use only:

  `ECOS_ADD_TARGET_LIB`

- **UseQt4**: Use Module for QT4

  Sets up C and C++ to use Qt 4. It is assumed that FindQt.cmake has already been loaded. See FindQt.cmake for information on how to load Qt 4 into your CMake project.

- **UseSWIG**: SWIG module for CMake

  Defines the following macros:

```
SWIG_ADD_MODULE(name language [ files ])
  - Define swig module with given name and specified
    language
SWIG_LINK_LIBRARIES(name [ libraries ])
  - Link libraries to swig module
```

All other macros are for internal use only. To get the actual name of the swig module, use: ${SWIG_MODULE_name_REAL_NAME}. Set Source files properties such as CPLUSPLUS and SWIG_FLAGS to specify special behavior of SWIG. Also global CMAKE_SWIG_FLAGS can be used to add special flags to all swig calls. Another special variable is CMAKE_SWIG_OUTDIR, it allows one to specify where to write all the swig generated module (swig -outdir option) The name-specific variable SWIG_MODULE_<name>_EXTRA_DEPS may be used to specify extra dependencies for the generated modules.

- **UsewxWidgets**: Convenience include for using wxWidgets library

Finds if wxWidgets is installed and set the appropriate libs, incdirs, flags etc. INCLUDE_DIRECTORIES, LINK_DIRECTORIES and ADD_DEFINITIONS are called.

USAGE

```
set( wxWidgets_USE_LIBS  gl xml xrc )
    # optionally: more than wx std libs
find_package(wxWidgets REQUIRED)
include( ${xWidgets_USE_FILE} )
... add your targets here,
... e.g. add_executable/ add_library ...
target_link_librariers( <yourWxDependantTarget>
                        ${wxWidgets_LIBRARIES})
```

AUTHOR

Jan Woetzel <jw -at- mip.informatik.uni-kiel.de>

Appendix D - Properties

Global Properties

The following global properties are available in CMakeLists.txt code:

- **DISABLED_FEATURES**: List of features which are disabled during the CMake run.

  List of features which are disabled during the CMake run. Be default it contains the names of all packages which were not found. This is determined using the <NAME>_FOUND variables. Packages which are searched QUIET are not listed. A project can add its own features to this list.This property is used by the macros in FeatureSummary.cmake.

- **ENABLED_FEATURES**: List of features which are enabled during the CMake run.

  List of features which are enabled during the CMake run. Be default it contains the names of all packages which were found. This is determined using the <NAME>_FOUND variables. Packages which are searched QUIET are not listed. A project can add its own features to this list.This property is used by the macros in FeatureSummary.cmake.

- **FIND_LIBRARY_USE_LIB64_PATHS**: Whether FIND_LIBRARY should automatically search lib64 directories.

  FIND_LIBRARY_USE_LIB64_PATHS is a boolean specifying whether the FIND_LIBRARY command should automatically search the lib64 variant of directories called lib in the search path when building 64-bit binaries.

- **PACKAGES_FOUND**: List of packages which were found during the CMake run.

  List of packages which were found during the CMake run. Whether a package has been found is determined using the <NAME>_FOUND variables.

- **PACKAGES_NOT_FOUND**: List of packages which were not found during the CMake run.

  List of packages which were not found during the CMake run. Whether a package has been found is determined using the <NAME>_FOUND variables.

- **TARGET_SUPPORTS_SHARED_LIBS**: Does the target platform support shared libraries.

  TARGET_SUPPORTS_SHARED_LIBS is a boolean specifying whether the target platform supports shared libraries. Basically all current general general purpose OS do so, the exception are usually embedded systems with no or special OSs.

Directory Properties

The following directory properties are available in CMakeLists.txt code:

- **ADDITIONAL_MAKE_CLEAN_FILES**: Addditional files to clean during the make clean stage.

  A list of files that will be cleaned as a part of the "make clean" stage.

- **CLEAN_NO_CUSTOM**: Should the output of custom commands be left.

  If this is true then the outputs of custom commands for this directory will not be removed during the "make clean" stage.

- **CMAKE_ALLOW_LOOSE_LOOP_CONSTRUCTS**: Allow loops to have non-matching closing statements.

If this is set then the closing statement of control structures in CMake will not require an exact match to the opening statement. For example IF(foo) will not require ENDIF(foo) but simple ENDIF() will work.

- **EXCLUDE_FROM_ALL**: Exclude the directory from the all target of its parent.

  A property on a directory that indicates if its targets are excluded from the default build target. If it is not, then with a Makefile for example typing make will cause the targets to be built. The same concept applies to the default build of other generators.

- **LISTFILE_STACK**: The current stack of listfiles being processed.

  This property is mainly useful when trying to debug errors in your CMake scripts. It returns a list of what list files are currently being processed, in order. So if one listfile does an INCLUDE command then that is effectively pushing the included listfile onto the stack.

- **TEST_INCLUDE_FILE**: A cmake file that will be included when ctest is run.

  If you specify TEST_INCLUDE_FILE, that file will be included and processed when ctest is run on the directory.

Target Properties

The following target properties are available in CMakeLists.txt code:

- **ARCHIVE_OUTPUT_DIRECTORY**: Output directory in which to build ARCHIVE target files.

  This property specifies the directory into which archive target files should be built. There are three kinds of target files that may be built: archive, library, and runtime. Executables are always treated as runtime targets. Static libraries are always treated as archive targets. Module libraries are always treated as library targets. For non-DLL platforms shared libraries are treated as library targets. For DLL platforms the DLL part of a shared library is treated as a runtime target and the corresponding import library is treated as an archive target. All Windows-based systems including Cygwin are DLL platforms. This property is initialized by the value of the variable CMAKE_ARCHIVE_OUTPUT_DIRECTORY if it is set when a target is created.

- **BUILD_WITH_INSTALL_RPATH**: Should build tree targets have install tree rpaths.

BUILD_WITH_INSTALL_RPATH is a boolean specifying whether to link the target in the build tree with the INSTALL_RPATH. This takes precedence over SKIP_BUILD_RPATH and avoids the need for relinking before installation.

- **CLEAN_DIRECT_OUTPUT**: Do not delete other varients of this target.

  When a library is built CMake by default generates code to remove any existing library using all possible names. This is needed to support libraries that switch between STATIC and SHARED by a user option. However when using OUTPUT_NAME to build a static and shared library of the same name using different logical target names the two targets will remove each other's files. This can be prevented by setting the CLEAN_DIRECT_OUTPUT property to 1.

- **COMPILE_FLAGS**: Additional flags to yse when compiling this target's sources.

  The COMPILE_FLAGS property sets additional compiler flags used to build sources within the target. It may also be used to pass additional preprocessor definitions.

- **DEBUG_POSTFIX**: A postfix that will be applied to this target when build debug.

  A property on a target that sepcifies a postfix to add to the target name when built in debug mode. For example foo.dll versus fooD.dll

- **DEFINE_SYMBOL**: Define a symbol when compiling this target's sources.

  DEFINE_SYMBOL sets the name of the preprocessor symbol defined when compiling sources in a shared library. If not set here then it is set to target_EXPORTS by default (with some substitutions if the target is not a valid C identifier). This is useful for headers to know whether they are being included from inside their library our outside to properly setup dllexport/dllimport decorations.

- **ENABLE_EXPORTS**: Specify whether an executable exports symbols for loadable modules.

  Normally an executable does not export any symbols because it is the final program. It is possible for an executable to export symbols to be used by loadable modules. When this property is set to true CMake will allow other targets to "link" to the executable with the TARGET_LINK_LIBRARIES command. On all platforms a target-level dependency on the executable is created for targets that link to it. For non-DLL platforms the link rule is simply ignored since the dynamic loader will automatically bind symbols when the module is loaded. For DLL platforms an import library will be created for the exported symbols and then used for linking. All Windows-based systems including Cygwin are DLL platforms.

- **EXCLUDE_FROM_ALL**: Exclude the target from the all target.

A property on a target that indicates if the target is excluded from the default build target. If it is not, then with a Makefile for example typing make will cause this target to be built. The same concept applies to the default build of other generators. Installing a target with EXCLUDE_FROM_ALL set to true has undefined behavior.

- **EchoString**: A message to be displayed when the target is built.

A message to display on some generators (such as makefiles) when the target is built.

- **GENERATOR_FILE_NAME**: Generator's file for this target.

An internal property used by some generators to record the name of project or dsp file associated with this target.

- **HAS_CXX**: Force a target to use the CXX linker.

Setting HAS_CXX on a target will force the target to use the C++ linker (and C++ runtime libraries) for linking even if the target has no C++ code in it.

- **IMPORT_PREFIX**: What comes before the import library name.

Similar to the target property PREFIX, but used for import libraries (typically corresponding to a DLL) instead of regular libraries. A target property that can be set to override the prefix (such as "lib") on an import library name.

- **IMPORT_SUFFIX**: What comes after the import library name.

Similar to the target property SUFFIX, but used for import libraries (typically corresponding to a DLL) instead of regular libraries. A target property that can be set to override the suffix (such as ".lib") on an import library name.

- **INSTALL_NAME_DIR**: Mac OSX directory name for installed targets.

INSTALL_NAME_DIR is a string specifying the directory portion of the "install_name" field of shared libraries on Mac OSX to use in the installed targets.

- **INSTALL_RPATH**: The rpath to use for installed targets.

  A semicolon-separated list specifying the rpath to use in installed targets (for platforms that support it).

- **INSTALL_RPATH_USE_LINK_PATH**: Add paths to linker search and installed rpath.

  INSTALL_RPATH_USE_LINK_PATH is a boolean that if set to true will append directories in the linker search path and outside the project to the INSTALL_RPATH.

- **LIBRARY_OUTPUT_DIRECTORY**: Output directory in which to build LIBRARY target files.

  This property specifies the directory into which library target files should be built. There are three kinds of target files that may be built: archive, library, and runtime. Executables are always treated as runtime targets. Static libraries are always treated as archive targets. Module libraries are always treated as library targets. For non-DLL platforms shared libraries are treated as library targets. For DLL platforms the DLL part of a shared library is treated as a runtime target and the corresponding import library is treated as an archive target. All Windows-based systems including Cygwin are DLL platforms. This property is initialized by the value of the variable CMAKE_LIBRARY_OUTPUT_DIRECTORY if it is set when a target is created.

- **LINKER_LANGUAGE**: What tool to use for linking, based on language.

  The LINKER_LANGUAGE property is used to change the tool used to link an executable or shared library. The default is set the language to match the files in the library. CXX and C are common values for this property.

- **LINK_FLAGS**: Additional flags to use when linking this target.

  The LINK_FLAGS property can be used to add extra flags to the link step of a target. LINK_FLAGS_<CONFIG> will add to the configuration <CONFIG>, for example, DEBUG, RELEASE, MINSIZEREL, RELWITHDEBINFO.

- **LOCATION**: Where a target will be written on disk.

  A read only property on a target that indicates where that target will be written. For libraries and executables this will be where the file is written on disk. This property is computed based on a number of other settings.

- **OUTPUT_NAME**: Sets the real name of a target when it is built.

  Sets the real name of a target when it is built and can be used to help create two targets of the same name even though CMake requires unique logical target names. There is also a <CONFIG>_OUTPUT_NAME that can set the output name on a per-configuration basis.

- **PREFIX**: What comes before the library name.

  A target property that can be set to override the prefix (such as "lib") on a library name.

- **RUNTIME_OUTPUT_DIRECTORY**: Output directory in which to build RUNTIME target files.

  This property specifies the directory into which runtime target files should be built. There are three kinds of target files that may be built: archive, library, and runtime. Executables are always treated as runtime targets. Static libraries are always treated as archive targets. Module libraries are always treated as library targets. For non-DLL platforms shared libraries are treated as library targets. For DLL platforms the DLL part of a shared library is treated as a runtime target and the corresponding import library is treated as an archive target. All Windows-based systems including Cygwin are DLL platforms. This property is initialized by the value of the variable CMAKE_RUNTIME_OUTPUT_DIRECTORY if it is set when a target is created.

- **SKIP_BUILD_RPATH**: Should rpaths be used for the build tree.

  SKIP_BUILD_RPATH is a boolean specifying whether to skip automatic generation of an rpath allowing the target to run from the build tree.

- **SOVERSION**: What version number is this target.

  For shared libraries VERSION and SOVERSION can be used to specify the build version and api version respectively. When building or installing appropriate symlinks are created if the platform supports symlinks and the linker supports so-names. If only one of both is specified the missing is assumed to have the same version number. For shared libraries and executables on Windows the VERSION attribute is parsed to extract a "major.minor" version number. These numbers are used as the image version of the binary.

- **STATIC_LIBRARY_FLAGS**: Extra flags to use when linking static libraries.

Extra flags to use when linking a static library.

- **SUFFIX**: What comes after the library name.

  A target property that can be set to override the suffix (such as ".so") on a library name.

- **VERSION**: What version number is this target.

  For shared libraries VERSION and SOVERSION can be used to specify the build version and api version respectively. When building or installing appropriate symlinks are created if the platform supports symlinks and the linker supports so-names. If only one of both is specified the missing is assumed to have the same version number. For executables VERSION can be used to specify the build version. When building or installing appropriate symlinks are created if the platform supports symlinks. For shared libraries and executables on Windows the VERSION attribute is parsed to extract a "major.minor" version number. These numbers are used as the image version of the binary.

- **WIN32_EXECUTABLE**: Used to specify Windows executable with a WinMain entry point.

  This can be set to indicate that a target is a Windows executable in contrast to a console application for example. This changes how the executable will be linked.

- **XCODE_ATTRIBUTE_<an-attribute>**: Set Xcode target attributes directly.

  Tell the Xcode generator to set '<an-attribute>' to a given value in the generated Xcode project. Ignored on other generators.

Test Properties

The following properties for tests are available in CMakeLists.txt code:

- **FAIL_REGULAR_EXPRESSION**: If the output matches this regular expression tes test will fail.

  If set, if the output matches one of specified regular expressions, the test will fail.For example: PASS_REGULAR_EXPRESSION "[^a-z]Error;ERROR;Failed"

- **MEASUREMENT**: Specify a dashboard meansurement and value to be reported for a test.

  If set to a name then that name will be reported to a dashboard as a named measurement with a value of 1. You may also specify a value by setting MEASUREMENT to "measurement=value".

- **PASS_REGULAR_EXPRESSION**: The output must match this regular expression for the test to pass.

  If set, the test output will be checked against the specified regular expressions and at least one of the regular expressions has to match, otherwise the test will fail.

- **TIMEOUT**: How many seconds to allow for this test.

  This property if set will limit a test to nto take more than the specified number of seconds to run. If it exceeds that the test process will be killed and ctest will move to the next test. This setting takes precedence over DART_TESTING_TIMEOUT and CTEST_TESTING_TIMOUT.

- **WILL_FAIL**: If set to true, this will invert the pass/fail flag of the test.

  This property can be used for tests that are expected to fail and return a non zero return code.

Sourcefile Properties

The following source file properties are available in CMakeLists.txt code:

- **ABSTRACT**: Is this source file an abstract class.

  A property ona source file that indicates if the source file represents a class that is abstract. This only makes sense for languages that have a notion of an abstract class and it is only used by somw tools that wrap classes into other languages.

- **COMPILE_FLAGS**: Additional flags to be added when compiling this source file.

  These flags will be added to the list of compile flags when this source file.

- **EXTERNAL_OBJECT**: If set to true then this is an object file.

If this property is set to true then the source file is really an object file and should not be compiled. It will still be linked into the target though.

- **EXTRA_CONTENT**: Is this file part of a target's extra content.

  If this property is set, the source file will be added to the target's list of extra content. This is used by makefile generators for some sort of Mac budle framework support.

- **GENERATED**: Is this source file generated as part of the build process.

  If a source file is generated by the build process CMake will handle it differently in temrs of dependency checking etc. Otherwise having a non-existent source file could create problems.

- **HEADER_FILE_ONLY**: Is this source file only a header file.

  A property ona source file that indicates if the source file is a header file with no associated implementation. This is set automatically based on the file extension and is used by CMake to determine is certain dependency information should be computed.

- **KEEP_EXTENSION**: Make th eoutput file have the same extension as the source file.

  If this property is set then the file extension of the output file will be the same as that of the source file. Normally the output file extension is computed based on the language of the source file, for example .cxx will go to a .o extension.

- **LANGUAGE**: What programming language is the file.

  A property that can be set to indicate what programming language the source file is. If it is not set the language is determined based on the file extension. Typical values are CXX C etc.

- **LOCATION**: The full path to a source file.

  A read only property on a SOURCE FILE that contains the full path to the source file.

- **MACOSX_CONTENT**: If true then this is part of a MACOSX bundle or framework.

MACOSX_CONTENT is a flag that if true this file will be copied to the bundle or framework.

- **MACOSX_PACKAGE_LOCATION**: Location for MACOSX bundles and frameworks.

MACOSX_PACKAGE_LOCATION is the property of a file within a mac osx bundle or framework that specifies where this file should be copied. This makes sense for things like icons and other resources.

- **OBJECT_DEPENDS**: Additional dependencies.

Additional dependencies that should be checked as part of building this source file.

- **OBJECT_OUTPUTS**: Additional outputs for a Makefile rule.

Additional outputs created by compilation of this source file. If any of these outputs is missing the object will be recompiled. This is supported only on Makefile generators and will be ignored on other generators.

- **SYMBOLIC**: Is this just a name for a rule.

If SYMBOLIC (boolean) is set to true the build system will be informed that the source file is not actually created on disk but instead used as a symbolic name for a build rule.

- **WRAP_EXCLUDE**: Exclude this source file from any code wrapping techniques.

Some packages can wrap source files into alternate languages to provide additional functionality. For example, C++ code can be wrapped into Java or Python etc using SWIG etc. If WRAP_EXCLUDE is set to true (1 etc) that indicates then this source file should not be wrapped.

Software Copyright

Copyright (c) 2007 Kitware, Inc., Insight Consortium. All rights reserved.

Redistribution and use in source and binary forms, with or without modification, are permitted provided that the following conditions are met:

- Redistributions of source code must retain the above copyright notice, this list of conditions and the following disclaimer.

- Redistributions in binary form must reproduce the above copyright notice, this list of conditions and the following disclaimer in the documentation and/or other materials provided with the distribution.
- The names of Kitware, Inc., the Insight Consortium, or the names of any consortium members, or of any contributors, may not be used to endorse or promote products derived from this software without specific prior written permission.
- Modified source versions must be plainly marked as such, and must not be misrepresented as being the original software.

THIS SOFTWARE IS PROVIDED BY THE COPYRIGHT HOLDER AND CONTRIBUTORS ``AS IS" AND ANY EXPRESS OR IMPLIED WARRANTIES, INCLUDING, BUT NOT LIMITED TO, THE IMPLIED WARRANTIES OF MERCHANTABILITY AND FITNESS FOR A PARTICULAR PURPOSE ARE DISCLAIMED. IN NO EVENT SHALL THE AUTHORS OR CONTRIBUTORS BE LIABLE FOR ANY DIRECT, INDIRECT, INCIDENTAL, SPECIAL, EXEMPLARY, OR CONSEQUENTIAL DAMAGES (INCLUDING, BUT NOT LIMITED TO, PROCUREMENT OF SUBSTITUTE GOODS OR SERVICES; LOSS OF USE, DATA, OR PROFITS; OR BUSINESS INTERRUPTION) HOWEVER CAUSED AND ON ANY THEORY OF LIABILITY, WHETHER IN CONTRACT, STRICT LIABILITY, OR TORT (INCLUDING NEGLIGENCE OR OTHERWISE) ARISING IN ANY WAY OUT OF THE USE OF THIS SOFTWARE, EVEN IF ADVISED OF THE POSSIBILITY OF SUCH DAMAGE.

See Also

The following resources are available to get help using CMake:

- **Home Page**: http://www.cmake.org

  The primary starting point for learning about CMake.

- **Frequently Asked Questions**: http://www.cmake.org/Wiki/CMake_FAQ

  A Wiki is provided containing answers to frequently asked questions.

- **Online Documentation**: http://www.cmake.org/HTML/Documentation.html

  Links to available documentation may be found on this web page.

- **Mailing List**: http://www.cmake.org/HTML/MailingLists.html

For help and discussion about using cmake, a mailing list is provided at cmake@cmake.org. The list is member-post-only but one may sign up on the CMake web page. Please first read the full documentation at http://www.cmake.org before posting questions to the list.

Summary of helpful links:

```
Home: http://www.cmake.org
Docs: http://www.cmake.org/HTML/Documentation.html
Mail: http://www.cmake.org/HTML/MailingLists.html
FAQ:  http://www.cmake.org/Wiki/CMake_FAQ
```

Mailing List

For help and discussion about using cmake, a mailing list is provided at cmake@www.cmake.org. Please first read the full documentation at http://www.cmake.org before posting questions to the list.

Index